D0272405

HOW TO COMMUNICATE ORALLY

PRENTICE-HALL INTERNATIONAL, INC.
London
PRENTICE-HALL OF AUSTRALIA, PTY. LTD.
Sydney
PRENTICE-HALL OF CANADA, LTD.
Toronto
PRENTICE-HALL OF INDIA (PRIVATE) LTD.
New Delhi
PRENTICE-HALL OF JAPAN, INC.
Tokyo

SECOND EDITION

HOW TO COMMUNICATE ORALLY

Glenn R. Capp

Professor of Speech

Chairman of the Department of Oral Communication

Baylor University

Prentice-Hall, Inc., *Englewood Cliffs, New Jersey*

Library of Congress Catalog Card No.:
66-16389

Printed in the United States of America:
40380-C

Current printing (last digit):

10 9 8 7 6 5 4 3 2 1

To my students—
past, present, and future

Preface

This revised edition preserves the same basic philosophy, direct style, and general organization of the first edition, but it includes a number of refinements. The three chapters of Part One have been condensed to two, and the chapter on listening has been moved from Part Four to Part One. This arrangement streamlines the background material on oral communication and integrates listening into the total communication process more effectively.

New illustrative material gives a freshness to the six chapters of Part Two on compositon and in a lesser degree to other parts. The entire text has been updated to reflect developments and writings in speech since publication of the first edition. The section titles in the Contents give a preview of the chapters, and the summaries at the end of the chapters emphasize the salient points as aids to learning rhetorical principles.

The fictitious Professor Doe meets his demise in this edition. The professor, athough an aid for linking chapters together and maintaining interest, seemed out of character with the fundamental philosophy of the text as a too obvious rhetorical device.

This edition retains the step-by-step arrangement that corresponds to the order in which one encounters the principles of oral communication. Part One explains fundamental concepts: a philosophy of speech education, the purposes of training in oral communication, the student's obligations toward the study, and how listening applies. Part Two discusses the preparation of a speech: its content and composition. This part, which continues to receive major emphasis, considers the factors of preparation and composition in chronological order. Part Three discusses the coordinated use of mind, body, voice, and language for effective presentation; and Part Four applies the principles of the first three divisions to discussion, debate, and speeches for special occasions.

This revision sharpens the emphasis on a twofold approach to oral communication: rhetorical and evaluative. Through a study of rhetorical principles, the student learns to organize and present his thoughts by acceptable standards of composition. Through the evaluative approach he learns to weigh carefully the validity and accuracy of his statements—to talk sense, not nonsense.

A minimum of advice and a maximum of explanation characterize this book. Instead of telling the student to use the library, the book shows him how to find and use the necessary materials. Rather than admonishing him to use accurate supporting material, it gives correct examples from speeches of history, contemporary speeches, and student speeches. In addition to explaining principles, the book includes examples which show how they operate, a practical approach which makes the principles meaningful.

The exercises and assignments follow this pattern: (1) questions on basic principles, (2) problems for applying the principles, and (3) assignments for classroom practice. The order of the assignments, from simple to complex, attempts to accustom the student gradually to the complexity of the total process of communication.

Grateful acknowledgment is made to many publishers and authors for permission to use copyrighted material and for permission to quote excerpts from speeches. Several of my present and former colleagues made valuable suggestions for the first edition: Professors Tom and Lee Abbott, George Stokes, Lola Walker, Chloe Armstrong, and Mary Booras. Professor Cecil May Burke gave invaluable assistance with the chapter on voice; Professor Edna Haney read and corrected the original manuscript; and my wife read and criticized the manuscript in each stage of its preparation. For helpful criticism of the first edition in preparation for this revision, I am indebted to Dr. Bernard C. Kissell of the University of Texas and to some twenty-five other professors who evaluated the first edition at my request.

G.R.C.

Contents

PART ONE

Background Concepts 1

PART TWO

Preparation and Composition 59

HOW TO COMMUNICATE ORALLY

PART ONE

Background Concepts

CHAPTER 1

Determine What Constitutes a Good Speech

You are beginning a study perhaps unlike any you have undertaken before. Facility in oral communication requires knowledge about speech-making and the acquisition of skills in composing and presenting a speech. It involves activities which require careful study, sustained practice, and dedication to purpose. Before you begin your study of the principles involved, you should first determine what constitutes a good speech. What do you hope to accomplish by your study? How will you know if you accomplish your aims? This chapter will help you answer these questions.

First you must dispel the popular notion that "speech is easy" and consists of a few "magic formulas" for controlling an audience. You must do more than master the techniques of "how to do it," as important as these factors may be. You must also develop yourself as an able person with a broad background of information. In short, your worth as a speaker will consist of what you know, the type of person you become, and the skills you acquire in organizing and presenting your ideas. To become an effective speaker you must acquire certain skills in arranging and presenting ideas as you develop a background of information and attributes of character that will identify you as an able person.

Where do we get our ideas of what constitutes good speaking? Who has the right or authority to say? Frankly, there are no absolute rules for good speaking whereby all persons can be run through the same mold and come out standard speakers. Would not speaking be tiring if all speakers did everything exactly the same way? All principles must allow for individual differences. Furthermore, there is no such thing as a "one-and-only" way to make speeches. There may be many equally acceptable ways.

Although no formal rules prevail, certain general principles have evolved during the two thousand years the subject has been taught. These principles include a body of information and skills which can be learned and which will help you develop your potential ability as a speaker. The principles come primarily from two sources: (1) the rhetoricians—those teachers and writers of oral communication since the Classical period who have set forth their findings and practices; (2) outstanding speakers—those who have used speech effectively throughout history. A brief insight into the contributions of these two groups will assist you in understanding what constitutes good speaking.

I. What the Rhetoricians Say

The Classical rhetoricians come to our rescue when we attempt to characterize a good speech. Although these men wrote over two thousand years ago, much of what they said forms the basis of modern-day speech. A review of their writings gives us at least four different, and sometimes conflicting, concepts of what good speech should do.

The Sophist Theory

The early Greek Sophists had their beginning in Sicily about 465 B.C., when Corax and his pupil Tisias first set down a system of rhetoric. The occasion grew out of legal disputes, primarily over land titles, for law trials had become public spectacles. Juries consisted of at least five hundred and one persons, and litigants pleaded their own cases. There were also numerous opportunities for speaking on public issues. Public measures were decided at town meetings open to adult male citizens, all of whom had the right to be heard, and much depended upon the effectiveness of their speaking. With this emphasis on competition of ideas, can you doubt that speech training became popular?

The Sophists advocated effecting persuasion by any means available. To them the ends justified the means; they cared little about the ethics of the speaker. Consequently, they taught methods that might easily deceive. In short, they taught a "bag of tricks" and measured the success of their speaking by the results obtained.

Measured by this standard alone, public speaking can be vicious. A speaker could be successful by complying with the prejudices of an audience, by avoiding the issue, or by simply getting an audible reaction from his hearers. He might even be declared successful in spite of the invalidity of his material if he succeeded in hoodwinking his listeners.

As unethical as this theory appears, much of this doctrine persists today. The average textbook on speech and many public-speaking courses deal solely with "how to be effective," with little concern about the ethics of the speaker or the value of what he has to say. Many ministers measure their success by how many people come forward at the invitation, without questioning the methods used to create an emotional state conducive to impulsive action. Many lawyers go on emotional tirades designed to conceal rather than to reveal the real facts of the case. Many politicians skillfully comply with the prejudices of their listeners to get their votes. Some speakers attempt to rush their audiences to thoughtless decisions. These speakers all say, in essence, "The results are tangible; therefore, the speaking must be effective." The Sophists said the same thing over two thousand years ago, and the belief is just as vicious today as it was then.

The "Knowledge Is Eloquence" Theory

Plato, 429-327 B.C., was the chief exponent of the theory which states that knowledge per se makes for eloquence. It regards formal training in oral rhetoric as unnecessary. Plato argued in part that knowledge brings eloquence automatically, that eloquence is implicit in knowledge.

Much of Plato's writings on rhetoric attempted to expose the Sophists. Most modern rhetoricians believe that he overstated his case in his zeal to expose the hypocrisy of the Sophists. The importance of subject matter seems apparent; it may be termed the requirement from which all others spring. That knowledge does not constitute the only requirement seems equally apparent. Many intelligent men fail to communicate their ideas and feelings because they do not analyze their audiences properly, speak so that they may be heard, or arrange their ideas so that they may be understood.

Recently a physician delivered the commencement speech at a

university. His knowledge of medicine and his maturity of judgment were unquestioned, but he read his speech poorly. He mumbled his words in a low tone and rarely looked up from his manuscript. In five minutes he lost his audience, yet he droned on for forty. Many persons expressed regret about the choice of speaker; however, an experienced teacher of speech, reading the speech at a later date, labeled it an outstanding written address. The fault lay in the speaker, not in the speech. He simply could not express himself orally. In short, knowledge of subject matter is essential, but it is not the only requirement for successful speaking.

The "Able Man" Theory

Quintilian was the chief exponent of the theory—although Cicero and other early rhetoricians discussed it—which stresses the moral qualities that reside in the speaker—his intelligence, character, and attitudes of good will. Thus a good speaker is an able man; he develops skill in speaking by developing himself as a whole. Quintilian stressed training for the speaker as a lifelong process of study, and asserted that a man cannot be a good speaker without this background. In his twelve books, he discussed what can be done to develop a speaker in this training "from the cradle to the grave." He contended that a good speaker must be both a good man and a wise man.

This theory needs more emphasis today among those who contend that effective speaking may be developed with a minimum of training and who make sweeping claims for short courses for adult groups. Speakers who restrict their training only to rhetorical skills could improve their speaking by reading the classical writers on this subject.

That no speaker is better than his intrinsic worth as a person can hardly be denied. That the concept covers an all-inclusive criterion for judging a speaker's worth should be questioned. The theory contains much sound advice, but it does not go far enough. Although a good speaker must be a capable man, a capable man may not be an effective speaker. He may be unable to communicate orally.

The Methods Theory

Aristotle was the original exponent of the methods theory, which measures a speech in part by the methods employed in arranging and presenting it. As developed by Aristotle, this theory embraces the other three already discussed. It evaluates a speech in part by the ethical factors that reside in the speaker and his knowledge of subject, but it adds the standard of skills in organization and presentation. The theory looks upon rhetoric as a science and an art that can be learned and can enable an otherwise capable person to become a competent speaker.

Most modern-day teachers of speech follow this theory, for it is, in fact, the basic idea upon which all training in oral communication rests. In short, training in speech offers a body of principles and skills for the arrangement and presentation of ideas that is not taught elsewhere in the modern school curriculum. A person who acquires a broad background of knowledge and a body of high ideals goes a long way toward becoming an able speaker, but he must also learn skills of arrangement and presentation to round out his training.

II. What Effective Speakers Do

The rhetoricians give us a solid basis for judging good speech. Those leaders in history who used speech accurately and effectively in accomplishing their programs also made significant contributions. Although few of these men ever set forth their theories for speech-making, they helped establish standards by usage. Thus we can learn about what constitutes good speech by studying the significant speakers and speeches of history. Chapter 6 lists the best anthologies of speeches both historical and contemporary. To supplement your study of the rhetorical principles in this text, analyze how some of these speakers applied the principles.

A poll was conducted among four hundred professors of rhetoric in American colleges to determine which speeches they considered the most famous in American history.[1] The two speakers that ranked highest may be compared to illustrate how great speakers help establish standards. For illustrative purposes, Abraham Lincoln's "Gettysburg Address" and Franklin D. Roosevelt's "Declaration of War" may be compared.

Perhaps no American statesman illustrates better the "able man" theory than does Lincoln. Born in a log cabin near Hodgenville,

[1] Glenn R. Capp, *Famous Speeches in American History* (Indianapolis: The Bobbs-Merrill Co., Inc., 1963), p. 3.

Kentucky, on February 12, 1809, his early environment and humble circumstances afforded him the opportunity for only one year of formal education. Yet his inquiring mind and zest for life caused him to educate himself beyond most men of his time. His awkward bearing, ungainly appearance, and high-pitched voice marred his effectiveness as a speaker, but his knowledge of human nature, his penetrating mind, and his clever repartee more than made up for his rhetorical deficiencies. In him the characteristics of an able man—intelligence, character, and good will—helped to establish principles of effective speaking.

Lincoln's "Gettysburg Address," presented at the dedication of the cemetery at Gettysburg, Pennsylvania, on November 19, 1863, commemorated those who had lost their lives at the Battle of Gettysburg. Edward Everett of Boston was the principal speaker, but President Lincoln was asked to give a "few appropriate remarks." Although his speech took no more than three minutes to deliver, he reemphasized his basic political philosophy that the equality of men must be preserved, that their rights must be protected, and that government of, by, and for the people must prevail. The speech was organized chronologically, emphasizing in turn that our nation was established on the principles of liberty and equality, that those principles were being threatened by the Civil War, and that they had met to dedicate the cemetery in honor of those who gave their lives for the protection of those principles. After paying homage to the dead, Lincoln stressed the task remaining—to honor their memory by protecting our original concepts of freedom and equality.

Many rhetoricians consider Lincoln's speech a masterpiece of arrangement and style. The text of the speech that follows, known as "the Bliss copy," is perhaps the most accurate of the several texts that exist. Study it as a model of excellence that helped establish standards, especially for the use of language.

> Four score and seven years ago our fathers brought forth on this continent, a new nation, conceived in Liberty, and dedicated to the proposition that all men are created equal.
>
> Now we are engaged in a great civil war, testing whether that nation or any nation so conceived and so dedicated, can long endure. We are met on a great battle-field of that war. We have come to dedicate a portion of that field as a final resting place for those who here gave their lives that that nation might live. It is altogether fitting and proper that we should do this.

But, in a larger sense, we can not dedicate—we can not consecrate—we can not hallow—this ground. The brave men, living and dead, who struggled here, have consecrated it, far above our poor power to add or detract. The world will little note, nor long remember what we say here, but it can never forget what they did here. It is for us the living, rather, to be dedicated here to the unfinished work which they who fought here have thus far so nobly advanced. It is rather for us to be here dedicated to the great task remaining before us—that from these honored dead we take increased devotion to that cause for which they gave the last full measure of devotion—that we here highly resolve that these dead shall not have died in vain—that this nation, under God, shall have a new birth of freedom—and that government of the people, by the people, for the people, shall not perish from the earth.[2]

Franklin D. Roosevelt's early life and training offer an interesting contrast with those of Lincoln. He exemplifies the methods theory because he not only was a man of wide knowledge and experience, but also was afforded the best training of his day for developing skills in speech-making. Born at Hyde Park, New York, on January 30, 1882, of wealthy and aristocratic parents, he received his early training from private tutors and extensive travel abroad. Later he attended Groton School, Harvard College, and the Columbia University School of Law. During his undergraduate days he was an avid debater, editor of the Harvard newspaper, and an enthusiastic student of history and government. These activities served him well in developing facility in oral communication, skills which he used extensively from the time he entered public life in 1910 until his death on April 12, 1945.

Roosevelt's "War Message" declaring war on Japan on December 8, 1941, was delivered before a joint session of Congress and members of the Supreme Court. Roosevelt had dictated his war message soon after the attack on Pearl Harbor, and it was delivered with only minor changes the next day.

This short speech, which took only six minutes to deliver, gives an excellent example of arrangement, style, and psychological appeal. Roosevelt's arrangement is, like Lincoln's, chronological; he started by a review of the attack on Pearl Harbor the previous day, discussed its present effect, and expressed confidence in the outcome of the war. The simple and direct style shows force and action. Although he showed restraint, the pathos of the occasion comes

[2] John G. Nicolay and John Jay, eds., *Complete Works of Abraham Lincoln* (New York: Appleton-Century-Crofts, 1894-1905), IX, 209-210.

through in his choice of language and reference to matters which the American people hold dear. A study of the text that follows will show how Roosevelt helped establish standards for good speech.

To The Congress of The United States: Yesterday, December 7, 1941 —a date which will live in infamy—the United States of America was suddenly and deliberately attacked by naval and air forces of the Empire of Japan.

The United States was at peace with that nation and, at the solicitation of Japan, was still in conversation with its government and its Emperor looking toward the maintenance of peace in the Pacific. Indeed, one hour after Japanese air squadrons had commenced bombing in Oahu, the Japanese Ambassador to the United States and his colleague delivered to the Secretary of State a formal reply to a recent American message. While this reply stated that it seemed useless to continue the existing diplomatic negotiations, it contained no threat or hint of war or armed attack.

It will be recorded that the distance of Hawaii from Japan makes it obvious that the attack was deliberately planned many days or even weeks ago. During the intervening time the Japanese government had deliberately sought to deceive the United States by false statements and expressions of hope for continued peace.

The attack yesterday on the Hawaiian Islands has caused severe damage to American naval and military forces. Very many American lives have been lost. In addition American ships have been reported torpedoed on the high seas between San Francisco and Honolulu.

Yesterday the Japanese government also launched an attack against Malaya. Last night Japanese forces attacked Hong Kong. Last night Japanese forces attacked Guam. Last night Japanese forces attacked the Philippine Islands. Last night the Japanese attacked Wake Island. This morning the Japanese attacked Midway Island. Japan has, therefore, undertaken a surprise offensive extending throughout the Pacific area. The facts of yesterday speak for themselves. The people of the United States have already formed their opinions and well understand the implications to the very life and safety of our nation.

As Commander in Chief of the Army and Navy I have directed that all measures be taken for our defense.

Always will we remember the character of the onslaught against us.

No matter how long it may take us to overcome this premeditated invasion, the American people in their righteous might will win through to absolute victory.

I believe I interpret the will of the Congress and of the people when I assert that we will not only defend ourselves to the uttermost but will make very certain that this form of treachery shall never endanger us again.

Hostilities exist. There is no blinking at the fact that our people, our territory, and our interests are in grave danger.

With confidence in our armed forces—with the unbounded determination of our people—we will gain the inevitable triumph—so help us God.

I ask that the Congress declare that since the unprovoked and dastardly attack by Japan on Sunday, December 7, a state of war has existed between the United States and the Japanese Empire.[3]

The study of these two representative speeches indicates that the way in which great men speak at crucial periods in history helps establish principles of good speech, as does what the rhetoricians say should be done. Both those who speak well and those who write about how to speak help establish standards.

III. Standards for Judging a Good Speech

As already suggested, a good starting point in your training consists of drawing up criteria for judging what constitutes a good speech. These standards will help you measure your own progress. The five following standards come partly from a study of the rhetoricians and partly from an analysis of significant speakers.

Do You Evaluate Properly What You Talk About?

You, like most Americans, cherish your right of freedom of speech. We think of freedom of speech as a basic American concept. Unfortunately, many speakers who proclaim this freedom the loudest do the least to assume their corresponding obligation to evaluate properly what they talk about. The public speaker has an obligation to present factually true information and mature ideas upon which his listeners may depend.

While on a vacation, a motorist drove into a gasoline station in an unfamiliar city to ask directions. The attendant, in a pleasing and effective manner, gave specific directions which carried the vacationists without difficulty across the city through heavy traffic over unfamiliar territory. They encountered only one hitch, but a vital one—upon arriving where they were instructed to go they found that they were farther from their destination than when they had started. The attendant had talked complete nonsense effectively.

[3] *Congressional Record,* Vol. 87, Part 9, December 8, 1941.

He rated "A" on method but "F" on evaluation. It matters little whether a speaker gives factually false information by design or ignorance; he still deceives his listeners.

Some speakers say what will be popular with an audience, rather than what needs to be said. They seek approval and applause, to make a favorable impression. Consequently, they choose facts in the light of how well they may be received, and they usually change them from time to time to correspond with the prejudices of their listeners. To illustrate: If a speaker has a choice among several examples, he selects the one most acceptable to his audience without regard to which is the most accurate. An example should represent a true sampling of all possible examples; choosing unrepresentative examples on the basis of popularity instead of accuracy deceives an audience.

Other speakers use ideas gained from collections of published speeches or other writings without giving credit for the sources of information. An almost nation-wide scandal occurred in college forensic circles several years ago when a young man won several original oratory contests with the use of a previously published speech. Others quote important men by taking statements out of their context, thus giving a false impression of the intent of the author. Some may quote persons popular with their listeners but who are not qualified to speak on the point at issue. These misleading devices result in a misevaluation of the subject and thus fail to measure up to the first criterion for judging adequate speech.

Let your first principle be—learn the facts, then speak. Recognize that you have an obligation as well as a right in speaking. Make sure that the information you give to your listeners is factually true.

Do You Make Your Basic Appeal on Rational Grounds?

In his writings on rhetoric, Aristotle deals with three factors important to the standard of rationality: (1) the ethical factors residing in the speaker, (2) his emotional appeal, and (3) the argument itself or the logical appeal. A good speech has an element of all three of these means of proof, but it will not center too largely on one to the exclusion of the others. The easiest way to evoke an immediate response from an audience is through an excess of emotional appeal. Almost any experienced speaker can work up an audience to an emotional state conducive to irrational action. Unfortunately, the quality of such impulsive decisions is low. A sensational revival preacher aroused his audience to such an emotional pitch over the use of tobacco that members of the audience marched down to the front and deposited their pipes, cigarettes, and cigars in containers, with firm resolves never to smoke again. Within a week after the close of the revival, the local stores reported sales of tobacco unparalleled in the history of the small community.

A defense lawyer went on such an emotional binge in a sensational criminal case that the jury recorded an eleven-to-one vote for acquittal within the first hour of their deliberations. Six hours later they brought in a unanimous vote for conviction, thanks to one juror who kept his head. After time for more mature deliberation, a person emotionally induced to take a particular stand may waiver or repudiate his impulsive decision. Excessively emotionalized speaking may accustom listeners to depend on emotional stimulation for decision, thus forsaking rational grounds in making decisions.

Logic depends primarily on evidence and reasoning. Evidence consists of the facts used to support ideas, and reasoning on the process of drawing inferences from the facts. The techniques of illogical reasoning consist of such devices as quoting unqualified authorities, presenting unrepresentative examples, citing limited statistics, drawing sweeping conclusions from meager evidence, making inferences from negative instances, and drawing conclusions by comparing objects not comparable. A good speaker avoids such fallacies and makes his basic appeal to logic.

Let your second principle be—avoid the overuse of emotionalized appeals; avoid mistakes in reasoning; appeal primarily to logic.

Do You Conform to Rhetorical Principles?

Scholars of rhetoric from the time of the Classical writers have treated of five factors of oral discourse: (1) invention, (2) arrangement, (3) style, (4) delivery, and (5) memory. An explanation of these factors as they apply today will help you understand rhetorical principles. A detailed development comes later; this discussion defines these principles.

Invention includes what you talk about in your speech—methods of argument, fallacies, logic, and proof. The term also includes forms of support—examples, analogies, illustrations, statistics, quotations from authority, explanation, and narration. In short, invention refers to the substance rather than the form of speech.

Arrangement means the composition of the speech. Organize your ideas into a simple, direct development of a completed idea so that your listeners will remember the central thought of your speech.

Style refers to the language used in expressing your ideas. Style, more than other skills, varies with changing times. Note the more ornate style of speeches of the nineteenth century as compared to those of the twentieth. Simplicity and directness form the keynote in style today. Language should conform to accepted standards of grammatical construction, but it should also be colorful, direct, and simple. Language indicates feelings about ideas as well as meanings of ideas.

Delivery treats the skills employed in presenting ideas orally—voice, bodily action, and poise. The voice should be pleasing in quality, distinct, and capable of being heard throughout the meeting hall. It should be free of affectations to avoid diverting attention from what you say. Bodily action refers to the movement of the whole body or parts of the body for the purpose of emphasizing and clarifying meaning. Correct bodily action never calls attention to itself but helps in making ideas meaningful and forceful. Poise refers to general bearing before an audience. A speaker shows poise when he gives the impression of self-confidence, without arrogance or condescension.

Memory pertains to the methods employed in recalling the ideas and material of a speech. Memory is less important today than during the Classical period because we have perfected methods of recording our ideas through written form. Facility at recall assists the speaker, however, for it makes frequent references to notes or manuscript unnecessary.

Let your third principle be—use rhetorical skills to communicate your ideas effectively; never use them for exhibition purposes.

Do You Present a Worthy Idea?

Unfortunately you may conform to the preceding requirements and still not make a worthwhile speech. Your idea may not be worth presenting in the first place; it may be trivial or immature. A worthy idea results from diligent research, careful thinking, and mature judgment. You waste the combined time of all your listeners, not simply your own, if you have nothing worthwhile to say. Thus, if you speak on a trivial subject for thirty minutes to five hundred people you waste two hundred and fifty man-hours. Consider the maturity of the idea of your speech as carefully as you do the preparation, arrangement, and presentation of it.

A worthy idea does not mean that you must have a completely arranged speech every time you speak. The circumstances of the occasion indicate the type of speech expected. Some occasions seek simply to maintain morale, as in a speech of the sales director to his salesmen, the alumnus before the university home-coming gathering, or the director of the fund-raising campaign before his solicitors. Such speeches take the form of a pep talk; if the speaker succeeds in arousing fervor for a worthwhile purpose, he fulfills the requirements of a worthy idea.

Some occasions call for speeches to provide interesting diversion, such as dinner occasions and social club meetings. At such meetings the speaker uses the speech situation to provide pleasantry. If he succeeds in entertaining his hearers, he accomplishes a worthwhile purpose.

Many occasions for speaking aim at presenting information, such as the teacher before his class, the lecturer at the study club, or the business executive before his employees. In these situations the speaker must be careful that he knows the facts and that he properly appraises his subject. If he gives accurate information, he presents a worthy idea.

In a free society numerous occasions arise for persuading others, like the lawyer before the jury, the statesman before the deliberative body, or the business executive before the board of directors. Democratic society could not carry on its activities without the able advocate. Unfortunately, some advocates distort the facts in attempting to make their positions sound convincing. If the speaker gives a distorted appraisal, he fails to meet the standard of a worthy idea. The able advocate gives a true-to-fact evaluation of his findings while arranging the most convincing case possible.

A persuasive speech may aim at stimulating an audience to think or to work toward solutions to problems. It may define an idea, teach mental skills, raise perplexing questions, present unsolved problems, or attempt to break through myths, prejudices, or dogmas. Such speeches challenge an audience to recall their experiences or to use their powers of reasoning. Speeches that generate criticism, analysis, and reflection meet well the standard of a worthy idea.

Let your fourth principle be—talk sense, not nonsense. Do something constructive for your listeners; never mislead an audience through design or ignorance.

Do You Accomplish What You Set Out to Do?

The final test for judging a good speech is—did it get results? Did it entertain, inform, persuade, or arouse the listeners? Much of the business of a free society is carried on through speech. The most effective speakers usually make the most noteworthy contributions.

You may say, "This standard closely parallels the Sophist doctrine." There is one basic difference. This standard is used in conjunction with four others equally as important. Furthermore, you are not justified in accomplishing your purpose by misleading an audience. The *end* never justifies the *means.* You do not need to deceive to be effective. The most effective speakers evaluate their facts properly, make their basic appeal upon rational grounds, conform to rhetorical principles, and present worthy ideas. Each of these standards is noteworthy individually; when applied together, they will help you attain the final standard of getting results.

As you begin your study to improve your communication, remember that you must develop yourself as an able person, increase your knowledge, and improve your skills in arranging and presenting ideas. You must accept your obligation to present factually true information and never purposely to deceive your listeners. By following these standards, you will eventually develop the ability to communicate ideas, information, and feelings effectively.

IV. Summary

Avoid short cuts to effective communication. Develop yourself as an able person, with a background of information, and with skills in speaking. The Classical writers gave us at least four theories upon which we may draw to formulate criteria for judging effective communication: (1) The Sophist theory judges a speech by its results. (2) The "knowledge is eloquence" theory judges a speech by the truth of the information presented. (3) The "able man" theory judges by the intrinsic worth of the speaker. (4) The methods theory includes the above theories but adds skills in rhetorical principles. Modern schools of speech hold to the latter theory because they believe that rhetorical principles can be taught and that learning them is important. Significant speakers of history have also helped establish standards by usage.

A set of standards for judging a good speech may be expressed in five questions: (1) Does the speaker properly evaluate what he talks about? (2) Does the speaker make his basic appeal on rational grounds? (3) Does the speaker conform to effective rhetorical principles? (4) Does the speaker present a worthy idea? (5) Does the speaker accomplish what he sets out to do?

Questions and Exercises

A. Answer the following questions about Chapter 1:

1. Why should you decide upon standards for good speech early in your training?
2. In the final analysis, of what will your worth as a speaker consist?
3. Briefly explain the principal contributions of the following Classical rhetoricians to oral communication: (1) Corax and Tisias, (2) Plato, (3) Quintilian and Cicero, and (4) Aristotle.
4. Why do modern students of speech follow the principles advanced by Aristotle?
5. What is your understanding of the following terms implicit in Greek rhetoric: (1) invention, (2) arrangement, (3) style, (4) delivery, and (5) memory?
6. To what extent do these principles have application to present-day students of oral communication?
7. How do famous speakers of history help establish principles of good speech?
8. Compare the speaking of Abraham Lincoln and Franklin D. Roosevelt.
9. Briefly explain the five principles advanced for judging good oral communication.
10. Do you consider these criteria adequate? Why?

B. To enable your professor better to evaluate your speaking, write out answers to the following questions about yourself:

1. Give your full name, address, and telephone number.
2. How are you classified? (Freshman, Sophomore, etc.)
3. Are you working for a college degree? What degree?
4. What is your major subject? Minor?
5. What business or profession do you contemplate?
6. How important do you consider speech to that business or profession?
7. Are you engaged in full-time employment? Where?
8. If you are engaged in part-time employment, how many hours per day do you work, what is the type of work, and who is your employer?

9. Did you take any speech courses in high school? If so, state briefly the nature and extent of such training.
10. Did you engage in any speech activities in high school such as debate, plays, readings, or radio announcing?
11. Did you receive any honors in high school speech activities? If so, explain briefly.
12. Have you had any other speech courses in college? If so, explain briefly.
13. Have you engaged in speech activities in college? If so, explain briefly.
14. List any honors received in college speech activities.
15. Have you had any speech courses taught by adult speech organizations?
16. Have you ever belonged to any self-teaching speech organizations such as the Toastmasters Club? If so, explain briefly.
17. Do you belong to any civic, fraternal, or church organizations that require you to speak in either formal or informal situations? If so, explain briefly.
18. What do you consider your principal weaknesses as a speaker?
19. What do you consider your principal assets as a speaker?
20. List what you consider the six outstanding qualities of a good speaker.
21. List what you consider the six principal shortcomings of public speakers.
22. Explain any special reasons that you have for taking this course. Include any special aims or purposes that will help your professor evaluate your progress.

C. Write a brief autobiography in which you relate such information as (1) whether you were born in a rural or urban area, (2) the economic and cultural environment in which you grew up, (3) how many brothers and sisters you have, (4) your father's occupation, and (5) any other information that you think will aid your professor in understanding you better.

D. Prepare a three-minute speech about yourself for oral presentation to the class. Attempt to cause your fellow class members to remember the following facts about you: (1) your name, nickname, and native state; (2) your major subject and some interesting facts about it; and (3) your future aims and aspirations. You may have notes, but try to avoid using them excessively. Attempt to make the speech interesting by injecting some humor and interesting incidents.

CHAPTER 2

Attempt to Become a Good Speaker

Now that you understand what constitutes a good speech, you need to consider four additional questions before taking up specific principles for developing yourself into a competent speaker and an efficient listener. These questions are: (1) What characterizes acceptable oral communication today? (2) What should you get out of a course in speech? (3) How can you develop yourself as a speaker? (4) How can you develop skills in organization and presentation?

I. What Oral Communication Means

Your professor has no desire to make you a silver-tongued orator; instead, he hopes to help you meet the everyday problems of both informal and formal communication. The old-time orator with his emphasis on high-sounding phrases and flamboyant style went out with the age of elocution (the latter part of the nineteenth century), but unfortunately memory of him remains. What then, you ask, characterizes acceptable oral communication today?

Good Speech Is Conversational and Communicative

The speech world today strives for a direct, communicative, conversational manner for the purpose of arousing thought and feeling. Do not regard speech-making as an occasion to exhibit your fine skills; rather, consider it as an opportunity to communicate ideas, information, and emotions. If what you do while speaking detracts from the subject matter of your talk, your skills defeat your purpose. Neither should you consider communication as a *delivery* of information. What you say is received in as many different ways as you have listeners. The audience relates what you talk about to their own experiences. At best, as a speaker, you express ideas, present information, and arouse feelings, compelling your listeners to further inquiry and thought.

To make your speaking effective, project yourself to your listeners. You talk *with* an audience, not simply *about* a subject. For example, suppose that you arrive early for your speech class and start talking with the one student present about your visit to Europe the past summer. Other students arrive and begin to listen. Soon your professor comes in and asks you to stand and continue your explanation to the entire class. When did the private conversation become a public speech? Was it when several students started listening? Was it when you stood, raised your voice, and started using gestures? Was it when you first realized that you were addressing an audience? There can be no correct answer because the fundamental process was the same at all times. The public speaker can talk in a direct, communicative manner before one person or a thousand people. The process before a large group is more formal than before a few people, but the aim of communication remains the same. Develop simple, direct, communicative, extemporaneous speaking for all occasions.

Good Speech Consists of Having Something to Say and Saying It Well

To be an effective speaker, you must have a balance between knowledge of subject and skill in organization and presentation. Some think that knowledge alone makes for effective speech. Others think that the way one talks overshadows what one says. Both concepts are equally fallacious. Since knowledge of the subject and presentation skill are both essential, their relative worth does not matter. Why argue whether the "heads" or "tails" side of a nickel is more important; both sides are essential to make the nickel legal tender.

Knowledge of the subject can hardly be overemphasized, yet knowledge without skill in presentation accomplishes little. The speaker may read from his prepared notes while his audience sleeps, looks out windows, or reads something else. If no one listens it matters little if the speech reflects maturity of judgment. Equally bad is the speaker who speaks well but says nothing. He may induce his audience to accept immature ideas, factually false information, and ill-conceived judgments. Knowledge of subject and maturity of judgment constitute prerequisites to the right to speak. Skills in speaking make a good speech accomplish its purpose. Each performs an indispensable function in developing a well-rounded speaker.

A minister and his wife each had reputations as excellent speakers, but were divergent types. He was noted for his wide knowledge, penetrating mind, and maturity of judgment; she, for her fluency, beauty of expression, and dignity. One professor remarked that the minister could tell his wife what to say and she could outspeak him, two to one. Another demurred, stating that knowledge of subject constitutes an essential part of speaking effectiveness. They agreed that if the minister and his wife each had the other's ability plus his own, each would possess the desired qualities. Having something worthwhile to say and saying it well constitute the goals for oral communication.

Good Speech Does Something Constructive to the Speaker's Auditors

The ultimate effect of a speech may be measured by what it does to its listeners or readers. What lasting effect does it have on the issues discussed? If a speech gives new insight into a problem, adds to the total of information on it, clarifies the audience's thinking, or affects the listener's attitude, it makes a measurable contribution.

The role effective speech has played during different periods of history probably accounts for the varying degrees of emphasis it has received. A study of the history of speech education shows that the emphasis placed on speech training varied in relation to the degree of democracy practiced. The greater the degree of democracy, the more emphasis speech receives.

Communication was the core of the curriculum for the schools of rhetoric in ancient Greece. And little wonder, for the Greek city-states represented pure democracy. Public measures were decided at town meetings, and litigants pleaded their own law cases.

When the center of civilization shifted to Rome, a gradual lessening of the emphasis on speech training resulted largely because individuals employed advocates to represent them in the courts and carried out their public business through representatives.

During the Dark Ages after the collapse of the Roman Empire speech training almost disappeared. With the decline of democracy, there was no reason for speaking because speech had little or no effect on public policy.

Democracy came back to its own in the Parliament of England. It regained power gradually, receiving its first major impetus by the founding of the House of Commons in 1265. With the union of England and Scotland in 1707, democracy became entrenched, and gained its full vigor in the latter part of the eighteenth century. Thus the reason for speaking came back.

Perhaps free speech gained its greatest vigor in the New World. The colonies were made up largely of Englishmen who brought with them ideas of self-government. All of the colonies had elective assemblies that provided endless occasions for public discussion. But speech-making was not confined to legislative halls. It took place on public platforms, in political campaigns, in town meetings, and in forums. Free speech flourished in America because speaking counts in a democracy. The good speaker does something constructive for his listeners by bringing ideas into focus, dispensing useful information, or influencing belief.

II. What You Should Get Out of a Course in Speech

You may next ask, "What should I expect to get out of a course in oral communication?" By setting up goals early in your study, you can direct your efforts toward attaining them.

Speech training offers a body of information and skills distinguishable from other fields, although it utilizes the subject matter of many fields. For example, studies in the social sciences aim at securing an understanding of subject matter, at assessing causes and effects, and at exploring different concepts. The student of public address strives for understanding too, but he goes further; he disseminates his acquired knowledge orally. He uses his knowledge for an added purpose. The student of English literature learns about great literature; the student of speech shares great literature with others through oral performances. The student of drama learns about dramatic literature; the actor portrays the characters to an audience.

The principle of communicating orally distinguishes speech training from other studies. The following skills should be developed by speech training.

How to Think Through a Problem

We must consider problems and make countless decisions each day. Some decisions may be of little moment, such as what suit we shall wear. Others are considerably more important, such as whom we shall vote for in the gubernatorial election, whether we should make the loan to the applicant, or whether we should expand our business. Still other decisions determine largely our lot in life, such as what profession or business we shall follow, what college we shall attend, or what church, political party, and organizations we shall join. Just how much intelligence do we exercise in thinking through such problems? Probably less than we care to admit. What about your opinion on major issues? Do you think that integration in our public schools in the South is the right policy, or do you subconsciously consider an educated Negro a potential threat to your future economic, social, or political position? Or do you think at all about the problem?

You will improve your ability to think constructively if you succeed in becoming a competent public speaker. Chapters 7, 8, 9, 14, and 15 will show you how. The public speaker develops the ability to think through a problem objectively and intelligently so that he may attain the goal of doing something constructive for an audience.

How to Investigate, Analyze, and Evaluate a Problem

A student council committee met to consider what could be done to alleviate the problem of automobile parking on the campus. One committee member moved immediately that parking permits be denied to freshmen and sophomores. Another member suggested that the committee investigate the question and bring evidence to bear on the problem. This suggestion prevailed and the chairman appointed subcommittees to investigate various facets of the problem and to report at a later meeting. These reports formed the basis for further deliberations and for the final decision of the committee.

Some people like to decide matters in a hurry. Impatient with investigation and deliberation, they prefer to get the matter settled at once regardless of the value of the decision. Others are overly cautious in making decisions. They say that they will not decide until all the facts are in, not realizing that such is an impossibility. Of course, during times of crisis decisions must be made in a hurry, but normally the wiser course calls for investigation and analysis prior to decision.

The public speaker usually has time for thorough investigation and analysis. He has learned how to find the facts, how to analyze them, and how to judge their worth. Chapters 6 and 7 bear directly on these skills, and other chapters treat them indirectly. The successful speaker has acquired the ability to separate the essential from the non-essential, the valid from the invalid, the facts from propaganda.

How to Organize Ideas

Some people have mature ideas and can find the facts, but they lack facility in organizing their thoughts for either written or oral communication. Thus the reader or listener must surmise what the writer or speaker means. No doubt the communicator has an idea, but he fails to organize a sequence of points that develop a central theme.

For example, some speakers attempt too much for a single speech. One statesman spoke on the eve of an election on "Ten Commandments for Successful Voting." The timeliness and appropriateness of his topic were excellent, but he had too many points. A few points thoroughly developed with illustrative material accomplish more than numerous ideas without adequate support.

Another common fault in arrangement comes from improper sequence of ideas. A student in a speech class spoke on "The Foreign Aid Program of the United States." He developed these three points: (1) the future of our aid program, (2) suggestions for reform, (3) the nature of the problem. These points were well chosen but poorly arranged; they did not follow in logical sequence. By reversing the order, an improvement becomes apparent: (1) the nature of the problem, (2) suggestions for reform, (3) the future of our aid program. Why discuss reforms before you show the need for them? The future of the aid program can best be discussed in the light of the speaker's suggested reforms.

Chapter 8 treats organization in detail and suggests several plans for arranging ideas. The instructions deal specifically with oral presentation but they apply as well to written communication.

How to Present Ideas Orally

Have you ever considered how much time you spend each day communicating with others? Estimate the time you spend during a typical day in talking and listening, reading and writing—the four principal methods of communicating. One student did so with the following results. He spent eight hours in oral communication—three hours talking and five hours listening. He engaged in written communication for six hours—four hours reading and two hours writing. These totaled fourteen hours; and note that he spent considerably more time in oral than in written communication.

Most of us spend a great deal of time in communicating, yet how much of it is effective? Why cannot we settle more of our conflicts by talking them through? Talk is not only an inexpensive method for settling problems, but it is also the most civilized. When talk breaks down, people resort to belligerent methods for settling their problems: labor strikes against capital, capital boycotts labor, friends get angry and will not speak, absenteeism runs high in industry, nations go to war. The causes for breakdowns in communication receive treatment in Chapter 14. It is sufficient here to call attention to the importance of improving your ability to communicate orally. This textbook concerns itself primarily with this aspect of communication.

How to Listen Critically

Listening and memory received more attention during the Classical period than they do today. Without methods of printing, ideas and information were passed on orally from generation to generation. Principles of listening and memory bulked large, therefore, in the ancient schools of rhetoric because they were essential to the preservation of knowledge. In the early history of America, listening also received major stress because oral communication was the principal means of disseminating ideas and information. With the coming of the printing press and advances in education, we relied heavily on the written word for mass communication. In recent years, the advent of radio and television has caused a shift back to the spoken word as the principal medium of communication. Recent studies indicate that most people listen more than they read. Furthermore, people devote a greater percentage of each day to listening than they may realize. Studies among various groups show the extent—nurses, 42 per cent; dietitians, 63 per cent; business executives, 40 per cent; students, 57 per cent; and a cross section of business and professional groups, 45 per cent.

Unfortunately many people hear but do not listen. Modern mass communication media have given rise to careless listening habits. One student insists that he must have his radio on to study effectively. Another requires the constant noise of his air conditioner to counteract other noises. Still another watches television, reads the evening paper, and eats his dinner all at once. Do you wonder that we have developed indifferent listening habits?

The slovenly listening habits of everyday living affect listening in audience-speaker situations adversely. Some students only half listen as the instructor lectures. They worry about their unfinished essay in English while attending their history lecture, work their mathematics problems in psychology class, and plan their social activities as the speech teacher lectures. The salesman plans his sales interview while attending the civic lecture series; the lawyer thinks about his law trial as the minister preaches; and the housewife plans her shopping trip during the lecture at her study club. The failure to listen prevents the speaker from attaining his purpose—the communication of ideas and feelings.

Who must assume responsibility for the loss of communication caused by poor listening? We formerly blamed the speaker exclusively. Members of an audience seem to say, "Here I am, Mr. Speaker; see if you can win out in the battle for my attention." More recently educators have contended that the listener must assume part of the responsibility. Many able people have worthwhile ideas, but their presentation skills are not effective enough to command the attention of the audience. By considering oral communication as a two-way process, its greatest potential may be realized.

You may ask, "How can a course in oral communication improve my listening?" Largely by two means: (1) by a study of methods and techniques for effective listening and (2) by providing exercises that encourage listening. Through a cooperative effort by speaker and audience, communication may be improved. A course in oral communication should help you become a more effective listener.

III. How You Can Develop Yourself as a Speaker

A good starting point in developing yourself as a speaker is to take stock of your own limitations. What do you consider your chief weaknesses in oral communication? Analyze your needs by answering the following questions.

Do you lack a background of knowledge on which to draw for ideas and subject matter? If so, the solution to your problem consists of cultivating an interest in and an inquiring attitude toward the many sources of knowledge. A program for acquiring such interests comes in Chapter 6.

Do you feel insecure in a speaking situation? If so, your problem may be caused by a lack of knowledge about speech-making or of experience in speaking. This entire volume proposes to familiarize you with the processes, while the class procedures will give you the opportunity to practice speaking before your class. Chapter 10 explains in detail how to gain confidence and poise.

Do you lack facility in presenting your ideas orally? Then, give special attention to Part Three of this textbook. Practice in speaking will cause you to get the feel of an audience; thus you can improve your ability to communicate orally.

Whatever your analysis reveals, your next question concerns what you can do to prepare yourself for oral communication. As explained in Chapter 1, a good speaker is an able man with a background of information and ideas. What can you do to develop these characteristics? Consider the following six suggestions.

You Must Desire to Improve Your Speaking

Without a genuine desire to improve your oral communication and a willingness to work hard, you have little chance of success. You learn to speak by speaking. The training program provides practice periods on subjects that lead you step by step through the necessary procedures. To succeed, your desire for improvement must exceed your inertia. This requirement does not mean an insatiable desire that drives you continually. It does mean that you must work intelligently to develop an analytical mind, an interest in research, an ability to arrange ideas logically, and an eagerness to improve your voice, language, bodily action, and poise. Regardless of your professor's ability and training, he cannot teach you to become an effective speaker unless you earnestly desire self-improvement. The impetus must come from you.

You Must Develop Yourself as an Able Person

Writers since the Classical period have stressed that able speakers develop themselves as a whole. You cannot be one type of person as a speaker and another type in other pursuits. Modern writers have given this principle a name—the able man theory.

As mentioned in Chapter 1, the able man theory includes the moral character of a person, as expressed in his regard for truth and good works, his sincerity of purpose, and his search for moral, spiritual, and social values. It also encompasses his qualifications to speak, his experience and knowledge, his maturity of judgment, and his skills in arranging and presenting ideas orally. Further, it relates to the type of person he becomes—his zest for life, his attitudes of good will toward people, his controlled emotional state, and his unselfish aspirations.

These ideas have been expressed in several ways by rhetoricians and speakers throughout history. Aristotle frequently refers to and discusses various phases of this theory in his *Rhetoric.* In one of his dialogues, Cicero has his character Cato state that "a good orator is a good man skilled in speaking." Seneca declared, "Whatever the man is, such is the orator." Quintilian lays major stress on this theory in his twelve books on rhetoric. Later writers Lew Sarett and William T. Foster said, "Speech is effective, other things being equal, in proportion to the intrinsic worth of the speaker." [1] Recent writers James H. McBurney and Ernest J. Wrage state, "Good speech reveals a person of competence, integrity, and good motives." [2]

Why is this concept important to the speaker? Members of an audience accept your ideas, in part, because of their impressions of you as a person. They accept your ideas because they consider that

---

[1] Lew Sarett and William Trufant Foster, *Basic Principles of Speech* (Boston: Houghton Mifflin Co., 1936), p. 18.

[2] James H. McBurney and Ernest J. Wrage, *The Art of Good Speech* (Englewood Cliffs, N.J.: Prentice-Hall, Inc., 1953), p. 43.

you know and properly appraise the facts and opinions you express. They believe that you have an earnest desire to communicate and that you would not purposely mislead them. Further, they form impressions that your training and experience have prepared you to speak with authority. If you get these positive reactions from an audience, your chances for a successful speech multiply several fold. Unfortunately, the audience may also get opposite impressions.

Upon what basis does an audience form impressions of you as a person? Some of the more important follow.

1. *You are judged in part by the reputation that precedes you.* Toward the end of his career, Dr. George W. Truett, former pastor of the First Baptist Church in Dallas, Texas, and President of the Baptist World Alliance, became so loved and honored throughout the South that he was received with respect wherever he went. Perhaps his originality and powers of discernment decreased with the years, but his reputation was never greater than in his declining years. His reputation had been earned by a life of useful works and service, and it stood him in good stead as a speaker. Persons of authority and accomplishments naturally have the advantage in this respect over younger people who have not yet made their marks in the world, but it behooves all who aspire to successful public speaking to keep in mind the fact that one's reputation affects audience receptivity.

2. *You are judged in part by your introduction.* If you are unknown to an audience, the person who introduces you may perform a real service by increasing respect for you. Properly done, the speech of introduction informs the audience of your qualifications to speak on your subject and creates good will toward you as a person. The person introducing you should tell who you are, your position, your experiences and training in the field of your subject, any outstanding accomplishments, positions of authority you have held, and sufficient human interest material that will cause an audience to like you. Where possible, a person who knows the speaker well should give the speech of introduction. The better known the speaker already is to the audience, the less need be said.

3. *You are judged in part by what you talk about.* "Speech is the mirror of the soul: as a man speaks, so is he." This statement by Publilius Syrus constitutes more than a maxim; it contains sound advice to the public speaker. If you talk about low and degrading things, your audience will be likely to consider you that type of

person; but if you express intelligent and mature thoughts, the audience will regard you as an able person. Some years ago a public relations man representing a large corporation spoke to a Lions Club meeting. Although his was an all-male audience, he not only resorted to off-color stories, but also engaged in rank vulgarity. The reaction of the audience was spontaneous: the men ceased laughing even out of courtesy. The display caused one speech teacher in attendance to label the speech as a new low in his twenty years of professional experience. Most male audiences can appreciate an occasional risqué story but will not tolerate situations that go beyond the bounds of common decency.

Substantial evidence, sound reasoning, and maturity of judgment not only affect the logical adequacy of the speech, but also the ethical adequacy of the speaker. A student was heard to remark following a speaking program, "If Mr. X does not find the facts to his liking, he simply changes the facts." Following a speech by Mr. Y at a ceremonial occasion, one listener remarked to another, "I am disappointed that the speaker did not give us a more substantial idea." The other retorted, "Mr. Y made it quite apparent that he does not have substantial ideas to give." What you talk about reveals much about you as a person.

If you choose illustrative material that expresses sordid or trivial thoughts, you create an atmosphere on that level. If you quote unqualified people, irresponsible sources, and questionable literature, your audience will question your scholarship and judgment. Conversely, if you give illustrations from good literature, quote men of scholarship and learning, and refer to responsible sources, your audience will form favorable impressions of you as a person.

4. *You are judged in part by how you speak.* "Mend your speech, lest you mar your future." This maxim aptly states the importance of speech skills in creating favorable impressions of you as a person. If you mumble your words, look away from your audience, show undue anxiety or extreme egotism, you will be likely to repel your audience. The way you conduct yourself on the platform creates impressions of your worth as a person. You should conduct yourself in a pleasant, business-like manner with neither a condescending nor a self-conscious attitude. By your manner of speaking strive to leave the positive impression that you are a person of integrity who is well qualified to speak on his subject; show that you have made thorough preparation, that you are in a good emotional state,

and that you have a sincere desire to communicate a worthwhile idea.

5. *You are judged in part by statements that evince ethos.* Some people may question the ethics of a speaker's using statements designed to induce approval of himself by the audience. Whether you use statements of your qualifications by design or by way of passing, such statements, judiciously used, do create favorable impressions. Examples follow: (1) statements of sources studied in your preparation; (2) references to special studies you have made which qualify you to know the facts, e.g., your membership in the student council's fact-finding committee; (3) statements of positions held, honors received, or other accomplishments which put you into a position to know the facts; (4) statements of places visited which bear on your subject, e.g., your visit inside the Iron Curtain in your speech on conditions in Russia. Such material will usually be brought into your speech by indirection, through illustrative material. It should never be given in a braggadocio manner.

References to matters which people hold in high esteem will usually create favorable impressions of you as a person. For example, if in your speech to the athletic association you illustrate a point by giving an incident involving your work in a boys' summer camp, your audience will know that you speak from experience. An incident relating your experiences on the honors program will show your academic attainment. An example pertaining to your work in the United Fund drive stresses your interests in civic activities. Such statements tend to create favorable impressions of you as an able man.

You Must Build a Storehouse of Information

To develop yourself as an effective speaker, you must have a storehouse of information and ideas upon which to draw. Acquiring such a background constitutes a lifelong process of interest and inquiry into the many sources of useful information. Many persons become experts in specific fields of knowledge, but their range of knowledge becomes too restricted for practical value to them as public speakers. A diversity of subject matter that comes from a continuous study of the liberal arts serves the public speaker well.

A distinction should be made here between *direct* and *indirect* preparation for speaking. Direct preparation consists of the specific research and planning you do for a particular speech. Indirect preparation comes from your general habits of reading and inquiry, your experience, travel, associations, and observations. The former consists of your preparation for a specific speech; the latter contributes both to a specific speech and to all your speeches.

Both types of preparation serve you well, but often people tend to overlook the importance of a broad general background of learning. Your general background may well make the difference between your making an occasional successful speech and your becoming a successful public speaker. The latter prepares himself by continuous study and intelligent thinking throughout his life. He can draw on the fields of literature, art, history, government, and philosophy for ideas and supporting material on many subjects. Broad inquiry also affects a person's attitudes, making him broad-minded, tolerant of new ideas, and willing to experiment. A program for acquiring a background of information and ideas comes in Chapter 6.

You Should Observe Great Speakers in Action

Time spent in listening to successful speakers, in analyzing their ideas, and in observing their skills serves the student of speech well. Do not, however, pattern your style after any one successful speaker. Do not try to become a second John Kennedy, Billy Graham, Winston Churchill, Lyndon Johnson, or David Brinkley. Although the observation and study of successful speakers should aid you in developing your own potential ability, you should develop your own potential abilities into an individual style.

Analyze successful speakers for pointers on both composition and delivery. What do they do that makes them effective? What distracting influences do you note? Can you reproduce the central idea of a speech several hours after hearing it? Apply the five standards of good speech discussed in Chapter 1 as you listen. These procedures not only will help you develop your own speaking ability but also will make you a better listener.

Do not restrict your observations to one or a few types of speakers; listen to diverse types. Analyze the minister's sermon on Sunday morning; go down to the courthouse and listen to an interesting criminal case; attend the lecture series sponsored by your university; hear a college debate or discussion; listen to the President speak on television; observe your professors' lectures critically. Make lists of good and bad techniques that you observe. These procedures should make you aware of your own shortcomings and inspire you to improve your speaking skills.

You Should Study the Great Speakers and Speeches of History

Read critically oratorical masterpieces of history, current representative speeches, and winning student speeches. This suggestion supplements the recommended program of listening to outstanding speakers. Analyze such masterpieces of history as Patrick Henry's "Call to Arms" speech, Daniel Webster's "Reply to Hayne," Abraham Lincoln's "Gettysburg Address," Henry W. Grady's "The New South," and the Lincoln-Douglas debates.

Although you cannot study presentation skills in published speech, you can study composition, language, forms of support, and reasoning. For the present, analyze famous speeches by the standards discussed in Chapter 1. After studying future chapters, you can analyze the three following rhetorical principles from a published speech. (1) *Organization*—Study the composition of the speech according to the principles discussed in Chapter 8. What type of organization does the speaker use? Can you follow his central idea easily? Does he support each idea well? (2) *Forms of support*—How effectively does he support his ideas according to the discussion in Chapter 7? Does he use a variety of examples, comparisons, statistics, and quotations? Which form does he use most effectively? (3) *Style*—Does the speaker's use of language comply with the principles discussed in Chapter 11? Does he express himself with preciseness of meaning? Does he use colorful language?

You Should Practice Speaking

The adage that "you learn to do by doing" applies especially to speech skills. Practice under the direction of a skilled critic, however, or your practice may simply make permanent, not perfect. Practice talks in speech classes prove more beneficial than those in private sessions; you get the "feel" of an audience by speaking before the class. Speeches before clubs, church organizations, and other classes offer realistic audiences. Accept as many such speaking assignments as possible during your period of training.

Practice periods, outside class, with your instructor or an advanced student as critic afford the opportunity for immediate criticism and appraisal. If possible, record some of your practice speeches. After receiving your criticism, play the record back and note your errors. Several sessions of this type will prove invaluable.

Practice your speech several times before giving it in class. Observe these rules in practice: (1) Use an empty room so that you can speak aloud. (2) Imagine yourself as speaking before your audience. (3) Speak through the outline extemporaneously from beginning to end. Do not stop and go back over a particular section. (4) Space your practice periods over several days. Several short sessions prove more valuable than one or two long sessions. (5) Force yourself to practice regardless of how artificial the rehearsals appear at first. (6) If you experience difficulty in expressing yourself, try writing out your first few speeches. Go over the written manuscripts and improve your choice of language and sentence structure. Do not memorize the speech but read your manuscript over several times.

IV. How You Can Develop Skills in Organization and Presentation

This textbook takes you step by step through the organization and presentation of a speech in the approximate order that you face each step. Since you will start making speeches immediately, a brief overall view follows for the purpose of helping you to get started. Each factor enumerated receives detailed treatment in succeeding chapters.

STEPS IN SPEECH PREPARATION

Preliminary steps
1. Analyze your audience and speaking occasion.
2. Select your subject and purpose.

Organization steps
3. Find and analyze your material.
4. Select your supporting material.
5. Organize and outline your speech.

Presentation steps
6. Develop skills in delivery.
    a. Develop poise and confidence.
    b. Develop a vocabulary for ready choice of language.
    c. Develop a pleasing voice.
    d. Use natural bodily action.

Analyze Your Audience and Speaking Occasion

To communicate effectively you must know about your audience and the details of the occasion. Determine your listeners' special interests, their attitude toward your subject, and their opinion of you. Learn the approximate age level, background of training and knowledge, and social and cultural background of your listeners.

Investigate the occasion. What is the purpose of the meeting? What ritual will prevail? How large will the audience be? What physical conditions will prevail? Knowledge of these facts about audience and speaking occasion will help you select a proper subject, effective supporting material, and a logical organizational pattern.

Select Your Subject and Purpose

What to talk about and how to treat your subject present perplexing problems. If the program commemorates some occasion, honors an outstanding person, dedicates a building, or pays tribute to graduates at commencement exercises, select a subject that conforms to the propriety of the occasion. When the audience assembles primarily to hear you on a subject of your choice, select a subject from your background of knowledge, interests, and convictions. Consider such limiting factors as the intellectual level of the audience, the time limit, the adaptability of the subject to oral presentation, and the probable size of the audience.

Next, consider the purpose of your speech. You may persuade, inform, or entertain your audience; but you should decide on the type early in your preparation to avoid wasted effort. After determining the type of speech, decide on the specific purpose you wish to accomplish.

Find and Analyze Your Material

Although the ideas and some of the material for your speech may come from your previous background knowledge, you will need to do additional research and study to clarify and support your ideas. Interview specialists and listen to speakers on allied subjects, analyze published speeches on similar subjects, obtain information through correspondence, discuss your ideas with others, and do research on your subject. In doing research, study source books, textbooks, and trade books first. Then read newspapers, magazines, encyclopedias, yearbooks, almanacs, biographical and literary references, professional and trade journals, and governmental documents. Also have available a good dictionary and bibliographic index.

To keep a record of your readings for ready references during the planning stage, adopt a systematic plan for taking notes. With the materials before you, analyze and evaluate your material, discarding irrelevant matter and arranging usable materials into an appropriate outline.

Select Your Supporting Material

As you do research on your subject, select specific items to support your points. The principal forms of support consist of explanation, statistics, examples, analogies, quotations from authority, and restatement. The forms of support give your ideas substance; they clarify, amplify, and help prove your points. Without the expanding process of supporting material, your outline becomes a mere skeleton and your ideas remain undeveloped.

Explanation constitutes the principal method for developing ideas in the informative speech and serves to give the necessary background for understanding arguments in the persuasive speech. Statistics, analogies, examples, and quotations from authority clarify explanations and support arguments. They serve a purpose in public speaking similar to that of evidence in courts of law and policy-determining bodies. They add probative force to your contentions. Restatement rounds out the points of speech by repeating and summarizing them, thus giving clarity and emphasis to ideas.

Two important factors govern the choice of forms of support—accuracy and effectiveness. In planning your speech, select only those forms of support that evaluate your points accurately and that have interest to your immediate listeners.

Organize and Outline Your Speech

Arrange your ideas simply and concisely to clarify the central idea of your speech. Divide your speech into three parts: introduction, body, and conclusion. The introduction establishes rapport with the audience, gains interest in the subject, and clarifies the plan for the speech. The body may be organized by several methods, depending upon the adaptation of the material and the purpose of your speech. First decide whether the general organizational pattern shall be deductive or inductive. The deductive method states the point first and develops it by various forms of support. The inductive method presents the details first and states the conclusion as a climax. Ideas may be developed in problem-solution form, by chronological arrangement, by simple enumeration, in logical order, from cause to effect, from effect to cause, or from familiar to unfamiliar.

The conclusion summarizes the speech and states the basic appeal.

Develop Skills in Delivery

Your final step in preparation takes patience and hard work. In practice sessions, attempt to improve your presentation skills. The delivery skills enumerated below are discussed in detail in Part Three of this textbook.

Knowledge of rhetorical principles and practice in speaking help improve self-confidence and poise. Tenseness can usually be brought under control by an understanding of the causes of the problem, by realizing that most conscientious people experience such feelings, by thorough preparation, by keeping physically fit, and by deliberately adopting a success attitude. Although tenseness cannot be eliminated, it can be controlled.

Strive to improve your vocabulary and use of language. The principal methods for improving vocabulary consist of reading good literature, of listening to educated people, and of writing and speaking. A study and discussion of new words also helps; try out new words in practice sessions.

Work to improve your speaking voice. An understanding of the speech mechanism serves as a good starting point. The essentials of good voice production consist of breathing deeply from the diaphragm, of relaxing the throat, of forward placement of the speech sounds, and of flexible speech modifiers.

Develop the ability to let your body help you speak. Bodily action consists of movements of the whole body, parts of the body (gestures), and facial expressions. Such movements help to express the meaning of what you say. Bodily action should come from an inner feeling or urge, and should not be planned and rehearsed. Unless the actions come naturally, they will not be appropriate and properly timed. Attempt to relieve inhibitions so that your bodily action will come naturally. Through practice with proper attention to bearing and poise, voice quality, vocabulary, and bodily action, you can improve your delivery skills to a marked extent.

V. Summary

Public speaking means the communication of ideas, information, and feelings to an audience. A good public speaker is conversational and direct, has something to say and says it well, and gives constructive ideas to an audience.

A course in speech should give a person skills in thinking through and investigating a problem, in organizing ideas and presenting them orally, and in listening effectively.

A starting point for developing yourself as a speaker consists of taking stock of your limitations. Your weaknesses may be considered in three categories: (1) lack of background knowledge, (2) insecurity in the speaking situation, and (3) lack of skills in presentation.

To attain oral communication skills, you must desire to improve your speaking, develop yourself into an able person, build a background of information and ideas, observe great speakers in action, study great speeches of history, and practice speaking.

Acquiring skills in organization and presentation requires a step-by-step procedure which includes the following: (1) analyzing the audience and occasion, (2) selecting a suitable subject and purpose, (3) finding and analyzing material, (4) selecting the best supporting material, (5) organizing and outlining the speech, and (6) developing skills in delivery. These steps receive detailed treatment in Parts Two and Three; the brief explanation in this chapter should enable you to start making speeches immediately.

Questions and Exercises

A. Answer the following questions on Chapter 2.

1. What is meant by, "Good speech is conversational and communicative"?
2. What are the principal differences between good conversation and good public speaking?
3. Which do you consider more important in oral communication: (a) having something worthwhile to say, or (b) being able to say it well?
4. What is meant by, "A good speech should do something constructive to the audience"?
5. What does the history of speech education reveal as to the emphasis on speech training in various stages of history?
6. What contributions should speech training make to individual skills?
7. On the basis of the discussion in this chapter, do you think you have the proper desire for starting a program to improve your communication skills?

8. What is meant by the statement that "a good speaker is an able person"?
9. On what basis do the members of an audience form opinions of "the worth of the speaker as a person"?
10. Distinguish between direct and indirect preparation for public speaking.
11. How important do you consider "a background of information and ideas" to success in oral communication?
12. What do you consider your chief weaknesses in indirect preparation? Rate yourself on this factor, using the scale: excellent, good, average, fair, poor.
13. How can you go about improving your background of information? Keep your answer to this question on file and compare it to the program outlined in Chapter 6 when your instructor assigns it.
14. List three present-day speakers in each of the following fields whom you consider able speakers: (a) religion, (b) politics, (c) labor, (d) industry, and (e) foreign service. Be prepared to defend your selection.
15. List ten persons in American history whom you consider able speakers. In what professions or businesses were they engaged?

B. Listen to a speech during the next week and answer the questions listed below about the speaker and his speech. Do not take notes during his speech, but listen carefully and write out your answers from memory. The speaker may be a business executive, one of your professors, a speaker at a civic club, or any other speaker. Reconsider this question after reading Chapter 3.

1. In a short paragraph, state the central theme of the address.
2. What were his main points in developing his theme?
3. Did you have difficulty following the organizational pattern of the speech? Explain.
4. How well do you think the speaker met the standards for judging a good speech as explained in Chapter 1? Make a brief comment for each standard.
5. Analyze the speech from the standpoint of (a) invention, (b) arrangement, (c) style, and (d) delivery.
6. What effect do you think this project had on your ability to listen intelligently to a speech?

C. For your second oral assignment prepare a simple reporting speech. Read an article in a current magazine and give a five-minute oral report on it in class. Remember that you are not responsible for the content or organization of the article; your only duty is to report it to the class. Proceed as follows:

1. State the title and date of the magazine, the author's name, and the title of the article.
2. Review the article.
3. Give a brief appraisal or evaluation of it.

CHAPTER 3

Acquire Listening Facility

Chapter 2 listed efficient listening as one of the five basic skills which the study of oral communication seeks to develop. Succeeding chapters will consider principles of composition and delivery primarily from the viewpoint of the speaker, but these principles also apply indirectly to listening. An understanding of the principles of oral communication not only assists the speaker to secure improved listening but also helps the listener to listen more intelligently.

Recent studies reveal a significant breakdown in communication between speakers and audiences—an average listener retains no more than 60 to 70 per cent of what the speaker says. What causes this breakdown? Most authorities believe that the speaker and the listener must share the blame. To help improve listening, consider the following questions: (1) Why listen? (2) What are the requirements for efficient listening? (3) How can you improve your listening habits?

I. Why Listen?

Listening and reading are the principal methods for acquiring knowledge. As discussed in Chapter 2, most of us listen more than we read. The teaching of listening has long been neglected, but most educators today realize that listening encompasses a body of knowledge and skills which can be learned and practiced. In short, listening can be improved. Furthermore, listening is as important to communication as speaking, reading, and writing. What are the principal purposes of listening?

To Acquire Facts

Scholars obtain most of their facts through research and experimentation. The average citizen spends little time in research and practically none in experimentation. He may read the daily newspaper, a few magazines, and an occasional book, but he gets most of his information from listening to the radio or television, from conversing with associates, from participating in conferences, or from listening to speeches. As a source for obtaining facts, listening proves invaluable for the average citizen.

Scholars and speakers also obtain some of their facts by listening. Suppose you decide to speak on juvenile delinquency. You may begin your study by interviewing a professor of sociology for facts about social aspects of the problem, a law professor for legal implications, the probation officer for facts on the extent of the problem, and the superintendent of schools and a minister for opinions on how education and religion apply. You may also listen to speeches, lectures, or panel discussions on aspects of the subject. You may discuss your ideas with members of your family, your roommate, or others. In each of these instances you obtain facts through listening. Wilson Mizner, celebrated wit and playwright, says, "A good listener is not only popular everywhere, but after a while, he knows something."

To Analyze Facts and Ideas

Finding facts constitutes an essential first step to understanding, but after acquiring the facts you must ask, "What do the facts mean?" The process of appraising the facts, of breaking a subject up into its constituent parts, and of assessing causes and effects is termed analysis. Chapters 6 and 15 explain the process of analysis in detail.

The point at issue here is "How does listening affect analysis?" Consider the mental processes of a critical listener. He constantly analyzes what a speaker says; he talks back in his own mind. The speaker sets up trains of thought which the listener considers in relation to his own knowledge and experiences. Speakers talk at a rate of 120 to 150 words per minute, but listeners can comprehend at a rate of 300 to 500 words per minute. A critical listener utilizes the time afforded by the speaker's slower rate to analyze the speaker's ideas and facts. In short, listening provides an occasion for analysis.

To Evaluate Facts and Ideas

Having determined what the facts and ideas mean, the listener asks next, "What are the facts worth? How accurate and valuable are they?" He may think, "I agree; what you say corresponds with my experiences and understanding." Conversely, the listener may think, "I disagree; your point contradicts my experiences" or "I am not sure; you still have to show me."

If the listener agrees with the speaker, he usually labels the speaker's ideas as mature and his facts as accurate. If he disagrees, he may consider the speaker prejudiced because of his economic, political, or social philosophy. He may think that the speaker has been influenced by propagandists or that his ideas reflect his own interests. He may believe that the speaker has made an immature evaluation of his subject, that he does not know what he talks about. He may conclude that the speaker's statistics cover only a limited phase of the subject, that his examples reflect extreme cases, that the objects he compares are not comparable, or that the authorities he cites are incompetent. In short, the listener passes judgment, weighs assertions, and evaluates facts and opinions.

For Inspiration

We sometimes listen, not for information or ideas, but to be inspired. Inspirational speeches abound in our society because they fulfill certain human needs. Professional people often attend conventions or institutes more from a desire to renew their enthusiasm than to acquire information.

A well-planned convention begins with a keynote speech designed to create enthusiasm or to inspire the delegates. Speeches of anniversary and dedication seek to increase listeners' respect for organizations or great movements in history. Sales managers, directors of promotional organizations, and campaign managers use inspirational speeches to promote their programs. Many religious services, patriotic rallies, and home-coming gatherings are based on the need for inspiration. In brief, the desire for inspiration constitutes a worthy reason for listening.

For Entertainment

We often listen for no other purpose than pleasure, for relaxation and entertainment. Enjoyment is a basic desire of humanity, a desire for release from the cares of everyday living. We listen to radio and view television basically for entertainment. We attend the movies, plays, and sport events for pleasure. We are entertained on many speaking occasions, such as banquets, club meetings, and parties. We derive entertainment from the human or light notes introduced into persuasive and informative speeches. In brief, entertainment serves a valuable purpose for listening.

To Improve Speaking

A perceptive person can improve his own speaking through observation, by listening to good speakers. To listen efficiently, he must have a plan for analyzing the speech and the speaker. The plan should include much that will be learned in this text: how the speaker conforms to the standards of effective oral communication, how he adapts his speech to his audience, how he composes his material and supports his points, and how he makes coordinated use of mind, body, voice, and language for effective delivery.

II. Requirements for Efficient Listening

The speaker must understand the prerequisites to efficient listening in order to improve communication. Upon what does efficient listening depend? Why do audiences listen attentively to one speech, yet fail to listen to an equally good speech? The answer depends on any one or a combination of the following factors: (1) the listener's attitude, (2) the listener's interests, (3) the listener's motivation, and (4) the listener's emotional state. In short, listening depends largely on the audience's readiness and willingness to listen.

Listening Depends on Attitudes

Probably no single factor affects efficient listening more than the listener's attitude. Efficient listening requires an objective, unprejudiced, cooperative attitude. If the listener has a biased attitude he may hear only those facts and opinions that conform to his beliefs.

Opinionated people usually make poor listeners. They refuse to listen to opposing views because of their prejudices. A person may be objective on some questions but subjective on others. Some years ago a university committee of departmental chairmen was appointed to revise the list of required courses. On many other questions these professors showed considerable objectivity; on the topic of required courses they were highly subjective because they feared that their own subjects might be left off the required list. Many people have difficulty maintaining an objective attitude when their interests are at stake.

Sometimes our political, economic, and social attitudes are formed early in life as a result of our environment. We do not want those fixed opinions challenged; questioning them disturbs our complacency. We, therefore, refuse to listen to ideas that might shake our beliefs. Because a person dislikes communism is no reason for him to refuse to listen to viewpoints opposed to his own. As will be explained in Chapter 6, we become unteachable when we think that we know the final answer to any question; we refuse to listen. We may consider our own opinions on such questions as segregation, religion, and prohibition. Do we find difficulty being objective on these topics?

Our attitudes may be influenced by our knowledge and experience with the subject discussed. An educated person usually is a more perceptive listener than an uneducated person. A perceptive listener relates what the speaker says to his own knowledge and experiences. Conversely, people with little knowledge often become passive listeners. They have little knowledge to which to relate the speaker's ideas, so they have difficulty in understanding them; they stop listening or only half-listen.

A person who wants to listen profitably neither strongly agrees nor strongly disagrees with the speaker early in his speech. Rather, he maintains a questioning, open-minded, creative attitude. He withholds final judgment until the speaker develops his subject.

Listening Depends on Interests

We listen to ideas that interest us. In Chapter 4 a distinction is made among primary, secondary, and momentary interests. The distinction also applies to listening. We have a primary interest when we have a direct stake in what the speaker talks about, when his proposal affects our daily living. We may consider some phases of education purely academic; but when the speaker suggests an increase in tuition rates at the university which our son attends, we become actively interested. The businessman may be mildly interested in the subject of taxation, but he becomes greatly interested when the speaker proposes an increase in taxes on his business. The professional man may show little interest in social security, but he becomes intensely interested when the speaker proposes that he be included in the program. We listen because what the speaker says relates to our primary interests.

We show interest also when the speaker appeals to our secondary interests. As citizens of a community we view the public works program of the federal government with fleeting interest; but when the President vetoes an appropriation bill which halts construction on our new dam, we become alive to the issue. When a speaker proposes a new civic center, we listen because the proposal affects our common interests. Many subjects relate to our secondary interests, and we show interest when a speaker refers to them.

Other matters may command our momentary interests. We show more interest during election year about the abolition of our two-party system than we do in an off-election year, just as we became intensely interested in our presidential succession provisions following the assassination of President John F. Kennedy. We are more receptive to the proposal to abolish football when a member of the local team suffers a serious injury than when the team enjoys a healthy and successful season. We show momentary interest in many matters of a temporary nature, and we listen when a speaker refers to those momentary interests.

We also show more interest in familiar than in unfamiliar things. Students are interested in campus problems, teachers in matters of education, businessmen in finance and investment, and lawyers in legal rights. The automobile worker in Michigan is more interested in the steel strike in Pennsylvania than in the longshoremen's strike in San Francisco. Similarly, the sharecropper in the Appalachian area shows more interest in President Johnson's program for alleviating poverty than does the steel worker in Pennsylvania. We become interested when speakers talk about familiar problems, matters close to us.

We are also interested in active and novel ideas. When a speaker shows enthusiasm, talks about striking and concrete things, and uses language of action, we show interest.

Listening Depends on Motivation

We listen when the speaker appeals to our basic desires and needs. We become interested when the speaker shows that his proposal means money in our pockets, increased prestige in our community, greater authority over our fellow man, or the preservation of things which we hold dear. The basic motives of man have been classified variously by many writers. A. E. Phillips, former director of Phillips School of Oratory in Chicago, gives us a comprehensive and workable classification as follows: (1) self-preservation, (2) property, (3) power, (4) reputation, (5) affection, (6) sentiment, and (7) taste.[1]

1. *Self-preservation.* Self-preservation is perhaps the most basic of all motives. Animals reflect the instinct to survive, and have characteristics that help make survival possible. Small animals have protective coloring and can conceal themselves effectively; others can move rapidly and avoid detection; still others have the strength and agility to protect themselves by force and dexterity.

Man is governed to a large extent by his desire to survive—to obtain food and shelter, to protect his health and comfort, to preserve his mind and body. Men lock up their homes to protect their possessions; they resort to the courts to protect their rights; and they go to war to protect their way of life. Self-preservation is a basic law of nature. When a speaker links his subject with the basic desire of survival, listeners pay attention.

2. *Property.* The desire for material things plays an important part in the lives of most people. We all desire land, goods, and money—things that we can call our own. Modern advertising often makes its basic appeal to this motive with the result that some people buy more than they can afford. Differences in the basic appeal of the government bond campaigns show how advertising uses the appeal to basic motives effectively. During the war, the basic appeal was made to self-preservation: "Buy bonds and help protect the American way." After the war, the basic appeal was to property: "Invest three dollars now and get four dollars back."

The desire for material things inheres in our system of free enterprise. It motivates people to devise more efficient ways of increasing profits. It causes merchants to sell at the lowest prices consistent with maximum profits to induce people to buy more. It causes laborers to form unions, capitalists to organize pressure groups, and

---

[1] A. E. Phillips, *Effective Speaking* (Chicago: The Newton Co., 1910), p. 48.

professional people to join associations. If a speaker can show his listeners how to increase their profits, how to do their tasks more efficiently, how to save money, or how to add to their material possessions, he makes them want to listen.

3. *Power.* Authority and influence are strong motivating factors with some people. Assistant managers strive to become managers; lieutenants work to become captains; and instructors seek professorships. Ambitious people strive to improve themselves. They seek responsible positions so that they may have power and authority over others.

The desire for power motivates students to strive for high academic records and excellence in extracurricular activities. It causes adults to take correspondence and evening division courses. It causes business and professional people to attend conventions and refresher courses. People desire to improve themselves so that they may extend their influence. The speaker who can show his listeners how to increase their influence and authority will increase their desire to listen.

4. *Reputation.* The desire for recognition and admiration is a universally compelling motive. Most people strive for social approval, to be respected by their associates. They accept positions of responsibility—civic, church, professional—because it increases respect for them among their associates. They wage political campaigns to be city councilman, mayor, member of the school board—positions that require much time and effort with little or no financial rewards—because they desire social approval. Students strive for medals, awards, and prizes in part because they desire the admiration of their fellow students.

The salesman appeals to reputation when he seeks to sell a new home, household furnishings, and the latest-model automobile. The real estate promoter stresses that the new subdivision is restricted to homes of distinction. The insurance salesman furnishes a list of influential citizens who have insured with his company. He stresses the importance of "keeping up with the Joneses." In the same way that the salesman gets acceptance of his product by an appeal to reputation, the speaker can get the idea of his speech accepted by showing how it will enhance his listener's reputation.

5. *Affection.* Love of family, friends, and country constitutes a strong motivating force. Love of family is perhaps the strongest kind of affection. The insurance industry was built largely upon this motive. Educational saving programs owe their popularity to love

for one's offspring. Attitudes of good will toward our fellow man have their inception in love of friends. Civic pride, school spirit, and church loyalty are based upon the warm feelings we have for members of our social groups. Love of country causes us to go to war. Men may criticize their fellow men, institutions, and country; but when these are threatened, they rally to their support.

Our ethical standards of fair play, personal honor, and respect for others are motivated largely by love and affection. Religious convictions arise from love for a supreme being. The speaker who appeals to affection causes audiences to listen.

6. *Sentiment.* Sentiment determines our sense of loyalty and patriotism. We go to great expense to establish museums, restore historic buildings, and preserve historical documents, largely for sentimental reasons. Sentiment occasions protests from the alumni when a college administration proposes to replace the original campus building with a more modern structure. We may be reluctant to move to a modern home out of sentiment for the old home place. We lament the passing of the local literary society because we have formed a sentimental attachment to it. Our sense of loyalty causes us to maintain friendships with people with whom we no longer have anything in common. The speaker who appeals to sentiment gives an audience an added inducement to listen.

7. *Taste.* The love of beauty, adventure, and new experiences forms a compelling motive for sensitive people. Not all our actions are motivated by practical considerations; some stem from aesthetic appreciation. We appreciate the works of the masters in painting, music, poetry, drama, and sculpture because they appeal to our aesthetic sense. Automobile manufacturers go to great expense to design streamlined cars with attractive colors and decorations; we call in interior decorators to harmonize the color and design of our new home; we vacation in the beauty spots of our country; we do all these things because of our sense of beauty and harmony. The speaker who defers to our aesthetic appreciation motivates us to listen.

Listening Depends on Emotional State

Our willingness and ability to listen depend in part on our emotional state. Undesirable emotional conditions for listening may be the result of an emotional upset, a reluctance in attending the speaking occasion, a lack of interest in the subject, or a crowding out of desire to listen by other pressing problems. On the other hand, failure to listen may result from attitudes toward the speaker. We may consider the speaker incapable of a constructive analysis of his subject because of his youth, his lack of training, experience, and prestige, or his immaturity of judgment. Something the speaker says may cause us figuratively to tune him out. The speaker may express extreme, illogical, or dogmatic statements that offend our sense of intelligence. He may make statements contrary to our political, economic, or social beliefs and thus antagonize us. He may fail to support his ideas with adequate evidence and thereby reveal his lack of knowledge. Any of these factors may cause us to stop listening or to listen with negative or antagonistic attitudes.

Another idea explained earlier in this chapter affects our emotional conditions for listening. We tend to listen to what we want to hear and refuse to listen to ideas contrary to our existing beliefs. We listen to what pleases us.

Professor Ralph G. Nichols of the University of Minnesota and free-lance writer Leonard A. Stevens, in their book *Are You Listening?*, state:

> In different degrees and in many different ways, listening ability in all of us is affected by our emotions. Like the troubled college student, we often "reach up and turn off" what we don't want to hear. Or, on the other hand, when we especially want to hear, we open our ears wide, accepting anything—truths, half-truths, or fiction.
>
> We might say, then, that our emotions act as filters to what we hear. At times they, in effect, cause deafness, and at other times they may make listening altogether too easy.
>
> When the emotions produce deafness, it can happen like this: If we hear something that opposes our most deeply rooted prejudices, notions, convictions, mores or complexes, our brains may become overstimulated, but not in a direction that leads to good listening. We mentally plan a rebuttal to what we hear. Or sometimes we formulate a question designed to embarrass the talker. Or perhaps we simply turn to thoughts that support our own feelings on the subject.
>
> When emotions make listening too easy, it usually results from hearing something which supports our deeply rooted inner feelings. When we hear such support, our mental barriers are dropped and everything is welcomed. We ask no questions about what we hear; our faculties are put out of commission by our emotions.[2]

---

[2] Ralph G. Nichols and Leonard A. Stevens, *Are You Listening?* (New York: McGraw-Hill Book Co., 1957), pp. 90-91.

In short, good listening depends upon the emotional state of the listener. The speaker should understand that his auditors listen best when they are free of emotional disturbances, when they disregard their strong prejudices and feelings, and adopt attitudes of willingness to listen.

In summary, efficient listening depends upon the attitudes, interests, motivation, and the emotional state of listeners. An understanding of these requirements will aid both the speaker and the listener in attaining improved listening.

III. How to Listen

Having learned the requirements for efficient listening and how the speaker may encourage listening, we now consider the listener who asks, "How can I improve my listening habits?" First, consider how listening differs from reading, as a basis for understanding the methods for efficient listening.

The reader depends upon the printed page exclusively. The listener receives impressions not only from what the speaker says but also from the way he says it. The speaker's poise, voice, and body action may be as meaningful as what he says.

The reader can stop to ponder or to reread ideas not fully understood at first reading. The listener must understand instantaneously; he cannot ask the speaker to repeat or to stop while he thinks of what has been said. The listener must work harder than the reader to comprehend; he must remain alert at all times. He either gets ideas and information the first time or he loses out.

Consider the following suggestions as aids to listening: (1) concentrate, (2) understand what to listen for, (3) listen critically, and (4) use mechanical aids for listening.

Listen with Concentration

To concentrate, you must prepare yourself to listen. Adopt a cooperative and objective attitude; create an interest in the subject; realize how the subject matter of the speech can help you; and turn off your emotional blocks. Try to anticipate the occasion; review what you already know about the subject; think through the topic and attempt to anticipate how the speaker may develop it. These suggestions will help you to concentrate.

To improve listening, you must realize that concentration requires effort. As explained earlier, listeners can comprehend at a faster rate than speakers can talk. The excess time should be used by the listener to think, weigh, and review what the speaker says. If you spend your time thinking of other matters, daydreaming, or solving personal problems, concentration becomes impossible. Nichols and Stevens stress this factor in concentration as follows:

> The brain deals with words at a lightning pace, but when we listen, we ask this brain to receive words at an extremely slow pace. It might seem logical to slow down our thinking when we listen. . . . But slowing thought processes is a difficult thing to do—almost painful. Therefore, when we listen, we continue thinking at high speed while the spoken words arrive at slow speed. In the act of listening, the differential between thinking and speaking rates means that our brains work with hundreds of words in addition to those we hear, assembling thoughts other than those spoken to us. To put it another way, we can listen and still have spare time for thinking.
>
> What do you do with your spare thinking time as you listen? The answer to this question holds the key to concentration in listening.[3]

Concentration requires continual, not spasmodic, attention. Some people listen attentively for a few minutes, think of other matters or daydream for a while, and then turn their attention again to the speaker. This irregular type of listening may be caused by one or more of many reasons: distracting influences such as outside noises or late arrivals, peculiarities of the speaker's manner or presentation methods, uncomfortable physical arrangements, or lack of interest in the subject. Regardless of cause, spasmodic listening prevents comprehension of the fully developed idea of a speech. The listener must try to ignore distracting influences.

In short, concentration constitutes a basic requirement for efficient listening. Concentration requires an attitude conducive to listening, a willingness to work at listening, and continual attention to the speaker. Listening is not a passive thing; it requires a great deal of effort.

Learn What to Listen for

To listen efficiently, you must know what to look for in a speech. Listening to speeches constitutes perhaps the most difficult type of

---

[3] *Ibid.*, p. 79.

listening, because properly constructed speeches develop several ideas, each based on the other; to miss part of the speech destroys the sequence of ideas. Conversation is more fragmentary and repetitive than speech-making. If you do not understand at first, you can ask your conversationalist to repeat or to expand an idea. An understanding of the process of speech composition will aid your listening materially, for then you will have a blueprint of what you should look for in a speech. Part Two treats the content and arrangement of speeches in detail. As you read this part of the text, consider how the principles apply to listening as well as to speech-making. Not all the principles discussed in Part Two apply to listening, but those that do may be summarized as follows.

1. *Determine the purpose of the speech.* Listen to determine if the main purpose is to persuade, to inform, or to entertain. The nature of the occasion or the statement of the topic usually suggests the purpose, or the speaker may reveal it in his introduction. For a persuasive speech, the critical listener demands adequate evidence and logical reasoning. For an informative speech, he asks for mature judgments and accurate evidence. For an entertaining speech, he wants humor in good taste. Understanding the purpose aids the listener in getting set to listen.

2. *Listen for the partition of the speech.* Listen to how the speaker reveals how he intends to limit and develop his subject, how he reveals the central theme, and how he defines technical terms and makes necessary explanations for an understanding of his subject. The partition may consist of but a few sentences, but they are important to listeners because here the speaker explains what will follow.

3. *Determine the central theme of the speech.* Listen for a central theme that provides a unifying force for the speech. Since the main points are built around this central theme, it aids the listener in keeping the speech in focus. The central theme may be stated in a concise sentence or two as part of the partition, or it may unfold as the speaker develops his main points.

4. *Determine the speaker's main points.* Since the main points consist of the three or four principal divisions of a speech organized in the several ways discussed in Chapter 8, listen to determine which method the speaker uses. The main points bring out or develop the central theme; they are the legs that support the table, the main ideas that support the thesis. A knowledge of how speakers arrange

their main points aids the listener because he knows what to look for in a speech.

5. *Listen for the forms of support.* Listen to determine how the forms of support fill in the structure of the speech, what types of support the speaker uses, and how much support he gives. The forms of support consist of such illustrative materials as examples, analogies, statistics, and quotations from authority. They aid the listener because they fill in the details essential to understanding a point or argument.

6. *Listen for restatement and summary.* Listen to determine how the speaker restates his points—verbatim, in different words, or through quotations. Listen for restatements of ideas within a point, at the end of a point, and at the conclusion of the speech. In the final summary, see if the speaker restates all the points and relates them to the central theme. Since almost all listeners fail to understand all that a speaker says the first time, restatement and summary serve the listener well in giving unity and coherence to a speech.

Listen Critically

Listeners can be classified into four groups: (1) Some do not listen; they "tune the speaker out" and think of matters foreign to the speaker's subject. They get little from a speech. (2) Some only half-listen; their spasmodic listening fluctuates all the way from careful attention to no attention. They understand fragments of the speech but they do not see the idea as a whole. (3) Some listen with passive acceptance; they accept all the speaker says without question. Because of their lack of discrimination, they add little to what the speaker says from their own experiences. (4) Some listen with discrimination; this critical type of listener gets the most from a speech. If you adopt the following measures you will soon find yourself a member of the last group.

1. *Relate what the speaker says to your own experiences.* As you listen, trains of thought will be set up in your mind which will stimulate you to think constructively. Relate what the speaker says to your own studies and experiences. You may agree with a speaker on some points because you have had similar experiences; you may disagree on some others because through your study you have come to a different conclusion. On still others you will find yourself reserving decision until you can give them further thought and investigation. By considering these relationships you will be practicing an impor-

tant aspect of critical listening—you will be thinking constructively.

2. *Review and arrange what you hear.* Draw together what the speaker says and your own thoughts, by summarizing and synthesizing the whole. Think ahead of the speaker and anticipate how he will develop his central theme. An intelligent speaker organizes his speech to bring out a well-developed theme; you help the speaker by summarizing previous points in your own mind, by predicting the next point, and by relating all points to the basic philosophy and central idea of the speech. Realize that communication is a two-way street; you, as a critical listener, participate actively in the communicative process.

3. *Analyze and evaluate what you hear.* Listen to understand, but do more than that—analyze and weigh what the speaker says. Neither believe nor disbelieve all that he says. Listen with discrimination. First, analyze by breaking down ideas to their constituent points, subpoints, and supports. Then, weigh the speaker's statements (1) to test the adequacy of evidence, (2) to test the validity of reasoning, and (3) to determine the speaker's true purpose. Apply these criteria:

1. Adequacy of evidence. Does the evidence come from reliable sources? Does it accurately represent what the speaker says it represents? Is it sufficient to justify his conclusions?
2. Validity of reasoning. Do the speaker's conclusions follow logically from his premises? Does he conform to acceptable rules for logical reasoning?
3. True purpose. Distinguish between subjective and objective material, propaganda and fact, dogmatic assertion and well-supported conclusions. Do you perceive any propaganda techniques, manipulations of language?

When you have completed this process, you will be able to assess the speech in its entirety. And you will know that if the speech embodied something of value, you have plucked it out for yourself; conversely, if the speech was a "hidden persuader," you will know that you have not been "taken in."

In summary, to be a critical listener you must understand the dual processes of communication—the sending and the receiving. You must participate cooperatively by adding to what the speaker says from your own experience: by reviewing, by synthesizing, by analyzing, and by evaluating what you hear. You must be active on the responding end of oral communication.

Note-taking as an Aid to Listening

The question arises, "Should I take notes as I listen?" The answer depends on what use you intend to make of what you hear. If you listen for inspiration, for entertainment, for an evaluation of the speaker's methods of composition and delivery, or to add to your general culture, notes serve little purpose. If you listen to get facts, to analyze what the speaker says, or to evaluate what you hear, notes will probably assist you. If you intend to use what you hear at a later date to pass an examination, to support a point in a speech, or to illustrate ideas in an essay, notes may be of great value.

Note-taking can aid listening by encouraging concentration, by providing materials for review, and by assisting recall. However, if the system of note-taking itself requires concentration, it can interfere with listening. Consider the following suggestions for efficient note-taking. These will also be useful in taking notes in course lectures.

1. Use an informal system, the simpler the better. The rules for outlining given in Chapter 9 are too detailed and cumbersome for note-taking. Use a simplified form of outlining that combines short paragraphs, sentences, phrases, and single words. The notes need be intelligible only to you.
2. Make your notes brief. Take down only the salient points and factual material. Take notes while the speaker makes transitions, when he restates his ideas, when he summarizes his points, and when he pauses.
3. Use abbreviations and symbols. Shorthand and speedwriting serve the note-taker well. If you do not know these systems, devise one of your own. Use symbols to represent phrases, and single letters or abbreviations for words. Try to cut the time spent in writing to a minimum.
4. Make your notes clear. In spite of the foregoing suggestions, make sure that your notes are intelligible to you. Then, if you want to later, you will be able to make a permanent record by expanding from your abbreviated class notes.
5. Mark important points for emphasis. Underscore or mark important points with asterisks. In scanning notes, such markings will help you recall the gist of your notes without having to read them fully.
6. Review your notes periodically. For class purposes, review your notes several times during the progress of the course. Relate your daily notes to the course units. Before final examinations, study your notes carefully and relate them to the course as a whole.

IV. Summary

Listening, the counterpart of reading, is an important part of oral communication. Knowledge about speech-making aids the listener because it teaches him what to look for in a speech. The answer to "Why listen?" is sixfold: (1) to acquire facts, (2) to analyze facts and ideas, (3) to evaluate facts and ideas, (4) to be inspired, (5) to be entertained, and (6) to improve speaking.

Requirements for efficient listening consist of four audience factors: (1) attitudes, (2) interests, (3) motivation, and (4) emotional state. The listener's attitude should be objective, unprejudiced, and cooperative. His interests in the speaker's subject are either primary, secondary, or momentary. The main motives that make listeners want to listen are self-preservation, property, power, reputation, affection, sentiment, and taste. Undesirable psychological feelings that prevent sustained attention may result from the listener's emotional upsets, his antagonistic attitudes toward the speaker, or his objections to statements made by the speaker.

To listen efficiently, the listener must listen with concentration, know what to listen for, listen critically, and take notes effectively. Concentration requires effort and a cooperative attitude. The listener should look for the principles of composition and delivery discussed in the two following divisions of this text. To listen critically, the listener must add to what the speaker says from his own experience, review and arrange what he hears, and analyze and evaluate what he hears. When performed effectively, note-taking aids efficient listening. For effective note-taking observe the following principles: (1) use an informal system, (2) make notes brief, (3) use abbreviations and symbols, (4) make notes clear, (5) mark points for emphasis, and (6) review notes periodically.

Questions and Exercises

A. Answer the following questions on Chapter 3.

1. How does listening relate to the total process of communication? What are the other basic factors of communication?
2. How can knowledge about speech-making aid the listener?
3. List and explain briefly six reasons for listening. How would you rank the reasons according to their importance?
4. List and briefly explain four requirements for efficient listening.
5. Discuss several motive appeals applicable to listening. What effect

do they have on listening? Which motivating factor do you consider most important? Why?

6. Discuss briefly the four suggestions presented in this chapter for improving listening. Can you add to the list?
7. What are the principal elements of concentration applicable to efficient listening?
8. List the factors that the listener should look for in a speech. Can you add to the list discussed in this chapter?
9. What are the essential features of critical listening? List and briefly discuss some types of listening besides critical listening.
10. List some advantages and disadvantages of note-taking as they relate to effectiveness in listening.
11. List several suggestions for efficient note-taking. Can you add to the suggestions discussed in this chapter?

B. You will have two weeks for this assignment. Listen to two types of public speeches and answer the questions below about them. For one speech, do not take any notes; listen carefully and write your answers within two days after listening to the speech. Take notes on the second speech, observing the suggestions made in this chapter. Use your notes in answering the questions listed below. You may attend any type of speaking occasion you desire—for example, a formal lecture, a church service, or a college debate—or listen to a radio or television speech.

1. What general purpose did the speaker have—to inform, to persuade, or to entertain?
2. Could you isolate the partition of the speech as a part of the introduction? Did the speaker define any technical terms? If so, what terms and how did he define them? Did he narrow or limit his subject? How?
3. In one or two sentences, state the central theme of the speech. Did the speaker state the central theme specifically or did it unfold as he spoke? In your opinion, did the speaker make effective use of the central theme?
4. How many main points did the speaker have? List them. In your opinion, were his main points well chosen? Did the main points develop the central theme adequately?
5. Did the speaker use a variety of the types of support? Did he seem to favor one form over others? In your opinion, did the speaker support each point adequately? Interestingly? Explain your answers.
6. Did the speaker restate ideas within a point? If so, on some points or on all points? Did he summarize at the end of each point? Did he give a detailed summary in the conclusion? Of the three types of summaries explained in this chapter, which type or types did the speaker use?
7. What effect do you think that this assignment had on you as a listener? Of the four types of listeners characterized in this chapter, how do you classify yourself?

C. For your third speaking assignment, read an editorial or a syndicated article in a newspaper or magazine and disagree with it in a speech limited to five minutes. Proceed as follows:

1. Briefly review the editorial or syndicated article and clearly state its central point.
2. State the reasons why you disagree.
3. Support each reason with statistics, examples, illustrations, or quotations.
4. Briefly summarize your points.

D. After presenting the above speech in class, evaluate yourself on the factors listed, according to the indicated scale: (1) excellent, (2) good, (3) average, (4) fair, (5) poor.

	Rating
1. Your choice of editorial or syndicated article	________
2. How well you adapted to your audience	________
3. The soundness of your reasons	________
4. How well you supported your reasons	________
5. The organization of your points	________
6. How well you held the attention of the class	________
7. Your poise and self-confidence	________
8. The distinctness of your voice	________
9. The quality of your voice	________
10. Your use of gestures and bodily action	________
11. Your choice of language	________
12. Your rate of speaking	________
13. Your volume adaptation to the room	________
14. Your fluency of speaking	________
15. Your over-all rating	________

E. Ask your professor to rate you by use of the same scale. On what factors did you and your professor agree? Disagree?

F. Make a list of your principal weaknesses as revealed by your self-analysis and your professor's analysis of you. Consider methods for correcting these weaknesses. Keep the list before you as you continue with the course and make a determined effort to improve.

PART TWO

Preparation and Composition

CHAPTER 4

Analyze the Audience and the Speaking Occasion

A professor received a telephone call requesting him to address a women's study club. He was busy when the call came, so he asked few questions about the occasion. Recalling that another member of the faculty had spoken to the club earlier, he asked him about the type of audience and the nature of the occasion. The friend said that the women met monthly to hear addresses on national and international problems and that they would expect a speech reflecting considerable research and thorough analysis. Consequently he prepared a speech on "The Possibilities of Peace through World Government."

He arrived at the meeting place only to discover that the women were staging their annual banquet, not a regular meeting. At this social occasion merriment formed the keynote. A hillbilly band and singer preceded his speech. He saw that his planned speech did not fit the occasion. Although he attempted to inject some humor before making his address, there was no getting around the inappropriateness of his talk. He simply had failed to analyze his audience and occasion properly.

The essential factors of any public-speaking situation include not only the speaker and his speech but the audience and the occasion as well.

I. Why Analyze the Audience and the Occasion?

The professor's unhappy experience reflects the importance of prior analysis of the audience and the speaking occasion in helping to decide upon the subject, the type of speech, and the choice of supporting materials. Consider these factors as an essential part of the total public-speaking occasion.

You do not deliver the ideas of a speech as the grocery boy delivers a loaf of bread. Different audiences will receive what you say in different ways; therefore, in addressing a particular audience you need to speak in terms that they understand, in terms of their experiences, training, and interests. To accomplish this, analyze the audience and occasion as you start your preparation. Include the following: (1) analyze the listeners, (2) analyze the occasion, and (3) analyze the physical conditions of the meeting place.

II. How to Analyze an Audience

Find out as much about your probable audience as possible when you accept an engagement. But you ask, "What should I know about them?" Consider the following factors.

Determine Audience Interests

A commercial photographer was asked to address a press club on the subject of commercial photography. He made careful preparation and felt that he made a good speech. Later a university faculty club asked him to make the same speech. This time he felt that he failed miserably. He gave the same speech; why the difference?

He planned the speech with the first audience in mind. He chose illustrative material and ideas that appealed to their interests. In short, he spoke their language. But the language of the first audience was not the same as that of the second; their interests and problems varied greatly. When you plan your speech, keep your specific audience in mind as you choose your ideas, supporting material, and elements of interest. What interest factors should you consider?

1. *Primary interests.* Attempt to determine if members of the audience have a common primary interest. Are they of the same

profession or business? If so, your problem is much simplified because people in the same profession have certain common interests. Relate your ideas and illustrative material directly to those interests; talk in terms that your listeners understand. A large propaganda organization considers audience interests of such importance that whenever its representatives have important speaking engagements, the organization sends an advance agent into the community to sound out local interests. The speech is then rewritten in view of his findings. High-salaried specialists write such speeches. These organizations realize the importance of audience interests. You can profit by their experience.

2. *Secondary interests.* If your listeners do not have common primary interests, determine if they have common secondary interests. Suppose you agree to speak at the annual banquet of the country club. Your audience will represent many professions with a variety of primary interests; but they have a community of secondary interest in recreation and entertainment. Choose your subject, ideas, and supporting materials from these fields. How about talking on the problem of leisure-time activities in America? In this technological age with short work days, this problem assumes major importance among thinking people. An annual banquet of persons engaged in a common social activity provides an excellent setting.

3. *Momentary interests.* If your listeners do not have common primary or secondary interests, consider their momentary interests. Discover matters of local concern that interest most persons in the community. Suppose you speak to a civic club in a city where the local university's football team enjoys a winning season. You can be assured that the businessmen will be interested in the team's victories. Capitalize on this momentary interest. Recently a visiting speaker gave the commencement address at a Southern university. He illustrated his points so well with instances of local common interest that his listeners were amazed and delighted with his knowledge and concern for them. The city had recently witnessed a devastating tornado. The speaker seemed to know as much about the details of the tragedy as did members of the audience. What members of the audience did not know was that the speaker had subscribed to the local newspaper for a month prior to the speech. Furthermore, he arrived in the city a day prior to his engagement and busied himself in seeking out local problems and interests. Speaking to an audience with a diversity of primary and secondary

interests, he did a remarkable job of supporting his ideas with matters of momentary interest in the community.

In short, never plan a speech to be given in a vacuum. Remember that you talk with people, not simply about a subject. Discover their interests and let these interests guide you in each step of your preparation.

Determine Audience Attitudes Toward the Subject

In a local-option election a speaker addressed an audience of temperance workers in the interest of their campaign. Although members of the audience favored the speaker's position, he berated them for over an hour on the horrors of strong drink. He shouted and raved with such vehemence that one listener remarked that he appeared to be full of his subject. Did this well-meaning speaker do his cause any good? Did he give the right type of speech for the audience? His unreasonable and dogmatic approach probably did his cause more harm than good. Some people were probably driven from their original positions. Did the speaker need to discuss the evils of drink? Obviously not, to a believing audience. Rather, he needed to discuss procedures for conducting the campaign and to emphasize the importance of active participation. Members of the audience wanted to know what they could do to forward the campaign, not to be harangued on a thesis with which they were already in agreement.

Consider the following possible attitudes that an audience may have toward your subject: (1) they may be favorable—in agreement with your thesis; (2) they may be hostile—opposed to your point of view; (3) they may be apathetic. To treat your subject the same way before these different types of audiences invites failure. What are some characteristics of these types?

1. *Favorable attitude.* Why speak before a favorable audience? You may need to strengthen their belief or increase their enthusiasm and fervor for the cause you represent. You may want to move them to action, to indicate how they may help in a common endeavor.

A businessman addressed several kinds of audiences when he campaigned for a place on the local school board. Since the election came soon after the Supreme Court's decision on segregation, this issue played an important part in the campaign. His first invitation to speak came from some Negro leaders. Since the candidate favored integration for the local schools, he simply explained his position and outlined how the Negro leaders could help in the campaign. He appealed to them on rational grounds and asked for a common-sense approach to the problem. He used little emotional appeal; the members of the audience already wanted to assist with the campaign. An emotionalized speech on the moral, social, and economic injustices of segregation would have been both unnecessary and unwise; it might have induced irrational behavior in certain members. This favorable audience needed a plan of action and admonition to show restraint in putting it into effect.

As a starting point for speaking, analyze the beliefs of your audience; then plan your speech to do something constructive for the listeners in view of their existing beliefs.

2. *Hostile attitude.* Consider an audience hostile to your position. Here you run a real danger of doing your cause more harm than good. The speaker mentioned in a preceding section had one speech on prohibition which he gave indiscriminately before temperance workers, liquor distillers, or any who would listen. You can imagine the effect he had on hostile audiences when he spoke as if all who opposed his position were stupid, evil people. He probably only increased the vigor of their opposition.

Yet some of the outstanding speeches in history have been those properly presented to hostile audiences. Henry W. Grady's "The New South" illustrates this point. Here we find a Southern editor addressing an Eastern audience during the Reconstruction period following the Civil War. The hostile feeling against the South had recently been intensified with the election of Grover Cleveland, a Democratic President, in 1884. The New England Society of New York City to which he spoke consisted of a highly conservative group who opposed Grady's defense of the South. Yet they arose at the end of his speech with an acclaim rarely accorded any speaker. How did Grady accomplish this difficult feat?

No doubt Grady's magnetic personality and attitude of good will helped. His psychological appeals also helped. He started his speech by quoting Benjamin H. Hill, a man respected by members of his audience. Then he expressed appreciation for being asked to address the society. He injected humor in excellent taste, some of which poked fun at himself as well as at his audience. He made a reference to fair play and emphasized that intelligent men should consider varying points of view. He paid a tribute to Abraham Lincoln and dealt with matters on which the audience agreed. He apparently succeeded in getting a series of "yes" responses from his audience and then led gradually into his defense of the South which he then developed on rational grounds. Grady's methods may be adapted to many hostile audiences.

3. *Apathetic attitude.* Quite a different problem arises when your audience is apathetic. Consider first how to awaken your listeners to the importance of your subject. Link it with the basic drives, needs, and desires in people. Show your audience why they should be concerned.

In the latter part of 1919, Woodrow Wilson was confronted with such audiences in his speaking campaign in the interest of the League of Nations. The nation had just concluded a devastating war, and most persons were trying to forget the problems of war and peace as they turned their thoughts to more personal things. They simply were not interested. In his speech at Des Moines, Iowa, on September 6, 1919, he attempted to shock them into concern. Note these words of his introduction, "My fellow countrymen, the world is desperately in need of the settled conditions of peace, and it cannot wait much longer. . . . The world is not at peace." He made an impassioned plea for the United States to take the initiative in formulating a permanent program of peace through the League of Nations, in order to show the way for nations not accustomed to freedom. Did his speaking program awaken the people from their apathy? Many would say "no" because we did not join the League of Nations. But who knows? Perhaps his efforts had a delayed effect that caused us to help establish the United Nations some twenty-five years later.

In summary, try to determine the attitude of the members of your audience toward the ideas of your speech. If it is apathetic or hostile, plan your approach to induce them to accept your ideas.

Determine Audience Attitudes Toward the Speaker

Several years ago an aged doctor gave a series of lectures to a university student body and faculty. He was one of the most beloved persons in the community, having devoted his life to unselfish service. A speech teacher was heard to remark that, although he did not hear a new idea in the lectures, he valued highly the opportunity to hear the speaker; the doctor exemplified "a good man, skilled in speaking." How different this comment was from one heard by a student after a lecture by a disgruntled professor: "The trouble with Professor X is that he stopped having ideas twenty years ago; how unfortunate he did not stop teaching then." What an audience thinks of you, the speaker, affects how your ideas may be accepted.

A young man before an audience of mature people faces a problem that a respected older man does not. Since the young man does not have the reputation to command respect, he must make sure that his speech reflects careful analysis, conscientious judgment, and rational appeals, and utilizes adequate evidence, to compensate for lack of maturity. Young speakers can command respect. Henry W. Grady was only thirty-six when he gave his famous speech, "The New South"; Booker T. Washington was under forty when he delivered his Atlanta Exposition Speech.

Consider these possible attitudes of the audience toward you: (1) favorable, (2) unfavorable, (3) neutral.

1. *Favorable attitude.* If members of an audience like and respect you, they will accept much of what you say because they want to; they respect your worth as an individual, your knowledge of your subject, and your ability to make mature judgments. This kind of reputation does not come easily; it usually comes from a life of useful works and sympathetic understanding of people.

Dr. Alexander Jerry Stoddard addressed a school board on the subject of educational television. He discussed problems that the group had previously considered, but he did so with such understanding that the group was able to decide on several problems largely through his influence. They respected his judgment partly because of his years of successful school administration in such places as Denver, Philadelphia, and Los Angeles. More important, they felt the influence of his personality, his kind and sympathetic understanding, and his humble and simple approach. He did not claim to know all the answers, but he gave the impression that his advanced years had dulled neither his inquiring mind nor his desire for more knowledge. He did not have to "act big," because he was "big."

Few speakers enjoy so high a regard from an audience as Dr. Stoddard. All should strive for better acceptance. Conversely, those who have attained favorable acceptance should be careful to appraise accurately what they talk about because an audience may accept their ideas at face value.

2. *Unfavorable attitude.* If an audience is unfavorably disposed toward you as a person, your approach should be twofold: (1) Attempt to create an atmosphere of fair play wherein the audience will withhold judgment pending the development of the speech. (2) Develop your speech through a preponderance of logical proof.

Note how Patrick Henry attempted to create an atmosphere of fair play in his *Liberty or Death* speech before the Virginia Convention at St. John's Church, Richmond, Virginia, on March 23, 1775. Preceding speakers had set a keynote unfavorable to Henry's position and many members of the convention were opposed to Henry as a person.

> Mr. President: No man thinks more highly than I do of the patriotism, as well as abilities, of the very worthy gentlemen who have just addressed the house. But different men often see the same subjects in different lights. . . . The question before the House is one of awful moment. . . . I consider it as nothing less than a question of freedom or slavery; and in proportion to the magnitude of the subject ought to be the freedom of debate. It is only in this way that we can hope to arrive at truth, and fulfill the great responsibility which we hold to God and our country. Should I keep back my opinion at such times through fear of giving offense, I should consider myself as guilty of treason toward my country. . . .[1]

Although the speech as a whole could hardly be classified as one based primarily on logical proof, Henry did show excellent skills in creating a tolerant atmosphere. Note that Henry showed a friendly attitude toward his opponents and the audience, appealed to their sense of fair play, showed where they had common interests and beliefs in the problem, gave evidence that his opinion came from careful study, and stated that he should speak out in justice to himself and the convention. These techniques may well be adapted to many unfavorable audiences.

3. *Neutral attitude.* If you are little known or consider your listeners neutral toward you, attempt to establish rapport by finding a common bond with them. In Senator Tom Connally's early years in the United States Senate, he spoke to a university student body whose president had been his roommate while in law school. Senator Connally delighted the students by relating incidents about

---

[1] William Wirt, *Life and Character of Patrick Henry* (25th ed., Philadelphia: Claxton and Company, 1881), p. 38.

escapades in which he and their president had engaged while students. His good-natured fun directed toward the dignified president won over the student body.

If the speaker is unknown to an audience, the person introducing him should furnish information about his training, experience, and accomplishments. A good speech of introduction helps to impress the audience with the speaker's credibility and authority, as do judicious statements by the speaker himself. For example, statements about special studies made by the speaker, honors received, and sources studied in preparation enhance the speaker's qualifications. Such statements should never be made in a braggadocio attitude, but should rather be brought into the discussion indirectly.

In summary, try to determine in advance the possible attitudes of your audience toward you as a speaker. Prepare your speech with this analysis in mind. Capitalize on a favorable audience by emphasis on subject matter, not by unnecessary introductory remarks. With unfavorable or neutral audiences, spend adequate time in establishing rapport with them so that you may create a favorable atmosphere.

Determine Facts About the Audience

To guide your choice of subject, purpose, interest appeals, and the idea of your speech, determine as much as possible about your audience in advance. Consider the following: (1) age, (2) background of training and knowledge, and (3) social and cultural background.

1. *Age.* Why determine the approximate age limits of your audience? Since you desire your audience to listen, you need to adapt your speech to appeal to the age levels of your audience. Consider the following psychological factors that apply to different ages, from young to old. (1) Young people respond to suggestion more readily than older people because they have less critical ability. They will be likely to accept much of what the speaker says because of his position of authority. Because young people require less logical proof and evidence than older people, a speaker should be careful to evaluate his facts and conclusions accurately. (2) Young people are usually more open-minded to new ideas than older people. Conservatism usually comes with age; perhaps the young have less to

lose by their liberal tendencies. Normally they are more willing to experiment with new ideas than are older people. Because the speaker need be less cautious in the adequacy of his facts and assertions, he should refrain from influencing young people on opinions that do not reflect maturity of judgment. (3) Young people usually require a more forceful and energetic presentation than do older people. Lacking background of ideas, information, and critical faculties, their attention may be easily diverted. When speaking to young people, consider the interest as well as the logical adequacy of material.

2. *Background of training and knowledge.* Determine the extent of training and knowledge of your anticipated audience. Are the listeners college graduates or uneducated people, highly skilled or unskilled workers, business or professionally trained personnel, widely read or poorly informed people? The failure to know such facts may cause you to talk above or below your audience's capacity to comprehend. Beware of "talking down" to an audience; most people can detect a condescending attitude and they usually resent it. Note these psychological factors in point: (1) The less experienced and trained are usually more suggestible; they accept your assertions with less proof than do people with advanced training. (2) The less educated require a more lively and forceful presentation; their attention may be diverted more easily than may that of the well educated.

3. *Social background.* What is the social background of your audience? The general environmental background of individuals often determines their attitudes toward social, political, and economic problems. Their interests and ability to understand vary with their social background. For example, an audience of factory workers would not be interested in, nor would they understand, references to mythology, poetry, or the classics. Such references would be appropriate to an audience of business executives or professional men. Those with poor social and cultural backgrounds are usually more suggestible and more susceptible to forceful presentation than are those with better backgrounds.

In short, determine the general age level, background of training, and social and cultural attainment of the members of your audience so that you can plan your speech with these factors in mind.

III. How to Analyze the Occasion

A business executive received a telephone call asking if he would participate in a panel discussion at a conference on leadership. Since he had discussed this topic on previous occasions, he readily consented. After arriving at the meeting, he discovered that his conception of a panel discussion was quite different from that of the program chairman. In educational parlance, the term "panel discussion" means an informal discussion without set speeches. To the layman, apparently, the term means whatever he wants it to mean at the moment. To the program chairman of this meeting, it meant a prepared fifteen-minute speech by each of the four panel members. The speaker was somewhat perturbed by this turn of events. Thereafter, he used more caution in determining the requirements of the occasion.

What would you do if you found yourself in similar circumstances? Avoid getting yourself into such a position by making the proper inquiry about the occasion and purpose of the meeting. What should you know about the occasion? Consider the following:

What Is the Purpose of the Meeting?

A school administrator was asked to give the commencement address at the summer exercises of a university. He chose as his subject, "How to Get a Position." He covered such points as the importance of combing your hair, pressing your trousers, and cleaning your fingernails in preparing for a job interview. His topic would have been appropriate to an eighth-grade class in hygiene, but it hardly met the propriety of the formal occasion of a university commencement program.

A speaker should know the purpose and circumstances of the speaking occasion. Is it a regular meeting of some organization, such as a civic club, that customarily includes speeches on the program? If so, the choice of subject and type of speech will usually be left to the speaker. Suppose you agree to speak at the laying of the cornerstone of the new school building. On this formal occasion you should treat some educational problem in a dignified manner. The type of speech required for a home-coming rally would be quite different from one prepared for a chapel program arranged by the same college. Be sure that plans for your speech conform to the reasons for the meeting.

Does the Occasion Call for a Regular Ritual?

A businessman accepted an invitation to speak at a church during the absence of the minister. Because of a mix-up in the church office, no program was printed. The businessman reported that he felt ill at ease because he was not sure how to proceed. Many speaking occasions have regular customs and rituals. To avoid embarrassment, you should inquire in advance about such matters. Will other speakers appear on the same program? Will a discussion follow your speech? Does the organization have a set procedure? Is the occasion formal or informal? How much time should you take? Knowledge of these facts will help you plan your speech intelligently.

Some programs may be so poorly arranged that the proper atmosphere will not be created for your talk. For example, one speaker planned a speech with a serious purpose, but the humorist who preceded him created an atmosphere of merriment. The speaker overcame this unforeseen difficulty by first fitting in with the mood created by the previous speaker and then gradually changing it to an atmosphere appropriate for his speech. The situation would not have occurred if he had found out beforehand the general plan for the evening or requested that the program be made specific.

What Will Be the Likely Size of the Audience?

If you have ever had the experience of planning a speech for a small, intimate group only to find yourself confronted with a large, formal audience, you will understand the importance of determining audience size. Consider the following reasons: (1) The smaller the group, the more unified it is in the several respects we have already discussed, and one must choose a subject and develop it accordingly. Before a small audience of experts in a particular field, for instance, one speaks in more technical language; given the same topic, one speaks in more general terms before a large audience of non-experts. Likewise, before a small group with unifying primary interests, one can develop an appropriate subject intensively, knowing the audience will comprehend; before a large group with a diversity of primary interests, one cannot go so deeply into the subject. (2) Meetings generally are held in rooms proportionate in size to the size of the audience. Small rooms are acoustically better than large; therefore, one can speak more rapidly in a small room, whereas one may have to speak at an unusually slow rate in a large room. This must be taken into consideration in planning the length of the speech, or, if there is a time limit, in planning how best to develop one's theme in the allotted time. (3) One's feeling of intimacy is stronger with a small group; with a larger group, one must plan to establish rapport before proceeding with the body of the speech. These differences make important your determination of probable audience size.

What Physical Conditions Will Prevail?

The less a speaker leaves to chance, the greater the likelihood of making a successful speech. This final analysis applies to the physical conditions likely to prevail. Although physical conditions cannot always be determined with accuracy in advance, by arriving a few minutes early a speaker has time for last-minute adjustments. Consider the following factors: (1) size and shape of the lecture room, (2) outside noises and disturbances, (3) platform equipment, and (4) provisions for visual aids.

1. *Conditions of lecture room.* Size and shape of the lecture hall may vitally affect your speaking. Experience in speaking in combination gymnasium-auditoriums, characteristic of many rural schools, shows that the acoustical factors may increase the time necessary to present a speech as much as twenty per cent. Usually no attention is given to acoustics in such buildings, and the echo produced makes necessary a decrease in rate of speaking. Often an increase in voice volume is required. Failure to consider acoustics may make your speech unintelligible. On other occasions a small audience may be scattered throughout a large auditorium; for best results, the speaker should ask the audience to move to the front of the room.

2. *Outside disturbances.* Where possible, avoid seating your audience facing windows since glare affects their vision and comfort. Face your audience away from entrance doors to minimize disturbances caused by late arrivals. Outside noises may materially affect your speaking. If you must compete with construction workers, power mowers, airplanes, or trains, do not show annoyance, for such feelings are contagious. If ringing class bells, telephones, or other temporary noises interrupt, pause until they subside. If they continue, proceed without calling undue attention to them.

During a speech by a British Consul to some college students, the loud-speaker blared forth with a recording by a popular pianist. After poking good-natured fun at the appropriateness of his musical accompanist, he paused temporarily to see if the music could be stopped. When informed that the control room was locked, he finished his address without showing annoyance. He received a standing ovation partly because of an excellent address and partly because of his good sportsmanship in continuing under adverse conditions.

3. *Platform equipment.* Stage equipment may also affect the plans for your speech. One speaker accustomed to keeping his notes in a loose-leaf notebook found that no lectern would be provided for his high school commencement speech. The speaker had to choose between speaking without notes or using a cumbersome system. He solved the problem by making brief notes on small cards, but he would have felt more at ease with his detailed notes. You need to consider, also, such factors as whether you will speak from a raised stage, whether loud-speaker equipment will be provided, and whether the audience will be comfortably seated.

4. *Visual aids.* If you plan to use visual aids, provide for their use in advance of the occasion. Some auditoriums do not have provisions for certain types of projectors or displays; others must provide trained personnel to operate the equipment. Where last-minute arrangements are possible, inconvenience may be caused for those sponsoring the program.

In summary, determine the physical conditions of the lecture hall in advance of your speech; attempt to adjust your plans to the size and shape of the auditorium, the outside noises, and the stage equipment; and provide for the display of visual aids.

IV. Analyze Audience Reactions During Speech

Rarely will your preliminary analysis of the audience and speaking occasion be entirely accurate. Hence, keep close watch on the reactions of your listeners during your speech. You may be able to make adjustments to correct inattention.

How do audiences show interest? An attentive person sits forward and moves occasionally; he shows interest by his face, by head and shoulder movements, and by eye contact. A quiet audience is not necessarily an attentive audience. Some experienced speakers can sense audience attention from signs of which they are not completely aware. If you feel the audience is losing interest, consider the following: (1) You may need to be more enthusiastic about your subject. You cannot expect audience interest unless you show enthusiasm yourself. (2) You may need to change the rate, volume, or pitch of your voice. A monotonous presentation invites inattention. (3) You may need to make your material more interesting by relating it to the interests of your listeners. Bring your speech close to your audience through illustrative material within their experiences. (4) You may need to define and explain technical terms or be less abstract. You may be speaking at the audience rather than communicating with them in terms that they understand. (5) You may need to correct peculiarities of presentation. Alter objectionable mannerisms or change your stance and position. Use bodily action to help express yourself. (6) You may need to correct faulty room ventilation. An overheated room is especially conducive to audience inattention.

In summary, conduct as thorough an analysis as possible of your audience and speaking occasion prior to your speech. Check on this prior analysis by observing audience reaction during your speech. Make the adjustments indicated when audience interest and attention lag.

V. Summary

To communicate adequately, you must understand the nature of your audience and the occasion. This understanding should include an analysis of your listeners, an analysis of the occasion, an analysis of the physical conditions of the meeting place, and an analysis of audience reaction during your speech.

You analyze audiences by (1) determining their interests; (2) determining their attitudes toward your subject; (3) determining their attitudes toward you, the speaker; (4) determining facts about their age, background of training and experience, and social and cultural background.

You analyze the occasion for your speech by determining the following: (1) What is the purpose of the meeting? (2) What rituals or customs will prevail? (3) What will be the likely size of the audience? (4) What physical conditions will prevail?

Analyze audience reaction during the speech. Determine the cause of inattention or unfavorable reaction and attempt to correct the cause during the presentation of the speech.

Questions and Exercises

A. Answer the following questions on Chapter 4.

1. What must be considered in planning a speech for the following different situations? (1) The American Institute of Banking plans to hold its annual convention in your city. They invite you to speak at the opening session. (2) The Masonic Lodge plans its state convention in your city. They invite you to speak. (3) You receive an invitation to speak at the Fourth of July celebration in the city park.
2. How would you analyze the above audience situations as to your listeners' primary, secondary, and momentary interests?
3. What would be the differences in your approach to the following types of audiences for a speech on "Segregation in Public Schools in the South"? (1) Your audience favors your thesis. (2) Your audience is hostile to your point of view. (3) Your audience is apathetic toward your subject.
4. Read Henry W. Grady's speech, "The New South." What techniques did he use in facing a hostile audience?
5. Your audience is neutral toward you as a person. What methods would you use to get a favorable hearing?
6. Suppose your audience consists of high school students. How would your approach to this audience differ from your approach to an audience of middle-aged people?
7. Suppose you are asked to speak to an audience of unskilled laborers on the subject of "atomic energy." How would your approach to this audience differ from your approach to an audience composed entirely of college graduates?
8. What would you want to know about the physical conditions likely to prevail at your speaking place? How would these factors affect your presentation?

9. If you note lack of interest in your audience as you speak, what might be some likely reasons? What could you do to improve interest and attention?

B. For your fourth speaking assignment, plan a *Problem-Cause-Solution* speech on a topic of your choice. For example, you may speak on traffic safety, apathy toward the franchise, juvenile delinquency, racial relations, inflation, hypocrisy in religion, military training, or any other problem of local, state, national, or international interest. Proceed as follows:

1. Point up the problem. Cite statistics, examples, comparisons, illustrations, or testimony to show that a problem exists. Support opinions by facts.
2. Explain what you think caused the problem. Beware of stressing only one cause if there may be several.
3. Point out how you think the problem could be solved or the situation improved. State the reasons for your ideas.
4. Summarize your points and end with a quotation, illustration, or appeal.

C. In preparation for the above speech answer the following questions about your class audience:

1. Do your classmates have a community of interests to which you can appeal?
2. Do you think that your audience will be favorable, neutral, or opposed to your point of view?
3. Do you consider your audience favorably disposed toward you as a speaker?
4. What is the approximate age level of your class members? Is there a wide range in their ages?
5. How well informed do you consider your audience on the topic you chose to discuss?
6. Will their cultural background be likely to affect their attitude toward your point of view?
7. Are the physical conditions of your classroom favorable or unfavorable for speaking?
8. Note the class response as you speak. Make whatever adjustment in your original plans you consider advisable for improving audience response.

CHAPTER 5

Select Your Subject and Purpose

Suppose that you receive two invitations to speak—one at your college annual honors award program and the other at a workshop sponsored by the Department of Business Administration of your university. What basic differences distinguish these two requests? For the awards program, the occasion and the subject constitute the main considerations; the propriety of the occasion limits the choice of subject. For the students' workshop, the speaker forms the main consideration; the students want to hear you on a subject of your choice.

I. Types of Subjects

The choice of speech subjects, then, depends first on whether the subject or occasion or the speaker predominates.

Where the Subject or the Occasion Predominates

In many speaking situations the audience assembles because of a particular occasion—to commemorate some great event, pay tribute to some outstanding person, lay the cornerstone of a new school building, honor the college graduates, or hear a particular subject discussed. These formal occasions, traditional in our way of life, call for speech subjects that conform to the occasion. How does this fact affect your choice of a subject?

You should speak on a subject that the occasion suggests. For your speech at the awards program, you should discuss some educational or cultural problem in a challenging manner and attempt to inspire your fellow students to lofty ideals. Usually a person receives invitations to speak on special occasions because of his knowledge of appropriate topics and his ability to adapt to the occasion. He should not disappoint or embarrass an audience by choosing inappropriate subjects or by failing to discuss the topic assigned.

You should select an idea from your knowledge and experience that serves your purpose. Your interest in education should give you a background of information on which to draw. Suppose that early in your study you chanced on an editorial entitled "All Dressed Up in Education with No Place to Go." The editorial developed the thesis that education receives too much stress today, that we find ourselves oversupplied with educated people who have no new fields to conquer. You disagree. "Surely," you say, "the demand for educated people increases with progress. Why does the claim of an oversupply not ring true?" The answer to this question can form the idea for your speech with the possible title, "New Frontiers in Education." Thus, you take a subject from your background of knowledge and adapt it to the occasion. This method usually constitutes the best course.

Where the Speaker Predominates

Your request to speak at the workshop of business students features you, the speaker. The nature of the workshop indicates certain limits for your subject, but not a specific topic. Many speaking situations permit the speaker to choose his own subject. Note the frequent requests for speakers by civic clubs, study clubs, school assemblies, church groups, and other organizations with regular meetings. They choose speakers with knowledge and reputations in certain fields and leave the choice of a specific subject to him. What factors should you consider when faced with these conditions?

1. *Choose a subject from your background of information.* Should you, a speech student, talk on subjects like property values, trends in home construction, or home financing for the workshop of business students? Probably not, because members of your audience will probably know more about these subjects than you. You should seek a subject in your field of specialization and apply it to the occasion.

A fundamental understanding of subject matter affects the speaking situation in many ways. Most important, it permits the speaker to express mature ideas and accurate information. It generates confidence, authority, and enthusiasm. After considering these factors, suppose that you decide to talk on "Effective Speaking in Selling." The audience will consist primarily of students in business administration; they should welcome ideas on how to improve themselves. Supposing that you are a speech major, you will be likely to know more about oral communication than will members of your audience. Thus you choose from your field of specialty a subject that vitally affects your audience. Apply these principles the next time you seek a subject for a speech.

As a student, you may sometimes have difficulty determining your fields of specialization. You may lack the training and experience from which to draw subjects. Consider the following questions to help determine your area of knowledge.

a. WHAT DO YOU READ DURING YOUR SPARE TIME? You usually read what interests you most; thus, in time you may become a specialist without realizing it. When you read a popular magazine, do you start with the first article and read through to the end? You probably turn first to the table of contents and select those articles that appeal to you most. When you go to the library in search of books for pleasure reading, what subjects do you select? The answers to these questions may reveal your specialty. We usually learn much from pursuits that give us pleasure.

b. WHAT SUBJECTS IN YOUR SCHOOL WORK INTEREST YOU MOST? Besides your required courses, what subjects do you take? What are your major and minor subjects? You probably have special knowledge in these areas. Suppose the local civic club invites you to speak. Perhaps you are majoring in economics. Look over your texts and notes to discover a topic; for example, the businessmen would be interested in an analysis of inflationary tendencies. Perhaps your major is art. What about a subject on the psychological effect of color on worker efficiency? The hard-fisted businessmen constantly seek methods to improve industrial efficiency. Many interesting and helpful topics may arise from your major subject.

c. WHAT ARE YOUR HOBBIES? Perhaps you like sports. Because of your interest you read considerably about sports in addition to participating in and observing them. How do sports apply to the problem of leisure activities? Because of increased leisure occasioned by shorter work days, the proper use of leisure has become an important social problem. It would serve for the subject of a constructive talk to an audience of social workers, the sociology club, or the school recreational directors.

You may have become interested in repairing and building things for your home. This interest may have led you to construct a workshop in your garage or basement. Several million citizens in the United States have done the same. The do-it-yourself addicts would welcome a novel idea on this subject. Your hobby may lead to informative and interesting subjects.

d. IN WHAT ACTIVITIES DO YOU PARTICIPATE? Do you participate in social welfare programs? If so, you could develop a worthwhile idea for the local chapter of the Society for Crippled Children, the Society for Mental Hygiene, or the university speech clinic. Consider your extracurricular activities. You chose these activities because of your interests and aptitudes. If you participate in the school's television program, you might talk on "The Future of Educational Television" or "Advertising by Television." If you belong to a fraternity or sorority, you might discuss the advantages or disadvantages of national social organizations. Your outside activities may suggest many topics for worthwhile and novel speeches.

e. WHAT PLACES OF INTEREST HAVE YOU VISITED? Have you made some interesting trips? One student visited the United Nations building in New York City and took some excellent photographs. Her visit increased her interest in the United Nations and caused her to make a special study of the organization. She made several speeches about the United Nations for civic and educational organizations and over the local television station. Slides prepared from her photographs added interest to her addresses. A veteran made movies and photographs while on duty in England. Several organizations invited him to speak at their meetings and show his slides.

As a sports enthusiast, perhaps you have visited the Baseball Hall of Fame in Cooperstown, New York. The local boys' club, YMCA, or athletic club would welcome more information on this program. Consider interesting places you have visited; they will suggest many subjects on which you have above-average knowledge.

2. *Choose a subject in which you have interests and convictions.* You chose the subject "Effective Speaking in Selling" for the workshop of business students because of your interest in the subject. Perhaps you have known salesmen who lessened their effectiveness

because of slovenly diction, incorrect grammatical construction, and poor voice qualities. You became enthusiastic about this subject because you felt you could give the business students some constructive pointers. Interest and enthusiasm in a subject affect a person's manner of speaking, giving him added confidence and desire to speak. He tends to forget himself, as he loses himself in the idea of his speech.

If you select a subject on which you have strong convictions, you will eagerly share your ideas. A student in an adult speech class chose for one of his class speeches, "Traffic Safety." His interest in the subject grew out of a tragic accident in which his brother had been killed. He spoke so well that the professor submitted his speech for publication. He did well because he was so convinced of his position that he eagerly shared his ideas with others. Consider subjects that you feel strongly about; they may affect your attitude toward your desire for speech-making.

In summary, where the choice of speech subject rests with you, consider a topic from your training and experience, one that interests you, and on which you have strong feelings.

II. Limiting Factors in Choosing Subject

Although your background of information, interests, and convictions may suggest many subjects, you should consider certain limiting factors. These limitations may affect your choice of a specific subject.

Is the Subject in Keeping with the Intellectual Capacity of Your Audience?

A scientist spoke to the freshman class of a university on the subject of nuclear weapons. He spoke in terms applicable to graduate physicists, not college freshmen. Dr. James B. Conant, then President of Harvard University and former chairman of the National Defense Research Committee, addressed the same group on atomic energy. He started with an elementary treatment and led gradually into technical matters for which his previous elementary treatment had prepared his audience. How did the two situations differ? One gave a speech; the other talked with people. Dr. Conant chose a subject which he could adapt to the persons present. A realization of this simple fact may mean the difference between success and failure in a public speech. Regardless of your thorough knowledge of a subject, you must choose one that will enable you to speak in terms that your audience understands.

Is the Subject Adapted to Your Time Limit?

A student in a beginning speech course received constant criticism from the instructor for failure to stay on his announced subject. He found the byways more interesting than the main road. Following an unusually severe admonition, the boy announced as his next subject "The Past, Present, and Future of Science, Literature, and Art." Thus he solved one problem, but he ushered in a new one. Even a college student experiences some difficulty in treating so broad a subject in five minutes. Do not decrease your effectiveness by trying to include all phases of your subject. Narrow it to permit adequate treatment in the time allotted.

Suppose that you decide to talk about the United Nations. If you could speak several hours, you could discuss previous attempts at world organizations, events leading to the United Nations, and its organization. For a twenty-minute speech you might narrow your subject to the organization and purpose of the General Assembly.

Is the Subject Appropriate for the Size of Your Audience and the Prevailing Physical Conditions?

Subjects suitable to small audiences with common interests and training may not be appropriate to large audiences with diverse interests. In general, a large audience requires a non-technical subject with universal appeal which coincides with the members' mutual secondary or momentary interests. An appropriate subject for a small audience would recognize its primary interests.

These variations do not mean that you must abandon your fields of interest; they do indicate that you may need to vary the treatment of your subject. If you speak in a large and uncomfortable auditorium, for instance, develop your speech through illustrative material and narration. If you speak in a small and comfortable room, you may develop the speech in a more technical manner through explanation and specific details.

In summary, choose your subject from your background of training and adapt it to your audience. Select a subject that interests you and in which you have convictions. In making your final choice, consider such limiting factors as the intellectual capacity of your audience, the time allotted, the size of your audience, and the prevailing physical conditions.

III. Selecting the General Purpose

You decided on an inspirational speech for the honors award program because this type is best for ceremonial occasions. You hope to persuade your listeners to continue their emphasis on education, that education has new objectives. For the workshop of business students, you decided on an informative speech because workshops aim at acquiring new methods and exchanging ideas.

Will Rogers, the American humorist, was invited to give an after-dinner speech for a group of clothing manufacturers. He spoke on "Settling the Corset Problem of This Country." You can easily imagine his purpose: entertainment. He was interested in neither persuading nor informing his listeners.

These instances exemplify the three basic purposes: (1) to persuade, (2) to inform, and (3) to entertain.

The Persuasive Speech

The ends sought in the persuasive speech may be classified as (1) to stimulate thought and emotions, (2) to gain assent, and (3) to move to action. Early in your preparation decide which you seek.

1. *To stimulate thought and emotions.* You do not seek overt action as a result of your speech to the honor students. Rather, you wish to stimulate the thinking of your fellow students, to indicate a point of view.

Ceremonial speeches often seek this response. For example, in "The Gettysburg Address" Abraham Lincoln paid tribute to those who lost their lives at Gettysburg and indicated the unfinished task that lay ahead. He called for a rededication to the task of preserving free government. He sought simply to stimulate the thoughts and feelings of the audience.

Franklin D. Roosevelt spoke at the ground-breaking ceremony for the Jefferson Memorial in Washington, D. C. in 1938. After explaining the circumstances that gave rise to the Jefferson Memorial, he sought to stimulate the nation's respect for Jefferson and for the contributions he made to free government.

Dorothy Thompson spoke at the commencement exercises at Russell Sage College on the subject, "Freedom's Back Is Against the Wall." She pleaded for greater respect for the freedom enjoyed by Americans and for dedication to the principle of protecting the spirit of freedom. She stimulated her audience's respect for freedom and indicated how Americans can assume their obligations to keep America free.

President Lyndon B. Johnson's address to the nation on Thanksgiving Day, November 28, 1963, sought to allay the grief of a nation over the assassination of President John F. Kennedy. He used this ceremonial occasion to pay homage to our beloved former president and to express his confidence in the future. Note these words: "A great leader is dead; a great nation must move on. Yesterday is not ours to recover, but tomorrow is ours to win or to lose. I am resolved that we shall win the tomorrows before us." [1]

None of the above speeches sought direct action; they meant to stimulate the listeners, to cause an increased dedication to high ideals. Speeches at home-coming gatherings stimulate alumni; the sales manager's talk stimulates his salesmen. Although the mildest type of persuasion, the speech to stimulate is the most common.

2. *To gain assent.* Some persuasive speeches seek to convince an audience. This purpose prevails in debates, at many forum meetings, and at some ceremonial occasions. Speeches to convince emphasize reasoned discourse and adequacy of evidence. The speaker usually shows that a problem exists, that his proposal can correct that problem, and that benefits will accrue.

William Trufant Foster gave the Scholarship Day Address at the University of Maine on the subject, "Should Students Study?" He developed the thesis that success in life can be measured largely by a student's academic attainment—that a positive correlation exists between high grades and success. Through reasoning and evidence, he sought to convince his audience of his position.

Former President Herbert Hoover gave an address over the network of the Mutual Broadcasting System on the topic, "A New Foreign Policy Is Needed." He showed first the problem presented by our foreign policy; then he outlined some criteria to govern our

---

[1] Lyndon B. Johnson, *A Time for Action* (New York: Pocket Books, Inc., 1964), p. 157.

foreign policy; finally he presented some specific proposals. He attempted to gain the approval of his audience for his proposed program.

On December 17, 1963, almost a month after he took office, President Johnson addressed the United Nations General Assembly. His purpose was more than to stimulate the thinking of the United Nations' delegates. Rather, he sought to convince them of the United States' continued support of the United Nations and of our desires for the future.

> We know what we want: The United States wants to see the cold war end, we want to see it end once and for all; the United States wants to prevent the dissemination of nuclear weapons to nations not now possessing them; the United States wants to press on with arms control and reduction; the United States wants to cooperate with all the members of this organization to conquer everywhere the ancient enemies of mankind—hunger and disease and ignorance; the United States wants sanity, and security, and peace for all, and above all.[2]

The speech that seeks assent makes its basic appeal on rational grounds and uses psychological appeal judiciously. Acceptance by the audience, not immediate overt action, constitutes the main purpose.

3. *To move to action.* The persuasive speech that seeks overt action constitutes the strongest type. The lawyer seeks a favorable verdict, the politician wants votes, the sales manager desires more orders, and the city manager wants the bond issue approved. Many occasions in a democratic society call forth the advocate. Without him, the business of free people could hardly be carried out.

The persuasive speech that seeks action should have a balance among logical, ethical, and emotional proofs. Usually the occasion for such a speech engenders an atmosphere of excitement and enthusiasm that makes for an aggressive presentation. Daniel Webster's reply to Hayne in the Senate in 1830 gives a classic example of the able advocate in action. Debate over the Foote Amendment, which proposed to limit sales of Western lands, developed into a bitter debate between Senators Webster and Hayne over federal versus state sovereignty. Webster championed the cause of federal supremacy. The speech consists principally of refutation of points raised by Senator Hayne. It bulks large in reasoned discourse, but it also contains ethical and emotional proofs. It attempted to influ-

---

[2] *Ibid.*, p. 167.

ence the vote of the senators on the Foote Amendment; thus it sought action.

On January 8, 1964, President Johnson presented his State of the Union Message to Congress. In this speech he sought action—to get his proposed budget adopted. After spelling out a ten-point program to justify the budget he concluded by calling for action.

> John Kennedy was a victim of hate, but he was also a great builder of faith—faith in our fellow Americans, whatever their creed or their color or their station in life; faith in the future of man, whatever his divisions and differences.
>
> This faith was echoed in all parts of the world. On every continent and in every land to which Mrs. Johnson and I traveled, we found faith and hope and love toward this land of America and toward our people.
>
> So I ask you now, in the Congress and in the country, to join with me in expressing and fulfilling that faith, in working for a nation—a nation that is free from want, and a world that is free from hate; a world of peace and justice and freedom and abundance for our time and for all time to come.[3]

The Lincoln-Douglas debates in the senatorial campaign of 1858 sought action. Each man was seeking the vote. The contrast between the speakers and their speeches forms an interesting study to students of public speaking. Stephen Douglas, a short but imposing figure, had a deep voice and a powerful delivery. Abraham Lincoln, a tall, somewhat awkward figure, spoke in a high-pitched voice and with a direct, conversational delivery. Douglas' speeches were polished and ornate; Lincoln's were homely and direct.

The Informative Speech

You reason that a persuasive speech would not meet the requirements of the workshop for business students. You, therefore, decide on an informative speech—to instruct your listeners on how good speech assists in effective salesmanship.

The workshop constitutes but one of many situations that call for the informative speech. Teachers' lectures consist largely of information and explanations. Speeches that explain a theory, demonstrate a process, give instructions, or report on surveys exemplify the informative speech. They are given before such groups as study clubs, civic organizations, and church meetings, where learning forms the keynote. In the informative speech, understanding con-

[3] *Ibid.*, p. 184.

stitutes the principal objective, although the audience may be stimulated, convinced, or entertained in the process of reaching the objective. Keep the end purpose—understanding—in mind to prevent deviation from the main course.

Ralph Waldo Emerson's address "The American Scholar," presented as the Phi Beta Kappa address in Cambridge, Massachusetts, in 1837, exemplifies the informative speech. He explained his educational philosophy and characterized what he considered to be the influences on man's thinking. Among these influences he included nature, the poet, and social intercourse. Although much of what he said was controversial, controversy was not his primary purpose. He sought understanding of his views on man's thought processes.

W. Stuart Symington, while Secretary of the United States Air Force, addressed the Air War College at Maxwell Field, Alabama, on the topic, "Our Air Force Policy." He stated that he proposed to explain the air force policy of the United States because many people do not understand its functions and purposes. He outlined the goals and concluded that they were being achieved. Instilling an understanding of our air force policy formed his primary purpose.

On speaking occasions where you desire to inform, keep understanding as your chief goal. Be sure that you appraise your facts properly and evaluate your material accurately.

The Entertaining Speech

After-dinner occasions, social gatherings, and some club meetings call for entertaining speeches. Entertaining speeches may make use of persuasion and information, but only as a means to the end of providing interesting diversion. Most entertaining speeches include humor, but humor does not constitute a prerequisite. An audience may be entertained by a talk on your visit to Europe, an unusual experience, or an interesting incident. The entertaining speech should be more than a string of unrelated stories or jokes; it should develop an idea in a light and pleasant manner. Heavy subject matter or controversial issues have no place in the entertaining speech. Alternatively, humor may be included in persuasive and informative speeches, but not as primary objective.

Mrs. E. M. Gilmer, who wrote under the name Dorothy Dix, addressed a meeting of the National Education Association on "Experiences of a Woman Columnist." Her speech consisted largely of humorous and unusual excerpts from letters written her for advice about matters of the heart. In a light and delightful manner, she developed the theme of changes in types of advice sought during her long experiences as an advisor to the lovelorn. No doubt her speech offered a refreshing "time out" from the serious speeches of the convention program.

Booth Tarkington talked on "Where We Come From" at an annual banquet of the Indiana Society of Chicago, Using exaggeration, he poked good-natured fun at those who bragged about their home states. Then he outdid them, but contended that he was simply giving facts. His burlesque provided entertainment and was well adapted to the occasion.

In summary, after deciding on the subject for your speech, determine your basic purpose—to persuade, inform, or entertain. Keep this basic purpose in focus as you prepare. For a thirty-minute persuasive speech, do not spend fifteen minutes giving background information. Rather, after a brief introduction, state your main contentions and develop them by reasoning and evidence. For an informative speech, do not dwell on controversial matters; stay with your purpose. An entertaining speech may take the form of persuasion or exposition, but entertainment remains the main purpose.

IV. Selecting the Specific Purpose

What specific purpose do you wish to accomplish in your honors award speech about education? You want to refute the indictment that education has no new objectives, no new and unsolved problems. So far your preparation has included the following:

Occasion:	Honors award program
Audience:	Honor students, parents, and townspeople
Subject:	Education
General Purpose:	To persuade
Specific Purpose:	To prove that education has new frontiers

For the workshop of business students, you want to show how good speech aids the salesman. Your plans thus far include the following:

Occasion:	Workshop for business students
Audience:	Students of business
Subject:	Speech
General Purpose:	To inform
Specific Purpose:	To show how good speech aids salesmanship

Will Rogers prepared an entertaining speech for the dinner occasion of the clothing manufacturers. His plans would have included the following analysis:

Occasion:	Banquet meeting
Audience:	Clothing manufacturers
Subject:	Importance of clothing industry
General Purpose:	To entertain
Specific Purpose:	To amuse the audience about corset manufacturers

A specific purpose assists in limiting the scope of the speech, adjusting to the time limit, guiding preparation, preventing rambling presentation, and selecting ideas and facts. It enables you to crystallize your thinking and your precise aims.

V. Phrasing the Title

Often the title of a speech appears on printed programs and in newspapers. The person who introduces you will need a specific title to announce. Between the time you select your subject and present the speech, therefore, formulate a specific title. Make the title interesting and provocative so as to increase interest. Consider the following suggestions.

Select a Title in Keeping with the Occasion

A dietitian chose as his title for an after-dinner speech to an audience of restaurant owners "The Social Implications of a Hamburger." Some student debaters presented a humorous debate at the annual banquet of the Forensic Club on the proposition, "Resolved, That Bachelors by Choice Should Be Compelled To Marry Old Maids from Necessity." The titles reflected the spirit of the occasions and helped create a pleasant atmosphere. A good title should do exactly that.

Nicholas Murray Butler chose as the title for his commencement address at Columbia University "Democracy Versus Dictatorship." Mr. H. H. Kirk used the title, "Academic Freedom: Are We Ready for It?" when he addressed the North Dakota Education Association Convention. C. M. Chester, former Chairman of the National Association of Manufacturers, spoke to the Congress of American Industry on the title, "How Liberal Is Business?" These were formal programs and the titles reflected the dignity of the occasions.

These examples of varying types of speeches show how the titles fit the occasion. A humorous occasion demands a humorous title; a formal occasion calls for a dignified title.

Select a Title Applicable to Your Subject

The title, "All Dressed Up and No Place to Go," would be provocative for your speech to the honor students, but it might prove misleading. The title, "New Frontiers for Education," meets the requirement of relevancy.

R. W. Jepson chose the title, "Potted Thinking," for a radio address. He characterized several illogical types of reasoning by which some people arrive at conclusions. He drew an analogy between these types of reasoning and foods we buy in potted form. The title applied directly to his subject.

During the depression, Owen D. Young spoke at the Charter Centenary dinner of the New England Mutual Life Insurance Company on the title, "Courage for the Future." He outlined a philosophy for the insurance people and suggested how they could rescue themselves during the depression. His title was descriptive of the theme of his address.

Although the title should apply directly to the theme of the speech, it should not state explicitly the main ideas. For example, Dr. John A. Schindler addressed an audience at Ohio State University on a medical subject, "How To Live a Hundred Years Happily." Compare this title with "Medical Science's Contribution to Longevity and the Resulting Problems of Leisure Activities." The first title relates specifically to the thesis of the speech; the second statement, while relevant, tends to spell out in detail the main points. It leaves too little to the imagination.

Compare "Paying the Parson" with "The Financial Plight of the Rural Minister in America"; "The Obligation To Talk Sense, Not Nonsense" with "The Obligation of the Public Speaker To Evaluate Properly What He Talks About in the Public-Speaking Situation"; "The Professor Talks Back" with "Educators' Answer to the Comparative Low Wage Scale of Teachers to Other Professions." The titles stated first seem best because they are relevant but do not state the theme of the speeches as explicitly as do the alternate titles.

Select a Provocative Title

Dr. Schindler's subject "How To Live a Hundred Years Happily" excites curiosity and makes the audience want to listen. A student in an adult speech course announced his title as "How To Add $1,200 to Your Annual Income." He gave pointers on the purchasing and selling of stocks and bonds. Another student used the title "Money in Your Pockets" for his talk on legitimate deductions often overlooked in filing income tax returns. These titles provoked audience interest.

The Reader's Digest uses provocative titles well. A copy chosen at random shows such interesting titles as "Nightmare on the 79th Floor," "Oh, Say, Can You Ski?" "Help Your Husband Stay Alive," "A New Way of Dying," and "They Swapped Everything but Their Wives." Such titles prick one's imagination and create an interest in the articles. A provocative title for a speech has the same effect.

What is your reaction to the sermon title, "Your Obligation to Your Church," to the professor's speech on "Problems of the School Teacher," or to the Chamber of Commerce representative's title, "Your Civic Duty"? Such titles show a lack of imagination and tend to repel listeners. Make your title excite curiosity and thereby increase interest.

Select a Brief Title

A brief title usually fulfills the foregoing requirements better than a long one. Most of the titles recommended in the preceding discussion consist of a few words arranged into a catchy phrase. Long titles tend to give away the theme of the speech and leave little to the imagination. The following titles are of winning college orations heard in recent years: "The Lie of War," "Cross Patches," "Believe It or Not," "Six Martyred Senators," and "A Rendezvous with Death."

In summary, after selecting your subject and purpose, give consideration to phrasing an apt title. A good title reflects the mood of the occasion, relates directly to the subject, excites curiosity, and is phrased briefly.

VI. Summary

Two principal types of speaking occasions affect choice of subjects: (1) where the occasion or the subject predominates, and (2) where the speaker predominates. The former limits the speaker to selecting a topic in keeping with the occasion; the latter allows a wider freedom of choice to the speaker.

In selecting a subject, take into consideration your background of information and your interests and convictions. In making a final decision, consider the following limiting factors: the intellectual capacity of your audience, the time allotted, and the probable size of your audience and the prevailing physical conditions.

After selecting your subject, consider your basic purpose: to persuade, to inform, or to entertain. The persuasive speech takes one of three forms: to stimulate, to convince, or to move to action. Next, decide on the specific purpose so as to limit the scope of your speech and to guide you in your preparation.

Finally, phrase a proper title for your speech. Consider these factors: the mood of the occasion, the application to your subject, its provocativeness, and its length.

Questions and Exercises

A. Answer the following questions on Chapter 5.

1. Distinguish between speaking occasions where the occasion or subject predominates and those where the speaker predominates. How does this distinction apply to your choice of topic?
2. In what field of knowledge do you consider yourself best prepared? List five topics from this field that you think would be appropriate at the weekly Rotary meeting. List five topics suitable for the local women's Thursday Study Club. List five topics appropriate for a meeting of sales managers.
3. Of what value is selecting a subject on which you have strong convictions? How would you distinguish between a conviction and a prejudice?
4. Select a subject about the United Nations suitable for a one-hour lecture to the International Relations Study Club. How would you narrow this subject for a twenty-minute speech for the Lions Club? How would you narrow it for a five-minute talk for a television program on United Nations Day?
5. What limiting factors may affect your choice of subject for a public speech?
6. Distinguish among the informative, entertaining, and persuasive speeches. Why should you select your general purpose early in your preparation?
7. Distinguish among the three types of persuasive speeches discussed in this chapter.
8. How does the specific purpose of a speech differ from the general purpose?
9. What factors should you consider in phrasing the title for your speech?

10. Phrase suitable titles that conform to the requirements you listed in answer to Question 9 from the following general subjects: (1) outer space, (2) atomic warfare, (3) juvenile delinquency, (4) the national debt, (5) international disarmament, (6) the welfare state, (7) the school crisis, (8) the armed services, (9) professional football, (10) the reading habits of Americans, (11) the poverty program, (12) the Great Society, (13) civil rights, and (14) medical care under social security.

B. For your fifth speaking assignment, give a personal-experience speech of not more than five minutes. Make this speech an interesting narrative. The following topics are suggestive:

1. An interesting place I have visited
2. An unusual person I have known
3. My most embarrassing experience
4. My most interesting game of sports
5. My most interesting vacation
6. My narrow escape
7. My first public speech
8. My introduction to politics
9. My home town
10. My major subject
11. My favorite hobby
12. My greatest accomplishment

C. Answer the following questions about the subject you select for your personal-experience speech.

1. Is the subject adapted to your time limit?
2. Does the title meet the requirements listed in this chapter?
3. What is the general purpose of your speech?
4. What is the specific purpose of your speech?
5. Did you get a good response from your audience?

CHAPTER 6

Find, Record, and Analyze Your Material

You should decide on the subjects for your addresses well in advance of the occasions in order to give yourself ample time to think about them. The most constructive preparation comes from thinking about plans for speeches at free moments, when ideas occur. Ideas may often come while waiting for the bus, dressing, or preparing to retire. Most good speeches evolve as the result of thought and deliberation. Rarely can you postpone the plans for a speech until a predetermined time set aside to prepare. The time may arrive without any inspiration or ideas.

We have already noted the mental processes that you should go through in selecting your subject, deciding on a general purpose, narrowing your subject to a specific purpose, and phrasing a provocative title. All these decisions must be made with your specific audience in mind. Now you are ready to begin your preparation. How should you proceed?

I. Sources of Material

To gather speech material: (1) survey previous background knowledge, (2) interview specialists and listen to speakers, (3) analyze published speeches on allied subjects, (4) collect material through correspondence, and (5) conduct research. A discussion of these sources follows.

Survey your Background Knowledge

After deciding upon your subject, think through what you already know about it. Make a tentative outline of a possible speech based on this background information. A preliminary analysis will reveal where you need more evidence. Then investigate and read for additional ideas and material. After reading for new information, think through your subject again. Revise your preliminary outline and incorporate the ideas and materials gained from your research.

How much you can rely on your previous knowledge will vary according to the subject. You probably know more about most subjects than you think. Through improved methods of communication—radio, television, forums, newspapers, magazines, books, pamphlets—we become exposed to the issues of many subjects. Our general knowledge may remain unused for long periods, but it can be recalled with conscious effort when needed.

Some speeches may be made mostly from background knowledge. Persons with inquiring minds, interests in information, varied experiences, and wide travel have much information on which to draw. They need only to utilize their acquired knowledge.

Daniel Webster's famous reply to Hayne consisted of some 30,000 words and took parts of two days to deliver. Yet he had only a few days to prepare. He replied when asked how he could prepare so eloquent a speech on such short notice, "Gentlemen, I have been preparing that speech all my life." In a sense this statement holds true for most great speeches.

But you reply, "I do not have a background of information on which to draw. How can I acquire such a background?" Neither did Daniel Webster in his youth, but he had an inquiring mind and an interest in learning that caused him to acquire it over the years. The supply of useful ideas to be learned is inexhaustible. Your daily habits of inquiry, reading, association with others, and travel can gradually build up a supply of ideas and information. Consider the following program as a starting point.

1. *Improve your reading habits.* If we devoted to general reading a part of the time that we waste each day, we would soon have a background of information upon which to draw. Some persons devote an hour or two to general reading before retiring at night; others utilize part of the noon hour or an early-morning period. The im-

portant thing is to acquire a regular habit. Consider the following suggestions:

a. READ A NEWSPAPER DAILY. Read with discrimination; not all parts of the newspaper will prove helpful. Follow the trends of domestic and international affairs by scanning the front page. Read the editorials and syndicated columns; observe the financial, sports, entertainment, and book-review sections. A good speaker will know what is going on in the world about him.

b. READ A NEWS MAGAZINE REGULARLY. Such weekly news magazines as *Time, Newsweek,* and *U. S. News and World Report* summarize and synthesize the previous week's happenings on the domestic, national, and international fronts. They give a more thorough treatment than do most daily papers. They carry special reports on financial conditions, the entertainment field, books, sports, and other subjects that serve the public speaker well. Read them with discrimination because they tend to reflect political, economic, and social philosophies of particular groups; but they contain information that can hardly be found elsewhere.

c. READ FROM SOME OF THE BETTER MAGAZINES REGULARLY. Such magazines as *Harper's, Atlantic, Scribner's, Forbes, Saturday Review, Fortune, American Economic Review, The National Observer, The Nation, The New Republic, The Reporter,* and *Vital Speeches* carry articles written by outstanding writers. Among these you will find articles that express varying concepts and attitudes. Your ability to discriminate and evaluate will increase the more you read.

d. READ FROM PROFESSIONAL MAGAZINES AND JOURNALS. Determine the professional journals in your field of interests and read the more important ones. For example, in the field of finance consult such publications as *Forbes, The Wall Street Journal,* the *Monthly Newsletter of the National City Bank of New York, Monthly Labor Review, Financial World, American Economic Review,* and *Barron's Weekly*. Many fields of specialization have their own journals that prove valuable to specialists. The speech student will find invaluable such publications as *The Quarterly Journal of Speech, The Speech Teacher, Speech Monographs, Theatre Arts, Players' Magazine, The American Educational Theatre Association Journal, The Journal of Speech and Hearing Disorders, The Journal of Speech and Hearing Research,* and state and regional publications such as *Today's Speech, Western Speech, Southern Speech Journal,* and *Central States Speech Journal.*

e. READ GOOD BOOKS REGULARLY. Acquire the habit of reading from some good book daily. Although you may find only a few minutes to read each day, the total mounts up in a year. Maintain a balance between fiction and non-fiction, prose and poetry, contemporary books and the classics. Form the habit of selecting books yourself rather than relying on some book club. In time your ability to discriminate will improve. Consult such sources as the book-review section of the *New York Times,* the *Saturday Review,* the weekly news magazines, and the book-review section of your local newspaper for leads on outstanding current books. Such books as Francis Xavier Meehan's *Living Upstairs: Reading for Profit and Pleasure,* John Mansfield's *I Want! I Want!,* John O'Donnell's *Much Loved Books,* and May Lamberton Becker's *Adventures in Reading* give excellent lists of the great books.

2. *Broaden your scope of interests.* Inquire into as many sources of information as possible. A ministerial student conferred with his counselor about his poor academic standing. He stated that he had little trouble with his courses in religion but that other subjects had little appeal for him. Further, he stated that he saw little reason for them because he planned to preach the gospel, not instruct in science, literature, and mathematics. Unless he changes his attitudes, he probably will not go far in his profession; and he may give warped and ill-conceived opinions on religion. How can he understand and evaluate the Bible without a knowledge of the many problems with which it deals? The minister who can draw on literature, history, government, and philosophy will not only understand better the truths of the Bible, but will make his sermons more effective by a variety of supporting material.

The lawyer must understand psychology, history, literature, and philosophy to represent his client adequately; knowledge of law alone will not suffice. Business demands people with a broad general education, not simply specialists in narrow fields. The failure to study broadly may make for narrow thinking, dogmatic assertion, and improper evaluation. The person who aspires to successful speaking will broaden his scope of knowledge and interests.

3. *Engage in varied activities.* The broader your interests, the more you learn about how others think and react. Such extracurricular activities in college as sports, debate, dramatics, band, university newspaper and yearbook, and study clubs not only provide sources of useful knowledge but also provide an opportunity for

association with others. These associations are an integral part of the educational process and increase your ability to speak well in public.

Travel will broaden your scope of interests and knowledge; it may provide incidents for use as illustrative material in speeches. Travel also broadens your experiences and increases your understanding of people—both invaluable to the public speaker. Photographs or motion pictures of places visited provide excellent visual aids to serve as illustrative material.

Participation in civic, religious, and educational activities will also increase your effectiveness as a speaker. Those who restrict their activities limit their scope of interests, knowledge, and understanding.

4. *Develop your social life.* Almost all great speakers are social in nature. They learn to know people and to appreciate their problems by associating with them. You must develop yourself not only mentally, physically, and spiritually, but also socially in order to have a well-rounded personality. Do not deplore time spent in conversation, club activities, participation in sports, attending football games or plays, and other worthwhile social activities. They are a necessary part of preparation for life and are a sound training for public speaking.

Interview Specialists and Listen to Speakers

Experts in the community may be able to furnish excellent ideas on your subject as well as leads for sources to study. For example, if your subject pertains to labor-capital relationships, plan interviews with some of the following: an economics professor who specializes in labor problems; a law professor, for legal implications of the problem; a history professor, for pointers on the history of the problem; the president of the local labor union, for labor's viewpoint; a local manufacturer, for capital's viewpoint; and the chairman of the local Chamber of Commerce, for facts on labor conditions in the community.

Plan your interview to cause the least inconvenience possible to the person interviewed and to obtain the exact information needed. Proper procedure follows: (1) request an appointment; (2) plan questions on the precise information needed; (3) explain what purpose the information will serve; (4) record accurately the statements of the person interviewed; (5) ask for opinions on ideas you have gained elsewhere; and (6) ask questions about materials for further study.

Listen to speakers on subjects closely allied to your topic. Check the programs of the local university-sponsored lecture series or the community-sponsored forums. Often civic organizations, study clubs, and church groups sponsor lectures and will welcome your attendance. Observe the radio and television logs in your local newspaper for the subjects and personalities on forum and lecture programs. Such sources may furnish excellent assistance in preparing speeches.

Analyze Published Speeches on Allied Subjects

Numerous collections of speeches are published, some annually. They furnish models for speech composition as well as ideas and information for oral assignments. Such volumes have long been used for courses in rhetorical analysis and an increasing number of professors now use them as supplementary texts for the beginning speech course; they add to the liberal arts content of these courses. Some of the more valuable collections follow:

Goodwin F. Berquist, Jr., *Speeches for Illustration and Example* (Chicago: Scott, Foresman and Co., 1965). This paperback volume contains fifteen speeches that focus upon five types of communication problems. Each speech is followed by a description of audience response, review questions, and study projects.

Haig A. Bosmajian, *Readings in Speech* (New York: Harper & Row, Publishers, Inc., 1965). This paperback book includes speeches articles, and essays about rhetorical principles under six headings. Study questions and suggested speech topics conclude each section.

Thomas A. Hopkins, *Rights for Americans: The Speeches of Robert F. Kennedy* (Indianapolis: Bobbs-Merrill Co., Inc., 1964). This hardback volume contains thirty-seven speeches on the subject of civil rights and is typical of numerous volumes containing speeches by a single man of prominence.

Glenn R. Capp, *Famous Speeches in American History* (Indianapolis: Bobbs-Merrill Co., Inc., 1963). This paperback volume contains eighteen of the most famous speeches in American history selected by a poll of leading professors of public address. It covers a two hundred year span, starting with Patrick Henry and ending with John F. Kennedy. The introduction explains how to analyze speeches. Each speech is preceded by a brief biography of the speaker, a discussion of the setting for the speech, and a short analysis of the speech.

Herbert W. Hildebrandt, *Issues of Our Times* (New York: The Macmillan Co., 1963). This paperback volume includes eighty articles and speeches of the contemporary scene. They are grouped under the headings of communication, education, and integration.

Edwin Black and Harry P. Kerr, *American Issues: A Sourcebook for Speech Topics* (New York: Harcourt, Brace and World, Inc., 1961). This paperback volume contains thirty-four speeches and essays that present conflicting points of view on current topics.

Carroll C. Arnold, Douglas Ehninger, and John C. Gerber, *The Speaker's Resource Book* (Chicago: Scott, Foresman and Co., 1961). This paperbound volume contains a collection of speeches with introductions, questions, and analyses. It also includes a brief manual of public speaking.

Lester Thonssen and William L. Finkel, *Ideas That Matter* (New York: The Ronald Press Company, 1961). This paperbound volume contains selections from 163 speeches and articles designed to provide ideas for student speeches.

Ernest J. Wrage and Barnet Baskerville, *American Forum: Speeches on Historic Issues, 1788-1900* (New York: Harper and Row, Publishers, Inc., 1960). This anthology contains twenty-six speeches, arranged chronologically in relation to basic historical issues. It includes several speeches not found in other volumes. *Contemporary Forum: American Speeches on Twentieth-Century Issues* (New York: Harper and Row, Publishers, Inc., 1962), a companion volume to *American Forum,* contains thirty-two speeches on controversial domestic and foreign issues. Each speech is presented in its historical context with a brief biography of the speaker.

A. Craig Baird, *American Public Address, 1740-1952* (New York: McGraw-Hill Book Company, 1956). This volume contains speeches by twenty-six speakers over a two hundred year period beginning with a speech by Jonathan Edwards in 1741 and concluding with Adlai Stevenson's acceptance speech in Chicago on July 26, 1952. It contains many of the great speeches in American history.

Lew Sarett and William T. Foster, *Modern Speeches on Basic*

Issues (Boston: Houghton Mifflin Company, 1939). This volume contains an excellent collection of speeches. It lists the speeches by type and subject matter, thus making it readily usable.

A. Craig Baird, *Representative American Speeches* (New York: H. W. Wilson, 1937-).[1] This collection, published annually, contains many of the best speeches made each year. It includes brief sketches of the speaker and the occasion.

William Hayes Yeager, *Effective Speaking for Every Occasion* (rev. ed., Englewood Cliffs, N. J.: Prentice-Hall, Inc., 1951). This volume includes an excellent collection of speeches by contemporary speakers as part of a textbook in public speaking. The brief instructions for each type of speech help you to analyze it. The speeches are listed according to types.

Harold F. Harding, *The Age of Danger* (New York: Random House, Inc., 1952). This collection of more than sixty speeches and discussions covers the period from 1946 to 1952. The volume is divided into three parts and classifies the speeches under eighteen topical headings. It is intended to furnish the student with materials as well as models.

W. M. Parish and Marie Hochmuth, *American Speeches* (New York: David McKay Co., Inc., 1954). This volume covers the period from 1741 to 1944, from Jonathan Edwards to Frankin D. Roosevelt. It contains a detailed analysis of Lincoln's First Inaugural Address.

Carl G. Brandt and Edward M. Shafter, Jr., *Selected American Speeches on Basic Issues* (Boston: Houghton Mifflin Co., 1960). This volume contains nineteen speeches with extensive biographical and background comments covering the period from 1850 to 1950. The volume is divided into three parts with an introduction to each part.

Other collections include William Brigance, *Classified Speech Models* (New York: F. S. Crofts and Co., 1938); James Milton O'Neill, *Classified Models of Speech Composition* (New York: Century Co., 1921); Ashley H. Thorndike, *Modern Eloquence* (15 vols.; New York: P. F. Collier, 1941); Mayo W. Hazeltine, et al., *Masterpieces of Eloquence* (25 vols.; New York: P. F. Collier and Son); Egbert Ray Nichols, *Intercollegiate Debates* (New York: Noble and Noble, 1919); *University Debater's Annual* (New York: H. W. Wilson, 1914); *Vital Speeches of the Day;* and the *Congressional Digest.*

---

[1] Professor Lester Thonssen became editor of this collection starting with Volume 32, 1959-60.

Be sure to give credit to the author when quoting from speeches. Do not use the ideas of others as your own. Analysis of other speeches may, however, give you valuable suggestions for the preparation of your own.

Collect Material through Correspondence

Supplement local sources of material by correspondence with individuals or organizations. A student in an adult speech course chose as his term speech subject "An Analysis of the Speaking Program of the American Medical Association." He wrote to the Chicago headquarters of the association and received letters from both the secretary and the director of public relations, a pamphlet, and suggestions about additional materials. Most organizations have public relations and research divisions that will send information on request. For the price of return postage, the extension division of many state universities will furnish materials on most subjects. A letter to your United States Senator or Congressman will get you materials on current problems pending before Congress. Address the Library of Congress, Washington, D. C., for governmental pamphlets.

A survey by means of questionnaires may serve a useful purpose in securing information not available elsewhere. A speech professor received a request to speak on "The Status of Speech Training in the Southwest." Since he could not find published material on the subject, he sent a questionnaire to the chairman of the speech departments in universities. The results of this survey provided the only source of information for the report.

Plan the questionnaire so as to get the exact information needed; do not ask for needless information. The questions must be sensible so that the person will want to answer. The greater the number of returns, the more representative and valid are your findings. Incorporate the following suggestions in planning your survey.

1. Accompany your questionnaire with a personal letter. State briefly what use the information will serve, and comment that confidential information will not be identified with the person or institution. Express thanks for the courtesy of a reply and agree to send a tabulation of your findings.
2. Type or mimeograph the questionnaire, observing the following procedures:
   (a) Make your questions unambiguous. Ask only questions pertinent to your subject, and avoid duplication of questions.

(b) Use only one side of the paper and space questions neatly on the page.
(c) Give specific instructions on how to fill in the answers.
(d) Provide sufficient space on the form for answers. Do not ask that numerous sheets be appended.
(e) Request approximations where exact information is not essential. Avoid the necessity of forcing the one providing the information to consult files, make telephone calls, or be otherwise inconvenienced.
(f) Keep to a minimum questions requiring written opinions and evaluations. For opinions, put your questions in multiple-choice form. Instead of asking, "What is your opinion of the proposed tax reform?" use the check method:
——— strongly for, ——— for, ——— neutral, ——— opposed, ——— strongly opposed.

3. Send your letters and questionnaires by first-class mail in sealed envelopes.
4. Enclose a self-addressed and stamped return envelope.
5. Send a second request within two weeks if you do not receive a reply. Emphasize the importance of complete returns and express appreciation for the courtesy of a prompt reply.

Conduct a Research Study

The sources of information discussed above will prove valuable, but the most important general source consists of books, periodicals, and other printed matter. The extent of reading and research necessary depends on your background of information and on how productive the sources already discussed may prove. Rarely will you speak on a subject in which some research will not be necessary. The following sources of research should prove helpful.

1. *Source books, textbooks, and trade books.* These sources will help you acquire a general understanding of your subject. Study the history and principles of your subject first.

To locate pertinent books, consult the card catalogue in the library. All books in the library are listed alphabetically by author, title, and subject. In the subject-matter listing, look under various topical headings. For example, if your subject pertains to the foreign-aid program of the United States, look under such headings as "The United States Foreign Policy," "The Marshall Plan," "The Point-Four Program," "Lend Lease," "Technical Assistance," "Foreign Aid," and "The National Budget."

2. *Newspapers and magazines.* These sources furnish valuable

current material on most subjects. To locate newspaper accounts, consult the *New York Times Index* if it is available. It is the only complete newspaper index in the United States. Most newspapers, however, will carry the same or similar accounts on approximately the same date. Releases disseminated by the Associated Press and the United Press International appear in most newspapers.

To find articles in magazines, consult the *Readers' Guide to Periodical Literature,* published since 1902, or *Poole's Index* for older articles. Like the card catalogue for books, the *Readers' Guide* lists magazine articles by author, title, and subject matter; and you must look under various allied headings to find articles through the subject-matter listing. The *Readers' Guide* is published monthly and bound into annual volumes by most libraries, and into three-year volumes by some. However, you must look in the monthly issues for the current year.

3. *Encyclopedias, yearbooks, and almanacs.* Encyclopedias provide a good source for beginning your study of unfamiliar subjects because they give a condensed history and discussion, an overall view. The encyclopedias are revised about every ten years; the revisions incorporate new material into the numbered volumes. Between revisions, annual supplements keep them up to date. For example, *Encyclopedia Britannica* publishes the *Britannica Book of the Year;* the *Encyclopedia Americana,* the yearbook *The Americana;* and the *New International Encyclopedia,* the supplement *The New International Yearbook.* Articles on most subjects list additional references at the end. Many special encyclopedias are also published, such as *The Encyclopedia of Social Sciences.*

Yearbooks and almanacs provide a wide range of factual material and statistics and give the sources of all data. Consult such volumes as *The World Almanac, The Statesman's Yearbook,* the *Statistical Abstract of the United States,* and various state almanacs.

4. *Biographical and literary references.* To find information about the authors of books and persons whom you might quote, consult any one of several biographical references. *Who's Who in America* and its companion volumes are perhaps the best known. *Who's Who in America—Living Authors* and *Who's Who in Education* exemplify specialized reference books. Also consult *Dictionary of American Biography* and *Webster's Biographical Dictionary.* Information on deceased persons may be found in *Who Was Who,*

Lippincott's Biographical Dictionary, and the *Dictionary of American Biography.*

For appropriate quotations and literary references consult such volumes as *Bartlett's Familiar Quotations,* Mencken's *A New Dictionary of Quotations, Oxford Dictionary of Quotations, Cyclopedia of Practical Quotations* by Hoyt, *The Speaker's Desk Book* by Lupton, *Brewer's Dictionary of Phrase and Fable,* and *Home Book of Quotations* by Stevenson. These books arrange quotations under topical headings or alphabetically by key words and phrases or by authors. Beware of frequent use of ready-made quotations. Instead, find quotations from reading the original source. One speaker quoted Shakespeare with fluency, but the more he talked the more apparent it became that he did not really know Shakespeare. Most people can detect whether a person speaks from understanding or merely from a surface knowledge.

5. *Professional and trade journals.* Most professions and businesses have their own journals which provide valuable material in specialized fields. For example, the medical profession publishes the *Journal of the American Medical Association* for members of the profession and *Hygeia* for the general public. Other large organizations that publish journals include American Bankers Association, American Bar Association, American Federation of Labor, the International Law Association, the National Association of Manufacturers, and the American Telephone and Telegraph Company.

The following indexes will help you find material in trade journals: *Agricultural Index, Art Index, Educational Index, Index to Legal Periodicals, Index Medicus, Index to the Quarterly Journal of Speech and Speech Monographs, Industrial Arts Index, Psychological Abstracts,* and the *Public Affairs Information Service.*

6. *Governmental publications.* The state and federal governments publish pamphlets and public documents on a variety of subjects. The *Congressional Record,* the official journal of Congress, carries proceedings of the debates in both houses of Congress. The appendix contains an extension of remarks, speeches made by legislators outside congress, and frequently speeches by others. Each senator and representative has a limited number of copies of the journal for distribution. Many libraries have them.

To obtain public documents and pamphlets, write the Division of Bibliography, Library of Congress, Washington, D. C., for a list of references. These lists specify the prices, usually reasonable. Check the pamphlets desired and send your order, together with a money order covering the charges, to the Superintendent of Documents, Library of Congress, Washington, D. C.

Many university libraries are depositories of public documents. Consult the *Catalogue of Public Documents* and the *Monthly Catalogue*. The latter gives descriptive information on each pamphlet along with the price and instructions for ordering.

7. *Dictionaries and bibliographic indexes.* A good dictionary provides indispensable help to the public speaker. The best known are *Webster's New International Dictionary, Webster's New World Dictionary,* Funk and Wagnall's *New Standard Dictionary, Oxford English Dictionary, A Dictionary of Contemporary American Usage* by Bergen Evans and Cornelia Evans, and the *American College Dictionary.* Webster's *Dictionary of Synonyms* and Roget's *Thesaurus* will also prove helpful.

To find additional information on your subject consult prepared bibliographies in *Bibliographic Indexes,* look for references at the ends of articles in encyclopedias and chapters in textbooks, and consult the *Reference Shelf* series published by H. W. Wilson Company.

II. Take Notes

A disconcerting part of speech preparation consists of failure to find a previously discovered piece of evidence, illustration, or idea. You can remember the library seat you sat in when you read the article and perhaps the pretty girl who sat across the table, but the exact article slips your mind. You need it; so you go back to the library and waste time trying to locate it. Perhaps you copied the title and magazine, but you forgot to list the author. Since you plan to use a direct quotation from the article you must go back to the library for only one piece of information. To prevent these frustrating experiences, acquire the habit of taking notes on what you read. Note-taking must be systematic, but it need not be tedious and unpleasant.

Take complete records for each article, book, or pamphlet that you read. For books, include the author's name, the title of the book, the facts and date of publication, and the page number from which the material came. To illustrate:

> John Doe and Peter Poe, *Practical Debating* (New York: J. B. Lippincott Co., 1949), pp. 11-15.

For magazines, bulletins, or pamphlets, use this form: author's name, title of article, name of publication, date, and page number. To illustrate:

John Doe, "General Semantics for the Debater," *The Southern Speech Journal,* XIX, No. 4 (May, 1954), pp. 295-303.

What should you include in your notes? One plan is first to write a summary of the article, including only enough to recall the gist of it. Since you can never be sure just what material you will need, the summary will indicate whether you should read the article again. Second, copy quotations and pertinent excerpts. In selecting quotations, observe these precautions: (1) Do not lift quotations out of context; they should accurately reflect the opinion of the author. (2) Delete parts of quotations not applicable by using three spaced periods . . . if the omission comes within a sentence, or four . . . . if at the end of a sentence, but be sure your deletions do not change the meaning of the author. (3) If you insert any explanatory statements, put the insertion in brackets within the quotation. (4) Enclose all direct quotations in quotation marks and give the page number from which they come. You may also find statistical information, illustrations, or other supporting data which you desire to copy. If so, make sure that such information means what you think it means before including it in your notes. Finally, a brief statement of your evaluation of the article may be helpful for future reference.

Be consistent in your methods of accumulating notes. Some speakers prefer to use cards, others prefer notebooks. Cards can be obtained in either three-by-five inch, four-by-six inch, or five-by-eight inch sizes. The larger sizes permit more notes on each card, but they may be inconvenient to carry about. The following form is suggested.

Author, Book, Facts of Publication, Page No.

Summary of part read

Quotations or Facts

Your evaluation

Cards permit an index arrangement and can be easily grouped and classified.

Notebooks are easy to carry about, and a sheet permits more

notes than a card. The loose-leaf variety has many of the advantages of cards as pages may be grouped and classified. The choice depends on individual preference, but do not copy notes haphazardly on whatever may be available at the time. Adopt a consistent plan and stay with it.

All the references used in composing your speech are to be added at the end of your outline when it is completed. If you decide to give the speech again, reread your references to renew your interest. This simple suggestion saves time and effort.

III. Analyze Your Material [2]

After gathering your material, relate it to your subject and purpose. What does the material mean, and how does it apply to your subject? The process of thinking the question through, relating one item to another, and breaking down the subject into its component parts is termed analysis. In short, you must differentiate main ideas from subpoints and subpoints from forms of support, and determine the relative value of items of evidence.

The ability to assess values increases as you read and think about your subject. Yet you cannot wait to collect ideas and facts until you complete your study. Begin by listing all ideas, forms of support, and arguments encountered in your study. List them without regard to value at first; the assessment of values comes later.

Consider the research for your speech to the honors award program, "Effective Speaking in Selling." Part of your original list of points, recorded as you might list them, follows. Actually, such a list will be longer, but this one will serve to illustrate.

1. Types of vocabularies—reading, writing, and speaking
2. Value of knowing subject well
3. Positive suggestion and salesmanship
4. How to improve vocabularies—read good literature, listen to educated people, write, and speak
5. Requirements of a good voice—breathing, relaxation, forward placement, flexible modifiers
6. Salesmanship and intrinsic worth of man
7. Errors in use of voice—volume, rate, distinctness, quality
8. Values of bodily action—increases self-confidence, helps hold interest, aids in clarity

[2] See Chapter 15 for a discussion of the preliminary steps in analysis. For a detailed discussion, see Glenn R. Capp and Thelma Robuck Capp, *Principles of Argumentation and Debate* (Englewood Cliffs, N. J., Prentice-Hall, Inc., 1965), pp. 86-100.

9. "A good speaker is a good man, skilled in speaking." (Cicero)
10. "Whatever the man is, such is the speaker." (Seneca)
11. The salesman's obligation to evaluate his product
12. Aristotle refers to "ethics" twenty-nine times
13. Alfred Korzybski—two easiest ways to get by in life—believe all that you read and hear, don't believe anything
14. Effects of skills on salesmanship
15. Procedures for proper evaluation of product
16. Psychology and salesmanship

Study this list and decide on the main divisions of the speech. Then study the list again to determine the subpoints within each main division. Finally, choose from the list the appropriate supporting material for points and subpoints. Note the following rearrangement of points on the original list as incorporated into your outline.

Main point	I. You develop yourself as an able salesman in proportion to your intrinsic worth as a person. (Point 6 on original list)
Support: Quotation	A. Cicero: "A good speaker is a good man, skilled in speaking." (Point 9)
Quotation	B. Seneca: "Whatever the man is, such is the speaker." (Point 10)
Main point	II. You develop yourself as an able salesman in proportion to your fundamental knowledge of your product. (Point 2)
Subpoint	A. The importance of proper evaluation of your product. (Point 11)
Subpoint	B. Procedures for proper evaluation of your product. (Point 15)
Main point	III. You develop yourself as an able salesman in proportion to the skills that you acquire. (Point 14)
Subpoint	A. Understand the psychology of dealing with people. (Point 16)
Support: Example	1. Example of shoe salesman.
Example	2. Example of a private selling war insurance.
Subpoint	B. Understand the principles of good speech.
	1. Develop a good vocabulary.
Support: Explanation	a. Types of vocabularies: reading, writing, and speaking. (Point 1)
	b. Improve your vocabulary by (1) reading good literature, (2) listening to educated people, and (3) writing and speaking. (Point 4)

	2. Develop a pleasing voice.
Explanation	a. Errors in use of voice: volume, rate, distinctness, and quality. (Point 7)
Explanation and demonstration	b. Improve voice by: deep breathing, relaxing throat and jaws, forward placement, and flexible modifiers. (Point 5)
	3. Develop relaxed bodily action.

You will note several items on the original list that were not used in the final outline. Normally you will read and take notes on more material than you can use. Do not consider this wasted effort, however, for all you read aids in your basic understanding of your subject. Understanding reflects itself in self-confidence, enthusiasm, and interest.

In summary, your analysis involves four steps: (1) think the subject through; (2) make a list of points, ideas, and supporting material gathered from your study; (3) arrange the pertinent material into main points, subpoints, and supporting evidence; (4) discard the points and material not applicable.

IV. Acquire Proper Attitudes Toward Research

The attitude assumed in research distinguishes the scholar from the propagandist. The scholar looks at data objectively; to him, factually true information constitutes an end within itself. He attempts to find the facts and disseminate them regardless of their effect on any social, political, or economic group. He seeks truth for truth's sake; his main concern is accurate evaluation.

The propagandist, on the other hand, is primarily concerned with the way in which he intends to use the outcome of his investigation. He seeks facts that support his cause. He starts his investigation with a predetermined end and searches until he discovers facts to support his purpose. He has a subjective attitude.

There exists a need for both types of attitudes in our democratic society, but the subjective attitude early in one's study defeats scientific investigation. Regardless of the ultimate use to which you put the findings of your study, maintain an objective attitude in initial stages to insure an accurate appraisal of your subject. To help maintain this objective attitude, consider the following factors.

Cultivate an Inquiring Mind

The truly effective speaker does not count the hours spent in study. He investigates new fields because he has a compelling interest in learning. While preparing, he discovers many more ideas and facts than he can use in his speech. You cannot see in advance what material will prove most helpful. It will, therefore, be necessary for you to follow many false trails in your efforts to acquire a fundamental understanding of your subject.

Some persons question the wisdom of finding a surplus of material. The tests applied to any idea or piece of evidence in assessing its worth for your speech make their contribution to your ability to evaluate. This carried-over material helps develop you into an able person and thus adds to your general preparation as a speaker.

Keep an Open Mind Toward Your Subject

If you begin a study with your mind already made up, you will read to strengthen existing beliefs. Once a person decides that he knows all the answers about a subject, he becomes unteachable. He refuses to look any further.

Some graduate students attempted to investigate this problem through an experiment. Together they composed a lengthy essay on the controversial subject of racial equality. By design, one-third of the statements in the essay favored racial equality, one-third opposed, and one-third were neutral or explanatory in nature. Then they recruited several hundred students to be subjects in the experiment. First the students' opinions on social equality were obtained by a public opinion test. On the basis of the findings, the students were divided into four groups, two favorable and two unfavorable. One favorable and one unfavorable group were given the graduate students' essay to read and were asked to write a lengthy summary of it. The summaries of each group were handed to the second group of students of like opinion with instructions to write summaries of the original summaries. The results showed that the second group favorable to social equality retained only favorable statements in the final summary while the second unfavorable group retained only unfavorable statements in their final summary. This experiment supports the belief that we find what we want to find when we do research on questions about which we have fixed attitudes.

The fixed attitude characterizes many people. Whether or not we like a speaker or writer depends largely upon whether he complies with our existing prejudices. The fixed attitude prevents scholarly investigation. The true scientist seeks and discovers; he has a flexible, not a fixed mind. He adopts a tentative, not a fixed attitude toward knowledge. The scholar accepts findings tentatively, subject to change if further investigation indicates it.

Cultivate a Discriminating Attitude

The ability to evaluate the findings of one's research constitutes an invaluable asset for the public speaker. Some naïve people believe everything that they read; they can vouch for its authenticity because they saw it in print. Others believe nothing that they read; they have a propaganda neurosis. Alfred Korzybski[3] states "The two easiest ways to slide through life are (1) to believe everything and (2) to believe nothing." Either attitude relieves us of the necessity of thinking and evaluating. A more intelligent approach asks that we develop our own ability to discriminate.

Present-day procedures encourage dependence upon others and discourage the cultivation of the ability to discriminate. Editorial boards choose what many will read through book-of-the-month selection clubs. Magazine editors select what they consider the best articles of the month and reprint them in digest form. The publishers of book-digest clubs choose certain books and reissue them in abridged form. Others view a play but wait until they read the review of the drama critic to decide if they liked it. If you purchase certain encyclopedias, the publisher will do your research for you upon request. Ghost writers will do your research and even write your speech for a fee. All these practices discourage us from developing the faculty of discrimination. Those desiring true scholarship will attempt to develop the ability to discriminate.

In short, the desired attitude for research calls for an inquiring mind, an open mind, and a discriminating attitude. These traits will help you develop yourself into an able speaker.

V. Summary

After deciding upon your topic and purpose, start preparation in earnest. The sources of material consist of previous knowledge,

[3] Irving J. Lee, *Language Habits in Human Affairs* (New York: Harper and Row, Publishers, Inc., 1941), p. xx.

interviews and listening to speakers, published speeches, correspondence, and research.

To gain a background of information from which you may draw improve your reading habits, broaden your scope of interests, engage in varied activities, and develop your social life.

In doing your research, read (1) source books, textbooks, and trade books; (2) newspapers and magazines; (3) encyclopedias and literary references; (4) professional and trade journals; (5) governmental documents; (6) dictionaries and biographic indexes.

Take notes as you read; include the complete citation of the source, a brief summary, specific material you think applicable, and a brief evaluation. Use a consistent system for note-taking. Next, analyze your material and organize it into usable form.

The proper attitudes for research include an inquiring mind, an open mind, and a discriminating attitude. These attitudes will help you develop yourself into a competent person and speaker.

Questions and Exercises

A. Answer the following questions on Chapter 6.

1. What advantages accrue from surveying your background knowledge on a subject before doing research on it?
2. Outline a program for improving your reading habits.
3. List what you consider the three best news magazines published weekly. The three best monthly magazines.
4. In what ways besides reading can you improve your background knowledge?
5. List five persons in your community whom you could interview profitably for a speech on taxation.
6. List several volumes that publish great speeches of history. What advantages accrue from reading great speeches?
7. List the steps that you would take in securing material on the subject of The Great Society from the Library of Congress.
8. List and explain the best procedures for securing material by use of a questionnaire.
9. In what three ways are books listed in the card catalogue of your library?
10. Explain how to use the *Readers' Guide* in finding articles in current magazines.
11. How would you go about finding articles published in magazines in 1895?
12. List three leading encyclopedias published in the United States. How are these encyclopedias kept up to date?
13. List five professional publications in the field of oral communication.

14. List what you consider three leading dictionaries published in the United States. List several distinguishing characteristics of each.
15. What advantages accrue from taking notes on your speech subject early in your preparation? What method of note-taking do you prefer?
16. What is meant by analysis of your material? Explain an acceptable method of analysis.
17. List several characteristics of the proper attitude for research.
18. Distinguish between subjective and objective attitudes in research.

B. For your sixth speaking assignment prepare a five-minute speech on some national problem for which you get most of your material through research. The speech may be either informative or persuasive. The following general topics are suggestive. They will need to be narrowed to your time limit.

1. Leisure-time activities in America
2. Possibilities of educational television
3. The Federal agricultural program
4. The nuclear-testing program
5. The national debt
6. Modern advertising
7. The problem of crime in America
8. Federal aid to education
9. The motion-picture industry
10. The Broadway theater
11. The 1964 civil rights act
12. Poverty in America
13. Extremist organizations in America
14. Presidential succession

C. Complete the following projects relative to the topic you select for your speech.

1. List three books on your subject that you secured through the card catalogue in your library.
2. List three magazine articles that you secured through the *Readers' Guide*.
3. List one reference from a professional magazine.
4. List one reference from a standard encyclopedia.
5. Find one newspaper reference on your subject.
6. Interview two specialists in your community and bring to class a summary of your interviews.
7. Find one speech on a closely allied subject from a volume of contemporary speeches.
8. Find one reference on your subject in a governmental publication.
9. Prepare a brief questionnaire that would be suitable for obtaining additional information on your subject.
10. List five persons of national prominence whom you consider authorities on your subject.

CHAPTER 7

Select and Evaluate Your Supporting Material

You can find an abundance of material for your speeches by following the procedures explained in the preceding chapter. Now you must select from that material various items to support your points. The main points and subpoints of a speech constitute its skeleton; the supporting material gives the speech substance. It clarifies, amplifies, or proves the points. Without the expanding process of supporting material, a speech would consist entirely of theoretical ideas, abstract and uninteresting.

I. How Forms of Support Apply

What types of supporting material should you seek? You will no doubt use a great deal of explanation, description, and reasoning. Then you will need to support those forms with examples, quotations from authority, statistical information, analogies, and reiteration. Although you will not use the same forms of support in every speech, attempt to use a variety of support in each speech.

The same forms of support apply to informative and persuasive speeches, but the manner of application varies. In the informative speech, the forms of support expand, explain, and develop an idea, giving it clarity and meaning. The persuasive speech uses these forms of support as a basis for inference, to prove a point. Note these differences in the discussions of the various types that follow.

R. W. Jepson used the analogy to make clear what he meant by

"Potted Thinking," the title to a speech that he gave over the British Broadcasting System. After characterizing several ways that people think, he said:

> Now, we have seen enough of this attitude . . . to give it a name. And I am going to call it Potted Thinking because the opinions it gives rise to seem to me rather like some of the food we buy in potted form. They are concentrated—easy to digest. And they save a lot of trouble. And the potted thinker saves himself a lot of trouble by acquiring his knowledge as well as his opinions in a potted form.[1]

In this analogy Mr. Jepson sought to clarify the term "Potted Thinking" by comparing it with something with which his audience was more familiar than the term he used. Later in his speech Mr. Jepson illustrated a type of potted thinker by an example. His point concerned the importance of reading beneath the headlines in our newspapers.

> . . . But the headlines may give quite a misleading impression by themselves. . . . I was badly taken in myself some months ago. I saw on the posters MUSSOLINI VOWS VENGEANCE. I thought at least I should find a fire-eating declaration that would set all Europe ablaze with war. But when I came to read the Duce's speech it was a very moderately worded statement of Italian aims and policy and at the end there was a rhetorical flourish—"We shall avenge our dead." But from the posters this might have been his chief theme.[2]

In short, to clarify ideas you must expand your explanations by citing examples, making comparisons, giving statistics, or quoting authorities. Ordinarily you will use several types of support for a single idea, the number depending upon the difficulty of comprehension of the point.

In persuasion, you support your points in order to prove them. Nicholas de B. Katzenback, Attorney General of the United States, used statistics in a speech before the House Judiciary Committee on March 18, 1965, to prove his point that recent Civil Rights Acts had failed to secure voting privileges for the Negro.

> What has been the effect of these statutes? It is easy to measure. In Alabama, the number of Negroes registered to vote has increased by 5.2 per cent between 1958 and 1964—to a total of 19.4 per cent of those eligible. This compares with 69.2 per cent of the eligible whites.
>
> In Mississippi, the number of Negroes registered to vote has increased at an even slower rate. In 1954, about 4.4 per cent of the eligible Ne-

[1] *Vital Speeches*, IV: 5 (December 15, 1937), 136.
[2] *Ibid.*

> groes were registered; today, we estimate the figure at about 6.4 per cent. Meanwhile, in areas for which we have statistics, the comparable figure for whites is that 80.5 per cent of those eligible are registered.
>
> And in Louisiana, Negro registration has not increased at all, or if at all, imperceptibly. In 1956, 31.7 of the eligible Negroes were registered. As of January 1, 1965, the figure was 31.8 per cent. The white percentage, meanwhile, is 80.2 per cent.
>
> The lesson is plain. The three present statutes have had only minimal effect. They have been too slow.[3]

Later in the speech Mr. Katzenback cited an example to further substantiate his point.

> I could cite numerous examples of how delay and evasion have made it necessary for us to gauge judicial relief not in terms of months, but in terms of years. For the fact is that those who are determined to resist are able—even after apparent defeat in the courts—to devise whole new methods of discrimination. . . . I could cite example after example, but let me . . . pick just one: Selma, Alabama.
>
> The story of Negro voting rights in Dallas County, Alabama, of which Selma is the seat, could—until February 4—be told in three words: intimidation, discouragement, and delay. . . .[4]

The use of the forms of support in a persuasive speech closely parallels the use of evidence in legal proceedings. What constitutes evidence in courts of law? Broadly speaking, two general types predominate—facts and expert opinions. Facts consist of physical objects and the circumstances surrounding an act. Physical objects consist of a lethal weapon, fingerprints, handwriting, photographs of tire skid marks, or any objects involved in the case. The circumstances of an act come from witnesses. Witnesses tell what they saw, not what they believe.

Expert opinion comes from persons qualified to make judgments on the basis of facts. For example, the handwriting expert testifies about whether two pieces of writing were written by the same person; the ballistics expert states whether the bullet was fired by a particular pistol; the medical doctor testifies about whether the poison could have caused death. These are judgments of experts based upon happenings.

Factual evidence applies to persuasive speeches much as it does in law cases. It takes the form of statistics and the circumstances of examples and analogies. Expert opinion comes from persons qualified through training and experience to give reliable judgments

[3] *Vital Speeches,* XXXI: 13 (April 15, 1965), 392.

[4] *Ibid.*

based on the circumstances. If your professor states that your final examination consists of ten questions, he makes a factual statement. If he states that the examination is difficult, he expresses an opinion. Both facts and opinions serve useful purposes in supporting ideas in a speech.

The courts strive for the best possible evidence. To protect the individual, many rules govern what constitutes evidence and what becomes admissible in a case. For example, Richard cannot testify about what John told him concerning Peter's actions, except under clearly defined circumstances. This violates the well-established *hearsay* rule. The best evidence would come from having John testify. His act of telling Richard removes the evidence one step further from the original source, and therefore injects an added possibility of inaccuracy. You cannot testify about the impressions in the bullet taken from the victim's body until you become qualified as a ballistics expert. Otherwise, the possibilities of ill-conceived judgments would be increased. Just as in law, in public speaking you should strive for only the best supporting material in your speeches. Unless you do this, improper evaluation may result.

II. Types of Supporting Material

From the foregoing discussion we can isolate several forms of support applicable to speech-making:

1. Explanation
2. Statistics (compilations of facts)
3. Examples (specific instances or detailed illustrations)
4. Analogy (comparisons)
5. Testimony (expert opinion)
6. Repetition and Restatement

In a broad sense, reasoning may be considered a form of support although it consists largely of inferences from the forms listed above. Reasoning is developed in detail in Chapter 15 and will not be considered as a separate form of support here.

The various forms receive a three-fold treatment: (1) their meaning, (2) their accurate use, and (3) their effective use.

Explanation

Explanation usually precedes the giving of other forms of support. It serves as the necessary background for examples, analogies, statistics, testimony, and reasoning. It explains the nature and purpose of the points; other forms then support and expand the explanation. Explanation may utilize other forms of support, especially analogy and definition, in making points clear.

To illustrate, note how Dr. Gerald Kennedy, Bishop of the Los Angeles area Methodist Church, used explanation to introduce a point in his address at the Human Relations Conference in Chicago on August 30, 1963.

> There was a ninth-grade student in a Texas high school who handed in a book report with this very perceptive statement, "I think the author was a pretty good writer not to make the book no duller than it was." Well, I think the generation is fortunate to be no worse than it is as it flounders about without very many examples of faith and courage and greatness. People who have no propositions to which they are dedicated, walk in darkness.
>
> So we come to a last thing which needs to be mentioned. The Christian Church must rediscover the main propositions of its Gospel and proclaim them with clear voice. Let us think again what it means when we say we believe in God who is the father of all mankind.[5]

1. *Definition.* In explanation, definitions play an important role. Dictionary definitions may not always be adequate. A dictionary defines words as a collective process; in a particular speech a word may be used in a selective way. The following methods of definition may prove helpful:

1. Definition by etymology
2. Definition by authority
3. Definition by exemplification
4. Definition by explication
5. Definition by negation[6]

Etymology treats the origin and development of words. Often meaning can be reasoned out by considering the derivation of words. Since words have a history and their meanings sometimes change, definition by this means alone may prove insufficient. For example, consider the meaning of the word *extemporaneous.* If we consider the Latin derivation, *ex* meaning "out" and *tempo* meaning "of the present time," we might reason that the term means speaking

---

[5] Lester Thonssen, *Representative American Speeches, 1963-64,* XXXVI: 4 (New York: The H. W. Wilson Co., 1964), p. 75. By permission of Dr. Gerald Kennedy.

[6] Glenn R. Capp and Thelma Robuck Capp, *Principles of Argumentation and Debate* (Englewood Cliffs, N.J.: Prentice-Hall, Inc., 1965), p. 94.

without preparation or on the spur of the moment. However, the term now means speaking through a prepared outline with choice of language made as one speaks. The study of the origin and history of words, however, may frequently lead to acceptable definitions.

Citing an *authority* to define a term may be useful. For example, to explain the term *extemporaneous speaking* one might quote from the textbook *Basic Principles of Speech* by Sarett, Foster, and Sarett:

> . . . an *extemporaneous speech* is one that has been thoroughly prepared through thinking, gathering materials from outside your own experience when necessary, outlining, and oral practice; but one that is not written out and memorized or read.[7]

For an example of how definitions may be made in a speech, note how Dr. John A. Schindler, formerly a physician of Monroe, Wisconsin, defined the word "emotion" in a radio address entitled "How to Live a Hundred Years Happily" as a part of the University of Wisconsin's Farm and Home Week program.

> . . . If we understand what an emotion is, we'll understand how thinking does things to our bodies. The best definition of an emotion comes from our own William James, who took the work of the physiologist Lange about 1888 and formed a definition that's still the best we have. Nobody has improved on it. Occasionally somebody tries but doesn't succeed. William James said that an emotion is the state of mind that manifests itself by a sensible change in the body.[8]

The authority should be a recognized expert within the field quoted.

Definition by *exemplification* means the selection of an individual case to represent the whole. The example must be representative and typical. The following statement illustrates this point:

> Confederation involves a definite organization. It is taken usually to mean an organization of nations. An example of an international confederation is the League of Nations. Another example of confederation was the League of Friendship under the Articles of Confederation. The basic unit of the organization is the state or nation. All final authority is thought of as being vested in the member states.[9]

---

[7] Lew Sarett, William Trufant Foster, and Alma Johnson Sarett, *Basic Principles of Speech* (Boston: Houghton Mifflin Co., 1958), p. 25.

[8] Goodwin F. Berquist, Jr., *Speeches for Illustration and Example* (Chicago: Scott, Foresman and Co., 1965), p. 104. Reprinted by permission of Mrs. John A. Schindler.

[9] Thelma Robuck Capp and Ralph Norvell, *Post-War Organization of Nations* (Waco, Texas: Baylor University Press, 1942), p. 47.

Definition by *explication* enlarges on bare statements and attempts to clarify a term by explaining it. The following explanation of the term *federation* illustrates this method.

> Federation involves a definite organization, but it involves much more. The distinguishing characteristic of this type of international organization is that its authority is delegated to it by member states or peoples. In the realms in which authority is delegated, it is supreme.[10]

Negation defines by explaining what a term does not mean. For example, the term *federation* may be defined by showing that it does not mean *confederation,* because in this type of world organization the supreme government acts directly on the member states, not directly on the people. It does not mean *regionalism,* because this type of organization provides for joint action of the nations in a region such as the Western Hemisphere. It does not mean *alliance,* because this relationship depends upon a definite agreement or treaty; the member nations pledge their honor to carry out an agreement. Federation means, therefore, the type of world organization that acts directly on the people. It has final authority in fields where it has been delegated power. Thus, by a process of elimination, an acceptable definition emerges.

2. *Visual aids.* Visual aids may be helpful in explaining difficult and technical materials. Numerous experimental research studies have been made to determine the effect of visual aids on learning, retention, and recall. In general, they show that a person learns more readily and retains information longer by a combination of visual and oral methods than by oral methods alone.

Visual aids may consist of drawings, diagrams, maps, printed materials, models, slides, motion pictures, or any physical objects. One student brought his pistol collection to class and demonstrated the principles upon which pistols operate. Others used such aids as blackboard drawings to demonstrate how the compass operates in an airplane, a map of the Middle East to explain the crisis there, a model of an altimeter to demonstrate how it acts in flight, and a diagram of a saw mill to show the processing of logs into lumber. Besides aiding in explanation, visual aids assist in gaining attention and maintaining interest.

Unless used properly, visual aids may confuse rather than clarify. When using visual aids, observe the following precautions.

---

[10] *Ibid.,* p. 48.

1. Adapt the visual aid to the size of your audience. A small model proves worthless unless members of the audience can gather around you as you demonstrate. Make your diagrams or drawings and lettering large enough to be seen by all. A visual aid that cannot be seen in detail distracts attention.
2. Stand to the side of the visual aid as you explain it to avoid obstructing the view of your audience or decreasing your communicative directness.
3. If you illustrate by drawings during your speech, explain the drawing as you draw it. Periods of silence permit interest to wane. If you plan to use complicated drawings, put them on the blackboard in advance.
4. Use a pointer to indicate specific references to parts of the visual aid as you explain it. A general reference to a visual aid confuses an audience.
5. Do not display your visual aid until you are ready to use it; an unused chart distracts attention.
6. Remove the visual aid when you finish with it. Remove any other visual aids displayed in the lecture room. They divert attention from your speech.

Statistics

1. *Meaning.* Statistics consist of compilations of numerical facts or occurrences. Numbers become meaningful when they show the proportion of instances of a specific kind. For example, the fact that the consumer price index stood at 109.6 per cent in May, 1965, means little unless we know that 100 per cent represents the average from the 1957-59 period. It takes on added significance when shown that the price index rose .3 per cent over the previous month. Thus the significance of the figure makes it meaningful.

To illustrate, note how Robert C. Weaver, Administrator of the Federal Housing and Home Finance Agency, used statistics in his speech "The Negro as an American," delivered before a symposium sponsored by the Fund for the Republic on June 13, 1963.

> The Negro here—as he has so frequently and eloquently demonstrated—is an American. And his status, no less than his aspirations, can be measured meaningfully only in terms of American standards.
>
> Viewed from this point of view what are the facts?
>
> Median family income among nonwhites was slightly less than 55 per cent of that for whites in 1959; for individual incomes, the figure was 50 per cent.
>
> Only a third of the Negro families in 1959 earned sufficient to sustain an acceptable American standard of living. Yet this involved well over a million Negro families, of whom 6,000 earned $25,000 or more.
>
> Undergirding these over-all figures are many paradoxes. Negroes

have made striking gains in historical terms; yet their current rate of unemployment is well over double that among whites. Over two thirds of our colored workers are still concentrated in five major unskilled occupations, as contrasted to slightly over a third of the white labor force.[11]

2. *Accurate use of statistics.* Of all the forms of support, statistics are the most easily abused. The adage, "Figures don't lie, but figurers often do," presents only part of the picture. Some speakers misrepresent the facts, not by design, but because they do not know their true meaning. The following are the more common causes for misrepresentation by statistics.

a. DETERMINE THE DEFINITION OF THE UNIT. The failure to define the unit upon which the statistics rest constitutes a common error. For example, what does this statement mean—"There are twenty million illiterates in the United States"? Does it mean anything per se? Not until we define the unit *illiterate.* Suppose the term were defined for a survey as "a person over ten years of age who cannot write in any language." Suppose another survey used the definition "any person over ten years of age who cannot write in English." Many people would be listed as literate under the first definition and illiterate under the second. Since high-level words like *illiterate, criminal, religious,* and *social* have no standard meaning, researchers can define them as they desire for a particular study. When using statistics in a speech, determine what the statistics actually mean. Otherwise, you may project your meaning upon the term. Consult the footnotes and explanations to determine how the compilers defined them.

b. COMPARE ONLY FIGURES BASED ON THE SAME UNIT. Comparing figures that are not comparable creates another abuse in the use of statistics. This error results when two sets of statistics, based upon the same high-level terms but with different definitions, are combined for comparisons and inferences. For example, suppose that the Department of Public Safety of State X issues figures showing five thousand automobile accidents in 1965. The figures of the Department of Public Safety of State Y show only one thousand accidents during the same period. At once the speaker jumps to several conclusions, such as: State Y has a better system of highways than State X, better traffic laws, a more effective inspection system, or newer automobiles. Suppose, however, that State X defined the

[11] Thonssen, *op. cit.,* pp. 59-60.

term *automobile accident* as a collision or upset in which at least twenty-five dollars' worth of property damage results and State Y defined the term as fifty dollars' worth of property damage. Thus none of the inferences apply because the two sets of figures have different meanings. The figures are not comparable.

c. USE UP-TO-DATE STATISTICS. Out-of-date statistics often lead to improper evaluation. In areas of rapidly changing conditions, current statistics must be used or false representation becomes inevitable. A student in a public speaking course in 1959 proposed to analyze the question of increasing college enrollments. He quoted the United States Office of Education as saying that college enrollments totaled approximately 2,360,000 and based his observations on that figure. In the criticism period, he discovered that he had unknowingly used 1949 figures. Enrollments by 1959 had increased approximately 20 per cent, according to the same source. Thus he gave a false evaluation of the current problem.

d. DO NOT MAKE MISLEADING INTERPRETATIONS. Unusual interpretations of statistics often lead to misunderstanding. Statistics lend themselves to abuse through misleading inferences. Averages may be particularly misleading. The boy and his dog, cat, and duck average three legs, but none has that particular number. A man drowned in a lake that averages only six inches in depth.

The way a conclusion is expressed may leave an erroneous impression. A country doctor, near the twilight of his career, treated only two patients one year. One recovered and the other died. He made his report as follows: "I had a very successful year. Fifty per cent of my patients completely recovered, and only one died." Beware of giving distorted impressions by the way you present statistics.

In summary, statistics constitute an effective form of supporting material, but they may be misunderstood. To help achieve accuracy in their use, (1) determine the definition of the unit, (2) compare only figures based on the same unit, (3) use up-to-date statistics, and (4) do not make misleading interpretations.

3. *Effective use of statistics.* To be effective, statistics must be made interesting. Citing long lists of statistical data without some embellishment will cause an audience to lose interest. The following factors apply to making statistics interesting and acceptable.

a. PRESENT STATISTICS IN ROUND NUMBERS when dealing with large numbers; they take less time and are more easily understood. Instead of stating that the national debt is $309,634,839,642.51, give it as approximately 310 billion dollars. Note the uninteresting and complicated treatment of statistics used by one student.

> Reductions (in illiteracy) in the poorer states from 1920 to 1930 were as follows: Mississippi, 17.2 per cent to 13.1 per cent, or a total reduction of 4.1 per cent; Arkansas, 9.4 per cent to 6.8 per cent, or a total 2.6 per cent; Louisiana, 21.9 per cent to 13.5 per cent, total 8.4 per cent; South Carolina, 18.1 per cent to 14.9 per cent, total 3.2 per cent; North Carolina, 13.1 per cent to 10.0 per cent, total 3.1 per cent.

Members of an audience would get lost in the maze of percentage figures. The following rearrangement shows improvement.

> Reductions in illiteracy in the five poorer states averaged approximately 4½ per cent from 1920 to 1930. Louisiana had the greatest reduction, with 8½ per cent; Mississippi, with 4 per cent, came next; North and South Carolina each had approximately 3 per cent, and Arkansas trailed with 2½ per cent.

b. MAKE STATISTICS VIVID AND GRAPHIC by relating them to matters familiar to the audience. The fact that the national debt approximates 310 billion dollars means little to the average citizen; but if one says "you owe the federal government two thousand dollars as your proportionate share," the figure becomes more meaningful. The speaker might also show how many highways this sum could build, how long it would take to count the sum in five-dollar bills, or how much of our tax money it takes to pay the interest. Newspapers and magazines make statistics interesting and meaningful through charts, graphs, and pictures. The speaker must do the same in word pictures.

c. CITE THE EXACT SOURCE OF STATISTICS. Since people have been deceived so often by statistics, you can dispel their doubts by giving the source of your facts. Avoid such phrases as these: "Statistics prove," "statistics gathered with great care show," "the undeniable facts prove," "facts don't lie," and "here are the facts." Say instead, "These statistics were taken from the book *The Problems of Lasting Peace* by Herbert C. Hoover and Hugo Gibson, page 212.

d. CHECK YOUR STATISTICS AGAINST OTHER SOURCES to test their authenticity. If you doubt the validity of statistics, check them against known reliable sources such as *The Statistical Abstract of the United States, The Statesman's Yearbook,* or *The World Almanac.* These sources publish objective data and are considered by most people to be reliable.

In summary, statistics prove an excellent means of supporting points for oral communication. They consist of statements that represent the number of occurrences of a particular phenomenon. Their accuracy may be assured by defining the unit, by combining and comparing only those statistics that use the same unit, by giving up-to-date facts, and by drawing valid conclusions from the facts. Statistics can be made interesting and authoritative by presenting them in round numbers, by relating them to the interests of the audience, by citing the source of facts, and by checking them against sources known to be reliable.

The Example

1. *Meaning and types.* An example may consist of a specific instance, a past happening, or a hypothetical situation used to support the points of a speech. It may be used to amplify explanations in the informative speech or as a basis for inference in the persuasive speech. For example, one cites the League of Nations and the United Nations as examples of the confederate type of world organization to explain how this type operates. In the persuasive speech, the speaker may contend that the confederate-type world organization has the greatest chance for success because the people have experienced this type. He cites the League of Nations and the United Nations as the types most acceptable under existing world conditions.

a. SPECIFIC INSTANCES OR DETAILED ILLUSTRATIONS. Examples may take the form of specific instances or detailed illustrations. The specific instance makes brief reference to one or several cases with little amplification. For example, in his speech for a declaration of war against Japan on December 8, 1941, Franklin D. Roosevelt cited these specific instances:

> Last night Japanese forces attacked Hong Kong. Last night Japanese forces attacked Guam. Last night Japanese forces attacked the Philippine Islands. Last night the Japanese attacked Wake Island. This morning the Japanese attacked Midway Island. Japan has, therefore, undertaken a surprise offensive extending throughout the Pacific area.[12]

The detailed illustration amplifies a case and presents it in detail. Note how the noted minister Harry Emerson Fosdick, in his sermon "Handling Life's Second-Bests," illustrates his point that success in life does not always consist of attaining our goals.

---

[12] *Congressional Record,* Vol. 87, Part 9, Dec. 8, 1941.

> Or consider Sir Walter Scott. We think of him as the novel writer whose stories charmed our youth so that for many years some of us would have voted *Ivanhoe* the best tale ever told. Sir Walter, however, did not want to be a novelist; he planned to be a poet, but Byron's sun rose and dimmed his lesser light. "Byron hit the mark," he said, "where I don't even pretend to fledge my arrow." Then he turned to writing novels. . . .[13]

b. REAL OR HYPOTHETICAL. Real examples come from history or experiences. They deal with actual happenings. The following example by Harry Emerson Fosdick illustrates this method:

> Whistler, the artist, for example, started out to be a soldier and failed at West Point because he could not pass in chemistry. "If silicon had been a gas," he used to say, "I should have been a major-general." Instead, he failed in soldiering, half-heartedly tried engineering, and then tried painting—with such remarkable results as one sees in the portraits of his own mother, Miss Alexander, and Carlyle.[14]

Hypothetical examples consist of imaginary happenings. They may or may not be based on actual cases. Booker T. Washington, outstanding Negro educator, used the hypothetical example in his Atlanta Exposition address:

> A ship lost at sea for many days suddenly sighted a friendly vessel. From the mast of the unfortunate vessel was seen a signal, "Water, water; we die of thirst." The answer from the friendly vessel at once came back, "Cast down your bucket where you are." And a third and fourth signal for water was answered, "Cast down your bucket where you are!" The captain of the distressed vessel, at last heeding the injunction, cast down his bucket, and it came up full of fresh, sparkling water from the mouth of the Amazon River. To those of my race who depend on bettering their conditions in a foreign land or who underestimate the importance of cultivating friendly relations with the Southern white man, who is their next door neighbor, I would say, "Cast down your bucket where you are"—cast it down in making friends in every manly way of the people of all races by whom we are surrounded.[15]

2. *Accurate use of examples.*[16] Although examples cannot be so easily manipulated as statistics, they can be misrepresented. Consider the following factors for properly evaluating examples.

---

[13] Harry Emerson Fosdick, *The Hope of the World* (New York: Harper and Row, Publishers, Inc., 1933), pp. 71-72.

[14] *Ibid.*, p. 69.

[15] Booker T. Washington, *Up from Slavery* (New York: Doubleday and Co., Inc., 1901), p. 219. Copyright, 1901, 1929, by Booker T. Washington. Reprinted by permission of Doubleday and Co., Inc.

[16] See Chapter 15 for a discussion of how examples apply to *generalization,* a process of reasoning.

a. CHOOSE ONLY REPRESENTATIVE EXAMPLES. Most persons select examples that most clearly illustrate their points, not the ones that are the most accurate among their choices. An example should represent all cases of a class. If a speaker selects extreme examples he misrepresents what he attempts to illustrate. For instance, one might challenge the need for formal college training by citing Henry Ford, who attained prominence in industry; Robert H. Jackson, who became a Supreme Court Justice; and Harry Truman, who attained the Presidency of the United States; all three were without benefit of a formal college education. Rather than exemplifying a general rule, these men more likely are exceptions to the rule. They were self-educated and probably attained pre-eminence in spite of their lack of formal training.

As a speaker, do not attempt to show that business is bad by citing the buggy industry, the hairpin manufacturers, and other industries adversely affected by technological advances. Select representative industries like the building trades, steel, and the clothing industry. In selecting examples, be sure that those chosen represent accurately the general rule, not the exception.

b. STATE THE DETAILS OF EXAMPLES ACCURATELY. Do not omit parts of the circumstances of an example to make it fit your assertions aptly. For example, if you decide to use the United States postal system as an example of governmental efficiency, do not omit the factor of costs, the deficit incurred annually. If you use the annual income of industrial workers now as compared with that of depression days to show the improved status of workers, do not omit the devaluation of the dollar. If you compare teachers' salaries now with those fifteen years ago to show how much they have increased, do not neglect to state that their salaries have increased less than those in any other major profession. Omitting such facts would constitute intellectual dishonesty and should be condemned.

A student quoted from a Supreme Court decision as an example of recent holdings of the courts on segregation. He was surprised when the professor pointed out that his quotation came from the dissenting opinion of the court. The student deceived his audience through failure to know the facts. Members of the audience were misled, however, the same as if he had deceived them intentionally. An ethical speaker learns the facts; then he presents the details of his example fairly and accurately.

c. GIVE A SUFFICIENT NUMBER OF EXAMPLES. Just how many examples should you give to support your points? The nature of your point and the time available constitute determining factors. If your point relates to explanation and you have an especially appropriate example, one might suffice. If your point concerns a controversial matter, several may be needed. When reasoning by example, you infer that what is true about the cases you present holds universally; they establish a general rule. Therefore, you must give a representative sampling.

Suppose your point to be that 1966 constituted a good year for the production of citrus fruit. You give as examples the yield in Florida, Texas, and California. On the other hand, suppose your point to be that 1966 constituted a good year for general agricultural production and you used the yield in the same three states to support your contention. Which point would be supported best? The first, because the examples are representative. Florida, Texas, and California produce most of the citrus fruit in the United States; their climatic conditions are similar to those in other states which produce fruit. The examples chosen represented accurately all those not chosen. The same three states would be poor choices for generalizing about agricultural production as a whole. They do not represent geographical distribution or different types of crops. Examples of states in the Northwest, Middlewest, and Northeast as well as Florida, Texas, and California would be needed to give a representative sampling. Thus, the nature of the point determines in part how many examples should be given.

The time available also affects the choice of specific instances or detailed illustrations. Several specific instances can be given in the time it takes to give one illustration. Yet the illustration may in some instances be more effective, especially in explanation. Several specific cases often prove more effective in persuasion than a few illustrations. In case of doubt, it is better to err on the side of too many rather than too few examples.

3. *Effective use of examples.* Like other forms of support, examples should interest the listeners. Accuracy comes first, but deference-to-interest factors cause an audience to listen attentively. The following factors apply in making examples effective.

a. MAKE CLEAR THE POINT TO BE GAINED. Some speakers seem to drag examples in by the heels; the examples may be interesting, but they hardly apply to the point. This condition often results when speakers take examples from collections of illustrations prepared especially for speakers and writers. It may result when one selects the examples first, then adapts the idea to fit the examples. The ideas constitute the most important part of speech-making; the supporting material should expand and clarify them.

b. CHOOSE VIVID AND TIMELY EXAMPLES. Make your examples vivid and graphic, swift-moving and timely. Talk about people and active things, not about inanimate objects. Note how Henry G. Roberts, a teacher of speech, does this well in his speech, "Thinking on Your Feet."

> Can you ever forget how your eyes almost popped out of your head the first time you saw a sleight-of-hand artist take a pigeon, two long-eared rabbits, and an American flag out of a tall silk hat? Can't you feel your heart skip a beat as the "bea-u-ti-ful young lady" vanishes before your very eyes in a puff of smoke? Not one of us in the audience could understand how it was done. . . .[17]

Familiar examples of recent date prove more effective than unfamiliar and outdated happenings. Talk in terms of your listeners' interests.

c. CHOOSE EXAMPLES CLOSE TO YOUR LISTENERS. Citizen Jones of San Diego shows more interest in how the Padres came out in their game than in how the New York Yankees fared. But he shows more interest in how his son did in Little League than in the Padres. People show interest in matters close to them, things that concern their everyday lives.

Some years ago two speech students spoke to the Junior Chamber of Commerce of Waco, Texas, on labor's right to strike. One student illustrated his points with examples of the coal strikes in Pennsylvania, the automobile workers' strikes in Michigan, and the longshoremen's strike in San Francisco. The other talked about the telephone workers' strike and the bus strike in Waco, Texas. The second speaker received better response because he talked about problems close to his audience. His listeners knew about these strikes because they had been inconvenienced by them. Other things being equal, choose examples close to your audience.

d. CHOOSE ACTIVE EXAMPLES. One Air Force officer lectured on the construction of the airplane. He divided his discussion into three parts: the engine, the fuselage, and the tail assembly. He discussed each division methodically and in detail. Another officer figuratively

[17] William Hayes Yeager, *Effective Speaking for Every Occasion* (Englewood Cliffs, N.J.: Prentice-Hall, Inc., 1951), p. 217. Reprinted by permission of Henry G. Roberts.

started up the motor and explained the various divisions with the airplane in motion. He evoked interest better because his material showed action. Action arouses attention.

In summary, examples may be specific instances or detailed illustrations, real or hypothetical. In choosing accurate examples, select only representative cases, give all important details, and select a sufficient number. Assure interesting examples by making the point clear, vivid, and graphic, close to the audience, active, and moving.

The Analogy

1. *Meaning and types.* An analogy as a form of support compares two or more things for the purpose of pointing out similarities and differences. The analogy applies especially well to explanation. One student explained how a world federal government would operate by comparing it with the government of the United States. The world government would have authority in matters delegated to it much like the federal government of the United States. The nations of the world would have a position in world federal government similar to that which the several states have in our form of government. They would have supreme authority in all matters not specifically delegated to the international government. Thus, the speaker compared world federal government with a government familiar to his audience.

Abraham Lincoln used analogies effectively. His statement in his second presidential campaign that "you should not trade horses in the middle of a stream" compared the dangers of changing presidents during a war to a situation with which his audience was familiar. His analogy that "a house divided against itself cannot stand" compared a division among the members of a family with a Congress divided over the slavery question.

In the persuasive speech, the analogy compares known features of two things for the purpose of drawing inferences about unknown features. We reason that likenesses in known features indicate likenesses in unknown features. We argue that because College X resembles College Y in enrollment, purpose, curricula, location, type of students, and social activities, the honor system will prove successful at College X because it has proved successful at College Y. Since they are alike in ways affecting the success of an honor system, they will probably also be alike in the degree of success of such a system.

a. LITERAL. Analogy may be divided into two types, *literal* and *figurative*. Literal analogy relates to similarities of two objects of the same class. It infers that objects resemble in points other than those compared because they resemble in known aspects. For example, an analogy often heard prior to the rocket probe to Mars early in 1965 was that Mars was probably inhabited because it was similar to the earth in atmospheric conditions, vegetation, and other aspects necessary for human habitation. We inferred that because Mars resembled the earth in certain aspects essential to life, Mars, like the earth, contained human habitation. Although the recent rocket probe raises questions of the validity of this conclusion, the process exemplifies the literal analogy.

b. FIGURATIVE. Figurative analogy compares objects in different classes. For example, in Christ's statement "Cast your bread upon the waters and it will not return unto you void," bread represents good deeds and waters represent life. Most speakers use literal analogy more than figurative analogy, especially in persuasive speeches.

2. *Accurate use of analogy*. Although less subject to abuse than either statistics or examples, analogies may be improperly used. The following factors apply to the accurate use of analogies.

a. THE POINTS OF SIMILARITY SHOULD OUTWEIGH THE POINTS OF DIFFERENCE. A large number of similarities between two things does not insure a good analogy. The strength of the similarities is more important than the number. Irrelevant details, even though they may be numerous, have little effect. For example, in the comparison discussed above, you might point out many differences between Colleges X and Y, such as size and beauty of campus, condition of buildings, and record of football team. Such differences hardly apply; they have little to do with the success of an honor system. The points of similarity outweigh the points of difference.

b. THE POINTS OF COMPARISON MUST BE TRUE. One student compared the conditions among nations today to the conditions among the thirteen original colonies in 1789 to prove that such differences as language and social, economic, and cultural problems are no greater now between nations than they were in colonial times between the several states. He contended that a world federal government, therefore, would be successful today because the federal government of the United States has been successful. His comparison overlooked the nature of the governing bodies. People came to the

New World dedicated to the concept of individual freedom and the dignity of the individual. Many were motivated to emigrate to escape the oppression of the mother country. Basically, the peoples had similar goals, although they differed in the methods for attaining them. Today, a basic difference exists among nations in the concept of the purpose of government. The world finds itself divided between those holding to the free-world concept and those holding to the collective management of the world's goods. The basic differences are, in fact, greater between nations today than between the states in Colonial times. The points of comparison must be factually true.

c. DIFFERENCES IN THE CASES COMPARED MUST BE ACCOUNTED FOR. Differences in the cases compared will not necessarily invalidate the analogy, provided they can be shown to be non-essential. For example, in the analogy that an honor system would be successful in College X because it has been successful in College Y, suppose you could show that the colleges differ greatly in capital investments. This difference would not be relevant to the point at issue. The types of student body, curricula, and the purposes of the colleges would be more important. If you can show that points of likeness are relevant and important and that no significant differences exist, the analogy will assist in the effective development of ideas.

3. *Effective use of analogy*. To insure effectiveness, select interesting analogies. Apply the following requirements.

a. COMPARE CASES FAMILIAR TO YOUR AUDIENCE. If you compare an unfamiliar object to one equally unfamiliar, you gain little from an analogy. The effectiveness of Abraham Lincoln's speaking came largely from the homely nature of his comparisons. "You should not change horses in the middle of a swift stream" had meaning to his largely agrarian audiences. It would be less effective to an audience of city dwellers who had never ridden a horse. The comparison of world federal government to the United States federal government would be more meaningful to an audience of college graduates than to an audience of unskilled laborers. The speaker who compared the principles of the hydrogen bomb with those of the atomic bomb did little to clarify his subject because the audience understood the principles of neither. Compare the unfamiliar object to matters familiar to your audience.

b. MAKE YOUR COMPARISONS VIVID AND COLORFUL. Stephen Vincent Benét wrote vividly of Abraham Lincoln as follows:

> Lincoln, six feet one in his stocking feet,
> The lank man, knotty and tough as a hickory rail,
> Whose hands were always too big for white-kid gloves,
> Whose wit was a coonskin sack of dry, tall tales,
> Whose weathered face was homely as a plowed field.[18]

Benét's comparisons of Lincoln's physical bearing to a hickory rail and his weathered face to a plowed field give a vivid picture.

Harry Emerson Fosdick once preached a sermon on the subject, "The Peril of Worshiping Jesus." He pointed out how people often worship Jesus but fail to practice the principles He taught. They avoid following Him by worshiping Him. Then he drew a parallel to this situation in the life of Abraham Lincoln as follows:

> Take the truth in a realm quite different from religion and consider Abraham Lincoln, who . . . comes as near being worshiped as any American. That began when he died. When he lived men tried to crush him by opposition. . . . When he died, however, they began using the other method to dispose of him. They adored him. They garnished his sepulcher. Nothing too marvelous could be said of him. But in the ten years after he died Congress put into effect a policy toward the South that denied everything Lincoln had stood for and wanted. . . . They alike adored Lincoln and refused to follow him, so they made the reconstruction era in the South one of the horrors of our history.[19]

The use, as illustration, of the way the people worshiped Lincoln and refused to follow him gives us a better understanding of people's attitudes toward Jesus. The colorful manner in which Fosdick presents the analogy commands interest.

In summary, an analogy consists of a comparison between two or more things to determine their similarities and differences. In a good analogy the points of similarity outweigh the differences, the points of comparison are true, and differences in the cases compared are explained. To use the analogy effectively, compare cases familiar to the audience and make them vivid and colorful.

---

[18] From *John Brown's Body* (New York: Rinehart and Co., Inc., 1928). Copyright, 1928, by Stephen Vincent Benét; copyright renewed, 1956, by Rosemary Carr Benét.

[19] Harry Emerson Fosdick, *op. cit.,* pp. 98-99.

Testimony

1. *Meaning and types.* Testimony consists of opinion statements of authorities. Opinions reflect conjecture or beliefs; although they do not constitute facts, they usually come from a person's evaluation of the facts. The speaker brings the authority's opinion into his speech by quoting him. Thus the term, *quotation from authority.*

You may quote a person for any one of three reasons. First, you may quote him as a source for factual material. Suppose Professor Jones made a survey and you desire to use his findings. You quote him for the information, not for his opinion. Second, you may quote a person to help you explain, describe, or clarify a matter. Suppose Professor Jones has a well-written explanation of the law of supply and demand in his textbook. Instead of putting the explanation in your own words, you quote the professor's explanation. Third, you quote a person for his testimony, for the effect that his opinion has in getting your contentions accepted. You desire his evaluation for its probative effect. Quotations of the first two orders should be subject to the tests for factual material already discussed. The third type, testimony, receives treatment in this section.

In one sense, opinion statements should have little probative effect on the acceptance of ideas. On most questions the experts disagree, especially on questions of public policy. An almost equal number of distinguished authorities hold to either side of controversial issues. The claim for logical effect comes from the inference that because an expert holds a certain opinion, you should also. Since the experts disagree, the inference does not count heavily.

Opinion statements should rarely be used without corroborating evidence. They may, however, have strong persuasive effect by lending prestige and dignity to your conclusions. If you reason well, support the reasoning with strong evidence, draw your conclusion, and then quote acceptable corroborating authorities, the quotations may help clinch your point.

Robert F. Kennedy used quotations effectively in a speech at the ceremonies celebrating the 175th anniversary of the Ratification of the Constitution at Independence Hall, Philadelphia, on June 21, 1963.

> In 1878, the British statesman Gladstone said that "The American Constitution is, so far as I can see, the most wonderful work ever struck off at a given time by the brain and purpose of man." And the same sentiments have been echoed time and again around the world.

> But perhaps no one has better defined the unique nature, the unique significance of these treasured papers than Woodrow Wilson. "The Constitution of the United States," he wrote, "is not a mere lawyer's document. It is a vehicle of life, and its spirit is always the spirit of the age."
>
> President Wilson's words have proved true through the governmental, industrial and social upheavals of two World Wars and a major economic Depression—for in each of those critical times the spirit of the Constitution did indeed become the spirit of the age.[20]

These quotations added prestige to Mr. Kennedy's contentions because of the prestige of the men quoted.

2. *Accurate use of testimony.* Speakers make errors in the use of testimony that approximate those made in modern advertising. To avoid the most common faults, consider the following.

a. IS THE AUTHORITY PREJUDICED? Representatives of propaganda agencies—political parties, industrial and labor organizations, and professional associations—issue statements designed to influence the public for the cause that they represent. They work to create good will for their organizations. They conduct subjective studies to find evidence to support their preconceived points of view. If they find unfavorable evidence, they may refuse to divulge it.

The opinions of many persons are governed by political, economic, or social considerations. Who ever heard of a Democrat's praising the policies of the Republicans, a labor leader's agreeing with the opinions of the National Association of Manufacturers, the Southern White Citizens Council's favoring a policy announced by the Americans for Democratic Action, or vice versa? Some writers of syndicated columns are always pro-administration, others always anti-administration. Given the topic and the writer, one can anticipate the writer's point of view.

Some years ago, when the national college debate topic concerned fair-employment practices, one forensic director received materials from twenty-five pressure groups, all containing biased information. Although much of the information was disseminated under the guise of objectivity, it took little analysis to detect its biased nature. Although pressure groups constitute an integral part of the democratic process, public speakers should know that they disseminate biased information. Avoid testimony from prejudiced sources.

---

[20] Thomas A. Hopkins, ed., *Rights of Americans: The Speeches of Robert F. Kennedy* (Indianapolis: The Bobbs-Merrill Co., Inc., 1964), pp. 165-66.

To avoid prejudiced statements, quote organizations engaged in objective research. The research divisions of universities and endowed research organizations constitute the principal agencies of objective research. They discover and disseminate true-to-fact information. They initiate studies to find the facts and hold no preconceived opinions on what they will discover.

b. IS THE AUTHORITY QUALIFIED BY TRAINING AND EXPERIENCE? A common error in the use of testimony comes from quoting persons incompetent in the fields quoted. Some speakers quote well-known persons in activities like motion pictures or athletics because of their popularity, not because of their competence. Modern advertising uses this method frequently. The popular motion-picture actress Glamor Doll attributes her beautiful complexion to Soapy soap, and infers that you too can have a beautiful complexion by using Soapy soap. No doubt Glamor Doll has certain characteristics we can admire, but her judgment of the chemical effect of compounds on the skin is hardly one of them. A dermatologist or a medical doctor would be a better authority. Muscles John, heavyweight champion, attributes his athletic prowess to his morning bowl of Tasty Chruncheys. Again, a nutrition expert would make a more qualified authority. Perhaps such practices sell soap and cereal, but they would not if the public were more discriminating.

An authority should be in a position to know the facts and to interpret them properly. Furthermore, he should be a specialist in the field in which he gives testimony. His training and experience should qualify him as an expert.

c. IS THE AUTHORITY MENTALLY AND MORALLY QUALIFIED? The fact that a person has attained high position does not mean that he qualifies as an authority per se. He may have attained his position because of an attractive personality or because of influential family connections. He may have been elected to public office because of good showmanship or because he capitalized on the prejudices of his constituents. He may have bought his position as mayor or inherited his position as president of the bank. The author's book may have become a best-seller because it dealt with the trivial so simply and sensationally that all could understand it.

To assess the value of an authority, consider the reasons he gives for his statements. Does he reason soundly? Does he support his reasons with acceptable evidence? Does he show evidence of maturity of judgment? You should be less interested in what a person says than in why he says it. Consider a quotation in relation to the context in which you find it. Does the book or article as a whole give evidence of the author's qualifications?

Further, consider the author's general reputation for truthfulness. Does he have a selfish outlook, or does he seem to consider the common good? Does he have a subjective interest in the matter on which he testifies, or does he give an objective evaluation? A person's mental and moral attributes go far in determining his qualifications as an authority.

d. DOES THE QUOTATION ACCURATELY REPRESENT THE OPINION OF THE AUTHOR? A speaker may give a distorted view of the intent of an author by taking isolated statements out of context and presenting them as the author's opinion. The author may have made the statement in discussing the side opposite to his beliefs or by way of explanation. The school board in a large city banned a civics textbook because they claimed some statements in the book indicated that the author had communist leanings. They released some of the statements to the press. The author replied that he wished that the school board had read the chapters from which the statements were taken, if they could not find time to read the entire book. Further, he stated that a reading of the textbook as a whole would show that he had complete confidence in free enterprise, but that any worthwhile textbook must acquaint students with the varying concepts and the many sides of all questions.

Before quoting an author, be sure that the statement represents his opinion accurately. Acquaint yourself with the entire writing, not the isolated statement alone.

3. *Effective use of testimony*. Although accuracy comes first, also consider how to use testimony effectively. The following methods apply.

a. QUOTE AUTHORITIES ACCEPTABLE TO YOUR AUDIENCE. Given a choice between equally qualified authorities, quote the expert best known and liked by your audience. Quote persons whom your audience will consider well qualified and unprejudiced. For an unknown expert, give facts about him that will establish his authority.

In a radio debate between students of Baylor University and the University of Texas, the following varying types of introductions to testimony were noted.

> We point to the fact that John Eyes, Professor of Economics at Kansas University and perhaps one of the best known economists in the nation, says. . . .
>
> Today, the Governor of Texas has said. . . .

> John Marshall tells us that the power to tax is the power to destroy. . . .
>
> According to Mr. L. A. Woods, Superintendent of Public Instruction in the State of Texas. . . .[21]

The debaters apparently considered that John Marshall and the Governor of Texas were too well known to a Texas audience to require qualifying statements. L. A. Woods was introduced simply as State Superintendent of Instruction, but Professor Eyes of Kansas received several statements about his qualifications because he was not likely to be well known in Texas outside academic circles. These cases exemplify the correct procedures for introducing opinion statements.

b. CHOOSING INTERESTING AND UNUSUAL QUOTATIONS. Quotations should be interest-provoking. Unusual, cleverly worded, or aptly stated quotations add to the interest of a speech. The following quotation by Dr. J. M. Dawson, prominent Texas minister, in his sermon, "Social Attitudes That Hurt or Help" illustrates this point:

> My friend, Charles Forbus Taylor, the evangelist, tells of a corner in Brooklyn that is known as Blindie's Corner, for a well-known reason: "on it stands an old blind man selling newspapers. You cannot buy a newspaper from any newsboy on that corner. A gentleman, not seeing the old man, one day called to a boy running with a sheaf of papers under his arm, 'Here, boy, a paper!' The boy never stopped. The gentleman was rather astonished, because these boys are usually very much on the job. He waited until he saw another boy, but the second boy did exactly as the first had done. The gentleman stopped a third boy and said, 'I have tried and failed to buy a newspaper from two different boys. Now, what's the idea? Don't you want to sell your papers?' The boy answered, 'No sir. Not on this corner, because this is Blindie's corner. . . .' "[22]

In summary, quotations from acceptable authority lend dignity and prestige to conclusions. To test the accuracy of testimony, determine if the authority is prejudiced, qualified by training and experience, and qualified mentally and morally; see that the quotation represents the opinion of the author accurately. Employ testimony effectively by quoting men acceptable to the audience and by choosing interesting and unusual statements.

---

[21] Egbert Ray Nichols, ed., *Intercollegiate Debates* (New York: Noble and Noble, Publishers, Inc., 1939), XX, 231, 232, 237.

[22] Joseph Martin Dawson, *Christ and Social Change* (Boston: The Judson Press, 1937), pp. 55-56. (Quotation from *The Riveter's Gang* by permission of the Fleming H. Revell Co., Publishers.)

Repetition and Restatement

Unlike the readers of written communication, members of your audience cannot turn back the pages and reread what they missed. Either they get the ideas as you talk or the continuity of your address becomes broken. It behooves you as a speaker to prevent this from happening. Repetition and restatement constitute your principal methods for accomplishing this purpose.

Repetition may be used to clarify an idea or to emphasize it. You may repeat your idea in the same language or restate it in different terms. Repetition may come immediately following a statement or it may come after intervening supporting material. You will usually find it better to vary your method, but use repetition and restatement liberally for clarity and emphasis.

Robert M. Hutchins of the Ford Foundation uses the various methods of repetition effectively in his speech, "What Is a University?"[23] Note how he repeats a statement verbatim in his opening paragraph.

> A university is a community of scholars. It is not a kindergarten; it is not a club; not a reform school; it is not a political party; it is not an agency of propaganda. A university is a community of scholars.

In the following excerpt Dr. Hutchins restates his idea in different terms by use of an idea from Socrates.

> Freedom of inquiry, freedom of discussion, and freedom of teaching —without these a university cannot exist. Without these a university becomes a political party or an agency of propaganda. It ceases to be a university.
>
> Socrates used to say that one thing he knew positively was that we were under a duty to inquire. Inquiry involves still, as it did with Socrates, the discussion of all important problems and of all points of view.

Again Dr. Hutchins restates an idea in different terms in his own words.

> It must be remembered that the purpose of education is not to fill the minds of students with facts; it is not to reform them, or amuse them, or make them expert technicians in any field. It is to teach them to think, if that is possible, and to think always for themselves. . . .

[23] Lew Sarett and William T. Foster, *Modern Speeches on Basic Issues* (Boston: Houghton Mifflin Co., 1939), pp. 51, 52, 54, 56. Reprinted by permission of Robert M. Hutchins.

In his conclusion Dr. Hutchins restates the central idea of his speech in the form of a challenge.

> In America we have had such confidence in democracy that we have been willing to support institutions of higher learning in which the truth might be pursued, and when found might be communicated to our people. We have not been afraid of the truth, or afraid to hope that it might emerge from the clash of opinion. The American people must decide whether they will longer tolerate the search for truth. If they will, the universities will endure and give light and learning to the nation. If they will not, then as a great political scientist has put it, we can blow out the light and fight it out in the dark; for when the voice of reason is silenced, the rattle of machine guns begin.

Thus through skillful use of repetition and restatement, the thesis of a speech unfolds and remains intact.

III. Summary

The forms of support clarify, amplify, and prove the points of a speech. They serve the same purpose in speech-making that evidence does in legal proceedings. Forms of support give the speech substance.

The principal forms of support consist of (1) explanation, (2) statistics, (3) examples, (4) analogy, (5) testimony, and (6) restatement. Explanation usually precedes the giving of other forms of support. It serves as a necessary background. It includes the various ways for defining terms: etymology, authority, exemplification, explication, and negation.

Statistics are compilations of numerical facts. Figures become meaningful when they signify relationships. To use statistics accurately, (1) define the unit upon which they are based, (2) compare sets of figures only when compiled upon the same unit, (3) use only up-to-date figures, and (4) refrain from drawing unusual or strained conclusions from them. To use statistics effectively, (1) present them in round numbers, (2) make them vivid and graphic, (3) cite their exact source, and (4) check their authenticity against other sources.

Examples take the form of specific cases or detailed illustrations. To use examples accurately, (1) choose only representative cases, (2) state the details accurately, and (3) give a sufficient number. To use examples effectively, (1) make clear the point to be gained; (2) choose vivid, active, and timely instances; and (3) select cases close to the audience.

An analogy is a comparison between two or more objects for pointing out similarities and differences. In persuasion, we infer that if two things are alike in pertinent known respects they will probably also be alike in respects not known. Analogies may be classified as literal and figurative. To use the analogy accurately, make sure (1) that the points of similarities outweigh the points of differences, (2) that the points compared are true, and (3) that differences in the cases compared can be explained. Use analogies effectively (1) by comparing cases familiar to the audience and (2) by making them vivid and graphic.

Testimony consists of opinions of persons, their beliefs and conjectures. A speaker may quote persons as a source of facts, for their explanations, and for their testimony. The person quoted should be (1) unprejudiced, (2) qualified through training and experience, and (3) mentally and morally qualified. The quotation should represent the author's opinion accurately. To make quotations effective, (1) quote authorities acceptable to the audience and (2) choose statements that are interesting and unusual.

Repetition and restatement are for the purpose of clarifying or emphasizing ideas. Repetition may be in identical language or in similar terms. It may come within an idea or at the end in form of summary. Restatement draws the central idea of a speech together, giving it coherence.

Questions and Exercises

A. Answer the following questions on Chapter 7.

1. How do the forms of speech support apply in speech construction? List the principal forms of support.
2. Define statistics. Explain four ways in which statistics may be used inaccurately.
3. Explain briefly how statistics may be used effectively.
4. Distinguish between specific instances and detailed illustrations, real and hypothetical examples.
5. Explain four ways to attain accuracy in the use of examples. Explain four ways to make examples interesting and effective.
6. What is an analogy? How does the analogy differ from the example?
7. Explain how to check an analogy for accuracy. How can the analogy be used effectively?
8. How valuable is testimony to speech support? What are some of its limitations?
9. State and explain four tests of the validity of testimony.
10. What value does repetition have to oral communication?

B. For your seventh speaking assignment, prepare a five-minute talk in which you sell an idea or in which you speak for a cause.

1. Follow this general plan:
   a. Plan an interesting introduction.
   b. State the idea that you champion.
   c. Support your idea with a variety of forms: explanation, statistics, examples, analogies, testimony, and restatement. Use at least four of these types of support.
2. The following topics are suggestions only; speak for any cause that you wish.
   a. Intercollegiate athletics should be de-emphasized.
   b. Taxes should be reduced.
   c. Fraternities and sororities should be abolished in American colleges.
   d. Public schools should provide religious instruction in the United States.
   e. The union shop should be outlawed.
   f. The Communist Party should be outlawed in the United States.
   g. Capital punishment should be abolished.
   h. The social security tax should be decreased.
   i. The United States policy in Vietnam should be changed.
   j. Civil rights is a federal responsibility.
   k. Poverty is a federal responsibility.

C. Problem in the use of supporting material.

1. Read the following excerpt from a student speech on "The Munitions Industry Should Be Nationalized." (The names of companies have been changed.)

   Munitions manufacturers cause the breaking of peace treaties to increase their armament sales. Article 170 of the Versailles Treaty prohibits the importation and exportation of arms, munitions, and war materials of every kind; yet this provision has been violated often by the private manufacturer of munitions. The Nye Investigating Committee's report shows that the Doe Company increased its sales of airplanes and engines enormously during 1933 and 1934 in violation of the treaty. The company's sales to Germany increased from $2,000 in 1931 to $6,000 in 1932, $272,000 in 1933, and $1,445,000 in the first eight months of 1934, according to the Foreign Policy Reports for December 5, 1934.

   Files of American corporations examined by the Nye Investigating Committee revealed that the peace treaties have been disregarded not only by the German arms industry but by private armament firms in France, Great Britain, and the United States. According to H. C. Engelbreath and F. C. Hannighen in their book *Merchants of Death,* "The treaty of Trianon has been broken by shipping of arms to Hungary in at least four instances: two in 1932 and two in 1933."

Not only do these companies violate peace treaties, but they play one nation against another to increase armament races. When Germany buys an order of arms and munitions, it automatically creates a market in France, Czechoslovakia, Italy, Belgium, and England because nations feel their security threatened. Sir Basil Zaharoff sold munitions to Greece prior to the war between Greece and Turkey in 1920 and by so doing he was enabled to sell armaments to Turkey also, which in turn resulted in increased sales to Greece. Thus an armaments race was fomented.

2. Answer the following questions on the above example.
   a. Did the student use a variety of forms of support? List the types used.
   b. Do you think the student should have qualified the Nye Committee by telling something of its status? Why?
   c. Were the statistics on increases in sales to Germany properly identified? Were they interestingly presented? Do you think the source would likely be questioned?
   d. Do you think the quotation from *Merchants of Death* helped support the point? Is it a factual or an opinion statement?
   e. Do you think the example of Sir Basil Zaharoff's activities in fomenting a war scare between Greece and Turkey helped develop the point? Would it have helped to document the example?
   f. Criticize the speaker's use of explanation and restatement. Was the transition between points adequate?
   g. Was sufficient evidence presented to convince you that munitions makers cause peace treaties to be broken? Explain your answer.
   h. Were the statistics up to date?
   i. What other suggestions can you make for improving the argument?

CHAPTER 8

Organize Your Speech

You have discovered many examples, analogies, statistics, and quotations to support your ideas by the methods learned in the two preceding chapters. Ideas on the central theme and treatment of your subject start to evolve from the time you decide on your subject. These ideas grow and become better solidified as you investigate the problem. By the time you complete the steps outlined in the preceding chapters, your thinking has become crystallized and you have decided on the central purpose, main and subordinate ideas, and forms of support for each point. Now you find yourself ready to arrange all these ideas, facts, and opinions into a workable organizational pattern. In short, you must now arrange and outline your speech.

I. Principles of Composition

You now raise the question—what principles should guide me as I set out to organize my speech? Consider these criteria:

1. A well-organized speech provides for the creating of a favorable mood, one conducive to the spirit and tone of the speech. It creates the proper atmosphere.
2. A well-organized speech provides for arousing immediate interest in the subject. The introduction of the subject compels the audience to listen.
3. A well-organized speech gives a clear explanation and partition of the speech, a division into its component parts. It provides for an early explanation of the intent of the speech and the necessary background for understanding the thesis.

4. A well-organized speech states the central idea in a simple, concise, orderly, and logical manner. It isolates the main purpose of the speech and limits the ideas and supporting material to the accomplishment of that purpose.
5. A well-organized speech keeps the specific purpose in focus. It divides the subject into a logical and convenient number of main points to develop or prove the thesis. It subdivides each main point into a sufficient number of subordinate points to explain or prove the main point.
6. A well-organized speech provides for a full, logical development of each idea. It uses a variety of supporting material, explanation, and restatement.
7. A well-organized speech draws the parts of the speech together by use of a summary and indicates the desired response.

With these principles before you, next turn your attention to how these standards can be achieved. You can include all of them in the traditional organizational pattern: (1) introduction, (2) body or discussion, and (3) conclusion.

II. The Introduction

The introduction paves the way for the body of the speech. A good introduction performs three functions: (1) creates a favorable atmosphere for the speech, (2) stimulates interest in the subject, and (3) clarifies and partitions the topic.

Create a Favorable Atmosphere

In most speaking situations, do not plunge immediately into the subject matter of your speech. Your audience will not be ready to listen. Consider the normal conditions of the members of your audience; they have divided interests. Perhaps the lady with the new hat wonders what kind of an impression she makes; another tries to remember if she turned the fire off under the roast; a man thinks of the par seventy-two he almost made in the golf game; an insurance salesman thinks over his list of prospects. You have about as many different thoughts among your audience as you have members. Undoubtedly, few have already focused their attention on you.

Your first task is to put your audience into the proper attitude to listen. You must create a receptive atmosphere that will make your audience want to listen. This cannot be done abruptly; gradually polarize their attention on yourself. On some occasions the proper atmosphere may have already been created by a previous speaker.

Perhaps the ritual for the occasion creates the proper atmosphere before you begin. Unless the occasion sets the desired keynote, you must do so before you develop your subject.

The proper keynote may be set in part by your manner of delivery, but what you talk about in your opening remarks also helps. Consider the following suggestions.

1. *Refer to momentary interests.* When speaking occasions arise as the result of crises, at the conclusion of a common endeavor, or where something of unusual interest has occurred, establish a bond between yourself and your audience by referring to that happening. You may capitalize on something that occurred in the meeting place prior to your speech.

On December 8, 1941, Franklin D. Roosevelt spoke to an emotionally charged audience when he addressed a joint session of Congress and the nation at large for a declaration of war against Japan. The subject matter of his speech was of such momentous interest that he needed only to refer to it:

> Yesterday, December 7, 1941—a date which will live in infamy—the United States of America was suddenly and deliberately attacked by naval and air forces of the Empire of Japan.[1]

The late Ambassador Adlai E. Stevenson, United States Representative to the United Nations, referred immediately to the event which was uppermost in the minds of all people following the assassination of President John F. Kennedy when he addressed the General Assembly Plenary Meeting on November 26, 1963.

> My privilege in this sad hour is to convey to you, Mr. President, to you, Mr. Secretary General, and to you, the assembled delegates of the world, the profound gratitude of the people of my country for what has been done and for what has been said here today. Our grief is the more bearable because it is so widely and so genuinely shared; and for this we can only say, simply but from the depths of our full hearts: thank you.
>
> President Kennedy was so contemporary a man—so involved in our world—so immersed in our times—so responsive to its challenges—so intense a participant in the great events and great decisions of our day, that he seemed the very symbol of the vitality and the exuberance that is the essence of life itself.[2]

2. *Respond to the mood of the audience.* Do not attempt to

---

[1] *Congressional Record,* Vol. 87, Part 9, Dec. 8, 1941.

[2] Lester Thonssen, *Representative American Speeches: 1963-64,* XXXVI: 4 (New York: The H. W. Wilson Co., 1964), 31.

change abruptly the mood in which you find your audience. If, for example, you have a humorous speech but find your audience in a somber mood, respond first to this mood and work gradually to change it. When Mrs. E. M. Gilmer (Dorothy Dix) addressed a convention of the National Education Association she began as follows:

> Not very long ago I received a letter telling me about all the harm I was doing. It read: "Dear Miss Dix: I wonder if you know how much harm you are doing in the world. I was in love with a man who did not notice me at all, and I wrote you to ask you how to attract him, and you told me how to do it, and I did, and married him, and now I wish I had not." [3]

3. *Refer to special interests of the audience.* If members of the audience have engaged in a common effort—attended a convention or workshop, or met regularly for a given purpose—begin by referring to the special interest. Martin Luther King, Jr., used this method when he addressed some 210,000 Freedom Marchers on August 28, 1963, during their March on Washington. His speech entitled "I Have a Dream . . ." was delivered on the steps of the Lincoln Memorial in Washington, D.C.

> Five score years ago, a great American, in whose symbolic shadow we stand, signed the Emancipation Proclamation. This momentous decree came as a great beacon light of hope to millions of Negro slaves who had been seared in the flames of withering injustice. It came as a joyous daybreak to end the long night of captivity.
>
> But one hundred years later, we must face the tragic fact that the Negro is still not free. One hundred years later, the life of the Negro is still sadly crippled by the manacles of segregation and the chains of discrimination. One hundred years later, the Negro lives on a lonely island of poverty in the midst of a vast ocean of material prosperity. One hundred years later, the Negro is still languished in the corners of American society and finds himself an exile in his own land. So we have come here today to dramatize an appalling condition.[4]

4. *Compliment the audience on some work well done.* If members of an audience have completed some project, succeeded in a campaign, or made a contribution to a worthwhile cause, open your speech by commending the audience for their contributions.

Booker T. Washington commended the persons responsible for

---

[3] *Proceedings of the National Education Association, 1937.* Reprinted by permission of the National Education Association.

[4] Thonssen, *op. cit.,* p. 44. By permission of Dr. Martin Luther King, Jr.

organizing the Atlanta Exposition and for the opportunities it offered his race in his speech in Atlanta, Georgia, in 1895.

> I but convey to you, Mr. President and directors, the sentiment of the masses of my race when I say that in no way have the value and manhood of the American Negro been more fittingly and generously recognized than by the managers of this magnificent Exposition at every stage of its progress. . . .[5]

Stimulate Interest in Your Subject

After polarizing the attention of your audience on yourself and creating a receptive atmosphere, make the first reference to your topic interesting and provocative. The following suggestions will help stimulate interest in your subject.

1. *Ask a stimulating question.* Ask a provocative question that will cause members of the audience to answer in their own minds, to think with you on your subject. The question should vitally concern the audience and be relevant to the central idea of your speech.

Harry Emerson Fosdick began a sermon with a question as follows:

> We face an old question this morning. How can we believe in a good God in a world like this? Job confronted it ages ago, and Sophocles wondered how the gods could look complacently down on so much suffering and pain.[6]

You may ask a provocative question in opening, hold it up to review during the speech, and reveal your answer as the climax to the speech. Such a device helps give unity and coherence to a speech.

2. *Ask a series of questions.* The desire of your listeners to discover the answers will help you get their immediate attention and maintain their interest. If the questions correspond to the main points of your speech, they will serve as a unifying force to your organizational pattern. Do not ask irrelevant questions simply as an attention-getting device; ask questions that apply specifically to your subject. Note how General Matthew B. Ridgway used this method on assuming command of the Eighth Army.

---

[5] From *Up From Slavery,* by Booker T. Washington. Copyright, 1901, 1929, by Booker T. Washington. Reprinted by permission of Doubleday and Company, Inc.

[6] Harry Emerson Fosdick, *Riverside Sermons* (New York: Harper and Row, Publishers, Inc., 1958), p. 247.

In my brief period of command duty here, I have heard from several sources, chiefly from members of combat units, the questions: "Why are we here?"—"What are we fighting for?"

What follows represents my answers to those questions.[7]

3. *Begin with an unusual statement.* Begin with one or several unusual or striking statements. The unusualness or beauty of expression compels interest. The following opening paragraph of a speech by Paul Geren, member of the United States Department of State, illustrates this point:

Thomas Carlyle, who had a way of going to the bottom of things, laid down a principle and demonstrated it in his work, *The French Revolution.* This was that principle: "All wrong is based upon falseness, upon hypocrisy." I have applied that principle to what must surely be the greatest wrong in all the world—war, and that greatest of wrongs is based upon the greatest of deceptions. War is a lie.[8]

4. *Begin with an illustration or narrative.* Stories from life and literature stimulate interest; they have universal appeal. The illustration must relate specifically to the central theme of the speech and command attention. Note the fast-moving action in the narrative of the opening paragraph of a speech by Frank Rosson, an attorney in San Antonio, Texas.

Early in the morning on a day in September, 1776, Nathan Hale was hanged in New York for spying on the British Army. General Washington was in need of information concerning the British Army stationed there, made known his need, and Captain Nathan Hale volunteered. He was entreated by his friends to forbear his dangerous mission; he refused their entreaties, disguised himself, and entered New York as a spy. He was discovered and sentenced by General Howe to be hanged. The next morning the body of Nathan Hale swung from a British gallows, a sacrifice for the founding of a nation.[9]

5. *Begin your speech with humor.* Humor, in good taste and relevant to the subject, often sends a speech off to a good start. Avoid long drawn-out anecdotes or humorous stories. The humor should be original, fresh, and entertaining.

Note how President Lyndon B. Johnson used humor in the introduction of his commencement address at Baylor University on May 28, 1965.

---

[7] Reprinted by permission of General Matthew B. Ridgway.

[8] Reprinted by permission of Paul Geren—a student speech.

[9] Reprinted by permission of Frank Rosson—a student speech.

> Mr. President, members of the Board of Trustees, faculty, student body, my fellow Americans:
> This is a moment I deeply wish my parents could have lived to share. In the first place, my father would have enjoyed what you have so generously said of me—and my mother would have believed it.[10]

6. *Start with a provocative quotation.* An interesting or unusual statement sparks interest. To be effective, it must state aptly the central theme of the speech. A statement may be quoted as a basis for examination and serve as a unifying force for the speech. A statement that makes a hypothesis or prophecy serves best. Note how Mr. George Ball, Undersecretary of State, used this method in a speech before the New York State Bar Association in New York City on January 31, 1964.

> Not long ago a distinguished statesman of a friendly country complained to me that Americans have "a sense of mission but no sense of history." I was willing to accept this as a neat aphorism, but not as a statement of elemental truth. I do not deny that we Americans have a sense of mission—any self-respecting people must—but I emphatically reject the suggestion that we lack a sense of history.[11]

7. *Present a hypothetical situation.* Creating a hypothetical situation in which the audience takes part in an imaginary way helps create and maintain interest. The hypothetical situation adds interest if it asks the audience to make a decision at the conclusion of the speech. Note how Lester Kamin, President of Public Radio Corporation, used this technique effectively in his speech entitled "In Defense of the Jew."

> I should like for you to picture a courtroom. You shall serve as the jury. Our chairman shall serve as the judge. Today's trial is a most interesting one, for we are trying the arch-enemy of all ages—the Jew. The prosecutor has just finished his case against the accused. I shall present the defense for the Jew. You shall render your verdict when I have finished.[12]

8. *Relate subject to special interests of audience.* By relating your topic to some special interest of your audience you show an awareness of your listeners' identities and thus command their respect. They feel that what you say would not be applicable to any other audience. Note how C. J. Humphrey, an attorney in Amarillo,

---

[10] *Waco Tribune-Herald,* May 29, 1965, p. 6-A.
[11] Thonssen, *op. cit.,* p. 78.
[12] Reprinted by permission of Lester Kamin—a student speech.

Texas, began his speech to a meeting of law-enforcement officers.

> On the cold bleak ground of the shell-torn fields of France, an American soldier lies in agony. He gasps for breath, rolls over, and is then still. He has helped to pay the price of American democracy.
>
> Twenty years later on a dim-lighted street in America, a human body lies, his face downward. From his back may be seen the pearl handle of a sharp sliver of steel which has pierced his heart. He has helped to pay the price of American crime.[13]

9. *Relate a personal experience.* A speech that arises from a personal experience commands attention. The experience should be unusual and pertinent to the subject. Some of your best speeches may grow out of experiences and incidents that created your interest in a subject. One student used an incident of a tragic automobile accident as the springboard for his speech on traffic safety. For an unusual speech on the subject of kleptomania a young lady used an incident in which her roommate was caught stealing. These students held the interest of the class because they were eager to share their ideas.

The opening paragraph of a speech entitled "Legal Death" deals with a personal experience that led to a speech on mental health.

> A week ago I observed a murder trial, the State vs. John H. Doe. I saw the experienced counsels examine and cross-examine their witnesses—skillfully bringing out points and information, and just as skillfully trying to conceal other points and information. I heard them sum up for the jury, heard them analyze minutely different items of evidence. . . . I recall the debate on whether John H. Doe was sane; whether he had sufficient presence of mind to know right from wrong.
>
> . . . John H. Doe committed a crime against life, but you have not heard of other awful hours and dark nights when life has been a crime to John Doe.[14]

10. *Refer to the problem.* The problem that occasions the meeting may be of such vital concern that an immediate reference to this problem gains prompt attention. Note how Donald M. Fraser, member of the United States House of Representatives from Minnesota, used this method in addressing the National Conference on South African Crisis and American Action at Washington, D.C., on March 22, 1965.

> Mr. Chairman . . . , no responsible citizen of this country can ignore

[13] Reprinted by permission of C. J. Humphrey—a student speech.

[14] Reprinted by permission of Thomas Webb—a student speech.

what is happening in South Africa. Actions taken by the Government of South Africa challenge our conscience and call into question our leadership among Western Nations. Every thoughtful person is on his own in attempting to plot our policies toward South Africa.[15]

11. *Explain a theory or principle.* Begin by explaining a theory or principle related to your subject. An unusual and dramatically presented theory compels attention and sustains interest. The theory or principle may be examined during the speech and thus serve as a unifying force. Note the use of this method in a speech by Senator Henry M. Jackson of the State of Washington entitled "The Will To Be Free," presented to the alumni of the Duquesne University School of Law in Pittsburgh, Pennsylvania on May 20, 1965.

> I greatly appreciate this opportunity to be with you for this special occasion. I do not know of a more appropriate group before which to discuss matters which affect the safety of the nation and the preservation of individual liberty.
>
> History is a most unsentimental judge of men and nations. One society after another has been tested, found wanting, and has sunk into the oblivion of a chapter or a footnote in the textbooks. History's judgment is coldly pragmatic: Does a society have what it takes to survive the challenges thrown in its path?
>
> As one reads history, or experiences it, one comes to understand that challenge and response are constants. Or, to put it another way, security is not a fixed condition, but a process.[16]

12. *Refer to the occasion.* Most ceremonial speeches can best be described as occasion speeches. They include such occasions as dedications of buildings and monuments, laying the cornerstones of buildings, paying homage to some outstanding person or organization, or paying tribute to the graduates at commencement exercises. You can best get attention by referring immediately to the occasion that brings the listeners together. Note how Abraham Lincoln refers to the occasion in his classical Gettysburg Address:

> Four score and seven years ago our fathers brought forth on this continent a new nation, conceived in liberty, and dedicated to the proposition that all men are created equal.
>
> Now we are engaged in a great civil war, testing whether that nation, or any nation so conceived and so dedicated, can long endure. We are met on a great battle field of that war.[17]

---

[15] *Vital Speeches,* XXXI: 13 (April 15, 1965), 398.

[16] *Congressional Record,* Vol. 3, No. 97, May 28, 1965, p. 11579.

[17] Nicolay and Hay, *op. cit.,* p. 209.

Clarify and Partition Your Topic

After creating the proper mood and stimulating interest, clarify your topic and disclose your intentions. You partition a speech by dividing it into its component parts, narrowing the subject to a central theme, revealing the main points, and defining technical terms.

Define and explain terms that might confuse the audience. Explain the meaning that you attach to terms that are subject to more than one interpretation. If you do not define your terms, members of the audience will project their own meaning on them. Use the methods of definition explained in Chapter 7.

Indicate how you intend to develop your subject, your central idea, and your attitude toward it. State your main points; give a foreshadowing of your plans. Your audience will thus know what to expect, and it can follow the central idea of your speech. Dwight D. Eisenhower partitioned and clarified his subject, "Crusade for Peace," in his first presidential campaign when he spoke at Detroit.

> In this anxious autumn for America, one fact looms above all others in our people's mind. One tragedy challenges all men dedicated to the work of peace. One word shouts denial to those who foolishly pretend that ours is not a nation at war.
>
> This fact, this tragedy, this word is: Korea. . . .
>
> Tonight I am going to talk about our foreign policy and of its supreme symbol—the Korean War. I am not going to give you elaborate generalizations—but hard, tough facts. I am going to state the unvarnished truth.
>
> What, then, are the plain facts? [18]

Judge Learned Hand addressed the Convocation of the Board of Regents of New York on the topic, "The Preparation of Citizens for Their Political Duties." He partitioned his speech as follows:

> The theme today is education, as to which you, the Regents of the University, have an overarching superintendence. What I have to say will be directed towards one aspect of your responsibility: the preparation of citizens for their political duties. I shall argue that the "humanities," instead of being regarded only as a solace, a refuge, and an enrichment of the individual—as indeed they are—are also an essential factor in training him to perform his duties in a democratic society. . . .[19]

---

[18] A. Craig Baird, ed., *Representative American Speeches, 1952-53,* XXV: 4 (New York: The H. W. Wilson Co., 1953), p. 93.

[19] *Vital Speeches,* XIX: 6 (Jan. 1, 1953), 173-74.

These speakers clarified their subjects and indicated their approach; they foreshadowed what the audience should expect.

In summary, a good introduction creates the proper atmosphere for the speech and focuses attention on the speaker, stimulates interest in the subject, and clarifies and partitions the speech. The emphasis on these factors depends upon whether the speaking occasion makes them necessary. Beware of wasting time in the introduction, but perform all three functions unless the nature of the occasion does one or more for you.

III. The Body or Discussion

The introduction prepares the way for the body of the speech; the body develops the ideas in detail. In developing a subject, do more than talk about it; explain a part of it, convince your audience on an issue involved, or entertain your audience with a novel idea. Develop the body through three steps: (1) disclose a central idea; (2) divide the central idea into main and subordinate points and arrange them into an organizational pattern; and (3) support ideas with explanation, reasoning, and evidence.

Develop the Central Idea

In Chapter 5 you learned about the importance and function of the general and specific purposes of a speech. To attain these purposes, you must have a basic idea underlying your reasons and evidence. The central idea consists of the principle upon which a speech rests, the justification for the speech, or the general philosophy underlying it. It differs from the main divisions in that you establish the central idea by developing the main divisions.

Suppose you decide to speak in favor of federal aid to education. Your general purpose calls for a persuasive speech; your specific purpose requires you to persuade your audience to accept the principles of federal aid. But what about the central idea? It may be expressed in a single statement, "to show that education in the United States is essentially a federal responsibility, a national problem." Why? Because the results of education transcend state lines and affect the nation as a whole. The benefits of education, or the penalties arising from lack of it, cannot be localized within the community or state where a person receives his education, because of migration between communities and states. Since the benefits of an educated populace accrue to the nation as a whole, the federal government should share in financing programs that equalize educational opportunity.

So far, the plans for your speech, after analyzing your audience and the occasion, take the following form:

Topic:	Federal Aid to Education
General Purpose:	To persuade my audience
Specific Purpose:	To cause my audience to favor federal aid to education for equalizing educational opportunity
Central Idea:	Unequal educational opportunity is a national problem that calls for a federal remedy.

Instead of a persuasive speech, suppose you decide on an informative talk on "The Characteristics of a Good State-Tax Program." Your general purpose will be to inform and your specific purpose to bring about an understanding of the characteristics of a good state-tax program. What central idea will form the principal philosophy? Two factors must be considered in making your decision. First, a good tax program will bear with representative equality on the four basic types of taxation—property, business, income, and consumption. Second, it will apply equally the two basic theories of taxation—the ability-to-pay theory and the benefits-received theory. No specific tax can be judged by itself; it must be considered in relation to the total tax program. The central idea of your speech, therefore, states that a good state-tax program must be equitable and that it must recognize with relative equality the theories of taxation. Thus your plans include the following steps:

Topic:	The Characteristics of a Good State-Tax Program
General Purpose:	To inform my audience
Specific Purpose:	To show what constitutes a good state-tax program
Central Idea:	A good tax program bears with relative equality on the types of taxes and recognizes the basic theories of taxation.

Develop Main Divisions, Subdivisions, and Organizational Pattern

1. *Decide on your main points.* After selecting the central idea, decide upon means to develop it. Expand the central idea by breaking it up into its component parts or the main divisions. Consider the persuasive speech on "Federal Aid to Education," discussed in the previous section. The central idea was stated, "Education is a

national problem that calls for a federal remedy." Why? What main points will prove that a program of federal aid to education should be accepted? A proposed reform should arise from a need. Unless a problem exists for financing education, why make a proposal? All reform measures have their inception in a felt need that arises from a problem.

"How to correct the problem" is the subject that arises next. A suggested reform must be practical; it must correct or improve the adverse conditions. Show how federal aid to education can improve the problems arising from state and local financing programs. Present a satisfactory plan for doing so. Show that the plan will bring about benefits as well as correct the problem.

Through this mental process you arrive at the following main divisions.

Main point 1: Unequal educational opportunity constitutes a problem.
Main point 2: Federal aid to education will equalize educational opportunity.
Main point 3: Federal aid to education is a desirable plan for equalizing educational opportunity.

Consider the main divisions for your informative speech on "The Characteristics of a Good State-Tax Program." How can you divide your speech into main points that will develop your central idea? Consider the basic types of taxes and the two basic theories of taxation already discussed. The main divisions or points for this informative speech may be:

Main point 1: An equitable tax program bears proportionately on the principal types of taxes.
Main point 2: An equitable tax program equates the basic theories of taxation.

Consider the following factors in selecting your main points:

a. THE MAIN POINTS MUST DIRECTLY SUPPORT THE CENTRAL IDEA. Unless a main point relates directly to the central idea, it should not be used as a main division. For example, in the proposed speech on federal aid to education, suppose your point to be "Cost per student varies greatly throughout the United States." Does this point relate directly to the central idea, "Education is a national problem that calls for a federal remedy"? No, but it does support directly the first main point, "Unequal educational opportunity constitutes a problem in the United States." Make it, therefore, a subpoint of the first main point. As such, it relates to the central idea indirectly.

b. THE COMBINED MAIN POINTS MUST DEVELOP THE CENTRAL IDEA. In the persuasive speech, the probative force of all the main points, properly developed, must prove the central idea. For example, to prove a case for federal aid to education you must show that a problem exists, that you can solve the problem, and that you can do so satisfactorily. The failure to advance and prove any of the main points leaves the central idea undeveloped.

c. THE MAIN POINTS SHOULD BE FEW IN NUMBER. The statesman who spoke on "Ten Commandments for Successful Voting" had a good organizational pattern but he advanced too many main points. An audience cannot remember so many main ideas in one speech. The number of main divisions depends upon your subject and purpose, but by limiting the scope of your subject you can limit the number of main points. From two to five main ideas serve best; an audience's ability to retain ideas drops sharply after five.

2. *Decide on your subpoints.* The combined subordinate points under a main point must develop or prove the main point. For example, to prove that unequal educational opportunities exist, show that they apply in several categories—expenditures per student, length of school terms, teachers' salaries, teachers' qualifications, and value of school property. Note the following arrangement of subpoints:

Main point: I. Unequal educational opportunities constitute a problem.
Subpoint: A. Inequalities exist.
Subpoint: B. Inequalities are detrimental.
Subpoint: C. State financing perpetuates these inequalities.

Assuming that you can support each subpoint with sufficient evidence, you have adequate development for your main point. Each main point in your speech must be developed in this manner. Each subpoint should relate directly to the main point which it supports; the combined subpoints should develop the main points.

3. *Decide on your organizational pattern.* The organizational pattern means the method of arranging points and subpoints. A study and analysis of the subject will suggest the best method for arranging ideas. No one method, in itself, can be claimed to be superior

to another. The choice may be partly arbitrary, but certain methods serve particular purposes better than others, as explained in the following discussion:

a. DEDUCTIVE AND INDUCTIVE METHODS. The *deductive* method states the point first and then supports it by explanation, reasoning, and evidence. Usually one states the points in the partition of the introduction, then develops them one by one in the body of the speech.

Francis H. Horn, President of the University of Rhode Island, used this method in his speech entitled "The Prospect for Civilization" in an address at a convocation at Ricker College, Houlton, Maine, on February 15, 1963.

> Several weeks ago I received a letter from the Ford Foundation's Fund for the Republic which said: "The world has just witnessed historic events that could have ended our civilization had not reason prevailed. [It referred to the Cuban crisis.] Mankind was saved. But can we count on such good fortune at the next confrontation of naked power and overstrained nerves? This is the overwhelming concern of every thinking person in our society today."
>
> I wish to direct your attention to this problem of the prospect for civilization. . . .
>
> In considering the future for mankind, I shall endeavor to make a case that though the world is teetering on the edge of an abyss, it will not only not tumble into it, but indeed move forward to the greatest future man has ever known. . . .
>
> Three major problems stand in the way of a better world for all peoples. The first is that of diminishing resources in the light of the so-called population explosion. . . .
>
> The second major cloud obscuring the hope for civilization is ethnic, racial, and religious prejudice. . . .
>
> The third and at present the most crucial problem clouding the future for mankind is war and the threat of war. . . .[20]

The *inductive* method starts with the speech details and from the examination of them draws a conclusion. The revelation of the point comes at the end, as a climax.

Attorney Raymond B. Fosdick's speech, "Middletown—and the Way Out," provides an example of inductive arrangement. The first part of the speech describes Middletown: ". . . a town in which money is pre-eminently the measure of value . . . a town where everyone conforms . . . a common pattern runs through the lives

[20] Lester Thonssen, *Representative American Speeches: 1962-63,* XXXV: 4 (New York: The H. W. Wilson Co., 1963), pp. 82-83.

of all the people . . . everybody is busy. . . . Idleness is a vice . . . it lives a standardized life." After this description, and near the end of the speech, he raises the question, "What is the way out?" He answers this question as the climax of the speech.

> I should like to suggest that the only life worth living at any time in any age is the adventurous life. Now, by the adventurous life I mean primarily a life that has a capacity to be different. I mean a life that is willing to cut loose from the past for the sake of the future, that will take chances in casting off from old traditions and old techniques. I mean by the adventurous life a life unwilling to remain tied up in any port, preferring to ride the high seas in search of fairer lands—a life that finds serenity in growth.[21]

b. THE PROBLEM-SOLUTION METHOD. This method develops a problem and advocates a solution. The method applies well to analyses of sociological and political problems.

Dwight D. Eisenhower used this organizational pattern in his speech on November 7, 1957, concerning the launching of Russia's "sputniks."

> First, let me tell you plainly what I am going to do in this talk and in my next.
>
> I am going to lay the facts before you—the rough with the smooth. . . . After putting these facts and requirements before you, I shall propose a program of action—a program that will demand the energetic support of not just the government but every American, if we are to make it successful.[22]

c. THE TIME-ORDER METHOD. Some speeches lend themselves to development by chronological order. The main points come in the order in which they occurred. For example, suppose you address the local bar association on the anniversary of Clarence Darrow's birth. You desire to inform your audience about his life and works. The main divisions of your speech may appear chronologically as follows:

1. Darrow's early life
2. Darrow's life as a corporation lawyer
3. Darrow's life as a criminal lawyer
4. Darrow's declining years

---

[21] Lew Sarett and William Trufant Foster, *Modern Speeches on Basic Issues* (Boston: Houghton Mifflin Co., 1939), p. 24. Reprinted by permission of Raymond B. Fosdick.

[22] A. Craig Baird, ed., *Representative American Speeches, 1957-58,* XXX: 4 (New York: The H. W. Wilson Co., 1958), p. 21.

d. ENUMERATION-ORDER METHOD. In some speeches the main points may be arranged as simple enumeration. Your subject lends itself to division, but with little indication of the order of presentation. In such cases, place the most interesting point first and the most important last. This permits you to get interest immediately and to build toward the most important factor.

For the speech on Clarence Darrow, suppose that, instead of a biographical sketch, you decide on a selective arrangement on the beliefs of Darrow. The following arrangement illustrates:

1. Darrow's beliefs on capital punishment
2. Darrow's beliefs on protection of minorities
3. Darrow's beliefs on religion

You might want to speak on the important cases in the career of Darrow, as follows:

1. The *Los Angeles Times* Building Bombing Case
2. The Loeb-Leopold Case
3. The Scopes Trial

e. THE LOGICAL-ORDER METHOD. Logical order may suggest the best position of points. For example, if you explain the construction of a house, you may divide the subject into main points that follow the order of construction, as follows:

1. Laying the foundation
2. Constructing the walls
3. Building the roof
4. Finishing the inside

For a persuasive speech favoring group medical plans you could follow the logical order—need, practical solution, most desirable solution. For example:

1. Medical distribution has created serious problems
2. Group medicine will correct the problem
3. Group medicine constitutes the most desirable solution

f. CAUSE-TO-EFFECT AND EFFECT-TO-CAUSE METHODS. In the cause-to-effect arrangement, start with circumstances sufficient for a cause and attempt to establish the probable effect. For example, you may anticipate an increase in inflation.

1. Labor is negotiating wage increases
2. Employment is greatest in our history
3. Credit restrictions are being lifted

   Therefore,

      Inflation will increase

In effect-to-cause arrangement, reverse the process; show an effect or existing condition and suggest the prior causes. To illustrate:

Inflation is on the increase today, for
1. Labor received wage increases
2. Unemployment decreased
3. Credit restrictions were eased

These patterns are based on the belief in causation—every effect must be produced by some cause and every cause will produce its effect unless interfered with by extraneous factors.

g. SIMPLE-TO-COMPLEX METHODS. By this method you start with the material easiest to comprehend and proceed to the more difficult. This method proves especially effective on subjects of a technical nature. For example, suppose your subject to be "Types of World Collaboration." Start with the method easiest to understand and conclude with the most technical method, as follows:

1. Cooperation
2. Alliance
3. Regionalism
4. Confederation
5. Federation

h. FAMILIAR-TO-UNFAMILIAR METHOD. This method starts with those ideas most familiar to the audience and leads to those least familiar. Suppose you desire to discuss the relative effects of raw materials, labor, and manufacturing on the price of commodities. If your audience consists of farmers, you would probably follow this order:

1. The effect of raw materials on prices
2. The effect of labor on prices
3. The effect of manufacturing on prices

If you addressed an audience of laborers on the same subject, the following order, from familiar to unfamiliar, would probably serve best:

1. The effect of labor on prices
2. The effect of manufacturing on prices
3. The effect of raw materials on prices

Support Your Ideas

The central idea forms the spinal column, the organization the skeleton, and the supporting material the flesh of your speech. The previous sections explained the purpose and function of the central idea and the organizational pattern. To complete the composition of your speech you must expand your ideas with the forms of support discussed in Chapter 7; namely, explanations, statistics, examples, analogies or comparisons, testimony, and restatement. The following illustration shows how the forms of support apply:

Main point: I. Unequal educational opportunity constitutes a problem in the United States.
Subpoint: A. Inequalities exist.
Support: 1. Explanation, and
2. Statistics, and/or
3. Examples, and/or
4. Analogies, and/or
5. Testimony, and
6. Restatement
Subpoint: B. Inequalities are detrimental
Support: (Support in same way as A.)
Subpoint: C. State financing perpetuates these inequalities.
Support: (Support in same way as in A.)
Main point: II. and III. (Support same as I.)

IV. The Conclusion

The heavyweight champion feels out his opponent in the early rounds and accustoms himself to his style; then he softens him in later rounds with repeated blows to the body and head; finally, when the softening-up process has served its purpose, he deals the knock-out punch. This procedure applies to speech construction. The introduction creates a favorable atmosphere for the speech, gains interest in the subject, and partitions the speech. The body develops the central idea through main points and subpoints supported by ample evidence and arranged into an acceptable organizational pattern. The conclusion rounds out the central idea and purpose. It may do so in three ways: (1) summarizing the main points, (2) amplifying the central idea, (3) indicating the desired action. Any one method or any combination of these methods may be used, depending upon the purpose of the speech.

Summary of Main Points

The summary may take three forms: a verbatim restatement of the main points, a paraphrase or abstract of the main ideas, or a quotation which epitomizes the central idea.

Dr. John H. Fisher, President of Teachers College, Columbia

University, used the restatement type summary in a speech at a conference sponsored by the United States Commission on Civil Rights in Washington, D.C., on May 3, 1962.

> To summarize then, briefly, what I have tried to say about the educational problems of desegregating schools:
> 1. The focus of sound teaching is always on the individual, for education is an intensely personal matter, having its principal effect always within the person.
> 2. If we are to achieve good education, we must respect the individuality of each student, relating his instruction to his background, his needs, his possibilities.
> 3. To achieve equality of opportunity within the whole of our culture, it may be necessary to offer those who are handicapped by their history or their current situation not merely equal, but compensatory educational opportunity.
> 4. In organizing education many considerations are important, many characteristics are relevant, but racial differences in themselves are not. In the administration of schools, therefore, the manipulation of pupils on purely racial grounds is irrelevant and improper.[23]

President Lyndon B. Johnson paraphrased his main ideas in his commencement address at Baylor University on May 28, 1965.

> In Santo Domingo the last month has been grim. The storm there is not yet over. But a new sense of hope is beginning. Across the angry arguments of the opposing forces, the voice of good sense is now beginning to be heard.
>
> As the Organization of American States recommits itself to the hard efforts of peace-making, the government and the people of the United States proudly pledge full support to the peacemakers.
>
> The path ahead is long, the way ahead is hard. So we must, in the words of the prophet, "Mount up on the wings of eagles, run and not grow weary."
>
> Thank you.[24]

In his inaugural address on January 20, 1965, President Johnson concluded with a quotation which restated his pledge to the American people.

> Is our world gone? We say farewell. Is a new world coming? We welcome it—and we will bend it to the hopes of man.

---

[23] Thonssen, *op. cit.,* XXXV: 4, p. 121.
Reprinted by permission of Dr. Fisher with this proviso: ". . . My views about the fourth point . . . have changed in the last three years . . . race . . . must be taken into account in decisions affecting schools and school systems." (Letter to author, August 5, 1965.)

[24] *Waco Tribune-Herald,* May 29, 1965, p. 6-A.

. . . I will repeat today what I said on that sorrowful day in November, 1963: I will lead and I will do the best I can.

But you must look within your own hearts to the old promises and to the old dream. They will lead you best of all.

For myself, I ask only, in the words of an ancient leader: "Give me now wisdom and knowledge, that I may go out and come in before this people: for who can judge this, thy people, that is so great." [25]

Restate and Amplify Central Idea

You may either expand and re-emphasize your central idea after the summary or use this method without a summary. Note how former President John F. Kennedy restated the central idea of his inaugural address held on the Capitol steps on January 20, 1961.

And so, my fellow Americans, ask not what your country can do for you: Ask what you can do for your country.

My fellow citizens of the world: Ask not what America will do for you, but what together we can do for the freedom of man.

Finally, whether you are citizens of America or citizens of the world, ask of us the same high standards of strength and sacrifice which we ask of you. With a good conscience our only sure reward, with history the final judge of our deeds, let us go forth to lead the land we love, asking His blessing and His help, but knowing that here on earth God's work must truly be our own.[26]

Indicate Desired Action

You may desire a physical response from your audience; for example, to subscribe the budget, vote the party ticket, or acquit your client. Such conclusions usually contain emotional appeal. Patrick Henry's conclusion in his "Liberty or Death" speech affords a classic example although we consider his style too elaborate today. The speech advocated that Virginia ready itself for war against England.

It is in vain, sir, to extenuate the matter. Gentlemen may cry peace, peace—but there is no peace. The war is actually begun! The next gale that sweeps from the North will bring to our ears the clash of resounding arms! Our brethren are already in the field! Why stand we here idle? What is it that gentlemen wish? What would they have? Is

[25] *Congressional Record,* Vol. 3, No. 13, January 20, 1965, p. 961.

[26] *Inaugural Addresses of the Presidents of the United States,* 87th Congress, 1st Session, House Document No. 218 (Washington, D.C.: United States Government Printing Office, 1961), pp. 267-70.

> life so dear, or peace so sweet, as to be purchased at the price of chains and slavery? Forbid it, Almighty God! I know not what course others may take; but as for me, give me liberty, or give me death! [27]

Other conclusions appeal for the acceptance of an idea, rather than for overt action. John F. Kennedy made such an appeal in his speech, "A Step Toward Peace," when he addressed a national radio-television audience on July 26, 1963.

> But now, for the first time in many years, the path of peace may be open. No one can be certain what the future will bring. No one can say whether the time has come for an easing of the struggle. But history and our own conscience will judge us harsher if we do not now make every effort to test our hopes by action, and this is the place to begin. According to the ancient Chinese proverb, "A journey of a thousand miles must begin with a single step." [28]

V. Summary

Organization means the arrangement of the central idea of a speech into main divisions, subpoints, and supporting data. The traditional organizational pattern calls for an introduction, body or discussion, and conclusion.

The introduction performs three functions: creates a favorable atmosphere for the speech, stimulates interest in the subject, and clarifies and partitions the topic. Numerous techniques may be employed to attain these purposes.

The body of the speech develops the central idea in detail. To develop the central idea, divide it into main divisions and subpoints and expand each with the various forms of support. Organizational patterns include several methods: (1) deductive and inductive, (2) problem-solution, (3) chronological, (4) enumeration, (5) logical, (6) cause-effect relationships, (7) simple to complex, and (8) familiar to unfamiliar.

The conclusion serves to round out the central idea and purpose, in one or all of three ways: (1) summarizing the main points, (2) amplifying the central idea, (3) indicating the desired action.

---

[27] William Wirt, *Life and Character of Patrick Henry* (25th ed.; Philadelphia: Claxton and Company, 1881), p. 42.

[28] Thonssen, *op. cit.,* XXXVI: 4, p. 29.

Questions and Exercises

A. Answer the following questions on Chapter 8.

1. List some principles of composition that should guide you in organizing your speech.
2. What three purposes does the introduction of a speech serve? Is it always necessary to perform all three functions? What determines your decision?
3. Why is it necessary to create a proper atmosphere early in your speech? List several techniques to accomplish this purpose.
4. Why should the opening remarks about your subject attempt to get immediate interest? List several techniques for stimulating interest.
5. What is meant by the partition or thesis of a speech? What should be included in the partition?
6. Distinguish between the central idea and the main points of a speech. Illustrate your answer.
7. State several principles that should govern the choice of main points. How do subordinate points differ from main points?
8. List nine organizational patterns for speech composition. What determines the choice of an organizational plan?
9. Distinguish between the deductive and inductive methods of organization.
10. How do the forms of support studied in Chapter 7 apply to the organization of a speech?
11. What purpose does the conclusion serve? What should be included in the conclusion?

B. For your eighth speaking assignment, prepare a five-minute demonstration speech in which you use some type of visual aid: the blackboard, a chart, a map, or any physical object. Choose any subject you like.

1. Consider the following suggestions:
   a. Demonstrate various collections in which you may be interested, such as stamps, coins, guns, or insects.
   b. Demonstrate some sport in which you are interested, such as football, golf, swimming, or tennis. Bring the materials to class or make drawings on the blackboard. For example, (1) show some interesting formations in football by blackboard drawings, or (2) demonstrate various golf strokes by using your clubs.
   c. Show how something is made, using a prepared chart or diagram.
   d. Explain the organizational plan of some company by a diagram or demonstration.
2. Observe these precautions:
   a. Make your demonstration a part of a well-developed speech. The demonstration should support your idea and should not be an end in itself.

b. Give special attention to organizing your speech. Follow the principles discussed in this chapter for introduction, body, and conclusion.

C. Using the topic, "Free Enterprise," make tentative outlines of the main points of speeches using the following organizational patterns: (1) deductive, (2) chronological order, (3) problem-solution pattern, and (4) simple enumeration.

D. Using the topic, "Principles of Business Administration," formulate the central idea of three possible speeches.

1. Decide on the main points for a possible speech using the deductive organizational pattern.
2. Subdivide each main point into two or three subpoints.
3. Decide on several types of support for each subpoint.

CHAPTER 9

Prepare Your Speech for Delivery —Methods and Outlines

Through the processes discussed in Chapter 8, you decided on the central idea for your speech and selected your main points, subpoints, and forms of support. You also chose the organizational pattern best adapted to your address. Now you are ready to approach the final step—the preparation of your speech for delivery. This step involves the method for delivery and the outline.

I. Methods of Preparing for Presentation

The way you prepare your speech for delivery may vary according to personal preference and the purpose of your speech, but the best plan for most occasions is to prepare for extemporaneous speaking. The four principal methods of presentation follow: (1) reading from the manuscript, (2) delivering from memory, (3) speaking impromptu, and (4) speaking extemporaneously. Consider the advantages and disadvantages of each method in relation to the purpose of your speech and the audience.

Reading from Manuscript

This method consists of writing out the speech and reading it. At least three occasions permit this type: (1) Officials in high governmental positions often read their speeches because deviation from the prepared manuscript might cause repercussions harmful to national policy. (2) Research reports before learned groups such as professional conventions sometimes utilize this method. If the speaker presents technical material, statistical information, and quotations of findings not well adapted to extemporaneous presentation, he may read his report. (3) Speeches prepared for radio may be read without prejudice to the speaker since he cannot be seen. However, the successful radio speaker cultivates the ability to read as though he were speaking extemporaneously. Some speakers read speeches for television by means of a teleprompter. The speech, printed in large type, is suspended before the speaker outside camera range. The device enables the speaker to give the appearance of looking directly into the camera as he reads. Its use often decreases audience projection because the stare of the speaker does not seem normal.

Although reading from the manuscript is not recommended for occasions other than those listed above, certain advantages do accrue: (1) It permits a careful choice of language for precision of meaning and beauty of expression. (2) It permits economy of expression because the manuscript can be edited. (3) It enables the speaker to develop more fluency than in extemporaneous speaking, for he does not have to choose his language as he speaks. (4) It prevents rambling and digressions. (5) It provides a manuscript for future reference or for publication.

The disadvantages of reading may be listed as follows: (1) It decreases audience communication because most speakers cannot read with the same directness with which they speak. (2) It lessens audience projection because the speaker cannot look at the audience so often as he can in speaking extemporaneously. He loses part of the effect of eye contact and freedom of bodily action, especially gestures. (3) It decreases flexibility because it cannot easily be adapted to changed conditions, such as more or less time than anticipated, or to preceding speeches. (4) More time is required to prepare the manuscript than is required to prepare the outline for an extemporaneous speech.

If you plan to read your manuscript, consider the following suggestions: (1) Outline your speech first and have your supporting material at hand when you start to write. The outline will help prevent rambling, and the supporting material can be inserted readily at the proper place. (2) Write as if you were speaking; imagine your audience present as you write. Oral style is more informal, repetitious, and direct than written. Some speakers retain these characteristics of oral style in preparing a manuscript by dictating or recording it. The transcribed manuscript can then be edited. Attempt to make the manuscript retain the freshness of extemporaneous discourse. (3) Read the speech several times aloud; imagine your audience present as you read. Think the thought as you read. Try to grasp whole sentences at a time. (4) Become sufficiently familiar with your manuscript that you can look at your audience frequently. Practice directness and projection as you read.

Speaking from Memory

Writing out speeches and committing them to memory finds favor with speakers who find difficulty in thinking on their feet. This was the favorite method during the period of elocution, for it freed the speaker to engage his presentation techniques.

Certain advantages do accrue. It allows for (1) precision in expression, (2) carefully planned development, (3) a colorful choice of language, and (4) more attention to presentation than the extemporaneous method. With most speakers these advantages are outweighed by the disadvantages: (1) difficulty of adaptation to changed conditions, (2) lack of directness in presentation, (3) more time required for preparation, (4) increased chances of forgetting, and (5) lack of apparent spontaneity. Too often the speech sounds memorized.

If you use this method, follow the instructions for preparing the manuscript explained in the previous section. Make the manuscript conform to oral rather than written form. For best results in memorizing, read the manuscript over in its entirety until you learn the speech as a whole. Do not memorize paragraphs, pages, or sections at a time. Space your practice sessions over several days. Most persons can memorize better with short practice sessions extended over several days, than with longer sessions over a shorter period.

The Impromptu Method

This method means speaking without specific preparation. Use the impromptu method only when called upon without prior notice. This will happen frequently in conferences but rarely in public-speaking situations. Experience in extemporaneous speaking and wide reading constitute the best preparation. In one sense, you never speak without preparation; rather, you speak from prior experience and out of your background of ideas and knowledge. Otherwise, you would not have anything to say. If you have nothing worthwhile to say when called upon without warning, by all means decline to speak.

When called upon without notice, rarely are you expected to make a lengthy speech; a few remarks or expressions of opinion usually suffice. When called upon, use deliberation in rising, make a quick analysis of your request, and decide on one or two main ideas. Your opening statement will usually concern the nature of the request or a reference to a previous idea expressed at the meeting.

Some speakers keep a few organizational patterns in mind for such occasions and attempt to put their remarks into these patterns. (1) "Past-present-future" indicates a chronological order. For example, if you are asked to talk on your future profession, the following ideas might serve: brief history of the profession, the status of the profession, your future plans. (2) "Problem-solution" may indicate facts about the problem and how you think it could be corrected. For example, you are asked how the problem of helping the indigent should be handled. (3) "Social-economic-political" may indicate an organizational pattern for a request such as your opinion on the advisability of a bond issue for building a new school building. (4) "Theoretical-practical" might indicate an organizational pattern, for example, for your opinion on whether the schools in your community should go on a twelve-month school year.

The advantages of impromptu speaking are: (1) It calls for an unpremeditated opinion that may more aptly reveal a person's true feelings than would a prepared statement. Industry's use of brainstorming sessions, as explained in Chapter 15, applies this principle. (2) The ideas and opinions must come spontaneously; they are, therefore, usually fresh and alive. (3) It encourages thinking on your feet. As a result, you communicate directly because you must think the thought as you speak.

The disadvantages outweigh the advantages in many persons' opinions. (1) It calls for speaking without complete preparation. Consequently, immature judgments may be expressed, based upon inadequate knowledge. (2) It encourages halting and non-fluent delivery. Many people cannot express themselves fluently on the spur of the moment. (3) It may result in poorly arranged ideas; without time for proper planning, speakers may ramble and present disconnected, incoherent statements. (4) It may induce stage fright. Without time for thought, a person may become emotionally disturbed.

The Extemporaneous Method

By this method you speak from a previously prepared outline and choose the phraseology of the speech as you talk. The speech should be prepared in advance, with a predetermined purpose, well-chosen main points, proper explanation and reasoning, and with adequate supporting material for each point. Extemporaneous speaking does not mean speaking without preparation, as you might conclude from considering the Latin derivation of the word. The word has changed its meaning through usage. Speaking without preparation is now termed impromptu speaking.

Final preparation for the extemporaneous speech does not end with gathering material and arranging it into an outline; it should include practice in presenting it. Start your practice by thinking through the outline until you can retain a mental picture of it. Then practice presenting it before your class or an imaginary audience until you attain fluency and a ready choice of language. During practice periods, stand and speak aloud as if the audience were present. Speak through the entire outline at each practice session; do not go back over certain sections or sentences. Complete the outline several days prior to the speech, if possible, so as to give yourself time to become familiar with the outline and to practice.

The advantages of the extemporaneous method may be listed as: (1) It encourages audience communication and directness. (2) It avoids an artificial and stilted manner because the speaker must think the idea as he speaks. (3) It permits flexibility; the speaker may shorten or lengthen his speech as the occasion demands or as he senses the need. (4) It permits apparent spontaneity; the speech does not sound memorized and rehearsed.

Disadvantages should be considered. (1) It permits inadequate preparation if one speaks from a hastily-made mental outline. (2) It encourages poor language choice since the speaker must choose his language as he speaks. (3) It lessens fluency by requiring an immediate choice of phraseology. (4) It allows for digressions when the speaker departs from his outline. (5) It does not provide a script for future reference or for publication.

Some speakers follow the practice of writing speeches out, reading them several times, but not memorizing them. This practice may aid in choice of language and in fluency. Others record their speeches during practice sessions and listen to the record for self-evaluation. These methods may prove especially helpful to the beginning student.

II. Outlining the Speech

Experienced speakers who talk on subjects in the field of their specialty may speak through a mental outline with success. For most speakers a well-prepared written outline proves an invaluable aid; for inexperienced speakers it is a necessity. The outline provides a blueprint of the speech. It assures realistic thinking on the subject and orderly arrangement of ideas. Speaking without an outline is like building a house without a blueprint; order and arrangement cannot be achieved. The complete-sentence outline distinguishes the relationships between main points and subpoints, and between subpoints and supporting data. The following procedures for outlining apply specifically to the sentence outline.

Rules for Outlining

1. *Divide the outline into three parts:* (1) *introduction,* (2) *body,* and (3) *conclusion.* The introduction includes opening remarks designed to set the keynote, a statement for getting immediate interest, and the partition. Opening remarks often may be suggested at the speaking occasion; to be safe, include a possible opening in the outline. The body of the outline develops the main divisions in detail. The main divisions are divided into subpoints and developed through the various forms of support discussed in Chapter 7. The conclusion summarizes the speech, restates the central idea, and makes the desired appeal. The parts of the outline for the introduction are illustrated in the sample outline near the end of this chapter.

2. *Use a consistent system of symbols.* The system of symbols may vary according to personal preference, but one system should be followed consistently. Changing the number and letter designations within an outline destroys the relationships between main

points and subpoints and between points and supporting data. The following system serves well.

I. ______________________________
  A. ______________________________
    1. ______________________________
      a. ______________________________
        (1) ______________________________
          (a) ______________________________
          (b) ______________________________
        (2) ______________________________
      b. ______________________________
    2. ______________________________
  B. ______________________________
II. ______________________________

3. *Arrange each division into heads and subheads.* Each subdivision of a main point should be designated by a separate symbol and proper indentation to indicate the relationship between points and subpoints. Failure to do so obscures the divisional sequence of ideas.

Wrong

It is necessary to distinguish between two types of research. That done by pressure groups or propaganda agencies, and that done by objective groups. Pressure groups are not interested in finding and disseminating factually true information; rather, they are interested only in those facts that serve their purpose. Objective agencies are interested in factually true information. They seek truth for truth's sake and are not interested in what the outcome of a research study may reveal.

Right

I. Distinguish between two types of research.
  A. That done by pressure groups—public-relation or propaganda agencies.
    1. Pressure groups are not interested in finding and disseminating factually true information.
    2. Pressure groups seek only those facts that serve their purpose.
  B. That done by objective groups—educational institutions and research organizations.
    1. They seek information for the sake of information.
    2. They seek all the facts and are not interested in what the outcome of a research study may reveal.

4. *Use one symbol only for each statement.* To designate a single statement by two symbols destroys the relationships between points and subpoints, and between points and supporting data.

Wrong

I. The findings of research studies are disseminated through classroom instruction and through publication.
   A. 1. Classroom instruction forms the more immediate function in meeting the needs of present students.
      2. An instructor may serve a valuable purpose by devoting all his time to this function.
      3. Some persons do not have the facility to serve as both classroom teacher and research scholar.

Right

I. The findings of research studies are disseminated through classroom instruction and through publication.
   A. Classroom instruction forms the more immediate function in meeting the needs of present students.
      1. An instructor may serve a valuable purpose by devoting all his time to this function.
      2. Some persons do not have the facility to serve as both classroom teacher and research scholar.

5. *Show a proper indentation for each statement.* Each statement subordinate to another should be designated by indentation, while statements of equal rank should show the same indentations.

Wrong

I. Unequal teaching loads can be corrected by the weekly service load.
A. Establish a normal work week applicable to all.
1. Extra duties such as administration, counseling, research, outside projects, public relations, and committee assignments can be evaluated in terms of hours per week.
2. The teaching load can be evaluated in terms of time spent in preparation and in the classroom.
   a. Laboratory courses should count more than non-laboratory classes.

Right

I. Unequal teaching loads can be corrected by the weekly service load.
   A. Establish a normal work week applicable to all.
      1. Extra duties such as administration, counseling, research, outside projects, public relations, and committee assignments can be evaluated in terms of hours per week.
      2. The teaching load can be evaluated in terms of time spent in preparation and in the classroom.
         a. Laboratory courses should count more than non-laboratory courses.

6. *Make each statement in the form of a complete sentence.* Do not mix sentences, clauses, phrases, and words in the same outline.

For the sentence outline, all statements should be made in the form of complete sentences.

Wrong

I. The purpose of a university is to discover, investigate, and disseminate knowledge, and to reveal varying and conflicting points of view.
   A. It includes both finding and disseminating information.
   B. Investigation
   C. What to think—how to think

Right

I. The purpose of a university is to discover, investigate, and disseminate knowledge, and to reveal varying and conflicting points of view.
   A. It includes both finding and disseminating information.
   B. It includes investigating all possible points of view.
   C. The purpose is to teach students not what to think but how to think.

7. *Avoid compound and multiple-idea sentences.* Confusion arises in dividing compound and complex sentences into subpoints. It may not be possible to determine to which part of the multiple-idea sentence a subpoint refers.

Wrong

I. Various plans can improve the status of research and classroom teaching.
   A. Sabbatical leaves would provide time for research.
   B. Limiting class size makes for greater individual attention to students.
   C. Were research funds provided, those with significant research projects could apply and get time off.
   D. Credit on teaching load for directing graduate theses would result in improved studies.
   E. Teaching assistants would relieve the teacher of administrative details and paper-grading.
   F. Review sessions scheduled outside the classroom period would assist the backward student.

Right

I. Various plans can improve the status of research.
   A. Sabbatical leaves would provide time for research.
   B. Were research funds provided, those with significant research projects could apply and get time off.
   C. Credit on teaching load for directing graduate theses would result in improved studies.
II. Classroom instruction can be improved.

A. Limiting class size makes for greater individual attention to students.
B. Teaching assistants would relieve the teacher of administrative details and paper-grading.
C. Review sessions scheduled outside the classroom period would assist the backward student.

Types of Outlines

The complete-sentence outline like that used to illustrate the preceding section, "Rules for Outlining," constitutes the best type for preparation. For presentation, the phrase and key-word outlines may serve best. The complete-sentence, phrase, and key-word outlines for a commencement address are illustrated below. The comments in the column to the left of the complete-sentence type explain the outline.

1. *Complete sentence.* The sentence outline helps to show the logical development of ideas. It also aids in choice of language since key sentences must be written out. The beginning student will find the sentence outline especially helpful. Study the following sample outline.

Topic:	NEW FRONTIERS FOR EDUCATION
	Introduction
Keynote statement:	I. Commencement time marks a period of beginning.
Interest statement:	II. A recent editorial stated, "Today we have too many people all dressed up in education with no place to go."
Explanation:	A. Do too many seek a college education?
	B. Does education have a place to go?
Partition:	III. Are there new frontiers for education?
Explanation:	A. Are the purposes of education realized?
	B. What new frontiers should guide future emphasis?
	Body
Main Point:	I. Much emphasis is put on education today.
Subpoint:	A. This emphasis is reflected in student enrollment.
Support: Statistics:	1. Total enrollment in colleges and universities last year was two and one-third million—greater by one-third than the prewar peak year of 1939-40.

Statistics:	2. Original estimates of the number of veterans who would be interested in the educational provisions of the federal government fell short by approximately 600 per cent.
Subpoint:	B. This emphasis is reflected in expenditures for education.
Support: Statistics:	1. More than three billion dollars were spent last year in educating public school students.
Statistics:	2. Expenditures of higher education have progressively increased since the war.
Subpoint:	C. Education is rapidly becoming America's number one enterprise.
Explanation:	1. We have many people dressed up in education.
	2. The percentage of high-school graduates who attend college is increasing annually.
Main Point:	II. The purposes of education may be broadly stated as threefold:
Subpoint:	A. The *acquisition of knowledge* comes first in order of time.
Subdivision:	1. Knowledge is necessary in an age of specialization.
Subdivision:	2. There is an aesthetic pleasure in knowledge.
Subpoint:	B. The second purpose is *training the mental faculties.*
Explanation:	1. Some courses are designed to teach people how to think.
Example:	a. This is true largely with law, which teaches through the case method.
	b. Such courses give knowledge plus a well-rounded mental development.
Explanation:	2. Many courses are concerned with both knowledge and reasoning facility.
Subpoint:	C. A purpose often minimized is *training in how to use* acquired knowledge and trained mental faculties.
Subdivision:	1. Failure to stress this purpose constitutes the crucial problem.
Subdivision:	2. Education, improperly directed, may be detrimental.
Examples:	a. Education gives us men who can perfect modern mechanical devices, but these cannot be used because of the effect on the labor market.

b. Education has given us men who can devise ways of using atomic power constructively in industry, but we use it on the battlefield.

Main Point: III. Education's new frontier is teaching people *how to live together.*

Subpoints: A. This involves working out a social order capable of coping with material advances.

B. It involves teaching people how to use existing knowledge in the field of social relationships.

Conclusion

Summary: I. Can education cross its new frontier?

Authority: A. Dr. E. Stanley Jones has said that our scientific life is fifty years ahead of our social order and that the next decade will witness a social awakening.

Emphasis of central idea: B. To realize this, we must utilize existing knowledge in the field of social relationships.

Action: II. Education's new frontier can be crossed by putting the proper emphasis upon the utility of education.

2. *The phrase outline.* The preceding sentence outline is here produced in phrases. The phrase outline may be intelligible only to the speaker, but it may be more usable to him for presentation than a sentence outline.

NEW FRONTIERS FOR EDUCATION

Introduction

I. Time of beginning
II. Recent editorial: "Today we have too many people all dressed up in education with no place to go."
III. New frontiers for education?
   A. Purposes of education realized?
   B. Future emphasis?

Body

I. Emphasis great on education
   A. Reflected in student enrollment
      1. Two and one-third million in 1948; one-third more than in 1939-40
      2. Original G. I. estimates 600 per cent short

B. Reflected in expenditures
  1. Three billion last year
  2. Costs increasing
C. Education number one enterprise

II. Purposes of education threefold
  A. Acquisition of knowledge
    1. Necessary in age of specialization
    2. Aesthetic pleasure in knowledge
  B. Training the mental faculties
    1. Some courses teach how to think
      a. Law as example
      b. Well-rounded mental development
    2. Some courses concern both knowledge and reasoning
  C. Training in utility of knowledge and mental faculties
    1. Failure to stress causes crucial problem
    2. Improperly directed, education may be detrimental
      a. Technological advances
      b. Atomic energy in industry

III. New frontier—how to live together
  A. Social order to match material advances
  B. Use of existing knowledge in field of social relationships

Conclusion

I. Can education cross new frontier?
  A. E. Stanley Jones—scientific life fifty years ahead of social progress.
  B. Apply knowledge in social relationships

3. *The key-word outline.* The key-word outline supplies a few words and phrases to guide the speaker. Experienced speakers may prefer the key-word outline, especially when talking on familiar subjects. It is not applicable as a preparation outline or for inexperienced speakers.

NEW FRONTIERS FOR EDUCATION

Introduction

I. Beginning time
II. Editorial statement
III. New frontiers?
  A. Purposes
  B. Emphasis

Body

I. Emphasis on education
  A. Student enrollment

B. Expenditures
C. Number one enterprise
II. Purposes
A. Acquisition knowledge
1. Material
2. Aesthetic
B. Trained faculties
1. How to think
2. Knowledge and reasoning
C. Utility
1. Crucial problem
2. Improperly directed
III. New frontier—live together
A. Material advances
B. Social relationships

Conclusion

I. Can education cross frontiers?
II. Stress utility

III. Speech Composition Restated

This chapter concludes the discussion of the steps in speech preparation and composition that started with Chapter 4. Figure 1 restates and summarizes these steps in graphic form.

IV. Summary

The final steps in speech composition consist of selecting the method for delivery and putting the speech into outline form. The four methods of speech presentation follow: (1) reading from the manuscript; (2) speaking from memory; (3) speaking impromptu, that is, without specific preparation; and (4) speaking extemporaneously. Extempore speaking, the recommended method, consists of speaking through a prepared outline as you phrase your ideas.

The last step in composition calls for putting the speech into outline form. The rules for outlining should be followed carefully. The types of outlines are: (1) the complete-sentence, (2) phrase, and (3) key-word. The complete-sentence outline serves best for preparing the speech. The phrase or key-word outline may suffice for presentation purposes.

Steps in Speech Preparation and Composition

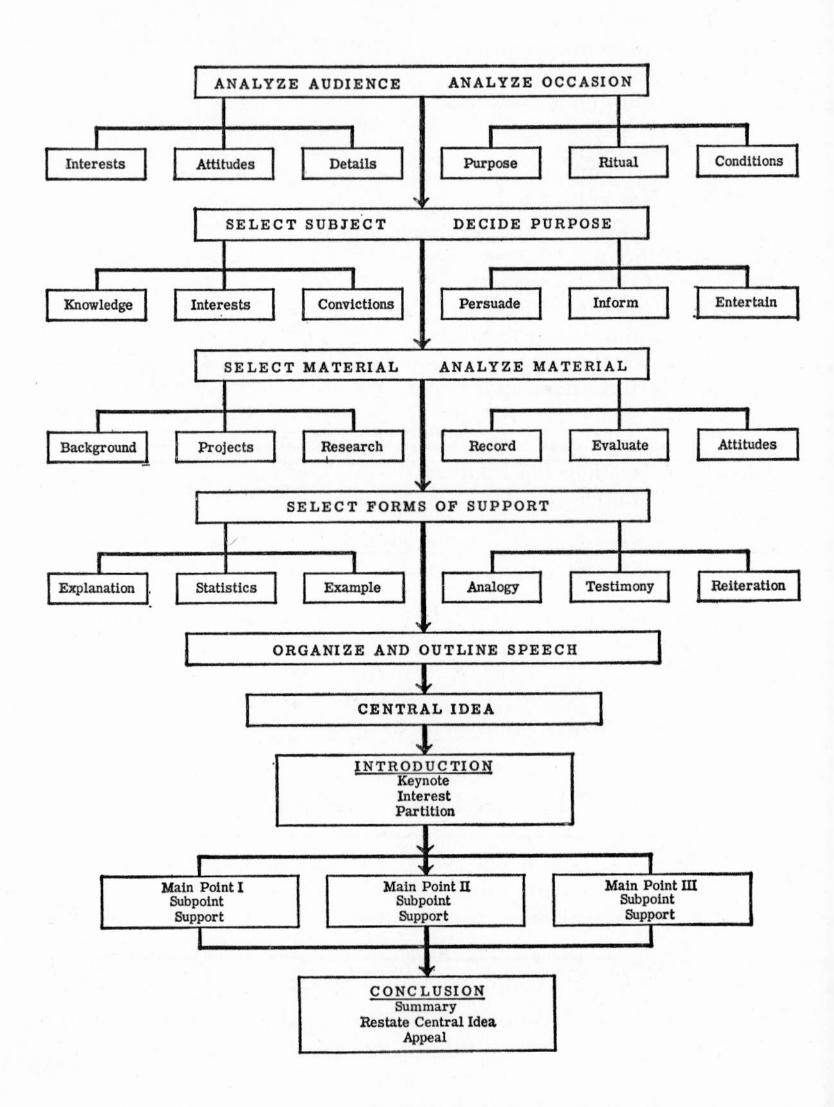

Questions and Exercises

A. Answer the following questions on Chapter 9.

1. List four ways that you may present your speech. Which method do you consider best? Why?
2. What occasions call for reading from the manuscript? List the advantages and disadvantages of this method. List some suggestions for preparing your manuscript.
3. What are some advantages and disadvantages of speaking from memory? Discuss several aids for memorizing a speech.
4. What constitutes the best preparation for impromptu speaking? How should you proceed when called upon without notice? Discuss several organizational patterns for such occasions.
5. What is meant by the extemporaneous method? What are its advantages and disadvantages? What procedures should you follow in preparing for extemporaneous speaking?
6. List several advantages for preparing a written outline for your speech. Why should the preparation outline be in the form of complete sentences?
7. Distinguish among the following types of outlines: (1) complete-sentence, (2) phrase, and (3) key-word. What should govern your choice of outline?
8. What should be included in the introduction of your outline?
9. List the rules for outlining. State the reasons for each rule.
10. What should be included in the conclusion of your outline?

B. Your ninth speech includes all the principles you have learned from studying Part II of this textbook. You will be given ten minutes for this speech. Observe the following suggestions:

1. Select a subject from your background of training and experience, one in which you have strong interests and convictions.
2. You may use as your purpose to persuade, inform, or entertain. Decide on this general purpose early in your preparation.
3. Make a tentative plan for your speech first, then find the following sources for study: (1) one source book or textbook, (2) a newspaper story or syndicated article, (3) one account in a news magazine, (4) one article in a monthly magazine, (5) one reference from a governmental pamphlet, and (6) at least one additional source explained in Chapter 6.
4. Interview three authorities in your community about your subject and quote them in your speech.
5. Use each type of support discussed in Chapter 7 at least once during your speech: explanation, statistics, example, analogy, testimony, and restatement. This suggestion will not preclude using a single form of support several times.
6. Use any organizational pattern discussed in Chapter 8 that you desire. Be able to justify your choice.

7. Decide on a central idea and state it under the title of your outline.
8. Write out a complete sentence outline. List the references that you used in preparing the outline.
9. From your sentence outline, prepare a phrase or key-word outline for use in presenting the speech.
10. Rate yourself and have your instructor rate you on the same basis explained in the exercises for Chapter 3.

C. At the conclusion of the above speech, write out the factors on which you think you have improved since your first speech. List the factors in which you consider you most need additional improvement.

PART THREE

Presentation

CHAPTER 10

Establish Poise, Confidence, and Attain Effective Delivery

Part Two of this textbook took you step by step through the process of composing a speech. The six chapters followed a logical sequence based upon the approximate order in which you encounter the principles of composition. The discussion started with an analysis of the audience and the speaking occasion. Through successive steps you received instructions on how to select an appropriate subject and purpose, how to find and evaluate material, how to choose supporting data, how to organize ideas, and how to outline and prepare a speech for delivery.

Now we must take the finished speech and see how to share ideas with others orally. Unless a speaker communicates clearly and understandably, the arduous task of preparation will have been in vain.

You sometimes hear people say, "Why take training in speech? We all talk! Why train to do something that comes naturally?" Some people do speak quite well without formal training in oral communication. Possessing forceful personalities, they develop skills in speaking on their own. You may learn to play golf the same way, but in doing so you may also develop some poor techniques. Correcting your bad habits may require more effort than learning the right techniques originally would have done. A potentially "par" golfer, you may achieve only "bogey" attainment because you did "what comes naturally" in the formative years. Persons with natural talents may do reasonably well without formal training, but it is logical to expect that they could do better with training. Those without natural aptitudes in oral communication find training a necessity.

Two incidents show why formal training for delivery does count. A large public relations organization planned a speech to be given by a nationally known businessman for a college assembly. The advance agent of the organization handed a manuscript of the speech to a speech professor the evening before the speaking occasion. The professor was impressed with the excellence of the speech; the manuscript showed extensive research and careful writing. However, the presentation by the organization's speaker fell far short of the excellence of the manuscript. The speaker had few attributes of effective delivery; he read the speech in a monotone, his voice was weak and high-pitched, he did not use overt bodily action, and he failed to adapt the speech to the interests of the students. His poor presentation caused the students to stop listening and to turn to more interesting pursuits such as reading and conversing with neighbors. An excellent written speech was rendered almost worthless by poor presentation; the speaker simply had failed to communicate.

At another occasion, a dedication ceremony for a new building, the speaker was chosen for his prestige, not for his speaking ability. His chief fault was that he could not be heard. The outdoor meeting required a vigorous and forceful presentation; the speaker read his manuscript haltingly and without animation. Those far back in the audience soon gave up trying to listen because it required too much effort. Later students in an advanced speech class analyzed a manuscript of the speech and rated it as excellent. It contained mature ideas, it was well organized, and the language was clear and forceful. Again, a good speech was rendered useless by ineffective presentation. The speaker failed to communicate orally.

From the preceding incidents we may conclude that effective presentation is necessary to make a good speech accomplish its purpose—the communication of ideas, information, and emotions. The means for attaining communication skills form the subject matter of the four chapters in this section. The chapters include establishing poise, confidence, and proper stage conduct; acquiring an accurate and colorful vocabulary; attaining an adequate and pleasing voice; and achieving coordinated use of the body for communicating ideas orally.

This chapter introduces you to the subject of delivery and develops the first requirement. The three divisions of the discussion include (1) understanding principles of delivery, (2) establishing poise and confidence, and (3) acquiring proper stage conduct.

I. Principles of Delivery

A good starting point in a study of delivery is a consideration of principles of effective presentation. These principles differ from the standards for judging effective oral communication discussed in Chapter 1 because they relate only to presentation, while Chapter 1 included the total process.

Effective Delivery Utilizes the Whole Man

A brochure advertising a course in speech by a high-pressure national organization extolled in glowing terms the benefits that would accrue to those who enrolled. For those who attended the five sessions of two hours each, seventeen major benefits were promised. These benefits included conquering stage fright, learning to understand people, cultivating a pleasing voice, building a large vocabulary, and holding an audience spellbound. The pamphlet boldly raised the question of how all these benefits could be guaranteed in so short a course. It answered its own question by stating that all non-essentials were omitted; only those techniques necessary to managing audiences received attention. Furthermore, the brochure claimed that learning the essential features was ridiculously simple. It inferred that one could become a spellbinder in five easy lessons.

We could wish that the process were so simple. Unfortunately, like other worthwhile accomplishments, facility in oral presentation comes as a result of long, arduous study and practice. Furthermore, you cannot learn presentation skills in isolation from other areas of development. Effective oral communication requires the development of the whole man. It includes the coordinated use of mind, body, voice, and language. To illustrate, we say that effective delivery calls for an alert, animated, and enthusiastic presentation. Yet you cannot manifest these traits effectively unless you truly feel enthusiasm for your subject. If your feeling comes from within, as a result of a thorough understanding and genuine interest in your subject, your animation will be sincere; if you must force enthusiasm, it will probably appear affected.

A normally pitched voice, controlled bodily action, and direct eye contact also characterize good delivery. Yet these factors do not operate independently of the whole person. As a speaker, you must have confidence in yourself, have ideas that you desire to share, and understand your subject well in order to make effective use of voice and bodily action. The factors of delivery work in conjunction with your emotional and intellectual state. You develop presentation skills as you develop yourself as a whole.

Effective Delivery Uses Both Visual and Auditory Signs

Audiences receive ideas from speakers through what they hear, feel, and see. Sometimes what they see is more revealing than what they hear and feel. You can manipulate words to give a false evaluation; you reveal your true feelings by the way you act. You may greet a friend with a loud "good morning"; but if you have a dour expression on your face and use little physical animation, your friend will not believe what you say. A person may reiterate his love for animals, but if his voice and bodily expressions do not indicate his true feelings, even a dog will not believe him. What you say and the way you act combine to reveal your true feelings; to attain maximum results they must be congruous.

You may have had the experience of reading a speech and later hearing it presented. How different were the impressions you received? During a political campaign a speech professor heard one candidate speak several times over the radio without being favorably impressed. Later, upon seeing him on television, his opinion of the speaker changed considerably because of his ready smile and animated action. The full force of his warm personality came through by the use of both visual and auditory means, but it did not by auditory means alone.

Visual signs come from bodily movements, facial expressions, posture, and gestures. Auditory impressions result from language and voice. Total impressions are conveyed by the coordinated use of both auditory and visual means.

Effective Delivery Considers the Total Speaking Situation

We learned in Chapter 4 about the importance of adapting to the audience and occasion as well as the importance of the speaker and the speech. Effective delivery considers all these factors.

The audience and occasion give rise to the purpose of the speaking situation. Plan your speech with the audience and occasion in mind. Attempt to communicate in terms that are proper to the occasion and that will be understood by your listeners. Determine what factors of interest and attention will appeal to them by the methods discussed in Chapter 4. Knowledge of your audience will affect your attitude and your eagerness to share your ideas.

The speaker and the speech, as parts of the total speaking situation, may be reconsidered here for their effect on delivery. If you choose significant subjects from your background of knowledge, you will usually speak with assurance. Perhaps nothing influences your mental attitude more than the knowledge that you know your subject thoroughly. This assurance increases your self-confidence and reflects itself in your voice quality and bodily action. If you feel that your audience respects you as a person and has confidence in your judgment, you will have the mental attitude essential for effective delivery. Knowledge of subject, respect for yourself, and an understanding of your audience give you an inner feeling that will help bring effective delivery skills into play.

Effective Delivery Communicates Ideas Without Calling Attention to Techniques

Effective presentation skills do not call attention to themselves; they assist in communicating ideas. Unlike the actor who attempts to portray the character of another, the speaker seeks to be himself. He uses himself as the medium for communicating ideas, information, and emotions to others. If he puts on an exhibition, he may impress his listeners without communicating with them. If his audience comprehends his ideas and information without being aware of his techniques of presentation, he has used skills of delivery effectively.

Suppose that you received several complimentary statements following a speech. Which of the following would you prize the highest? (1) "Your voice was pleasing." (2) "Your meaningful gestures helped me understand your ideas." (3) "I have never heard a better organized speech." (4) "Would you mind if I used your vivid illustrations about the business executive?" (5) "Your ideas gave me something to think about. Could you suggest other materials on the subject?" Consider your answer before reading the next paragraph.

The first four statements indicated effective use of individual presentation skills, but they also show that the skills called attention to themselves. The fifth statement indicated that you communicated the ideas of your speech effectively and created a desire for further information. If you accept the philosophy expressed in this textbook, you will accept this statement as the most complimentary of the five.

Effective delivery is simple, natural, and unaffected. It reflects an earnest endeavor to communicate ideas. It is direct, communicative, and conversational, never exhibitionistic.

Effective Delivery Establishes Rapport with the Audience

Effective delivery consists of a two-way communication system. The speaker does all the talking out loud, but members of the audience talk back in their own minds. The speaker expresses ideas that set up responses in the minds of members of the audience. Each member of the audience adds to what the speaker says from his own experiences and knowledge. In short, the speaker directs the thinking of the audience.

A responding audience forgets about presentation techniques as it reacts to the speaker's ideas. The speaker forgets himself because he feels the response of the audience; he loses his anxiety because he stops thinking about himself and concentrates on his ideas. He uses bodily action in an endeavor to express himself adequately. He uses variety in force and rate according to the importance of the idea. In short, presentation techniques are motivated from a feeling within. A speaker uses skills naturally because he has established rapport with his audience.

Effective Delivery Controls and Utilizes Tensions

Effective delivery utilizes nervous energy; it puts tensions to constructive use. Almost all conscientious people feel some degree of nervous tension when facing an audience. Beginning speakers often testify that this feeling constitutes their most perplexing problem. Although experience in speaking tends to lessen the degree of tenseness, few speakers ever lose the feeling completely. Instead they learn to bring the feeling under control; they learn not to show the outward signs of tensions.

More important, they learn to put their tensions to constructive use. A feeling of anxiety increases a person's desire to do well. It, therefore, prods him to prepare adequately. It also causes him to be alert and energetic while speaking. It speeds up his thinking processes and causes him to become sensitive to audience reactions. The control of tensions receives detailed treatment in the following division.

II. Confidence and Poise

Tenseness before an audience has been discussed periodically since the time of the Classical rhetoricians. Volumes have been written about the subject without settling it, but an open discussion of tenseness helps most students; they learn that their feelings of anxiety are not abnormal.

Tenseness is usually more apparent to the speaker than to his audience. Excessive anxiety, reflected in signs apparent to an audience, may be termed stage fright. Students in speech classes taught over a twenty-year span were asked to indicate the degree of anxiety that they experienced while speaking. Their feelings ranged all the way from slight apprehension to extreme stage fright that prevented them from continuing. They were also asked to rate other class members on their poise and confidence. Almost without exception the students ranked themselves lower than did their classmates. Professor E. C. Buehler of the University of Kansas conducted a survey on positive and negative factors in effective speaking among 1,750 students in speech classes and 77 nationally known speech educators. The results showed that the students considered lack of self-confidence as a more serious problem than the teachers did. "The widest difference between experts and beginners occurs on 'self-confidence.' Experts rank it at the bottom of the scale, beginners rank it at the top." [1]

These and other studies indicate that beginning students tend to magnify the problem of anxiety out of proportion to its importance. That the problem is real cannot be disputed; that it produces the harmful results considered by some students must be questioned.

---

[1] E. C. Buehler, "Progress Report of Survey of Individual Attitudes and Concepts Concerning Elements Which Make for Effective Speaking." Mimeographed Report. University of Kansas, August, 1958. For details of study, see E. C. Buehler and Wil A. Linkugel, *Speech: A First Course* (New York: Harper and Row, Publishers, Inc., 1962), pp. 388-91.

The question arises, "Will taking speech courses help one overcome feelings of anxiety in speech-making?" Speech students answer yes. Of more than two thousand students surveyed over a twenty-year period, only four students felt that they experienced more tenseness after taking a course than before. The degree of improvement reported ranged from slight to almost complete control.

Ernest Henrikson of the University of Minnesota concluded, after a survey, that speech training tends to promote confidence both in and out of the classroom. Two hundred and five students were asked to indicate on a ten-point linear scale the degree of stage fright that they experienced in speaking. On the scale, *one* indicated no apprehensions; intensity of apprehension increased with each succeeding number, with *ten* denoting extreme stage fright. The students reported an average gain in confidence of 6.67 points on the scale as the result of a speech course extending over a quarter term. The students were also asked to indicate what they considered the reasons for their decrease in feelings of anxiety. Practice in speaking led the list, with 68.8 per cent listing this factor.[2]

Tenseness may be explained in part by the fact that most persons fear that which they do not understand. As a beginning student you realize that speech-making constitutes a complex process that you do not fully comprehend. Inasmuch as speech courses familiarize you with the process and give you an opportunity to practice before a sympathetic and critical audience, you may normally expect gains in self-confidence. This chapter considers tenseness from three standpoints—signs, causes, and controls.

Signs of Tenseness

Internal signs are reflected by rapid beating of the heart, dry lips and mouth, and discomfort in the stomach. In some cases a speaker may experience a lapse of memory that makes recall of his outline difficult.

External signs are indicated by excessive perspiration, fast breathing, twitching muscles, nervous swallowing, and a flushed face. These feelings may cause such mannerisms as shifting of the eyes, looking away from the audience, clasping and unclasping the hands, and unnatural variations in rate, pitch, and bodily actions.

Excessive apprehension may account in part for variations in

[2] Ernest Henrikson, "Some Effects of Stage Fright of a Course in Speech," *Quarterly Journal of Speech,* XXIX: 4 (December, 1943), pp. 490-91.

fluency as reflected by increases in rate, excessive use of "ers, ahs, and uhs," and a general reluctance to pause. Thus the timing of one's speaking may become affected, causing improper emphasis. The speaker may give the impression of racing through his speech to get it over with.

Undue anxiety may be reflected in the voice as indicated by unnaturally high pitch, lack of adequate volume, and breathlessness. Extreme cases may result in a tremble in the voice. In an attempt to prevent these signs from showing, some speakers force their voices, causing huskiness and hoarseness.

Signs of tenseness may be indicated by such mannerisms of bodily action as too formal posture, swaying body, shaking knees, trembling hands, excessive leaning on the lectern, aimless movements, or restless playing with a pencil or other article. To cover up these signs, some speakers assume an unnaturally slouchy posture. They may sit on the desk, slouch over the speaker's stand, rest their weight on one leg, or move aimlessly about with their hands in their pockets. In either extreme, the speaker focuses his attention on what he does rather than on what he says. The mannerisms described here may come from causes other than anxiety, but anxiety is often indicated by these signs.

Causes of Tenseness

Some psychologists and physiologists disagree on the causes of tensions. Usually tensions result from a multiplicity of causes, and perhaps no two people react in exactly the same way. In spite of the varying nature of apprehensions, certain causes can be isolated and explained. An understanding of the causes should precede attempts at control. Consider the following four causes.

1. *Some tenseness is a normal condition.* Tenseness is a normal, natural condition of many conscientious people. As a speaker, you realize the importance of directing the thinking of the members of your audience. You realize that the success of your speech depends largely upon your own ability. Psychologically, almost all people have a certain fear of failure and a desire for success. Directing the thinking of a group constitutes a high type of activity. Because of these factors you desire to succeed but may doubt whether you can measure up to your assignment. Capable people experience these normal reactions.

As a beginning student you may take heart from the story about a great singer who became unusually tense at an important performance. He stopped in the middle of his performance and said: "Yesterday ven I was in ze bath tub I zang zo gloriously I pat myself on ze back and zay, 'Oh, how I vish I vere on ze platform zinging.' Now zat I am on ze platform, I vish I vas back in ze bath tub." His audience laughed with him, and he felt more relaxed during the remainder of the concert.

Some tenseness is not only normal, but desirable. To relieve yourself entirely of apprehensions would deprive you of an important stimulant for your best efforts. Look upon it as nature's way of causing a person to be alert. One does better work under controlled emotional stress than when placid or unconcerned. Nevertheless, although tenseness may be normal, excessive nervousness manifested by outward signs mars speaking effectiveness.

2. *Excessive tensions may be caused in part by poor physical condition.* Poor physical condition may cause a person to become nervous while speaking. Lack of sleep, improper diet, and lack of physical exercise affect the nervous system. Persons who neglect their physical health decrease their chances of gaining control over their physical mechanism.

Busy people may put off preparing. Since they are not properly rested, they become nervous.

Persons with chronic poor health or physical exhaustion may brood over the seriousness of the speaking assignment and magnify it beyond its importance. Such people may have acquired physical habits that encourage tensions.

3. *Tensions may be caused in part by lack of proper preparation.* If you feel unsure of your material, fail to make adequate preparation, and neglect organizing your speech properly, you have reasons to be apprehensive. Feelings of uncertainty about your subject and preparation may well be the greatest causes of anxiety, especially if you consider your audience well informed on your subject. Poor choice of subject, shoddy preparation, and inadequate organization may build up tensions in experienced speakers; they most certainly will cause apprehensions for inexperienced speakers.

4. *Tensions may be partly psychological.* Anxiety may come from a general feeling of insufficiency or inferiority. Such feelings may be due to one or a combination of factors. The speaker who has a physical defect or ungainly appearance, whose economic condition has forced him into inferior environmental conditions, whose efforts

have been ridiculed, or whose social aspirations have been thwarted may have inadvertently developed feelings of inferiority. Some unpleasant experience or questionable action in his life may cause him to fear exposure. These feelings of inferiority may be carried over to the platform and cause him to show fear, or he may attempt to cover up his real feelings by an arrogant and blustering manner.

Outward signs of anxiety may be more apparent in some than in others. Some people do not believe sufficiently in themselves. They find trouble adjusting to any social situation and often feel inferior to people less capable than themselves. They find difficulty in adjusting to new situations. Since speech-making involves a complex activity, they doubt their ability to cope with its complexity and cannot cover up their feelings. Knowledge about speech-making and practice in the classroom help to allay these fears.

Control of Tenseness

The control of excessive tenseness must start with correcting the causes. Consider the following suggestions:

1. *Realize that tenseness is natural.* Students in speech classes often request conferences with their professors to discuss their problems of anxiety. Many of them seem disturbed and consider themselves abnormal because of their apprehensions. When the professor explains that their feelings are normal, they seem relieved. With many, this fact serves to start them on the road to control of their tensions.

Like these students, you must accept your tensions as normal for many beginning speakers. Try first to control only the outward signs of tenseness; then as you gain more experience in speaking and greater understanding of the process, your feelings of anxiety will become less severe. Consider tenseness as a matter to be controlled, not eliminated.

2. *Realize that excessive tenseness can be brought under control.* Sometimes students who request conferences with their professors report that they still feel apprehensive after the second or third speech in class. They seem impatient with the slowness of their progress and want results immediately. Unfortunately, a program for bringing tensions under control may be a slow and tedious process. It can be done, but it takes time and effort. If you expect miracles from your course in speech, you are likely to be disappointed. With some the progress may be so slow as to be hardly perceptible; others

make rapid progress. Above all, keep trying. Look upon each new assignment as an opportunity to progress toward your goal of complete control.

Many professors can look with pride on the progress made by some of their students. On his first speaking assignment, one student became so nervous that he could not finish. He asked to try again before the class period ended and this time managed to stumble through, but without distinction. On succeeding assignments he always asked to be first and welcomed each opportunity to participate. He later joined the forensic group, where he made such progress that during his senior year he won the award as the outstanding debater. At the annual banquet concluding the forensic year he stated, "When I first started taking speech, I could hardly talk for shaking. Now after taking ten courses, I have learned to talk while shaking." A student who can look on the humorous side of the problem has a better chance for progress than one who takes the matter too seriously. Professors sometimes make an assignment to determine which student can appear more nervous. Unfortunately some students do not have to act, but the assignment gives the class an opportunity to look upon the lighter side of the problem.

Many great speakers and performers of history have testified to extreme stage fright. In the Classical period Demosthenes and Cicero wrote of their efforts to overcome excessive tensions. Such outstanding speakers as Disraeli, Daniel Webster, Abraham Lincoln, Booth Tarkington, Eleanor Roosevelt, and Booker T. Washington have discussed their apprehensions in print. William Jennings Bryan refused to eat before important speaking assignments for fear his anxiety would make him ill. Lily Pons, Madame Schumann-Heink, and Eva Le Gallienne have written of their tenseness at public performances. All these outstanding people and others had one thing in common—they put their tensions to constructive use as they brought their apprehensions under control.

3. *Prepare thoroughly.* The realization that you know your subject well increases your feelings that you can give your audience properly appraised facts and mature judgments. You feel confident because of superior understanding.

The processes of preparation form the subject matter of Chapters 4 through 9. The application of these processes also affects your feelings of confidence, for you know you have prepared properly. A program of preparation starts with an analysis of your audience and the speaking occasion. An awareness that you conform properly to the occasion gives you a feeling of social well-being. Knowledge about an audience assures you that you will communicate in terms that your listeners understand. Such knowledge tends to build up your confidence.

Your choice of subject also affects your self-confidence. You will be more confident if you discuss subjects from your experience and background of knowledge than if you speak on subjects developed entirely from research. Familiar subjects give you an inner feeling of confidence of your ability to appraise them intelligently.

Do not confuse time spent and time spent properly in preparing a speech. Proper preparation consists of more than spending many hours in forced preparation. The best preparation comes from thinking through your subject at varying times when ideas occur. The longer you think about your subject, do research on it, and discuss your ideas with others, the more confident you will become of yourself. When the idea of your speech evolves, it becomes a part of you. You no longer fear that you may forget your speech, for the outline has become mental as well as written.

In developing your subject, observe the following steps: (1) think the ideas through and form a tentative outline; (2) do research to correct original impressions and to gain factual information; (3) revise your original plans in keeping with your investigation; (4) think through your outline and practice your speech. Through careful preparation you help develop a feeling of self-confidence.

4. *Keep physically fit.* College students who put off studying an assignment and then neglect their sleep in last-minute preparation may increase their tensions. Making speeches is hard work; it burns up more energy than manual labor for some people. When confronted with the increased emotional strain of speaking under conditions of physical fatigue, the result may be stage fright. Prepare your speech sufficiently in advance of its delivery to permit proper rest.

Relaxation aids in maintaining proper physical condition. Overtensed muscles may cause uncontrollable shaking of hands and knees. If you feel yourself stiffen, attempt to relax by conscious effort; take several deep breaths, put the weight of your body on your heels, or lean your weight on the table or lectern. If you tend to become excessively nervous, attempt to keep physically fit and rested; take time out for rest and recreation; refrain from brooding over your assignment.

5. *Adopt a success attitude.* If you feel a lack of confidence in

yourself, try giving yourself a mental pep-talk occasionally. Think in terms of success, not failure. Concentrate on those speaking occasions when you did well, not on those when you felt that you had failed. Think of pleasant experiences, not unpleasant ones. You cannot experience opposite types of emotional reactions at the same time. Thinking in terms of success helps overcome feelings of inferiority.

As you await your turn to speak, focus your attention on your subject matter, not on yourself; think through your outline, not about what impression you may make. Instead of thinking, "How am I doing?" say to yourself, "This subject is important and needs to be discussed. I have prepared my subject thoroughly and can get my point of view understood and accepted." For speeches outside the classroom, remember that you have earned the right to speak; otherwise you would not have been selected.

Attempt to get a physical response from your audience early in your speech. The response may be laughter at an amusing story, applause for a striking statement, or nods of approval for statements with which the audience agrees. Once you feel the response of an audience, you will concentrate on what you have to say and forget to think about yourself. Thus you will bring your tensions under control without being aware that you have done so.

III. Acquiring Proper Stage Conduct

Students sometimes ask how they should conduct themselves at speaking occasions. Are there any rules of etiquette peculiar to the speaking situation? Perhaps the best advice consists of following the customs of courtesy applicable in any social situation. The following discussion considers some of the factors applicable to situations of oral communication.

Before the Speech

Proper stage conduct begins before you speak. It consists of the way you look and act. Initial appearances may go far toward creating the proper atmosphere for your talk. They cause an audience to form impressions of you as a person, and thus affect the reception of your ideas. Consider the following:

1. *Dress appropriately for the occasion.* Avoid affectations in

manner and dress for speaking occasions. Dress conservatively and in good taste to avoid calling attention to yourself. A dark suit, white shirt, dark tie and socks, and well-shined black shoes serve men best. For formal occasions, wear a tuxedo or formal dress suit. Women should avoid excessive make-up, too much jewelry, and clothing or ornament that detracts from what they talk about. Good taste in dress and grooming indicates a person whose evaluations can be trusted. Appropriate dress, therefore, helps you to get off to a good start.

Appropriate dress also affects your self-confidence. We may be amused at the lady who buys a new hat to boost her morale, but it often has that effect. A well-groomed appearance gives a feeling of well-being that helps you forget your apprehensions.

2. *Be punctual for your engagement.* If possible, arrive at the meeting place a few minutes before the time set for the program so that you can meet the chairman, receive instructions, look over the meeting hall, note the type of lectern, check the public-address system, and inquire about the acoustics of the auditorium. In instances where the speaking conditions vary greatly from those you anticipated, a new cause for tension arises. By arriving early, you have time to allay your anxieties by changing your plans to meet the changed conditions.

You show discourtesy by keeping an audience waiting past time for the meeting. Late arrival without good cause indicates disrespect and will be so interpreted by many people. It indicates an arrogant attitude that does much to decrease your appeal. Show proper respect for your audience by being punctual and friendly.

3. *Be pleasant and businesslike as you await your turn to speak.* On some occasions the program participants are seated on the platform as the audience gathers. In most cases they are ushered to the stage after the audience assembles. The chairman usually assigns the seats in advance and leads the procession to the stage. The program participants follow in order, the main speaker immediately after the chairman. Upon reaching the platform, the chairman steps aside to let others be seated. He then takes his place behind the speaker's stand and starts the program.

While waiting your turn to speak, do not call attention to yourself by the way you sit or act. Attempt to avoid appearing ill at ease or self-conscious. If you sit rigidly with both feet planted firmly together on the floor, you appear as unnatural as if you slump in your chair. Strive to maintain a natural position, somewhat between these two extremes.

Avoid engaging others in conversation, reviewing notes, or looking away from the proceedings. Although you may desire to think through your outline as you sit on the platform, do nothing that will attract undue attention.

During the Speech

Many students encounter difficulty in getting started. Unfortunately, your listeners form more impressions of you during the first few minutes than they do later in the speech. Getting off to a good start also affects your poise and self-confidence. If you feel an audience respond early in your speech, you tend to lose your feelings of apprehension as you gain interest in your subject. Consider the following suggestions:

1. *Use deliberation in beginning.* Upon being introduced, rise slowly and walk to the speaker's stand with a firm step, an erect body, a pleasant expression, and a direct and assuring look at your audience. If you slouch up to the speaker's stand, you may give the impression that your speech will be as listless as your walk. If you look away from your audience, you announce that you are sure of neither yourself, your material, nor your desire at the moment. Conversely, do not leap from your chair and charge to the stand like a warrior to battle. Your audience will be likely to conclude that you are apprehensive. Either extreme in approaching the speaker's stand calls attention to itself and causes unfavorable impressions.

Upon taking your position at the speaker's stand, pause momentarily before beginning your speech. Arrange your notes on the lectern, adjust the microphone, or put your watch on the table. A brief pause causes your audience to turn their attention from their thoughts of the moment and to polarize their attention on you. Sometimes speakers start talking before an audience is ready to listen. This condition is likely to happen if you start speaking as you walk to the speaker's stand. Show deliberation in beginning your speech.

2. *Use the public-address system provided.* Thirty years ago many speakers prided themselves that their powerful voices could rattle the back rows. A common technique of such speakers was to ask, "Can you hear me back there in the rear?" Then they beamed with pride because they already knew the answer. No longer must we put

such a premium on volume alone; the public-address system has come to the rescue of those whose voices have less volume. Almost all auditoriums today have public-address systems. Although you think that you can be heard without the loud-speaker, use it if one has been provided; you may overestimate the force of your voice. Furthermore, those making the arrangements may be offended if you refuse to use the equipment.

Most microphones for public-address systems are permanently fixed behind the speaker's stand. For effective use of the loud-speaker, stand directly behind the lectern and vary your position but slightly. If you move from one side of the speaker's stand to the other, you will cause annoying variations in volume. Speak at your normal volume with only slight variations; the amplifier will increase the volume so that all can hear. Avoid sharp increases in volume to prevent a blasting sound in the amplifier. The public-address system is invaluable for maintaining a conversational and communicative manner.

3. *Use an informal salutation.* Students often ask, "Whom should I address in beginning my speech?" The procedure varies with the formality of the occasion and the manner of the speaker. For informal occasions before small audiences, no verbal salutation may be needed. To give a long formal salutation would appear ludicrous. Begin with a friendly smile and nod to your audience or express appreciation to the person introducing you or to the audience for inviting you.

On ceremonial occasions that call for speeches, such as dedications, anniversaries, or tributes, a brief formal salutation will suffice. To illustrate, Franklin D. Roosevelt used the following salutation at his first Inaugural Address on March 4, 1933: "President Hoover, Mr. Chief Justice, My friends." Dwight D. Eisenhower said simply, "My friends," at his first Inaugural Address. When Adlai Stevenson accepted the Democratic nomination for the Presidency in 1952, he began: "Mr. President, Ladies and Gentlemen of the Convention, my fellow Citizens."

During the period of elocution, elaborate salutations followed the ornate, stylistic trends in speech-making. Speakers included long lists of dignitaries and their titles. Today's informal, conversational type of speaking makes such formal salutations appear out of place. If a salutation seems necessary, the traditional "Mr. Chairman, Ladies and Gentlemen" can hardly be improved upon.

4. *Be direct and enthusiastic.* Physical directness and enthusiasm indicate respect for your listeners. Look directly at your audience; include the entire audience in your vision; be pleasant and enthusiastic in your opening remarks.

Your face indicates attitudes almost as much as your words do. If you have cordial feelings toward your listeners and an interest in your subject, such feelings will be evident unless you experience undue anxiety. The insincerity of the fixed smile of professional good will, the arrogant attitude, and the bored feeling cannot be easily camouflaged. Show your enthusiasm, sincerity, and interest by a friendly smile and a pleasant manner.

Often speakers let their notes interfere with their directness of presentation. They begin by looking at their notes and refuse to look at the audience; they appear to speak at their notes, not to their audience. You cannot project to your audience properly if you focus your attention on your notes. You give the impression that you are more interested in your material than in your audience.

Notes may serve a useful purpose if used properly. They relieve you of the necessity of committing to memory the sequence of ideas, lengthy quotations, and statistical information. They also may allay your fears of forgetting. Once you get audience interest, you can make brief references to your notes without breaking eye contact with your listeners. Do not use your notes as a substitute for looking at your audience.

5. *Comply with the instructions for the occasion.* Some programs feature several speakers on different phases of a subject. Usually those who arrange the program divide the subject to permit a logical development and to avoid duplication. You should understand the part assigned you and avoid discussing those phases of the subject assigned to other speakers. Hardly anything can be more provoking to a speaker than to have his topic discussed by a previous speaker. You can help prevent this situation from happening by understanding the plans for the division of topics.

A speaker shows poor taste by ignoring the time limit for his speech. At a convention program the adjournment hour came, with one thirty-minute speech yet to go. One speaker, impressed with the sound of his own voice, used double his assigned time. Fortunately, the last speaker sensed the situation, cut his speech to five minutes, and released the audience. An audience at a commencement program was not so fortunate. The principal speaker was given thirty minutes but took an hour. Since other parts of the program could not be omitted, the audience had to remain overtime. Such speakers apparently attempt to stake their claim for immortality by going on interminably. The spirit of a well-planned program can be ruined by failure to conform to instructions.

After the Speech

Certain amenities prevail as you conclude your speech and at the end of the program. Observing them helps you clinch a good impression. Consider the following:

1. *Conclude your speech with force and poise.* End your speech with force and poise; do not simply let it die a natural death. A student, when asked his opinion of a speech, said, "The speech was fine, but the speaker passed up several excellent opportunities to stop." Some speakers seem unable either to quit or to add to the subject; like Old Man River they just keep rolling along. Do not give your audience a false lead by saying "in conclusion" unless you are going to conclude. One speaker started a series of "in conclusions" fifteen minutes before he finally made good on his promise. If you organize your speech properly, the audience will sense when you near the end. The term "in conclusion" is rarely necessary; but if you use it, mean it. Simply summarize, state your appeal, and stop.

After concluding, return to your chair in the same businesslike manner in which you approached the speaker's stand. Do not use the last fraction of time allotted you to grab your notes and mumble "I thank you" as you rush from the stand. If you finish falteringly, you may destroy whatever good impression you have made. To clinch your idea with force, summarize, pause momentarily, show a pleasant expression, and walk back to your chair with poise, a firm step, and an erect body.

2. *Participate willingly in the question-and-answer period.* Some speaking occasions include an open forum in which members of the audience ask questions and make comments. These informal periods provide an excellent opportunity for the speaker to improve speaker-audience relationships and thus to increase the audience's estimation of the value of his talk. Attempt to determine in advance if the program includes an open forum; but if the forum develops at the last minute, accept the assignment willingly and with poise.

If the program includes an open forum, the last speaker should return the meeting to the chairman following his speech and let him start it. He will probably comment on the speeches, ask the first question, and then ask for questions from the audience. After a question or two, he may step aside and permit members of the audience to direct their questions to the speakers.

Do not use the question-and-answer period as an occasion for further speech-making. Answer questions briefly and to the point. If you do not know the answer to a question, state that you do not know, frankly and without hesitation. You cannot be expected to answer all questions about your subject, especially questions of fact. On opinion questions, you may want to give tentative or qualified answers. Do not attempt to deceive an audience into believing you know the answers to questions when you do not. They will respect your integrity.

By your manner encourage members of your audience to ask questions. Never belittle a questioner for asking trivial questions if he shows seriousness of purpose. If a person asks heckling or patronizing questions, you may be justified in answering in kind. A spirit of lively exchange and friendliness makes for successful open forums.

Do not drag out the question-and-answer period beyond time for adjournment. After a brief expression of appreciation to the audience, return the meeting to the chairman and resume your chair.

3. *Remain after the speech to accept felicitations and answer questions.* Do not hurry from the meeting hall after your speech without giving members of the audience an opportunity to congratulate you and ask further questions. Speaking situations are looked upon as social occasions in some places, especially in small communities, with you as the honored guest. In the interest of good public relations make yourself available for conversation as long as members of your audience remain.

IV. Summary

This first chapter in Part Three introduces the subject of effective delivery—the means of communicating your finished speech orally. Training in the principles and practices of effective delivery is necessary to complete the processes of oral communication.

The basic principles of delivery stress that effective delivery (1) utilizes the whole man, (2) uses both visual and auditory means,

(3) considers the total speaking situation, (4) communicates ideas without calling attention to techniques, (5) establishes rapport with the audience, and (6) controls and utilizes tensions.

To establish poise and confidence, attempt to bring your tensions under control. Almost all speakers experience anxiety in facing an audience. Excessive anxiety is termed stage fright. The signs of stage fright are both internal and external. Tenseness is (1) partly a normal condition, (2) partly a result of poor physical condition, (3) partly a result of lack of proper preparation, and (4) partly psychological.

To control tensions (1) realize that tenseness is natural, (2) realize that excessive tenseness can be controlled, (3) prepare thoroughly, (4) keep physically fit, and (5) adopt a success attitude.

The speaker observes proper stage conduct before, during, and after the speech. Before the speech, he makes a good impression with appropriate dress, punctuality, and a pleasant and businesslike attitude while waiting to speak. During the speech he uses deliberation in beginning, uses the public-address system effectively, uses an informal salutation, is direct and enthusiastic, and complies with the instructions for the occasion. Following the talk, he concludes with force and poise, participates willingly in the question-and-answer period, and remains after his speech to answer questions.

Questions and Exercises

A. Answer the following questions on Chapter 10.

1. Explain effective delivery as it applies to the total process of oral communication.
2. Can delivery skills be acquired? Explain your answer.
3. What does the statement, "Effective delivery utilizes the whole man," mean? Do you think it possible for a person to be an effective speaker without being a capable person? Explain and defend your answer.
4. How does a speaker express his ideas, attitudes, and emotions? Are you more likely to form opinions of a person's emotional state by what he says or by how he acts? Explain.
5. Explain the statement, "True art conceals itself." How does this principle apply to effective delivery?
6. What is meant by establishing rapport with an audience?
7. Define and explain some signs of stage fright. Do you think it possible to eliminate all feelings of anxiety in facing an audience? What benefits may accrue from controlled apprehensions?
8. List and discuss some causes of stage fright. Can you add to the list

discussed in this chapter? Which cause do you consider the most important?

9. Outline a program that will help one cope with his apprehensions. Can you add to the suggestions discussed in this chapter?
10. Discuss several factors of etiquette and stage conduct that you should consider prior to your speech. How does appropriate dress affect a speaker?
11. What factors of stage conduct should you consider during your speech? Give some precautions for using a public-address system.
12. What amenities prevail at a speaking occasion after you finish your speech? List some advantages of a forceful conclusion.

B. For your tenth speaking assignment you will use a microphone. The instructor will record a part of your speech and play it back to the class at a future session. Observe the following instructions.

1. Prepare an incident speech on the theme of overcoming fear or using fear for constructive purposes. The incident may be either a personal experience or one that you have read or heard. The following specific topics are suggestions only.
   a. A narrow escape
   b. My most harrowing experience
   c. The time I almost drowned
   d. Caught in a snow storm
   e. Lost in the mountains
   f. My near accident
   g. My first speech
   h. Called on the carpet
   i. Hunting big game
   j. Getting my first job
   k. My conference with the boss
   l. How overcoming fear helped shape history
   m. An incident in the life of a great man or woman
2. Take notes on your instructor's criticisms and consider them as he plays your recording.
3. Make the incident you relate interesting and dynamic. Use some of the elements of interest discussed in Chapter 7.
4. Try to give this speech without notes. You may have notes, but use them only if necessary. Keep them in your pocket or face down on the speaker's stand.
5. Limit your speech to five minutes.

C. After presenting the above speech, rate your degree of confidence, using the discussion in this chapter as a basis. Give yourself a number from "one to ten" on a continuum scale in which ten denotes such stage fright that you could not complete your speech and one indicates an absence of apprehensions. To illustrate, if you experienced considerable anxiety but were able to finish, rate yourself between seven and nine. If you experienced average anxiety, rate yourself five or six. If you felt confident but not completely at ease, rate yourself three or four. If you were hardly aware of anxiety, rate yourself one or two.

1. Your instructor will ask each member of the class to rate you on self-confidence, using the same scale. Average the ratings of your class members and compare their ratings with yours.
2. Make a list of the signs of anxiety that you experienced while speaking.
3. Review the section of this chapter on causes for anxiety. Which cause or causes do you think apply to you?
4. After reviewing the section in this chapter on how to cope with anxiety, outline a program of future action for yourself.

CHAPTER 11

Use Language Accurately and Effectively

One student asked his roommate, "Did you hear the speaker last night?" His roommate replied, "Yes, I heard him; now I am trying to decide what he meant." To be heard does not necessarily mean to be understood. Language serves to convey thought: it has no end within itself. If you use language to convey information, ideas, and feelings accurately to others, you use language effectively. If you use language to confuse or simply to impress your listeners, you do not use language to serve its purpose.

A properly organized speech is a prerequisite to effective oral communication. Careful organization, however, is not enough. To communicate your ideas, you must develop your outline with simple, understandable language. For language to accomplish its maximum usefulness, it must express your ideas precisely and accurately. Furthermore, as a speaker you have an obligation not to mislead your audience by manipulating words, because you can use words to give improper evaluations as easily as to evaluate ideas accurately.

How can you develop your use of language so that it will realize maximum usefulness? Consider two approaches: (1) the general semantics approach—using language that accurately represents what it is supposed to represent; (2) the rhetorical approach—using language that conforms to acceptable standards of grammatical construction, word choice, and structure. Both approaches must be considered if you wish to develop effective use of language.

What happens if you master one approach without the other? Consider these examples. While an uneducated man awaited his turn in the doctor's reception room, the doctor came by and said to him, "How is the treatment going, Sam? Do you feel any better?" Sam responded, "Yes, doc, I are feelin' some better. I was afraid it wouldn't work. I had went too long before doin' nothing. I jest trust the Lord and come to you and now I think I git well." Sam's rhetorical skills left much to be desired, but he apparently gave an accurate account of how he felt.

Contrast Sam's effort to communicate with Peter's: "Chicago, the largest and most picturesque city in America, lies peacefully on the shores of the blue Danube two hundred miles south of Moscow." Peter's rhetorical efforts far exceeded Sam's, but he talked nonsense, pure gibberish. In fact, one can talk nonsense with as much rhetorical skill as one uses to express mature thoughts. Rhetorical principles contain no built-in features that distinguish gibberish from profound pronouncements. We must go outside the principles of rhetoric to attain accurate evaluation.

I. General Semantics Approach

Have you ever thought of how much of your life you spend associating with words? The average American spends more than seventy per cent of his waking hours using words, either speaking and writing or listening and reading. College students spend from twelve to fourteen hours per day communicating. *Webster's Third New International Dictionary* contains some 550,000 words, but the average person uses only a few of them. In the words of Professors Mawhinney and Smith, "There is little doubt that English has the richest vocabulary of any language. Yet the average American uses a vocabulary of about 3,000 words, a businessman uses about 8,000 words, and a professional person uses about 20,000 words." [1]

In view of the vast number of words, we should be able to express ourselves more effectively. Why don't we? First, we do not develop an adequate vocabulary. Second, we do not develop our ability to use language accurately and understandably. As a result, we fail in day-to-day personal relationships, conferences break down and fail to solve problems, written reports do not present information accurately, and formal speeches do not get results.

What can we do to improve our use of language? The rhetorician and the general semanticist each has much to offer. The rhetorical

[1] Clara Krefting Mawhinney and Harley A. Smith, *Business and Professional Speech* (New York: American Book Co., 1950), p. 51.

approach to language relates to the style of speaking and writing. It considers the skills employed in using language effectively so that the communicator avoids errors in composition and presentation. General semantics is a study in how to talk accurately, how to fit words to actual things, how to eliminate language habits which lead to confusion and misunderstanding, or how to talk sense. The late Irving J. Lee of Northwestern University said,

> It [general semantics] has to do with whether or not what a speaker says properly evaluates the situation to which he refers; whether or not what he says is an adequate representation of the actual facts or happenings of which he speaks, . . . with the whole process whereby men in speaking evaluate properly the happenings, objects, feelings, labels, descriptions, and inferences with which they are dealing.[2]

Consider the following suggestions from the general semanticist.

Consider Words as Symbols

Irving J. Lee said, "We live in two worlds which must not be confused, a world of words, and a world of not-words." [3] The words in our "world of words" are merely symbols by which we may talk about things in our "world of not-words." Words are not the things themselves.

Words have denotative meanings which include all that strictly belong to the definitions of the words. They also have connotative meanings which include all the ideas that are suggested by the words. Thus, the denotative meaning of a university includes "An institution organized for teaching and study. . . ."; the connotative meaning may suggest football games, bull sessions, and dances. Words are merely symbols by which we talk about things, regardless of people's interpretations of those symbols. To avoid confusion, we must realize that people do add their own connotations to those symbols.

Confusion arises when we consider that certain words may not have the same meaning to our listeners as they have to us. Our understanding of words is affected by our experiences with the things that they represent. There is nothing in words to differentiate the varying experiences that people have with the things that words represent.

---

[2] Irving J. Lee, "General Semantics and Public Speaking," *Quarterly Journal of Speech,* XXVI (December, 1940), 597.

[3] Irving J. Lee, *Language Habits in Human Affairs* (New York: Harper & Row, Publishers, Inc., 1941), p. 16.

Professor Andrew T. Weaver, formerly Professor of Speech at the University of Wisconsin at Madison, states the matter aptly,

> Satisfactory communication is more rare than we realize. We naively assume that, since what we say is clear to us, it therefore will be equally clear to others. We fail to comprehend the fact that the speech signs we make have to be filtered through the nervous systems of other persons, on their way to minds made up of experiences different from our own.[4]

A middle-aged man related an incident of how, as a child, he became ill when he slipped into his mother's pantry and ate an entire box of shredded coconut. He reported that forty years later he still became almost nauseated when he so much as heard the word coconut. Yet to most people the word recalls pleasant associations—delicious pies, cakes, and salads.

An army officer related an incident in which several officers' wives from the South were driven to an army post each week for their club meeting by a personable young private from the station motor pool. Since he drove several officers' wives on the same trip, one lady rode in the front seat with him and enjoyed engaging him in conversation. That is, she did until she learned that the driver was part Negro. Then she refused to ride in the front seat with him any more. She reacted favorably to the young man as a person, but she so reacted to the word which labeled him that her actions were affected.

A lady complimented her hostess on the delicious chicken which she served for dinner. Upon being told that she had not eaten chicken at all, but rather that she had eaten frogs' legs, the lady reacted so unfavorably that she became physically ill.

In short, confusion arises when we fail to distinguish between things and the words we call those things. Consider words as symbols, as ways of representing things much as maps represent the terrain. The listener must realize that the speaker may not use terms as he understands them. The speaker must recognize that listeners may not receive his ideas as he has them in mind. Both must realize that words are not things but are symbols for representing things.

Locate the Level of Talk

High-level words cause confusion because they may be interpreted in many ways. Low-level words have specific meaning because they

[4] Goodwin F. Berquest, Jr., ed., *Speeches for Illustration and Example* (Chicago: Scott, Foresman and Co., 1965), p. 5. By permission of *Vital Speeches of the Day* (Feb. 1, 1961).

refer to objects and events. For example, suppose that a speaker states, "All criminals should be electrocuted." What exactly did he mean by the word *criminal?* A criminal means anyone guilty of a crime, and a crime is any act forbidden by statute or contrary to the public welfare and punishable by law. Crimes may be classified broadly as felony or misdemeanor. Felony refers to the major crimes such as murder, armed robbery, arson, and rape; a misdemeanor refers to less serious crimes. *Felony* and *misdemeanor* are, therefore, more specific words than *crime.* If the speaker meant that all persons guilty of a felony should be electrocuted, he will get agreement more readily than if he meant those guilty of a misdemeanor. The word *murder,* as a type of felony, is more specific than the word *felony;* yet there are types of murder. Some states classify murder as first, second, and third degree. First degree murder consists of premeditated acts with malice aforethought. Second degree murder consists of killings without premeditation, on the spur of the moment. Third degree murder means unintentional killings without malice. The term *first degree murder* is, therefore, a lower-level word than *felony.* Did the speaker mean that all persons who committed first degree murder should be electrocuted?

Misdemeanors also constitute crimes, and traffic violations are misdemeanors. Did the speaker mean that you should be electrocuted because you ran a red light? In fact, we do not know what he meant. But we do know that if the speaker was thinking "first degree murder" and the listener was thinking "traffic violation" when the speaker said, "All criminals should be electrocuted," the listener will consider the speaker a very stupid fellow.

Suppose the speaker says, "Religious people are narrow-minded." Did he mean Christians, Mohammedans, Buddhists, or others? If he meant Christians, did he mean Catholics or Protestants? If he meant Protestants, did he mean Baptists, Methodists, Presbyterians, or others? If he meant Baptists, did he mean Southern Baptists, Northern Baptists, Negro Baptists, or another branch of Baptists? If he meant Southern Baptists, did he mean Orthodox Baptists, Fundamentalists, or hard-shell Baptists? If he meant Orthodox Baptists, did he mean the Baptists in Birmingham, Dallas, Atlanta, or some other place? If he meant the Orthodox Baptists in Birmingham, did he mean John Doe, Peter Poe, Richard Roe, or whom? In fact, John Doe, Peter Poe, and Richard Roe may all be narrow-minded, religious people, but their being so does not necessarily mean that all religious people are.

To be sure, we cannot avoid using high-level terms, but as listeners we can realize that when a speaker uses high-level terms he may not mean what we think he means. As speakers, we can seek specific rather than general terms; but if we must use general terms, we must realize that listeners may think at one level while we talk at another. The simple realization of the levels of talk should minimize confusion and misunderstandings occasioned by communication.

Locate the Time to Which You Refer

The things we talk about change rapidly; the words we use to talk about changing things remain static. The chair in which you sit is not the same today that it was last year, and it will be much different when you come back to the home-coming celebrations twenty years hence. Things change, but words may not indicate the change.

A middle-aged man related an incident of how he returned to his boyhood home after thirty years' absence. He remembered his boyhood home as a large, white castle that sat upon a hill in the suburbs of the city. What he saw thirty years later was a large, dilapidated rooming house in the middle of an industrial district. The house had changed considerably in thirty years; the words *boyhood home* had not changed at all. *Boyhood home* (1935) did not mean the same as *boyhood home* (1965).

Students in a speech class were asked to characterize Clarence Darrow. Their comments included such descriptions: "a famous criminal lawyer," "a champion of the little man," "a liberal," "one who hated capital punishment," "an atheist." The professor then characterized him as "a corporation lawyer of renown," "a champion of large corporations," "a conservative," "one who was little concerned with capital punishment or religious beliefs." Who characterized Darrow correctly, the students or the professor? In fact, both the students and the professor gave accurate evaluations, but they were thinking of different periods in the life of Darrow. Darrow (1890) was a corporation lawyer who represented the Chicago and Northwestern Railway Company; the professor was thinking of that period. The students were thinking of Darrow (1925). The man Darrow changed much in thirty-five years, but his name did not change.

If a speaker refers to Sigmund Freud's theories of psychoanalysis, you should ask yourself, "Of what period does he speak?" Freud's theories of psychoanalysis changed from his early to his later writings. If a speaker talks about "principles of speech training," does he refer to the ornate, stylistic principles taught in schools of elocution in 1870 or to the direct, communicative principles taught today?

When we wish to use words which in themselves do not indicate change with time, we must be careful to use other words that will refer to the time of which we are speaking. Thereby we help prevent confusion and misunderstanding.

Be Aware of Abstracting

We cannot talk about all aspects of anything. We abstract and use some of the details and omit others. Writers of history must select certain events and omit others. To write a complete history would be impossible.

Can two people testify honestly but differently about an automobile accident which they witnessed? Court trials indicate almost daily that people do. You cannot see all the details of an accident. What you see depends upon when you start looking, where you stood when you looked, and what part of the whole commanded your attention. If you saw the cars approach the intersection, you probably witnessed more of the details than if the impact of the crash attracted your attention. You probably saw more of the details if you stood on the street corner where the crash occurred than if you were a half block away. Your testimony will reflect the details you abstracted from the almost infinite number of details that occurred.

Some three hundred organized religious groups exist in the United States, consisting of religions, denominations, and sects. Does any one of these groups include all the details about religious beliefs in their creeds and doctrines? Each uses a number of the total of religious beliefs and omits others.

Lincoln characterized our form of government as being "of the people, by the people, for the people." It is that and more too. A dictionary defines democracy as a "government in which the supreme power is retained by the people and exercised either directly or indirectly through a system of representation." That definition gives us the most pertinent details of democracy, but it does not give us all the many finer details.

Not only do we abstract from the total of what could be said about a subject when we talk, but we must also remember that the listener is also abstracting selectively from the various possible meanings of our words. Although the general meaning and detailed meanings of the term *labor union* are known to both the laborer and the contractor, each, on hearing the term, may abstract those details for consideration which fit in with his viewpoint. In the same way, the overseas veteran may abstract a set of detailed meanings from the word *war* quite different from those selected by the defense-plant worker. What a speaker talks about sets up varying trains of thought in the minds of his listeners. They abstract from the total of what the speaker says or from the total meanings of words according to their interests and experiences.

Some people are more receptive and at the same time more discriminating than others. They have inquiring minds and an interest in ideas. These people are able to grasp total meanings, and they are also able to recognize when and why a speaker has abstracted details.

In brief, both speakers and listeners should realize the impossibility of one's saying all that could be said about anything. All communication consists of abstracting some details and omitting the others. A consciousness of abstracting serves to minimize confusion and misunderstanding and thereby aids proper evaluation.

Professors Gray and Wise, Professors Emeritus at Louisiana State University, state,

> Abstractions are unavoidable in the use of language. . . . What is important is that in our use of words we should be conscious of the fact that they are abstractions. . . . Unless we are especially conscious of how far we have gone in our abstracting . . . our language will be meaningless, even to ourselves.[5]

In summary, in choosing language we should first be sure that our words convey our ideas accurately. To help achieve this goal we must consider words as symbols, locate the level at which we talk, consider the time of which we are speaking, and be aware that we are abstracting some details and omitting others.

II. Rhetorical Approach

Although accurate use of language comes first, the effective use of language also aids communication. You will go far toward getting

[5] Giles Wilkeson Gray and Claude Merton Wise, *The Bases of Speech*, 3rd ed. (New York: Harper and Brothers, 1959), p. 507.

your ideas accepted by choosing clear, understandable, and vivid language. Choose language to communicate clearly and precisely, not to display your vocabulary. Like other phases of rhetorical principles, language is for communication, not exhibition.

Oral style is more informal, repetitious, and direct than written style. A writer has time to edit his manuscript, to choose among many words and phrases. A reader may turn back the pages and reread ideas not immediately clear. Not so with the speaker and listener; the extemporaneous speaker chooses his language as he speaks; the listener either comprehends instantaneously or loses the speaker's idea.

What characterizes effective oral style? Language should be clear, appropriate, vivid, and free from affectations.

Oral Language Should Be Clear

Above all, language should be clear and unambiguous. An adequate command of language enables a speaker to choose from the many ways of expressing an idea the one way which expresses his thoughts with greatest precision. Consider the following factors for achieving clarity.

1. *Use specific language.* Specific terms convey meaning with greater clarity than do general terms. They aid the speaker in saying precisely what he means and thus in decreasing misunderstanding. Consider the word *communications* in the sentence "I am taking a course in communications." The term *oral communication* is more specific than *communications* because it distinguishes oral from all other methods of communication. Oral communication includes several divisions of study such as public address, interpretation, radio and television, speech correction, and acting. Public address encompasses many courses such as rhetoric, public speaking, discussion, debate, and persuasion. Rhetoric may be divided as classical, medieval, and contemporary. Specificity is achieved, therefore, in inverse order as discussed above: (1) classical rhetoric, (2) rhetoric, (3) public address, (4) oral communication, and (5) communications.

The *chemistry building* is more specific than the *classroom building*, but the *classroom building* is more specific than the *campus building*. *Dog* is more specific than *mammal*, but *mammal* is more specific than *animal*. *Debate* is more specific than *forensics*, but *forensics* is more specific than *extracurricular activities*. *Los Angeles* is more specific than *California,* but *California* is more specific than the *West Coast. He stole my watch* is more specific than *he robbed me,* but *he robbed me* is more specific than *he is a thief.* Abstract terms may be useful for expressing general principles, but specific terms help achieve clarity and avoid misunderstanding.

2. *Use simple words.* If you accept the principle that "speech is for communication, not exhibition," you will understand the value of using language understandable to your listeners. Children first learn simple words to express their wants. Through long association, these words remain more meaningful than those learned later in life. Some speakers seem to think that big words indicate a mastery of language and profound ideas. Actually, knowledge of a limited number of big words indicates less mastery of language than a thorough knowledge of simple words.

Big words increase the chances of misunderstanding, the failure to communicate properly. Adapt your choice of words to your audience, but do not use big words simply to impress under any circumstances. Consider the following list of simple words in relation to their more complex counterparts:

Complex words	*Simple words*
imbibe	drink
consume	eat
individuals	persons
domicile	home
inaugurate	begin
expedite	hasten
edifice	building
purchase	buy
endeavor	try
antagonist	foe

3. *Avoid technical terminology.* Specialists often use terms which lay audiences do not understand. The specialist becomes so accustomed to using the special vocabulary of his profession that he forgets that his terminology has little meaning to others. The more highly specialized a person becomes, the greater risk he runs of using technical terms without adequate explanation. An experienced professor of economics used the following terms without explaining them in addressing a lay audience: *technocrats, blue-sky laws, marginal industries, protected industries, parity prices, union shop,*

closed shop, and *economic equilibrium.* Students in an introductory speech course, who composed part of the audience, were later asked to explain the terms. Only forty per cent of the students understood more than half of the terms.

The dean of a university addressed the freshman class at its orientation program. At a later session, a freshman counselor found that some of his students did not understand the following terms used by the dean in his address: *honor credits, humanities, liberal arts, median score, exceptional child, overlaid function, honors program, positive correlation, statistical certainty, academic freedom,* and *scientific attitude.* Academic terms understood by college professors may not be understood by college freshmen.

Almost all professional groups have specialized vocabularies. How many of the following terms, common to specialized professions, do you understand: law—*fee simple, hearsay rule, writ of mandamus, malice aforethought,* and *common law;* ministry—*Holy Ghost, apocalyptic order, millennial, redemption, cataclysmic creed, transfiguration,* and *exorcism;* medicine—*encephalitis lethargica, protozoa, hydrotherapy, psychoneuroses, dementia praecox,* and *agraphia.* In speaking about your field of specialization to a group outside your field, put technical terms in simple language so that your listeners can understand.

4. *Strive for economy of expression.* Let one word do the work of two, a phrase the work of a clause, and a sentence the work of two or more sentences. Wordiness may decrease clarity by making the thought vague, by injecting irrelevant ideas, and by prolonging the development of a point.

To illustrate, compare the following first draft of a paragraph in a manuscript with the revised paragraph that follows.

> The logical development of a speech depends primarily on evidence and reasoning. Evidence may be considered as the material or facts one uses to support his ideas; and reasoning, the process of drawing conclusions or inferences from the facts. Examples of illogical development consist of such devices as quoting one or two unqualified authorities, presenting isolated or unrepresentative examples, quoting statistics covering a limited phase of the subject, and drawing sweeping conclusions from meager evidence. The same may be said for making inferences from negative instances and drawing conclusions from comparisons when the things compared are not comparable. A good speaker will attempt to avoid such fallacies in reasoning as he attempts to make his basic appeal upon rational grounds.

The above paragraph consists of five sentences of 120 words. The revision that follows reduces the paragraph to 4 sentences of 79 words, a reduction of over 30 per cent.

> Logic depends primarily on evidence and reasoning. Evidence consists of the facts used to support ideas, and reasoning of the process of drawing inferences from the facts. Examples of illogical reasoning consist of such devices as quoting unqualified authorities, presenting unrepresentative examples, citing limited statistics, drawing sweeping conclusions from meager evidence, making inferences from negative instances, and drawing conclusions by comparing objects not comparable. A good speaker avoids such fallacies and makes his basic appeal to logic.

In each instance one or several words were substituted for phrases or clauses. For example, in the second sentence, the adjective *limited* does the work of the phrase *covering a limited phase of the subject.* By combining the second and third sentences, the introductory phrase for the third sentence, *the same may be said for,* becomes unnecessary. Superfluous modifiers and unnecessary repetitions were deleted: for example, why use two adjectives, *isolated* or *unrepresentative* examples, when one gives the same meaning? Since the nouns *conclusions* or *inferences* are similar, use only one. The term *one or two* in the third sentence slows the reader and adds nothing to the meaning of the sentence. In brief, by deleting forty-one words, the paragraph seems smoother and expresses the meaning better than the original paragraph.

Wordiness is more easily detected and corrected in writing than in speaking because the writer can edit his manuscript. Skill in editing written speeches will, however, eventually improve your language for extemporaneous speaking. To correct verbosity, write and edit several speeches, record and play back some speeches for self-analysis, and transcribe some recorded speeches for editing. The carry-over in language improvement from written to oral communication will soon be apparent by use of these suggestions.

5. *Use repetition and restatement.* Although wordiness should be avoided, oral style must be more repetitious than written style. The writer indicates divisions of ideas by titles and subtitles; he writes in paragraphs and sections. The speaker must state his point, develop it, summarize it, and make a proper transition to the next point. The speaker uses questions to point up an idea. He illustrates his points in many ways—through examples, comparisons, statistics, explanations, and narratives. Since spoken language must be instantly intelligible to listeners, a speaker must restate ideas in many ways to insure understanding.

Note how Franklin D. Roosevelt used repetition effectively in his message to Congress on January 4, 1939.

> Dictatorship, however, involves costs which the American people will never pay: The cost of our spiritual values. The cost of the blessed right of being able to say what we please. The cost of freedom of religion. The cost of seeing our capital confiscated. . . . If the avoidance of these costs means taxes on my income; if avoiding these costs means taxes on my estate at death, I would bear those taxes willingly as the price of my breathing and my children breathing the free air of a free country, as the price of a living and not a dead world.[6]

In summary, clarity is achieved in oral communication by using specific terms, by using simple words, by avoiding technical terminology, by avoiding wordiness, and by judicious use of repetition.

Oral Language Should Be Appropriate

To be appropriate, language must be adapted to the personality of the speaker, to the type of speech, to the audience, and to the occasion. An enthusiastic person naturally uses more colorful and lively language than a reserved person. The language for a speech at a home-coming gathering would be more forceful than that for a speech at a study club. The language for a speech on a formal occasion shows more restraint than one for a social occasion. In spite of these variations, certain principles apply to all occasions.

1. *Avoid triteness.* Acceptable language becomes trite by overuse. Modifiers such as *lovely, adorable, very, most, tremendous, exceedingly,* and *gorgeous* fall into this category.

Many expressions which once were apt, original, and colorful have lost their freshness through repetition. Thus, they have become dull, unimaginative, and commonplace. Speakers use them automatically to relieve the necessity for thinking.

Terms which have become trite and hackneyed are called clichés. Some shopworn phrases pass into this classification each year depending on the frequency of their use in certain occupations, geographical locations, and age groups. The following typical list is by no means exhaustive: too funny for words, last but not least, conspicuous by its absence, at a loss for words, it stands to reason, goes without saying, it gives me great pleasure, no sooner said than done, method in his madness, they gave their all, with singleness

[6] Lew Sarett and William T. Foster, *Modern Speeches on Basic Issues* (Boston: Houghton Mifflin Co., 1939), p. 126. Reprinted by permission of the estate of Franklin D. Roosevelt.

of purpose, sturdy as an oak, dead as a doornail, straight as an arrow, sleeping like a log, and hard as a rock.

2. *Use slang judiciously.* Slang consists of words or terms of a colloquial type that have not been accepted as cultivated speech by educated people. Distinctions in types of slang are noted by Bergen and Cornelia Evans as follows:

> In slang the creative forces that shape language are often exceedingly active and much slang is vivid and clever and forceful. Much more of it, however, is merely faddish and infantile and its consistent use does not display the fullness of expression that the user thinks it does but rather a triteness and a staleness that the user is apparently unaware of. Slang ages quickly and nothing so stamps a total lack of force or originality upon a man or woman as the steady use of outmoded slang.[7]

We cannot rule out slang entirely because some of it arises from a need for more expressive terms than exist. It enriches language and aids in conveying meaning. When slang words become generally accepted, they are incorporated in the dictionaries. For example, such words as the following are in common usage today but were formerly considered slang: *jailbird, tightwad, bootleg, racketeer, push-over, crack down,* and *O.K.* Other terms like *cool boy, yeah man, square, get hep, scram, dig that song,* and *that's cat kid* are considered low-grade slang of temporary usage.

Although the judicious use of slang adds color and force to language, its overuse indicates a limited vocabulary and careless thinking. Avoid low-grade or temporary slang altogether, and avoid all types on formal occasions.

3. *Use foreign phrases sparingly.* Foreign words and phrases should seldom be used when an English equivalent exists, especially when addressing lay audiences. They may be understood by specialists in a particular field but not by the general public. For example, the use of the following terms by a lawyer would have little meaning outside his profession: *caveat emptor*—Latin for "let the buyer beware"; *habeas corpus*—Latin for "bring the body before the court"; *compos mentis*—Latin for "of sound mind"; and *de jure*—Latin for "according to law." The same would be true for the minister if he used the following foreign terms: *ecce homo*—Latin for "behold the man"; *grâce à Dieu*—French for "thanks to God"; *Iesus Nazaremus*—Latin for "Jesus of Nazareth." Members of a lay

[7] From *A Dictionary of Contemporary American Usage,* by Bergen Evans and Cornelia Evans. Copyright © 1957 by Bergen Evans and Cornelia Evans. Reprinted by permission of Random House, Inc.

audience would not only fail to understand the terms, but they would probably consider the speaker an exhibitionist.

Some foreign words and phrases have been used so extensively that they will be understood by most educated people; for example, *chef*—"head cook"; *cum laude* and *magna cum laude*—graduation "with praise" and "with great praise"; *de facto*—"in fact"; *de luxe*—"of special elegance"; *en route*—"on one's way"; *laissez faire*—"non-interference with trade"; *nouveau riche*—"one newly rich"; *per se*—"of itself"; and *prima facie*—"at first view." The safest course for beginning speakers is to avoid use of foreign phrases. Concentrate on the use of acceptable English words.

4. *Avoid vulgarisms and off-color words.* Vulgarisms consist of words and phrases used in colloquial speech by uneducated and uncouth people; for example, *where at, ain't, hadn't ought, that there, could of, afeared,* and *can't hardly*. Vulgarisms should be distinguished from faulty grammar, although they may sometimes include improper grammatical construction. For example, in the sentence "Them words hadn't ought to be teach because they ain't nice," *them* and *teach* violate standard grammar; *hadn't ought* and *ain't* are vulgarisms. The adjective *those* should replace the pronoun *them,* and the past participle *taught* should be used for the transitive verb *teach. Should not* should replace *hadn't ought, are not* should be substituted for *ain't,* and *appropriate* should be used for *nice.* As corrected, the sentence reads, "Those words should not be taught because they are not appropriate."

When a speaker uses vulgarisms, his listeners consider that he is either an uncouth person or that he underestimates the intelligence of his audience. Listeners like to consider speakers as intelligent leaders, and they resent being talked down to. Avoid the use of vulgarisms on all occasions.

Off-color words, obscenity, and profanity should not be used at all. Some speakers like to shock their listeners or show their worldly-wise ways by using off-color words and stories. Perhaps the profanity found in modern novels causes this tendency. Most people will tolerate or even enjoy obscenity in literature because reading is private; they resent off-color expressions by speakers because speaking is public. Listeners will consider a speaker who uses off-color material as a person of low character and poor judgment, and they will not be receptive to his talk.

5. *Avoid name-calling.* Name-calling means giving bad names

to things we do not like or good names to things we like. If the name-caller does not like a person's political beliefs, he calls him a *Communist,* a *Red,* or *an extremist.* If he wishes to cast aspersions at his superior intellect, he calls him an *egg-head,* a *brain-truster,* or a *brain.* If he dislikes a co-worker he calls him a *rabble-rouser,* a *troublemaker,* or a *goldbrick.* If he resents his employer he may call him a *dictator,* a *demagogue,* or a *dirty capitalist.*

Although name-calling usually attaches "bad" labels, it may be used positively by labeling things favored as "good." Thus we label the proposal for labor reform as the *American way,* and its proponent as a *defender of freedom,* or *protector of democracy.* We say that particular proposals uphold *states' rights, free enterprise,* or *separation of church and state.* The name-caller relates his proposal to principles revered by his listeners and thus evokes an immediate desirable emotional response.

The techniques of name-calling encourage uncritical acceptance and permit easy repetition through short, slogan-like phrases. The detrimental effect of name-calling lies in the fact that it short-circuits the reasoning processes, makes for oversimplification of complex matters, and discourages the critical evaluation of facts. That name-calling succeeds in getting immediate results cannot be denied; that extensive use of name-calling perverts intellectual honesty seems equally obvious.

6. *Avoid euphemisms.* Euphemisms consist of the substitution of mild or indirect words or expressions for those which might offend or suggest something unpleasant. For example, for *died* one might use such euphemisms as "passed away," "gone to the great beyond," or "passed on to his reward"; for *leg* he may substitute "limb"; for *eat,* "partake of the evening meal"; for *lie,* "prevaricate" or "falsify"; for *steal,* "appropriate" or "filch." The propagandist or advertiser often uses euphemisms to avoid unpleasant associations. Although a speaker should avoid offending sensitive listeners, the excessive use of euphemisms irritates thinking people.

In summary, appropriate language is adapted to the speaker, the speech, the audience, and the occasion. Although language usage varies with the speaking conditions, for all occasions avoid (1) triteness, (2) excessive slang, (3) foreign phrases, (4) vulgarisms and off-color expressions, (5) name-calling, and (6) euphemisms. The appropriate choice of language increases listeners' respect for the speaker and what he has to say.

Oral Language Should Be Interesting

Language may possess clarity and appropriateness and yet not command attention or hold interest. To attain maximum usefulness, language must be vivid, graphic, and impressive. It must make use of imagery and must appeal to basic desires so that listeners will want to listen. Oral communication aims at a specific audience, not general readers. Language should, therefore, be adapted to the interests and desires of the immediate audience. Reread Chapter 4 for a review of the elements of interest to which you should appeal. In addition, consider the following suggestions for making language interesting.

1. *Speak directly and personally.* Try for a direct, conversational, communicative style. Make your language say that the speech is intended for your immediate listeners, that it could apply to no other audience. Use language that causes your listeners to recall their experiences, that relates to their interests, and that appeals to their wants. Consider the following opening paragraphs for a speech on traffic safety.

> It is well that the people throughout our great nation be informed on the problem of traffic safety in America. It is reported that a family of five was killed last night in one of our neighboring states by a drunken driver who disregarded traffic regulations. This incident should serve as an example to call the problem of traffic safety to our attention. Think with me for a few minutes on the seriousness of the problem.

This wordy, unimaginative, indirect introduction could apply to any audience; neither the language nor the material has direct or personal application to the immediate audience. Compare it with the following introduction.

> At nine o'clock last night a tragic accident befell our fellow citizen, Dr. M. D. Roe. While driving across Broadway at Fifth Street, Dr. Roe, his wife, and his three children were killed instantly by a drunken driver who disregarded all traffic signals. What can we do to prevent such needless tragedy?

Oral language is more direct than written language. It uses personal pronouns like *I, me, we, you, they,* and *ours.* Instead of saying, "Each person must do his part to alleviate traffic accidents; it is a personal problem," say, "We must do our part to prevent traffic accidents; the problem is ours." Oral language uses short, idiomatic words like *think* instead of "contemplate," *eat* instead of "consume," and *me* instead of "myself." Instead of saying, "In order to help the solution of the traffic problem, each person must give his support to the law-enforcement officers," say, "To help solve the traffic problem, support your enforcement officers." Oral language employs contractions like *won't* instead of "will not," *isn't* instead of "is not," and *don't* instead of "do not." Instead of saying, "Will not you help us encourage traffic safety by driving safely?" say, "Won't you help encourage traffic safety by driving safely?"

The rhetorical question makes oral language more direct and personal than written language. It motivates an audience to think about the question. For example, instead of saying, "We must consider the seriousness of traffic violations; we must work to solve the problem," say, "How extensive are traffic violations? How can we solve the problem?"

2. *Use colorful words.* Simplicity of language does not mean dull and colorless language. The language of oral communication should indicate attitudes and opinions as well as meaning. Oral communication uses loaded words judiciously, words that call up emotional associations and indicate attitudes. For example, consider the following colorless sentence, "The man walked down the street." How can we indicate attitudes and feelings about *man?* Try substituting some of the following loaded words for man: *dictator, miser, savage, guy, robber, baron, father, dad, sportsman, cheapskate, piker,* or *chiseler.* The verb *walked* is also colorless and indicates little. Consider substituting some of the following loaded words: *strutted, ran, shuffled, danced, sped, staggered, swaggered, tiptoed, wandered, slunk, toddled,* and *skipped.* The word *street* is also colorless; loaded words with more meaning are these: *thoroughfare, alley, road, highway, lane, footpath, boulevard, avenue,* and *pike.* Thus, "The piker slunk down the alley" has quite a different connotative meaning from "The man walked down the street." Beware of using loaded words as substitutes for facts or for name-calling; use them to make your language colorful and forceful.

Onomatopoetic words lend color to language; they indicate attitudes and feelings by their sounds. They may enhance meaning by creating a mood or by suggesting an idea. Bergen and Cornelia Evans explain this type of words as follows:

> Onomatopoeia is the technical name for the formation of a name or a word by imitating some sound associated with the thing designated. *Cuckoo* and *whippoorwill* are probably examples. *Bang, fizz, burp, rattle, smack, flop, sneeze* are others.[8]

3. *Use figurative language.* Figures of speech use words out of their literal sense to suggest an image or a comparison. They add color and interest to language. Their effective use depends upon originality, vividness, and relevancy to the implied thought. Unlike forms of support such as examples, statistics, analogies, and testimony, figures of speech do not prove or explain an idea; they describe emotions in terms of concrete objects. Winston Churchill's "Blood, sweat, and tears" is more colorful and interesting than "life, labor, and sorrow." William Jennings Bryan's "You shall not crucify mankind upon a cross of gold" is more forceful than "You should not force labor to accept the gold standard." Franklin Roosevelt's "We have nothing to fear but fear itself" is more forceful than "Our economic concern has no real foundation." Figurative language stays in the listener's memory; it relates new concepts to familiar beliefs.

Of the numerous forms of figurative language, simile, metaphor, antithesis, and personification are used most frequently in oral communication. The simile makes direct comparisons between one thing or idea with those of a different kind, usually by use of *as* or *like*. "He is as cross as a bear," "Her smile is like the flowers of Spring," and "My love is like a red, red rose" illustrate the simile. The metaphor resembles the simile except that the comparison is implied; it drops the connecting word. One thing resembles another; we indicate the resemblance by attributing to one an action which belongs to another. "He is a sly fox," "Window of my soul," "The hounds of Spring are on Winter's traces," illustrate the metaphor. Antithesis sets contrasting phrases opposite each other for emphasis. The contrasting statements are parallel and balance, as: "Governments do not determine man's ideologies; man's ideologies determine his government." "When discussion ends, debate begins." "The idealist has ideas; the realist puts ideas to work." Personification attributes to inanimate things the attributes of living things; objects without life are spoken of as if they were living. The following illustrate:

---

[8] Bergen Evans and Cornelia Evans, *A Dictionary of Contemporary American Usage,* p. 388. Reprinted by permission of Random House, Inc.

Carl Sandburg speaks of Chicago as the "City of the Big Shoulders"; Eugene Field stated, "The old moon laughed and sang a song"; William Jennings Bryan insisted, "Avarice paints Destiny with a dollar mark."

Although figures of speech add color and interest to oral communication, they should not be far-fetched or contrived. They should suggest associations and comparisons without calling attention to the method used. They should not be used as a substitute for facts or reasons; rather they should be used to embellish them. They should conform to the tone of the content of the speech; an informal speech calls for simple figures of speech. Although the content of speech comes first, figures of speech aid in making the content interesting and colorful.

4. *Use action words.* Make your language move by using active words. Do not say, "He was watching when the airplanes collided in the air"; say, "He looked on with horror as the planes crashed in midair." Do not say, "The speed of the automobile was ninety miles per hour as it went down the street"; say, "The automobile raced down the street at ninety miles per hour." Instead of "The engine operates well," say, "The engine runs smoothly"; instead of "It is well to analyze the use of language," say, "Analyze your language"; instead of "It is believed that we should all vote," say "We know we should vote."

What principles govern active language? First, consider verbs. Use the active voice with verbs that represent their subjects as doing or being something. For example, say, "I believe the theory." The passive voice represents its subject as acted upon; for example, "The theory is believed." For oral communication, "My opponent refuted the argument with logic" is better than "My argument was refuted with logic by my opponent"; "John won the election" shows better action than "The election was won by John."

Beware also of using noun substitutes for verbs; instead of "It is my belief that the theory is sound," say, "I believe that the theory is sound." Instead of "High wages are a cause of inflation," say, "High wages cause inflation."

To keep your language moving, cut the use of adjectives and adverbs to a minimum. Use definitive adjectives like "*All* men are created equal," "*High* wages cause inflation," and "*Fallacious* reasoning should be avoided"; choose also qualifying adverbs like "Come *early*," "Step *lively*," and "Speak *louder*." Avoid modifiers like "The argument is *so very* logical," "The play was *most* unique,"

"Where did you get that *exquisitely adorable* hat?" "He shouted for help" shows more action than "He called loudly for assistance."

Make liberal use of dialogue. Dialogue arouses interest by appealing to the familiar and holds attention by putting people into motion. In a sense, effective speakers simulate the give-and-take spirit of dialogue by asking questions, issuing challenges, and making accusations. They seek to make their listeners respond—to think, to answer, to argue.

Note how the late W. J. Cameron of the Ford Motor Company shows action largely through dialogue in his speech entitled "Too Soon to Quit."

> Young persons sometimes ask Mr. Ford, "How can I make my life a success?"—as if anyone could answer that question half as well as the one who asks it. But occasionally Mr. Ford does give a valuable tip . . . : "If you start a thing, finish it. . . ."
>
> "Yes," one says, "but the thing may not be worth finishing." Of course, when he says, "Finish it," Mr. Ford isn't thinking about the thing at all, he is thinking about you—you, Miss Maiden, and you, Sir Youth. In the preparatory time of life the real job is not what you are working on, but what it is doing to you. You start it with a great gush of interest—you miss your meals for it—then suddenly it goes stale—and you quit. Or you find that your plan is wrong—and you quit. And all that you have as profit from your effort is the knowledge of *how to quit!* "Well," you say, "the thing wasn't worth it." Quite probably, *but you are,* and that's the whole point.[9]

Note how Edward F. McGrady of the Radio Corporation of America created a sense of dialogue with his listeners in the opening paragraph of his speech entitled "What Does Labor Want?"

> What does labor want? Will labor ever be satisfied? The answer to the first question is that the wants of labor vary from time to time. Once it had the status of serfs and asked for liberty. After a long struggle freedom was secured; then it asked for wages. Later it asked for the right of organization. Then came the quest for shorter hours, better working conditions, and the right to have its organizations recognized.[10]

In summary, to make oral language interesting (1) speak directly and personally to your listeners in a conversational, communicative style; (2) use colorful words that indicate attitudes and feelings as well as meaning; (3) use figurative language that implies comparisons; and (4) use language of action and force.

---

[9] Sarett and Foster, *op. cit.,* pp. 41-42. Reprinted by permission of the Ford Motor Company, Dearborn, Michigan.

[10] *Vital Speeches,* III (April 15, 1937), 398-401.

III. Improving Oral Style

An understanding of the principles of the general semantic and rhetorical approaches to language is the essential first step toward improving oral style. The acquisition of rhetorical skills will also help in vocabulary-building and language usage.

Understanding Language

Understanding is the principal method for securing proper evaluation, because few skills are involved. Rather, accurate evaluation results from proper attitudes—delaying and questioning attitudes. Listeners must ask, "Is the speaker saying what he seems to me to be saying?" Speakers must ask, "Is the listener receiving my ideas as I have them in my mind?" Each must ask, "Do we have a 'meeting of minds' or do our communications bypass each other?" Each must realize that communication goes beyond the mere spoken word—its ultimate effect comes from the total impact of language, the responses it invokes.

Rhetorical skills involve more than understanding; they involve doing as well as knowing. How can you improve your use of language by improving rhetorical skills?

Improving Vocabulary and Language Skills

We have four types of vocabularies: (1) reading, (2) writing, (3) hearing, and (4) speaking. Our reading vocabularies are the largest because some unfamiliar words have meaning within a context. We understand the meaning, at least partially, of many words that we never use in writing or speaking. Our writing vocabularies are next in size. We use some words in writing that we never use in speaking because pronunciation presents no problem. If we are not sure about the meaning of a word, we can look it up in a dictionary. Some words that we do not use in speaking we understand when we hear. Unfortunately for oral communication, our speaking vocabularies are the smallest. We do not use many words with which we have partial acquaintance because we are unsure either of their exact meaning or of their pronunciation. Our goal in oral communication should be to make these four vocabularies as nearly alike as possible.

How can we improve our vocabularies? Techniques and formulas abound in this field. Some say, "Learn a new word each day," but few will carry through with this suggestion. Others suggest that you look up each new word when you encounter it, but this suggestion often proves impractical. Others suggest, "Look it up; write it down; use it seven times within the day, ad infinitum." It may be difficult, however, to maneuver the conversation so that you can use new words seven times within the day. In fact, most formulas have some validity, but rarely does one carry through with them. Several practical suggestions follow.

1. *Vocabulary-building.* The principal methods for improving vocabulary follow: (1) read good literature, (2) listen to cultured people, and (3) speak and write. An objective study of words helps; but such a study will never supplant reading, listening, speaking, and writing.

Reading good literature introduces one to new ideas. Since we think by use of words, we must learn new words to comprehend new ideas and to communicate those ideas to others. Exposure to new ideas motivates one to consult a dictionary, to think about words, and to use new words in communicating. Herein lies the advantage reading has over formula methods; you learn and use new words because you have a purpose in doing so. By reading poetry, you acquire new concepts of imagery, of colorful words, of figures of speech, of forceful language. By reading prose you acquire new ideas, new words, and new methods for using them effectively. By reading masterpieces of oratory, you gain ideas on how to use language effectively for oral communication. By reading aloud, you learn new rhythmical patterns as well as the pronunciation and meaning of new words. Reread the parts of Chapter 2 on how reading assists one to develop into an effective speaker. Review Chapter 6 on how to improve your reading habits. Through reading, introduce yourself to new words. Associate with them, play with them, eat with them, sleep with them, make friends with them.

Associating with and listening to educated people also aids vocabulary-building. Like reading, educated people introduce you to new ideas and to acceptable methods for expressing them. Through exposure, one gradually absorbs some of the language style of those with whom one associates. Cultured people may open up whole new fields of learning with their new terminology. One student commented on the many new words that he learned from the lectures of his professor in biology. From the classroom, from the pulpit, from the courtroom, and from the public platform, cultured people express new ideas with skill and force. Radio and television offer countless opportunities for listening to persons who use language effectively. Regardless of our opinion of the low caliber of some programs, radio and television have had a beneficial influence on the language habits of the average citizen.

The adage, "We learn to do by doing," has special application to improving language style. New words become a permanent part of our vocabularies when we learn to put them to use through speaking and writing. Speaking and writing have much in common; excellence in one leads to improvement in the other. A careful writer gives attention to each word, phrase, clause, sentence, and paragraph by editing, revising, and rewriting. He chooses, from the many words available to express an idea, the one that expresses it with greatest precision and effect. The laborious task of editing leads to improved methods of writing which gradually make revision and rewriting less necessary. Improved writing skills carry over to extemporaneous speaking. The knowledge of new words and skills in expressing ideas lead to improvement in the ready choice of language for oral communication. There is no substitute for speaking and writing for improving oral style.

2. *Acquiring skills.* An objective study of words aids the primary methods for improving vocabulary. The following suggestions make a sort of game of vocabulary-building and word usage. They stress the ready choice of the most appropriate word for extemporaneous speech.

a. FIND WORDS WITH SIMILAR MEANINGS. Words with similar meanings are called synonyms. Knowledge of synonyms aids the speaker to choose the right word to express shades of thought. Practice in choosing them makes for ready choice during extemporaneous speaking. The following illustrate:

bright: shining, beaming, radiant, gleaming, luminous, effulgent, refulgent, sparkling, scintillating, glittering, glowing, glaring, dazzling, glistening, shimmering, lustrous, brilliant, splendid, resplendent, quick-witted, clever, smart, intelligent, precocious, animated, vivacious, lively, gay, cheerful, favorable, promising, encouraging, auspicious, propitious.

expert: proficient, adept, connoisseur, master, authority, specialist.[11]

[11] H. G. Emery and K. G. Brewster, eds., *The New Century Dictionary* (New York: Appleton-Century-Crofts, Inc., 1959), pp. 2267, 2301.

Find synonyms for the following words and check your list in any standard dictionary:

bad	fury	prove
bare	holy	shout
confuse	innocent	uncouth
elevate	move	young

b. FIND WORDS WITH OPPOSITE MEANINGS. Words with opposite meanings are termed antonyms. Practice in selecting antonyms will improve your immediate choice of words to express precise meaning. The following are antonyms for the words used as examples in the preceding section:

bright: dull, lusterless, dim, dark, gloomy.
expert: novice, tyro, beginner, amateur, smatterer, bungler.[12]

Find antonyms for the following words:

averse	fame	pardon
beautiful	good	proud
calm	large	rich
dim	misfortune	sad

c. FIND WORDS WITH MANY MEANINGS. Many words can be used in several ways. In some instances the same word may have antithetical meanings; for example, *strike* means "to miss" in baseball, but it means "to hit" in bowling. Some words have different meanings because they serve as different parts of speech; for example, the conference is *brief* (adjective), but the lawyer files a *brief* (noun) of his case. Practice in thinking of the many ways that a word may be used aids the speaker in word choice and helps prevent misunderstanding. Note the several meanings of the word *spade:*

1. To spade the garden (dig it up)
2. To play the spade (playing card)
3. To use a spade (cutter's tool, shovel, two-edged sword)
4. To call a spade a spade (plain talk)
5. An instrument to check recoil on a gun
6. A measure of space
7. A spade-fish (type of fish)

Find several ways in which the following words may be used:

bite	enter	jog
crown	find	kill
detect	grate	mate
drive	hang	pattern

---

[12] *Ibid.*

d. FIND COLORFUL WORDS FOR COLORLESS WORDS. As explained in an earlier section, words may indicate attitudes and feelings as well as meaning. Colorful language helps the speaker get attention and maintain interest. Note the following examples:

ruler: dictator, monarch, autocrat, despot, tyrant, czar, rajah, sovereign, king, queen, emperor, president, governor, chief, lord.
worker: artisan, craftsman, handicraftsman, toiler, slave, journeyman, peon, coolie, roustabout.

Find colorful words for the following words:

act	cry	person
animal	event	run
bit	flood	show
capture	mad	top

e. FIND SUBSTITUTES FOR TRITE WORDS. Use fresh words for those usually employed to excess. The following illustrate:

great: large, big, immense, numerous, countless, important, eminent, renowned, famous, lofty, noble, excellent.
lovely: attractive, amiable, beautiful, charming, pretty, handsome.

Find substitutes for the following trite words:

adorable	marvelous	really
darling	most	stupid
exceedingly	nice	tremendous
gorgeous	precious	very

3. *Using the dictionary.* The foregoing methods suggested for vocabulary-building make use of the dictionary. To acquire facility with language, you must acquire the "dictionary habit." Although we add to our vocabularies primarily from reading, writing, listening, and speaking, these methods will be aided greatly if we look up unfamiliar words and study their meaning. When you hear a speaker use an unfamiliar word or when you encounter one in your reading, look the word up in a dictionary as soon as feasible.

Review Section II, 1 of Chapter 7 for an explanation of how to define words and terms. Dictionaries give the derivation of many words; by studying roots, prefixes and suffixes, synonyms and antonyms, and etymologies of words, you should improve your vocabulary rapidly.

Look up the following words in a standard dictionary; consider their different meanings and use each in a sentence.

ambiguous	embellish	prescribe
conjugate	genealogy	propaganda
connotative	linguistic	provincial
culinary	predict	vague

In short, you can improve your use of language by thinking about words, studying them, and experimenting with them. Make frequent use of a dictionary. These suggestions supplement the primary methods of vocabulary-building—reading, listening, speaking, and writing.

IV. Summary

This chapter discusses two approaches to oral style: general semantics—fitting words to actual happenings, and rhetorical—using words correctly.

The general semantics approach considers words as symbols, locates the level of talk, locates the time to which the speaker refers, and recognizes the principle of abstracting. A consciousness of these principles decreases misunderstanding and confusion.

The rhetorical approach stresses that oral language should be clear, appropriate, and interesting. Clarity is achieved by (1) using specific terms, (2) using simple words, (3) avoiding technical terminology, (4) striving for economy of words, and (5) using repetition and restatement. To assure appropriateness, one should (1) avoid triteness, (2) use slang judiciously, (3) use foreign words sparingly, (4) avoid vulgarisms and off-color words, (5) avoid name-calling, and (6) avoid euphemisms. Make language interesting by (1) being direct and personal, (2) using colorful words, (3) using figurative language, and (4) using active words.

Oral style can be improved by understanding the principles of language and by practicing language skills. We have four vocabularies—reading, writing, listening, and speaking. For oral communication, we should strive to make our speaking and hearing vocabularies approximate the size of our reading and writing vocabularies. The principal methods for vocabulary-building are: read good literature, listen to educated people, and practice speaking and writing. Skills in using language may be improved by studying (1) synonyms, (2) antonyms, (3) varying usage of words, (4) colorful words, and (5) substitutes for trite words. Consult the dictionary frequently for the meaning of words.

Questions and Exercises

A. Answer the following questions on Chapter 11.

1. Distinguish between the general semantics and the rhetorical approaches to oral style.
2. What is meant by Professor Lee's statement, "We live in two worlds which we must not confuse, a world of words, and a world of not-words"?
3. What is your understanding of "The level of talk"? "The time of talk"? "Abstracting"?
4. What is meant by the rhetorical approach to language?
5. List and discuss briefly five methods for making language clear.
6. List and discuss briefly six methods for insuring appropriateness in choosing language.
7. List and discuss briefly four ways for making language interesting.
8. What can you do to secure more accurate evaluation of language?
9. What types of vocabularies do we have? Which type is the largest?
10. What are the principal methods for improving vocabulary?
11. Discuss several methods for improving language skills.
12. How would you rate your language skills in relation to those of other members of your class—superior, average, inferior?

B. Below is a list of one hundred words which a committee of teachers believes should be in the speaking vocabulary of college freshman students. Go over the list and label each word with the following code: *a,* meaning known positively; *b,* meaning doubtful; *c,* meaning not known. Look up those labeled *b* in a standard dictionary and check the dictionary definition with your definition. Look up and write definitions for those labeled *c;* then use each word in a sentence. After studying the sections of Chapter 12 on pronunciation, return to this list and label each word again with the following code: *x,* pronunciation known positively; *y,* pronunciation doubtful; *z,* pronunciation not known. Check your pronunciation of those labeled *y* with the pronunciation given in a standard dictionary. Look up and write the diacritical markings for those labeled *z.*

auspices	clientele	discern
averse	combatant	disputants
bravado	comely	economic
chagrin	concrete	eczema
inflammable	condolence	emanating
chastisement	controversial	decisive
chic	coupon	defect
cache	decadent	deluge
clique	decadence	despicable
comparable	decorative	discretion
data	decorous	eccentric
dais	demise	err
debris	details	exquisite

finale
gala
extraordinary
frustrated
formidable
gallant
gamut
granary
grievous
grimace
heinous
wrestle
pianist
precedence
perspiration
pique
poignant
romance
robust
quintuplets
veterinary
chiropodist
impotent
hospitable
lamentable
barbarous
bona fide
vice versa
caramel
virile
bade
comptroller
February
forehead
frequented
gratis
height
horizon
hundred
children
ignominious
tenets
impious
juvenile
lingerie
mischievous
luxury
larynx
pharynx
inquiry
vehicle
vehement
incognito
lamentable
obligatory
longevity
short-lived
penalize
rough
superfluous
tarpaulin

C. For your eleventh oral assignment choose one man or woman from the list below as the subject of a five-minute biographical speech. Tell about the person's life, about his influence on history, and about his ability as a speaker. If you can find a published speech by the person you select, analyze his language style according to the principles discussed in this chapter.

Socrates
Mahatma Gandhi
St. Paul
Franklin Delano Roosevelt
Albert Schweitzer
Douglas MacArthur
Julius Caesar
George Washington
Abraham Lincoln
Thomas Jefferson
Edward Everett
Daniel Webster
Henry W. Grady
John C. Calhoun
Booker T. Washington
Ralph Waldo Emerson
Samuel Gompers
Theodore Parker
Eugene Debbs
Carrie Chapman Catt
Konrad Adenauer
Marshal Tito
Jawaharlal Nehru
Harry Truman
Susan B. Anthony
Claire Booth Luce
Eleanor Roosevelt
Madame Chiang Kai-shek
Helen Keller
William Jennings Bryan
Nikita Khrushchev
James Bryant Conant
Woodrow Wilson
Patrick Henry
Josef Stalin
Adolf Hitler
Winston Franco
Francisco Franco
Charles de Gaulle

CHAPTER 12

Develop an Adequate Speaking Voice

The victim testified that he recognized the voices of the culprits although he had never seen them. His testimony was the most damaging in a chain of circumstantial evidence that brought conviction. The oil magnate had been kidnapped and held captive for three days by two men and a woman. He had been hit from behind as he dozed in a chair of his study and had been kept blindfolded throughout his captivity. He knew his captives only by the sound of their voices. Yet, his identification of their voices proved damaging to the culprits' defense.

Your voice may prove almost as accurate an identifying factor as your handwriting or fingerprints. It gives strong indications of your personality and emotional state.

As an experiment, try blindfolding yourself and listening to a discussion program over television. After listening for a while, write down the impressions you have received of each participant from the sound of his voice. Then view the program and check your visual impressions against the oral impressions you listed.

No doubt you successfully identified the sex of each person. With less accuracy you probably came to conclusions about each speaker's age, size, emotional state, general personality, race, cultural background, and enthusiasm for his subject. A person's state of health may also be reflected in his voice, although you may be unable to check the accuracy of such observations.

A distinct and pleasing voice constitutes an important part of effective delivery. You sometimes hear it said, "What does voice matter so long as you have something to say?" Conversely, one might also ask, "Of what value is having something to say if you cannot be understood?" Voice is not the only element in effective delivery, but it is an integral part of it. Thus a person with a poor voice can make an acceptable contribution in oral communication only if his delivery is otherwise competent. He makes a worthwhile contribution in spite of his poor voice.

An adequate voice does not insure effective communication, but it helps a good speech accomplish its purpose. A poor voice proves irritating, invites inattention, obscures meaning, and lessens the pleasure of the listener. A good voice commands respect; it helps in holding attention, in securing understanding, and in gaining acceptance of ideas.

I. Requisites for an Adequate Voice

An adequate voice is not an end within itself; it serves as a means to the end of communicating ideas, information, and emotions. If the voice calls attention to itself, it detracts from communication. Properly used, it aids communication. What are the principal characteristics of an adequate voice? Consider the following requisites.

An Adequate Voice Is Intelligible

A good voice is understood easily throughout the meeting hall. In auditoriums that have public-address systems or excellent acoustics, making one's self heard presents no serious problem. Other halls such as combination gymnasium-auditoriums may present serious difficulties. Some speakers, accustomed to favorable speaking conditions, find difficulty adjusting to less favorable conditions. Since they become accustomed to speaking with little force when using a loud-speaker, they tend to use insufficient force when speaking without one. A rapid rate may be easily understood in a well-constructed auditorium; the same rate may prove unintelligible in a poorly constructed hall. One student described his experience while speaking in a hall with poor acoustics as "my voice came back and hit me in the face." He had to decrease his normal rate and volume to be understood.

To be heard does not necessarily mean to be understood. Distinctness of utterance also counts. You should strive for clarity of diction; do not omit or slur syllables. Good articulation is as important to intelligibility as proper volume.

An Adequate Voice Has Pleasing Quality

A poor voice may be characterized as raspy, guttural, breathy, thin, harsh, whining, or monotonous. Desirable voice characteristics include flexibility, modulation, animation, as well as controlled melody, pitch, rate, and force. Why does one speaker have a pleasing voice while another does not? The difference is due partly to training; by putting into practice the principles discussed in this chapter, one should develop a more pleasing voice quality. More important, a warm, pleasant, sympathetic voice is the product of a warm, pleasant, sympathetic person. A person with a zest for life, with a desire for knowledge, and with attitudes of good will normally reveals these attributes in his voice. Pleasant voice quality has close connection with the able-man theory discussed in Chapter 2.

An Adequate Voice Is Free of Affectations

When a speech teacher's colleague from another department heard a particular student speak, the colleague remarked, "That young lady sounds just like a speech major." Regardless of how the professor meant the statement, it was not complimentary to the speech teacher. The young lady used overly precise diction, artificially rounded tones, and other affectations that called attention to her speech and detracted from what she said. Her use of voice represented the antithesis of the goals sought.

A good voice does not call attention to itself. It makes the ideas of a speech understandable in a manner pleasing to the ear. Some beginning speech students and other improperly trained speakers show affectations in voice because they have not perfected voice control. They may be in the "show off" stage when they make a major production of all they do. Saying "Pass the biscuits, please" with the same oratorical flourish that Maurice Evans would pronounce Hamlet's "instructions to the players" will make one appear ridiculous. True art conceals itself; properly used, one's voice aids in accomplishing one's purpose without calling attention to itself. It is free of affectations and passes unnoticed in any cultured group.

An Adequate Voice Is Flexible

A speaker with an unusually strong voice delighted in displaying its full force on every occasion. He used the same loud volume when talking in a room seating fifty people as he did in an auditorium seating five thousand. He proudly boasted on many occasions that he developed his strong voice calling pigs on his father's farm. What he did not learn was that the ears of most human beings are apparently more sensitive than those of pigs. The characteristics of successful pig-calling do not of themselves insure success in public speaking.

Some speak in a monotone throughout their speech. Others use the same rate at all times, whether explaining Einstein's theory of relativity or describing a heavyweight fight. Many use little or no variation in pitch regardless of subject matter. Still others acquire a singsong or stereotyped pattern. All these types create monotonous patterns that prove irritating to listeners.

A well-managed voice shows variety in keeping with the content of a speech. The speaker varies the volume, rate, pitch, timing, inflection, and pattern of speech to bring out his subtleties of thought and feelings. He strives for a conversational manner and a flexible voice that aids in communication.

II. Variations in Voices

What accounts for variations in voices? Some people have better voices without training than others have with training. Some people make more progress in training than others. A few people seem to have pleasing, natural voices. Franklin D. Roosevelt's many attributes as an able man and speaker included a voice with a warmth that helped attract millions. His fireside chats over the radio introduced a new era in which a president discussed policies of his program directly with the people. These speeches did more to allay the fears of some people during the depression of the 1930s than the legislation that he advocated. On the other hand, Abraham Lincoln had a high-pitched, whining voice that repelled listeners. His speeches read better than they sounded. Consequently, he relied less on speech-making than did many presidents. Why these differences in voice? The variations may be accounted for on the four bases that follow.

Variations Are Partly Physical

Some people have better physical equipment for voice production than others. We do not have a voice mechanism separate from other life processes. Voice is produced as a secondary function of several structures whose primary functions are essential life processes. Variations in health and size of these organs from one individual to another account for some vocal variations. The length of the vocal cords accounts in part for vocal variations, as do the size and condition of the resonating chambers of the nose and mouth. A person with a flexible tongue and lips, well-formed palates, and well-aligned teeth has good physical equipment for articulation.

The general state of a person's health also affects voice production. A strong, healthy body gives vitality and force to one's voice. Chronic ill health or fatigue usually causes weak and indistinct voices that project poorly.

A few people have organic difficulties that prevent the production of normal speech. Studies reveal the total to be between 5 and 10 per cent in the United States, depending upon the definition of a speech defect. The organic difficulties may range all the way from poorly spaced teeth to complete vocal paralysis. Almost all defects can be improved under the guidance of speech pathologists and doctors. Their analysis and suggested treatment are not within the scope of this text, but those with speech defects should by all means consult a specialist.

Variations Are Due Partly to Environment

Speech is learned, not inherited. Although we are born with the physical mechanism for producing sound, the making of sound into speech must be learned. Since a child learns to use his voice largely through imitation, he acquires the voice characteristics of those with whom he associates during his early years. Later, his playmates, teachers, and performers in radio, television, and the movies exert an influence. So powerful is environmental influence that some children acquire slight impediments in speech from early associations.

Since vocal habits are learned and some vocal characteristics acquired, it stands to reason that we can correct some of our faults. The changes do not come easily, however, for poor vocal practices may have been developed over a long period. Persistent efforts will result in improvements.

Variations Are Due Partly to Personality Characteristics

We learned in Chapter 10 that chronic feelings of inadequacy affect communication abilities, including the voice. A tense person fails to relax his throat; thus the tension prevents free vibration of the vocal cords. Stage fright usually affects a person's breathing and in turn causes an uneven rhythm and breathiness. A timid person tends to speak either indistinctly in a high-pitched voice or in a blustering manner in an attempt to cover up his feelings of inferiority. Conversely, a relaxed person usually uses breathing, resonance, and articulation in a natural manner because the voice makes coordinated use of the organs of speech production. In one sense, proper voice production may be considered partly as social adjustment.

Your voice indicates your temperament and emotional attitudes. An aggressive, high-strung, hard-working person tends to speak rapidly, forcefully, and emphatically. An easy-going person usually speaks with moderate rate, normal force, and an even emphasis. An irritable, troubled person often speaks in a high-pitched voice that may approach whining. Since your voice tends to indicate your general temperament, beware of attempting radical changes in a short time. A hard-driving, aggressive person will probably never acquire the slow rate, moderate force, or even rhythm of an easy-going person, but by conscious effort he can bring undesirable voice qualities under control.

Variations Are Due Partly to Improper Use

We sometimes acquire poor habits of voice for reasons not directly attributable to any of the foregoing causes. We acquire poor techniques because of a lack of knowledge about proper voice control. The young man with a natural high pitch may force his voice down into his throat in an endeavor to acquire a deep voice. The young lady with a naturally thin voice may force her voice almost to a shout in an attempt to get more force. A person who thinks more rapidly than he speaks may acquire a halting, uneven rhythm. Some persons may attempt to emulate the voices of speakers or performers whom they admire when they have no natural propensities for such use. These types use their voices improperly from lack of knowledge about proper control.

The following sections of this chapter relate to the physical characteristics and methods for improving voice. With an understanding of voice production and methods for improvement and with conscientious practice, any normal person can develop an adequate voice.

III. The Process of Voice Development

Voice development consists of (1) controlled breathing—regulating breathing habits for the initiation of sound; (2) phonation—relaxation of the throat and jaws to permit unhampered vibrations of the vocal folds; (3) resonation—taking full advantage of the resonating chambers of the throat, mouth, and nose; (4) articulation—shaping of the jaws, tongue, and lips for forming different speech sounds; and (5) ear training—learning to hear one's voice.

Breathing

Breathing is perhaps the most important factor in tone production. It exemplifies speech as an overlaid function. We do not breathe in order to speak but to supply our bodies with oxygen and rid them of carbon dioxide. In short, we breathe to live. Speech is a kind of by-product of breathing since we use the outgoing breath to make vocal tones. To use the outgoing breath to the best advantage, we must exercise control over our breathing habits. Lower-chest or diaphragmatic breathing serves speech best because it permits easier control, requires less effort, and results in less tension in the throat than does upper-chest breathing.

Breathing for speech requires more air than does breathing for life. Exhalation must, therefore, be controlled. In breathing for life we breathe regularly, rhythmically, and deeply about fifteen times a minute. In breathing for speech the rhythm is irregular. We fill our lungs comfortably with air and keep them filled. We use the amount of air necessary to speak a phrase; we inhale quickly through our mouth instead of our nose and take in as much air as we have just used. Through this process we keep a reserve supply of air in our lungs at all times. This type of breathing gives the speaker a

The Human Voice Organs*

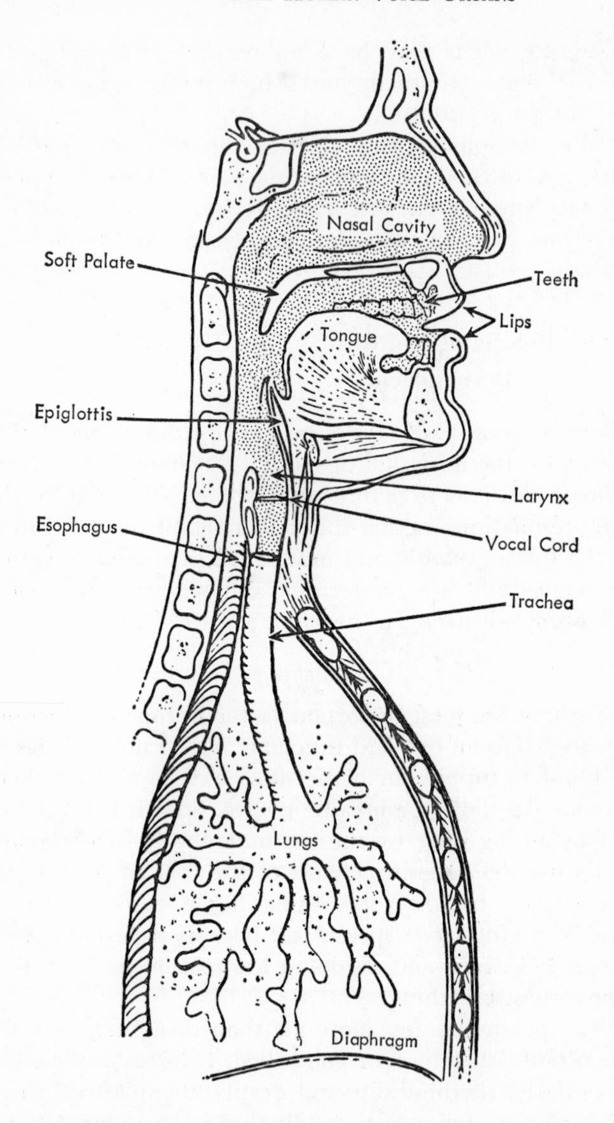

* "The Speech Chain" by Peter B. Denes and Eliot N. Pinson. Copyright Bell Telephone Laboratories, Inc.

feeling of adequacy. He realizes that he has sufficient reserve breath to make himself heard easily; he therefore feels no need to strain or tighten the muscles of his throat in order to produce an adequate tone. Excessive muscular tension results in the hoarseness and "tired throat" we so often associate with evangelists and teachers and all those who speak often in public.

To motivate proper breathing habits, we should understand the mechanics of breathing. Air is taken into the body because of the expansion of the chest cavity. When the respiratory muscles contract, the diameter of the cavity increases from side to side because of the lifting of the ribs; it increases from top to bottom because of the contraction of the dome-shaped muscle called the diaphragm. The increase in the size of the chest cavity causes a decrease in the pressure within. Air rushes into the nose or mouth and fills the lungs with enough air to equalize the pressure. Upon the completion of inhalation, an elastic recoil of the muscles occurs and the air is squeezed out of the lungs. If the upper rib-cage is held high and allowed to participate little in the breathing process, the work of breathing must be done by the lower ribs and the diaphragm. Since the lungs are passive organs and can be acted upon only by the ribs and diaphragm, it follows that so long as the upper rib-cage is held high there will be a reserve supply of air in the lungs.

The floor of the thoracic cavity is a dome-shaped sheet of muscular fibers called the diaphragm. It separates the thoracic from the abdominal cavity. When the diaphragm contracts to draw breath into the lungs, it pushes down upon the organs of the abdominal cavity, resulting in a slight bulge of the upper abdomen. In exhalation, the diaphragm and the muscles that control the elevation of the ribs relax; the abdominal organs return to their normal position, and the air is forced out of the lungs. An understanding of this process helps the speaker exercise conscious control over the breathing mechanism.

The abdominal muscles are used in the controlled exhalation necessary for proper use of the voice. They press upon the viscera which in turn press upon the diaphragm. In this manner the abdominal muscles regulate the pressure and distribute the portions of air necessary to support tone production. Thus, they help control the rate at which the air leaves the lungs.

Proper breathing habits must be developed outside the public-speaking situation. If the speaker concentrates upon the control of breathing rather than upon what he says, he will not communicate properly. The audience will be conscious of the speaker's mechanics of delivery and will not concentrate upon what he says. Ideally, proper breathing habits should become so thoroughly learned that the speaker will use them at all times, even in conversation, without being conscious of how he breathes.

Drills and exercises will help one acquire proper breathing habits. Practice the following:

1. Good posture is conducive to proper breathing. The following exercises, if practiced several times a day, will improve posture.

a. Stand with the heels, buttocks, and shoulders pressed against a wall. Press the middle of the back firmly against the wall until the spinal column is straight. With the upper part of the body relaxed, try to walk away from the wall, keeping the back straight.

b. Stand relaxed with the eyes closed. Take a fold of the skin at the base of the throat between the fingers and lift straight up. Keep the shoulders relaxed. Pull the body up tall. Keep the heels on the floor but imagine the whole body as being lifted. Lift the chest up from the waist. Feel a stretch between the lower ribs and the hip bones.

2. Place the hand flat on the upper abdomen. Pant quickly like a tired dog. Feel the alternate bulging and relaxation of the abdomen as the diaphragm pushes down to draw in air and relaxes to release it. Do this several times. Now pant slowly. Push hard with the hand and with the abdominal muscles on exhalation. Feel the thrust of the muscles as air is expelled from the lungs.

3. With the shoulders relaxed, place the heels of the hands flat on the lower ribs with the fingers touching over the abdomen. Inhale, pushing out against the hands with the lower ribs and abdomen. Make the fingers separate as far as possible. Exhale slowly through the mouth, prolonging the breath as long as possible. Push all of the air out of the lungs by tightening the abdominal muscles. Do this several times, working for greater expansion under the hands each time.

4. In the same position as in the above exercise, inhale until the lungs are comfortably full of air. As you exhale push with the hands and abdominal muscles but do not allow the upper chest to move. Keep the upper rib-cage high. Exhale only that air which can be controlled by the diaphragm. Inhale a short breath. Exhale as you keep the upper ribs from participating noticeably in the breath-

ing process. Work at this exercise each day until you feel that all breathing activity takes place in the center of the body.

5. Start with the same position as for the two previous exercises. Inhale on the mental count of three. Push out against the hands. Hold the breath as you count three silently. Inhale again on the count of three and again hold your breath while you count three. Inhale again, taking in enough air to fill the lungs. Hold the breath while you count ten. Attempt to remain relaxed. To aid relaxation, roll the head around on the shoulders as you hold your breath. Let the breath go slowly, exhaling the air through rounded lips and prolonging the exhalation as long as possible. Again push out all the air by contracting the stomach muscles. If done properly, the upper abdomen will bulge a little on the first inhalation, a little more on the second, and still more on the third. It will remain without motion when the breath is held.

6. This exercise is the reverse of the last one. Start with the same position. Inhale until the lungs are comfortably full. Exhale as you count three, pushing against the abdomen with the fingers. Hold the breath as you count three. Do not cut off the breath at the glottis. Stop exhaling by stopping the action of the breathing muscles. Now exhale again on three, hold the breath on three, and finally push all the air out of the lungs by pressing the contents of the abdomen against the diaphragm. The upper rib-cage should be held high, the throat and shoulders relaxed.

7. This exercise correlates breathing and tone production. Fill the lungs comfortably with air. Hold the upper ribs high. Do not allow them to move any more than necessary. Push the air out with the abdominal muscles as you need it. Keep the throat and shoulders relaxed. Breathe quickly through the mouth, taking in as much air as was used to form the preceding phrase. Count aloud—one, two, three, breathe; one, two, three, breathe; one, two, three, breathe. This time count to five before you take a breath. Now drop back to a count of two. Be sure that the ribs remain high.

8. Using the same technique as in Exercise 7, read the following passage; take a quick breath through the mouth at the places marked with a diagonal line.

> This is the man all tattered and torn/ who kissed the maiden all forlorn/ who milked the cow with the crumpled horn/ that tossed the dog/ that worried the cat/ that killed the rat/ that ate the malt/ that lay in the house that Jack built.

Phonation

The second step in tone production is the initiation of tone by the vibration of the vocal folds in the larynx. Air pushed up from the lungs passes through the bronchi, through the trachea, and finally to the larynx or voice box. The larynx is a shield-shaped box of cartilages situated at the top of the trachea. Stretched across the larynx are two tendinous folds or bands. These are not cords or muscular strings as some people believe, but folds or ledges of tough fibrous muscle.

Phonation aims at a free, open, relaxed throat which offers no impediment to the easy vibration of the vocal folds. A speaker can do little to bring this state about except consciously to relax the muscles of the neck, throat, and shoulders. The muscles that control the tensions of the folds operate automatically; they cannot be knowingly controlled. Any adjustments made in the larynx that improve vocal tone come through trial and error. The speaker must attempt to recognize a desirable tone and endeavor to reproduce the conditions which produced it, although he may not understand fully how he brought the condition about. He must rely on his ability to hear variations in tone.

A free, open throat during phonation is essential to proper tone production. Tensions caused from an endeavor to produce an adequate tone without sufficient breath support interfere with free vibration of the vocal folds. They rub against each other as they vibrate; this condition may cause irritation and a loss of tonicity. Tensions which give rise to this condition may arise from stage fright or excitement such as that felt at a football game.

The following exercises for improving phonation should help in achieving relaxation of the muscles of the throat, neck, shoulders, and jaws.

1. To relax the upper body, first swing the arms around vigorously in a full circle a dozen or more times. Then reverse their direction and continue to swing in a full circle until the arms are tired. Next, drop the head on the chest as you relax your shoulders. Let your arms, which should be feeling heavy at this point, pull your body over. Relax your back one section at a time until your upper body is hanging inert from the waist. Now begin again to take possession of your body; straighten the lower back, now the middle back, then the shoulders, and last the head. This exercise not only promotes

relaxation but also results in an increase of the blood supply to the brain. It serves well in relieving tensions.

2. Drop the head vigorously from side to side until the jaw waggles loosely. Now take the chin between the thumb and first finger and move it up and down. Do not allow the jaw to offer any resistance to the fingers. Shake the head again to loosen the jaw and try again to move the chin using only the fingers.

3. Yawn widely. With the mouth open at its widest, say "Ah-a-a-a-" and gradually close your mouth. Attempt to recognize the sensation of an open, relaxed throat. Now go through the motions of yawning without really doing so. Open your mouth wide, keep the tongue low in the mouth, and intone "Ah." Do the same with "Oh" and "Aw."

4. Keeping the same open throat and relaxed jaw, read the following selections quietly and easily. Do not worry about purity of tone. Think of the air's being pushed up from the center of the body and vibrating through the folds with no effort exerted in the throat.

SWEET AND LOW

Sweet and low, sweet and low,
Wind of the western sea,
Low, low, breathe and blow,
Wind of the western sea!
Over the rolling waters go,
Come from the dying moon, and blow,
Blow him again to me;
While my little one, while my pretty one, sleeps.

Sleep and rest, sleep and rest,
Father will come to thee soon;
Rest, rest, on mother's breast,
Father will come to thee soon;
Father will come to his babe in the nest,
Silver sails all out of the west
Under the silver moon;
Sleep, my little one, sleep, my pretty one, sleep.[1]

ANNABEL LEE

For the moon never beams without bringing me dreams
Of the beautiful Annabel Lee;

[1] Alfred, Lord Tennyson, *The Works of Alfred, Lord Tennyson* (London: Macmillan and Co., 1884), p. 41.

And the stars never rise but I see the bright eyes
Of the beautiful Annabel Lee;
And so, all the night-tide, I lie down by the side
Of my darling, my darling, my life and my bride,
In her sepulchre there by the sea—
In her tomb by the sounding sea.[2]

Resonation

The tone initiated in the larynx is thin and weak. To be adequate for communication, it must be amplified and reinforced. Amplification comes through resonating the tone in the cavities of the head.

The first resonating cavity after the larynx is the pharynx. The muscles of the pharynx are flexible and capable of changing the shape and the texture of the walls of the organ. If the walls of a resonating cavity remain soft, they tend to soften the high overtones and to reinforce the more pleasing low frequencies. If you were to place an alarm clock in a large tin pan and allow the bell to ring, the noise would be unpleasant. Line the same pan with pillows, thus softening the resonating walls, and the alarm bell would lose much of its unpleasantness. The walls of the larynx function somewhat like the pan. If the muscles of the larynx are tense, the vocal tones become unpleasant. Conversely, a soft-walled pharynx causes pleasing original tones. A relaxed throat helps create the proper condition for the pharynx.

A flexible resonator can direct the flow of air toward the front of the mouth or focus the tone forward. Although we frequently hear the term "tone placement," we know that physically a tone cannot be placed. The vowel *ah* or consonant *k,* for example, would lose their identity if made anywhere except in the back of the mouth. We also know, however, that the quality of a tone can be improved when it is "thought forward." This improvement is due in part to the directing of the air forward in the pharynx and the rounding of the lips to focus the tone.

The mouth is the largest resonating cavity. It aids resonance because it can change its size and shape by action of the tongue, jaws, and velum. To gain the most from resonance, one should keep the mouth open so that it may function properly. If one speaks habitually with tight jaws and with the teeth almost meeting, he leaves little room for oral resonance.

---

[2] Edgar Allan Poe, *The Works of Edgar Allan Poe* (New York: Harper and Row, Publishers, Inc., 1849), IV, 50.

The nasal cavity also aids in resonating the tone. In making all of the vowels and most of the consonants, the velum or soft palate rests against the back of the pharynx, thus directing the flow of air into the mouth. In making the nasal consonants *m, n,* and *ng,* the velum relaxes and leaves a passage for the air to enter the nasal cavity where it is resonated.

Some people tend to nasalize vowels when they occur before or after a nasal consonant. A speaker who produces a clear "a" in *cat* may nasalize the same vowel in the word *man.* We tend to practice economy of effort. It hardly seems worthwhile to make an adjustment of the velum after the "m" and again after the "a," so we frequently send all three speech sounds through the nose, to the detriment of quality.

For the most effective resonance we must gain control of the velum. There must be full passage into the nose for the consonants *m, n,* and *ng*; but in the formation of the vowel sounds, the velum must be so controlled that only that amount of air which makes for a pleasing quality in our own particular vocal process be allowed to pass. Again, we see the necessity for ear training. We must hear, recognize, evaluate, and regulate the amount of nasal resonance in our own vocal tone.

The following exercises should improve resonance.

1. With the throat relaxed, open the mouth wide and sing "Ah." Now with the teeth almost together sing "Ah." Listen to the difference in quality.

2. Intone "m," "n," and "ng," using a great deal of force. Make the nasal cavity vibrate with sound, but do not tighten the throat.

3. Place the heels of the hands under each side of the chin, the little fingers along the nose, and the other fingers spread over the temples and upper jaws. Intone "ah," "oh," and "oo." Fill the head with sound so that it vibrates under your fingers.

4. To check the amount of air that goes through the nose, try this exercise: Place a small lighted candle about an inch under your nose. Hold a sheet of stiff paper over the mouth so the air from the mouth will not reach the candle. Now count vigorously from one through ten. The candle flame should flicker on one, seven, nine, and ten but should remain unaffected during the counting of the other numbers.

5. Say "Jack goes to high school." Now hold the nose tightly and repeat the sentence. Since there are no nasal consonants in the

sentence, there should be noticeable change in quality. Try the candle test described in Exercise 4 on this sentence. The candle flame should not waver.

6. Intone "hung-ah-ng-ah-ng-ah-ng." Sense the relaxation of the velum on "ng" and the "pulling down" on "ah." Sense the "ng" in the back of the throat. Place the "ah" forward toward the front of the mouth. There should be no noticeable nasal resonance on "ah."

7. Prolong the vowel in the words below. Be sure that no air comes through the nose; then relax the velum on the nasal consonant and send the air out through the nose.

home	loan	sing
ten	sun	lawn
hung	fan	tong

8. Direct the column of air toward the front of the mouth as you say the phrases listed below. Open the jaw wide, relax the lips, and "think the tones forward." Think of projecting the tones as you say each phrase several times.

"Focus tones forward."
"Fee, fi, fo, fum."
"Most men make money."
"Ten top tunes."

Articulation

Rather than thinking of articulation as the last step in tone production, consider it as the shaping of the resonated tone into the sounds of speech and as joining these sounds together in words and phrases. These processes are accomplished by the articulatory organs—the lips, jaws, tongue, and velum—and must be accomplished with lightning-like speed. Each speech sound requires a different adjustment of the many muscles controlling the articulatory organs. For example, consider the word *adventure;* it has seven different speech sounds and each sound requires its own particular adjustment of the muscles which produce it. We can pronounce this word in half a second. Imagine a sentence containing a half dozen such words. The pronunciation of the sentence, requiring perhaps five seconds, involves so many intricate, delicate, and precise resonance and articulatory adjustments that one wonders how the mechanism is capable of producing it in so short a time. Is it any wonder that it usually takes a child from four to seven years to perfect speech?

If the individual sounds are not clearly made, mumbling and indistinct speech will result, requiring careful concentration from an audience. Poor articulation arises from one or more of the following conditions: (1) lazy, inactive lips; (2) stiff jaws; (3) a thick, clumsy tongue; or (4) a flaccid, inactive velum.

We must develop flexible articulators and learn to control them quickly to produce articulate speech. The following exercises should help in this process.

In the following exercises, keep the jaws and throat relaxed. Direct the air forward in the mouth. Think of all the words in the exercises as made in the front of the mouth. Practice proper breathing while you do them. Keep the chest high, and take a quick breath through the mouth when you have exhausted the air controlled by the lower ribs and diaphragm.

1. Bite the tip of the tongue lightly until you feel the pressure of the teeth. Flip the tongue rapidly back and forth against the front teeth. Pass the tip of the tongue over the hard palate and on back until it touches the soft palate. Stretch it as far as it will go.

2. Keep the mouth open as wide as possible without strain as you say:

"La lay lee ly low, la lay lee ly low, la lay lee ly low."

"Rah ray ree ry row, rah ray ree ry row, rah ray ree ry row."

3. Trill the "r's" in this sentence: "Around the rocks the ragged rascal ran."

4. Attempt to keep each sound clear as you say the following rapidly.

"Tip o' the tongue, tip o' the tongue, tip o' the tongue."

"Thistle zither, thistle zither, thistle zither, thistle zither."

5. Keeping the jaws relaxed, exaggerate the action of the lips as you repeat the following:

"Lippity lippity lop, lippity lippity lop, lippity lippity lop."

"Linoleum, linoleum, linoleum, linoleum, linoleum, linoleum, linoleum."

"Ee dee ee do, ee dee ee do, ee dee ee do, ee dee ee do, ee dee ee do."

"Oh ah, oh ah, oh ah, oh ah, oh ah, oh ah, oh ah, oh ah, oh ah, oh ah, oh ah."

6. Open the mouth as wide as possible and sense the action of the velum with the following:

"Gurgle, gurgle, gurgle, gurgle, gurgle, gurgle, gurgle, gurgle."

"Ng uh, ng uh, ng uh, ng uh, ng uh, ng uh, ng uh, ng uh, ng uh."

7. Observe all the things you have learned about breathing, relaxation, and articulation in saying the following tongue twisters; say each three times rapidly:

(1) "She sells sea shells on the sea shore."
(2) "He saw six slim, sleak, slender saplings."
(3) "Rubber baby buggy bumpers."
(4) "A big black bear ate a big black bug."
(5) "Sam shipped six slippery, slimy eels in separate crates."
(6) "The ship's masts were splintered by the sharp September blasts."
(7) "The little lowland lubber was a lively lad, lucky, liberal, and likable."
(8) "Tell the tall tramp that there's advantage to him and to the community if he keeps on traveling."
(9) "Two terrible, tedious, tiresome talkers took advantage of the debating team."
(10) "The sharp, shrill shriek of the bat shatters the shadowy silence."
(11) "While we waited for the whistle on the wharf, we whittled vigorously on the white weatherboards."
(12) "Some varieties of fish are fiercely vicious, fighting vigorously and often inflicting physical hurt on the fishermen."
(13) "The view from the veranda gave forth a fine vista of waves and leafy foliage."
(14) "He mangled his ankle as he bungled a shot out of the bunker."
(15) "We climbed up the high incline, deciding to visit the shrine reminding mankind not to be unkind."
(16) "We apprehensively battled with the bragging apprentices, but they broke away from our blows and beat a poor retreat."
(17) "Sid said to tell him that Benny hid the penny many years ago."
(18) "Three gray geese in the green grass grazing; gray were the geese and green was the grazing."
(19) "The seething sea ceaseth and thus the seething sea sufficeth us."
(20) "Fanny Finch fried five floundering fish for Frances Fawlie's father."
(21) "The sixth sheik's sixth sheep's sick."
(22) "Limber Lena leaped laughingly after Lazy Lally."
(23) "Meaninglessly meandering Melina managed to master Monday's memory work."
(24) "Grass grew green on the graves in Grace Gray's grandfather's graveyard."

Ear Training

Voice training includes ear training; you must first hear your voice. You must train yourself to listen to it analytically and critically.

Perhaps you have always taken your voice for granted much as you have your nose or hair. To improve your voice for speech, you must learn to listen to it objectively. The tape recorder is invaluable for this purpose. No one can tell you exactly how to produce a good tone. You can learn how to support the tone with well-filled lungs, how to round the lips, how to relax the jaw, and why you should open your mouth; but in the end you must listen to the resulting tone to evaluate it. Then you must either try to repeat a well-made tone or change the relationship of the different parts of the process in order to achieve more pleasing results. This trial-and-error method applies when trying to overcome nasality, harshness, breathiness, or any unpleasant defect in tone production. Through ear training you will eventually acquire a proper auditory image so that when you finally produce a good tone you will recognize it as such.

In summary, tone production starts with breathing. Proper breathing for speech results from the control of an adequate amount of air. When the outgoing breath strikes the vocal folds, sound is initiated. Relaxation of the body, especially the throat and neck, helps to avoid strain and thus aids phonation. The initial vibrations are transmitted to the resonating chambers of the throat, mouth, and nose, where the sound becomes amplified. Relaxation also aids in this amplification process. Finally, through use of the organs of articulation—the tongue, teeth, jaws, lips, and palates—sounds are formed into words. Proper voice training starts with ear training; one must learn to hear his own voice so that he can analyze, evaluate, and improve it.

IV. Variety in Vocal Utterance

To gain the most advantage from your voice, avoid monotony in its use. Variety may be achieved in quality, time, pitch, and force.

Quality

Variation in voice quality is determined by emotional understanding and response. If the speaker learns to control his voice mechanism, if he has a clear understanding of the logical and emotional content of his material, and if he has no physical defects to mar the timbre of his voice, he may attain variety in voice quality.

The emotional aspect of quality cannot be attained by mechanical means. All other things being equal, an emotionally responsive and uninhibited person will produce the desired emotional aspect. Emotional responsiveness may be developed, in part, through real and vicarious experiences. The speaker who reads, understands, and responds to the emotional content in good literature will be greatly aided in attaining emotional responsiveness. A healthy body and a healthy mind aid the speaker in developing emotional color in his voice.

Time

Speakers usually have so much material to cover and so little time in which to cover it that they tend to acquire a rapid rate of speech. This rapidity, which gives little time for pause, may defeat the speaker's purpose. Any discussion of time should include a consideration of rate, phrasing, and pause. Time aids the expression not only of logical content but of emotional content as well.

Rate means the speed of utterance, the number of words spoken per minute. The normal rate for most speakers is from 120 to 150 words per minute. Variations in rate depend upon such factors as the importance of the material, the desire for emphasis, and the mood of the content. One would not describe the dire conditions of poverty in city slums at the same rate that he would describe a horse race. Neither should a speaker race through point after point simply because he considers his message important. Actually the audience would be more impressed by two or three well-developed points delivered at a normal rate than it would be by ten points hastily developed and more hastily given.

Proper phrasing makes clear the speaker's meaning. "For every selection or speech paragraph there is a maximum number of words beyond which one cannot go without destroying meaning." [3] Phrases may be defined as thought units. If a speaker ignores these thought units and groups words together regardless of their meaning for the convenience of breathing, he decreases his chances for presenting a successful speech. He should group words according to meaning and control his breathing so that he can pause slightly at the end of the phrase and get a breath at the same time.

Pauses serve not only to help the speaker control his general rate, but they also provide him the opportunity to emphasize and point

[3] C. H. Woolbert and J. F. Smith, *The Fundamentals of Speech* (New York: Harper and Row, Publishers, Inc., 1934), p. 221.

up a thought. A speaker pauses to give his audience time to get the full significance of what he says. While a speaker speaks, he has a threefold task: he must think, he must organize his thoughts, and he must choose words that express his thoughts. Pauses also permit the speaker to think ahead, to weigh the significance of what he plans to say next, to anticipate and empathize with the next thought. An occasional pause will give him time to do these things well. It is better to hesitate a moment in order to choose the right word than to say the first word that comes to mind.

If a speaker fails to pause often enough or long enough, he gives the audience a feeling of frustration. While the listener attempts to digest an idea, the speaker leaps ahead before the listener is ready for another idea. The amateur speaker often fails to pause because he fears that if he stops talking the audience will think he has forgotten his speech. A rapid rate with few pauses indicates lack of poise. A speaker's failure to pause may cause his audience to stop trying to listen.

Pitch

Pitch means the key or place of the voice on the musical scale and the variations up and down the scale. The pitch of the voice grows higher as one becomes aggressive or excited. A noticeable rise in pitch level decreases effective delivery. Conversely, a voice kept on the normal key at all times becomes monotonous. A speaker should attempt to find his normal pitch level and vary the level in keeping with the emotional content of his material.

To bring out fine distinctions in meaning, make use of key variations, or inflections and steps. A rising inflection within a word or phrase or at the end of a sentence denotes incompleteness of thought, indecisiveness, or doubt; a falling inflection denotes finality and completeness of thought. For making the finest distinction between logical and emotional meaning, however, a combination of the two may come within a single syllable. For example, the word "yes" means an affirmation when spoken with a downward or falling inflection; when spoken with a rising inflection it denotes doubt or question; when given a combination of the two, a circumflex, it may mean "no" or "yes" with reservations. Beware of developing an inflection pattern, a preponderance of either falling or rising inflections. To help correct an inflection pattern, make a voice recording for the purpose of self-criticism.

Inflection relates primarily to gradual changes in pitch within a word or syllable; the *step* concerns abrupt changes in pitch between words and phrases or sentences. No speaker wants to bore an audience by speaking all of his words, phrases, and sentences in the same pitch. For example, "Give me liberty or give me death," would vary widely in range. To say all the words of such a sentence at the same pitch level would destroy its full meaning.

Force

Force or stress applied to individual words and phrases helps to convey meaning. For example, "I am going to town" may be made to mean that *I,* not somebody else, will go to town by stressing the word *I*: "*I* am going to town." The same sentence may be given a note of defiance by stressing the word *am*: "I *am* going to town." Still different meanings may be given by stressing the words *going* and *town.*

Variety in force applies as well as variety in other aspects of voice. One who speaks in a bombastic tone or with explosive force throughout a speech will be likely to wear his audience out. The audience will be unable to hear what he says because of the noise he makes. The person who continually speaks with little vocal energy or force will not be heard well and will lose audience attention. The audience feels that such a speaker is convinced neither of the importance of his material nor of his desire to communicate.

Your voice can be one of your greatest assets. To make the most of your natural ability, spend much time developing your voice and learning to use it advantageously.

V. Acquiring Acceptable Pronunciation

Although articulation means the producing and joining together of speech sounds, pronunciation concerns choosing the correct sound and placing the proper stress upon the syllable or syllables to be accented. One cannot know, just by looking at a word, how to pronounce it. The English alphabet is not consistently phonetic. A letter may be pronounced one way in a certain word and another way in a different word. The letter *a,* for example, is pronounced differently in each of the following words: *rain, apple, autumn, among, what,* and *care.* Although certain rules for pronunciation prevail, the great number of exceptions make the rules practically useless. The only way to determine the pronunciation of a word is to look it up in a dictionary.

The compilers of a dictionary do not decide pronunciation arbitrarily. Instead they record the pronunciation currently in use by the majority of educated people. If usage justifies, they record two or more pronunciations. Some dictionaries record the pronunciations without any thought to preference; others record first the pronunciation used by most people. The trend toward multiple pronunciations is greater today than formerly.

The majority of words have only one pronunciation other than the normal deviations within a phoneme, a family of related speech sounds. We have only to consult the dictionary to know the correct pronunciation. But students often hear two or more pronunciations of the same word, and they find more than one pronunciation given when they look it up. They may insist on knowing which is right. In fact, all are correct. Although one may choose the desired pronunciation, the best choice consists of that pronunciation used by the majority of educated people in one's particular section of the country. The best pronunciation passes unnoticed in any cultured group. An unusual pronunciation for a particular region, although given in the dictionary, calls attention to itself and sometimes interferes with audience concentration.

We do not have one standard American pronunciation in the United States as do some other countries. In France, a standard pronunciation is used by those who speak so-called Parisian French. In Spain, the educated classes speak Castilian Spanish. In England, the dialect used by Oxford and the public schools, the pronunciation of Southern England, is considered standard. In the United States we have regional standards instead of one standard dialect.

Almost all writers divide the speech of the United States into three groups, based on the geographical regions where they are used: (1) Eastern dialect, spoken in eastern New England and New York City; (2) Southern dialect, spoken in those states usually considered the "Old South"; and (3) General American dialect, spoken elsewhere in the United States.

Since approximately two-thirds of the people of the United States use General American speech, the national television and radio systems use this dialect. Dictionaries also record the General American pronunciation since they base pronunciation on that used by the majority of the cultured population. For the same reason, the use of Southern British diction for the American stage is rapidly disappearing.

Some people think that Southern and Eastern dialects will slowly be assimilated by the General American and that eventually we will have one standard American pronunciation. Many people regret this trend because they like the variations of the crisp, brisk accent of the Bostonian and the mellow, resonant drawl of the Southerner. Standardization would destroy much that we consider distinctively American.

PHONETIC AND DIACRITIC EQUIVALENTS*

Consonants

I.P.A.	*Merriam*[a] *Webster*	*American*[b] *College*	*Webster's*[c] *New World*	*Standard*[d] *College*	Key Word
p	p	p	p	p	pep
b	b	b	b	b	bib
t	t	t	t	t	tot
d	d	d	d	d	dead
k	k	k	k	k	kick
g	g	g	g	g	gag
f	f	f	f	f	fat
v	v	v	v	v	van
θ	th	th	th	th	thin
ð	th̲	tħ	*th*	th̲	these
ʃ	sh	sh	sh	sh	she
ʒ	zh	zh	zh	zh	leisure
m	m	m	m	m	me
n	n	n	n	n	not
ŋ	ŋ	ng	ŋ	ng	sing
l	l	l	l	l	let
r	r	r	r	r	run
j	y	y	y	y	yet
w	w	w	w	w	we
h	h	h	h	h	hot
hw, ʍ	hw	hw	hw	hw	when
s	s	s	s	s	see
z	z	z	z	z	zeal

* Cecil May Burke, *A Phonetic Primer* (Berkeley: McCrutchan Publishing Corp., 1964), pp. 56-57. Reprinted by permission of Professor Burke.

[a] By permission from Webster's Third New International Dictionary. Copyright © 1963 by G. and C. Merriam Co., Publishers of the Merriam-Webster Dictionaries.

[b] Reprinted from *The American College Dictionary*, Copyright 1947, © Copyright 1965, by permission of Random House, Inc.

[c] From *Webster's New World Dictionary* of the American Language, College Edition. Copyright © 1964 by The World Publishing Company.

[d] From *Funk and Wagnalls Standard® College Dictionary*. Copyright © 1963 by Funk and Wagnalls Company, Inc. Reprinted by permission of the publishers.

PHONETIC AND DIACRITIC EQUIVALENTS* (Continued)

I.P.A.	*Merriam*[a] *Webster*	*American*[b] *College*	*Webster's*[c] *New World*	*Standard*[d] *College*	Key Word
		Affricates			
tʃ	ch	ch	ch	ch	church
dʒ	j	j	j	j	judge
		Vowels			
æ	a	ă, â	a, â	a, a	cat
ɑ	ä, ȧ	ŏ, ä	o, ä	a, a	what
ɔ	ȯ	ô	ô	ô	fall
e	ā	ā	ā	ā	chaotic
ɛ	e	ĕ, â	e	e	set
ɪ	i	ĭ	i	i	sit
i	ˈē, ˌē, ē	ē	ē	ē	neat
o	ō	ō	ō	ō	obey
ʌ	ˈə, ˌə	ŭ	u	u	cup
ə	ə	ə	ə	ə	connect
ʊ	u̇	o͝o	oo	o͝o	cook
u	ü	o͞o	o͞o	o͞o	cool
ju	yü	ū	ū	ū	you
ɝ	ˈər, ˌər	ûr	ũr	û(r)	burn
ɚ	ər	ər	ẽr	ər	persuade
		Diphthongs			
eɪ	ā	ā	ā	ā	vein
oʊ	ō	ō	ō	ō	soul
aɪ	ī	ī	ī	ī	time
aʊ	au̇	ou	ou	ou	owl
ɔɪ	ȯi	oi	oi	oi	toil

Pronunciation is represented in print by several methods. The International Phonetic Alphabet provides the most accurate and scientific method. This alphabet uses a symbol for every sound in the language and only one symbol. The national news services use a system of respelling and capitalization to show pronunciation. The most common method, that used by most dictionaries, indicates pronunciation by means of diacritical marks. Diacritical marks are signs added or placed adjacent to a letter to distinguish it from another or similar form. Dictionaries give a chart of diacritical symbols and illustrative words with diacritical marks; some dictionaries also give the corresponding phonetic symbols. An aural recognition of speech sounds and the ability to record them by means of phonetic symbols or diacritical marks should improve one's pronunciation.

Many words in the English language are commonly mispronounced. They may be classified and analyzed according to the divisions that follow. Look up each word in the dictionary and write the pronunciation in diacritical marks as explained in the guide to pronunciation for your dictionary.

1. Words mispronounced because of improperly placed accent:

admirable
alias
awry
beneficent
comparable
coupon
electoral
genuine
horizon
impotent
mischievous
police
positively
superfluous
theatre
vehement
vehicle

2. Words mispronounced because of a reversal of sounds:

cavalry
children
hundred
larynx
modern
perspiration
pharynx
prescription
tragedy

3. Words mispronounced because of adding a sound or syllable:

athlete
business
calm
drowned
elm
film
miniature
mischievous
parliament
umbrella

4. Words mispronounced because of omitting a sound or syllable:

accurate
antarctic
believe
bona fide
candidates
capital
carburetor
chocolate
circular
company
diamond
different
experiment
generally
geography
history
interesting
literature
popular
positively
really
regular
regulate
sophomore
suppose
usually
vice versa

5. Words mispronounced because they are pronounced as they are spelled:

chic
flaccid
handkerchief
hiccough
salmon
victuals
Worcestershire

6. Words mispronounced because of an awkward repetition of sound:

February	horror	secretary
governor	library	terror
government	mirror	usury

7. Words mispronounced because of improper association with a word or part of a word which is similar but pronounced differently:

column (volume)	grievous (previous)	penalize (penalty)
comely (homely)	hearth (earth)	pronunciation (pronounce)
despicable (despise)	height (length)	put (but)
February (January)	impious (pious)	

VI. Summary

An adequate voice aids in communicating ideas; it also gives cues to one's personality and emotional state. Although not an end in itself, a good voice serves as a means to an end—the communication of ideas, information, and emotions. An adequate voice is intelligible, pleasing in quality, free of affectations, and flexible.

Variations in voices are due (1) partly to physical characteristics, (2) partly to environmental conditions, (3) partly to personality characteristics, and (4) partly to improper use. Some speakers have better natural voices than others, but most people can improve their voices by conscientious efforts.

One does not have a separate speech mechanism; all organs of the body used in producing speech have other important life functions. An adequate voice requires proper breathing, phonation, resonation, and articulation. To develop an adequate speaking voice, try to acquire controlled breathing, a relaxed body, flexible articulation, and acute hearing.

Variety in vocal utterance comes by learning to control quality, time, pitch, and force. Proper control helps in avoiding monotony and in causing the voice to realize its maximum effect for oral communication.

Acceptable pronunciation is that used by the majority of educated people in a given region. Phonetic symbols and diacritical marks are the best guides to pronunciation. Acquire the dictionary habit for improving pronunciation.

Questions and Exercises

A. Answer the following questions on Chapter 12.

1. What advantages accrue to a speaker from a good voice? List several disadvantages of a poor voice.
2. What is meant by the following statement? "An adequate voice is never an end within itself; it serves as a means to an end." What is the end that a good voice serves?
3. List four requisites of an adequate voice for oral communication. Discuss each briefly. Do you think the requisites discussed in this chapter are adequate? Explain.
4. What is your opinion of the following statement? "Some people have better voices without training than others have with training." Justify your answer.
5. List and discuss four causes of variations in voices. Can you add to the causes discussed in this chapter?
6. Discuss briefly the process of voice production. Of what significance is the fact that all organs of the body used in producing voice have other important life functions?
7. In what ways can one develop variety in use of the voice?
8. What should determine variations in rate for oral communication? What is the average rate in words per minute for most speakers?
9. What relationship does pause have to rate of speaking? Discuss the importance of pause in expressing meaning and in attaining emphasis.
10. How does pitch relate to variety in vocal utterance? Distinguish between inflection and step.
11. How does force apply to gaining variation in vocal utterances? What should determine variations in force?

B. Exercises for voice development.

1. Review Section III of this chapter. Practice the exercises given in this section for diaphragmatic breathing, relaxation of throat, resonance of tones, and flexibility of modifiers.
2. Apply the principles of pronunciation to the list of commonly mispronounced words contained in the exercises for Chapter 11.

C. For your oral speaking assignment, choose a novelist, playwright, or a poet from the list below. Make a five-minute speech, using this outline: (1) a brief biographical sketch, (2) a brief discussion of his principal writings, and (3) a critical evaluation of one of his works.

Novelists

Saul Bellow	Willa Cather
Theodore Dreiser	John Updike
Sinclair Lewis	Graham Greene
Ernest Hemingway	Somerset Maugham
John Steinbeck	James Baldwin
William Faulkner	Mark Twain
Rebecca West	Thomas Mann

Playwrights

George Bernard Shaw
Eugene O'Neill
Samuel Beckett
Sir James M. Barrie
Maxwell Anderson
Terence Rattigan
Arthur Miller
Edward Albee
Tennessee Williams
Clifford Odets

Poets

Carl Sandburg
Robert Frost
T. S. Eliot
Archibald MacLeish
William Butler Yeats
Ezra Pound
W. H. Auden
Edna St. Vincent Millay
Marianne Moore
John Ciardi
Edward Arlington Robinson
Edgar Lee Masters
Amy Lowell
Wallace Stevens

CHAPTER 13

Develop Bodily Action and Avoid Delivery Mannerisms

One of the basic principles of delivery discussed in Chapter 10 states that effective delivery uses both visual and auditory signs. An audience accepts your ideas in part by what you say and in part by what your actions indicate. When your language and your bodily action are congruous the audience usually believes what you say. If language and action contradict each other, your audience may accept what your actions indicate. You may solicit your audience to vote for the bond issue, but if you speak with your eyes focused on your notes, your hands thrust in your pockets, and your body draped over the lectern, your listeners will probably conclude that you do not believe what you say. The old adage, "Actions speak louder than words," applies to speaking situations.

I. Bodily Action in Oral Communication

Meaningful bodily action comes spontaneously from inner feelings; it is self-motivated. An uninhibited person uses his body to help him express his ideas and feelings without realizing that he does so. If you describe in a "bull-session" with your friends the exciting football play that you witnessed, you use your arms and hands, your facial expressions, and indeed your entire body to dramatize the play, to express your thoughts and feelings. Watch any group of children at play; they use uninhibited movements and gestures without thought of how they appear. The least educated man helps to make his meaning clear by using his arms, hands, shoulders, head, and face. People naturally speak with gestures and the whole body; only when people become inhibited do their bodily actions appear unnatural.

Yet, frequently when people get on the platform, they seem paralyzed and refuse to make gestures and use their bodies; or they make only half-gestures or inhibited bodily movements which appear unnatural. They say one thing, but their bodies indicate something else. These incongruous bodily actions detract from what one says; the listeners' attention is called to the action because the body movements appear weak, indefinite, poorly timed, and unnatural. Effective bodily action assists the speaker in clarifying ideas and in expressing emotions because it reinforces what he says.

Purposes of Bodily Action

Bodily action can help your speaking in three ways: (1) by conveying meaning, (2) by holding attention, and (3) by increasing your energy and self-confidence.

1. *Helps convey meaning.* Bodily action helps convey meaning in part by describing the size and shape of things. To say that the airplane propeller is three feet from the ground gives a word explanation; but if you hold your hand about three feet from the floor, you also give a visual picture. A statement that the get-away car raced down the highway at ninety miles per hour gives some indication of high speed; but if you strike the air rapidly with your hand as you make the statement, you emphasize the high speed. If you say that the box is two feet square, your audience will visualize the size better if you hold your hands about two feet apart vertically and then horizontally. Descriptive gestures reinforce your language and help express meaning.

Bodily action also aids in expressing attitudes and feelings. A shrug of the shoulders may convey your attitude better than a paragraph of words. You may say that you are pleased by being asked to speak, but a smile and pleasant manner indicate your true feelings better than your statement. If you want your audience to feel your alarm about world conditions, show alarm in your face, shoulders, and whole body.

The whole person should react in every type of behavior. Your voice should not indicate one emotion, your language another, and your body still another. They should work in coordination to give a total impression. Your posture, facial expressions, gestures, and movements must also work in coordination. Delivery may be explained in terms of activity of the whole body. An uninhibited body acts with mind, voice, and language to express meaning and emotion.

2. *Aids in holding attention.* The human body tends to imitate muscularly what it sees and feels. This we call empathic response. The enthusiastic spectator strains practically every muscle in his body to help his team push across the goal line. The great drama tires you physically because you react to the actors. The lecturer describes the bloody battle, and your body reacts covertly with the actions of the warriors. In short, as an active speaker you make an audience become alert. If you use little or no bodily action you seem sluggish, and your audience becomes apathetic. They sense that you do not feel what you say.

You walk down the sidewalk without noticing the automobiles parked by the curb; but one races by and your attention becomes immediately drawn to it. The coach explains the new football formation while the players doze; but when he diagrams it on the blackboard and acts out each player's duty, he receives careful attention. A moving object attracts attention and holds interest; so does an active speaker.

3. *Increases energy and self-confidence.* A tense person helps rid himself of tautness by physical activity. The athlete engages in warm-up exercises before the game to loosen up his muscles and help him forget his apprehensions. Some speakers take long walks before important engagements. They understand the importance of physical activity in relieving nervous tensions. By providing useful action during a speech, bodily movements release nervous energy. A step forward to emphasize a point or a step backward at the completion of an idea assists in emphasis and transitions; they also provide useful movement that helps release muscular tensions.

Action generates fervor, which in turn results in more action. Soon the speaker becomes active and enthusiastic about his ideas and forgets himself. Bodily action may be both a cause and an effect. If a person knows his subject well and has enthusiasm for it, he will normally use bodily action. Thus, action may be considered the effect of the enthusiasm for one's subject. Conversely, if a speaker uses action deliberately at first, he provides the physical activity essential to relieve muscular tension. As his tensions become released, increased fervor for his ideas results. This enthusiasm in turn causes him to forget his inhibitions and to concentrate his attention on his ideas. Thus, bodily action may be the cause of increased energy and self-confidence.

Types of Bodily Action

The types of bodily action discussed in this section may be overt or covert. Overt action comprises the easily discernible movements of the arms, head, shoulders, legs, or the whole body. The slightly discernible movements of the muscles of the arms, shoulders, face, or body that indicate the muscular tone of the entire body constitute covert action. Both overt and covert action play an important part in oral communication, but covert action may give an audience more accurate indications of the speaker's feelings and attitudes than overt action. Covert action cannot be easily camouflaged; from these actions listeners form opinions, sometimes subliminal, of the speaker's responsiveness, sincerity, decisiveness, sympathy, and confidence.

Bodily action may take the form of movements of the whole body, movements of parts of the body, facial expressions, and posture. These four types of bodily activity work together for total body expression, but they may be considered separately for better understanding of their relationships.

1. *Movements of the whole body.* Purposeful movements from one place on the platform to another will assist your delivery. Random movements call attention to themselves and detract from what you say. Random movements result from nervous tension; besides aimless pacing, they include such movements as shifting the weight from one leg to the other, and slouching over the speaker's stand. To avoid these distracting movements, consider the following descriptions of natural and purposeful movement.

When and how does one move naturally? He moves the whole body during transitions or to emphasize points. A forward movement stresses an important point. Suppose you state, "Vote 'yes' on the bond issue. Our schools must keep pace. Accept the challenge for better schools." A step or two forward with both arms raised, palms up in a giving gesture, reinforces your verbal appeal by your bodily movements. Suppose you say, "Vote 'no' on the bond issue. Taxes are already exorbitant. Defeat the proposal for needless waste." A backward step or motion accompanied with a downswing of your arms indicates rejection as well as does your language.

A backward step or two denotes the conclusion of an idea. It says to the audience that it can relax briefly. This movement would follow such statements as these: "Now you have considered the pro's and con's of the bond issue. I hope you are apprised of the facts. The decision on how you vote is yours."

Lateral movements indicate transitions from one point to another. They accompany such statements as, "You have heard the issues of the bond election discussed from both sides. Perhaps you have already decided how you will vote. Now let us consider how to mark the ballot." The lateral step would come as you speak the final sentence. It indicates that you are leaving one idea and taking up another.

When speaking behind a lectern or desk, you may occasionally move slightly to one side of the lectern, back to the original position, then to the other side, but do not pace aimlessly back and forth.

When using a public-address system, make your movements slight to avoid moving outside the range of the microphone. As discussed in Chapter 10, variations in amplification irritate an audience. You can move the body slightly without stepping outside the area of amplification of the microphone, but you must not turn away from it; keep your voice directed into the microphone.

2. *Gestures.* Gestures consist of movements of parts of the body for the purpose of emphasizing thought or emotion or for reinforcing oral expression. The principal gestures are made with the arms and hands, but they may be made also with the head and shoulders. Specific gestures bring out finer distinctions in meaning than do movements of the whole body, especially when gestures are combined with whole-body movements.

An objective study of gestures may help one understand their use, but gestures should not be used in a studied, formal, and precise manner. They should be natural and spontaneous, not mechanical. If gestures come from an urge within to help express feelings, they are likely to be natural.

Above all, do not plan gestures in advance to accompany certain statements. Let them come naturally; then in practice sessions correct those that detract from effective delivery. The right use of gestures is a matter of correction and control, not of objective planning. A study of the basic principles of gestures may aid inexperienced speakers in overcoming the initial hesitancy to use them. Beginning students often say that gestures do not come naturally. Gestures must come from feelings and impulses or they will appear unnatural, but it may be necessary to force yourself to use them in practice periods. A study of the following classification and principles governing gestures should help you free yourself from self-consciousness and show you how to use your body more effectively.

Some movements of the hands and arms have been used so long to indicate a given reaction that they may be classified as *traditional* gestures. Other gestures of the head, trunk, and shoulders are used to emphasize ideas and feelings and may be termed *emphatic* gestures. Others enforce what the speaker says by imitation and have been termed *descriptive* gestures. The distinguishing characteristics of these types and their uses need further elaboration.

a. TRADITIONAL GESTURES of the hands and arms will not be used in exactly the same manner by any two speakers, but they denote in a general way the expression they accompany.

The clenched fist indicates extreme feeling, determination, or emphasis. This gesture would be used with such statements as, "We must fight to the last man to protect our freedom. We must destroy the dictators. We must put every ounce of energy into the fight."

The hand held in a vertical position and moved from side to side indicates the separation of ideas or facts. Sometimes termed the division gesture, it would be used with such statements as the following: "We should become neither too liberal nor too conservative in our thoughts." "The advantages of this procedure are many; yet we must consider the disadvantages." "On one side we have freedom; on the other, slavery."

Pointing the index finger calls attention to objects, emphasizes statements, or indicates direction. This gesture could be used with such statements as the following: "We must go forward to keep pace with changing conditions." "Freedom is the essence of democracy. Freedom-loving men will never surrender their heritage." "In the words of Abraham Lincoln, ours is 'a government of the people, by the people, for the people.' "

The palm upward in an extended position indicates giving or receiving. If you hand a book to another or receive an object, you extend your arm with the palm up. This movement asks an audience to accept an idea. The gesture accompanies such statements as these: "We must fight or give up our heritage." "Freedom of speech carries with it certain obligations. To protect our freedom we must accept these obligations."

The palm downward denotes rejection. It indicates disapproval or suppression of a proposal. It would accompany such statements as the following: "The idea has no foundation." "The theory is worthless." "To protect our freedom, we must reject the proposal."

b. EMPHATIC GESTURES of the head, trunk, and shoulders, when used in coordination with traditional gestures of the hands and arms, emphasize feelings and ideas. A nod of the head may emphasize a point or indicate approval or disapproval; a shrug of the shoulders may denote dislike or contempt; leaning forward slightly from the waist may suggest emphasis or show keen interest. These gestures may be used to advantage, but none should be used too often. Too many gestures detract from what one says because the audience becomes aware of the movement. A speaker's constant shrugging of the shoulders, nodding of the head, or bending from the waist may wear an audience out physically.

c. DESCRIPTIVE GESTURES indicate the size and shape or distance and movement of objects by imitation. One uses his arms, hands, and body to assist his oral expression. For example, the speed of the rocket may be indicated by a swift, sweeping movement of the arm and hand. The height of the boy may be indicated by holding the hand as if at the top of his head. The vigor of a blow can be shown by a swift striking of the palm of the hand with the fist. The size of an object may be illustrated by imitative hand gestures that indicate its shape. The spiraling of prices may be indicated by describing the upward movement with the hands and arms.

3. *Posture.* Posture relates to the position or stance of the speaker while standing or sitting on the platform. Just as we have fads in slang, we also adopt fads in posture. These range all the way from ridiculous nonchalance to stiff military rigidity. A speaker should no more stand rigidly with both feet planted flat on the floor than he should slouch forward from apparent lack of ability to stand upright. The ideal posture permits the speaker to keep his head erect, his chin up, his chest out, his shoulders relaxed, and one foot slightly advanced with the weight on the forward foot.

"What shall I do with my hands?" perplexes many beginning speakers. They say that their hands get in their way. While sitting on the platform, they drum on their chair with their fingers, adjust their clothing, nervously clasp and unclasp their hands, or run restless fingers through their hair. While speaking, they clasp their hands behind them, grasp the lectern, put their hands in their pockets, or hold on to their lapels. Constant actions call attention to the mannerism and cause distractions.

None of the hand positions described above detract from delivery unless used excessively or unnaturally. In beginning your speech, you may rest your hands on the lectern. Later use them to gesture and to help express ideas. As you concentrate on your ideas and become engrossed in your speech, you will tend to forget about your hands; then their actions become natural.

Do not maintain the same posture throughout your speech; changes in position come with emphasis on ideas. All instructions about bodily action must allow for individual differences, but changes in posture normally should come during transitions. Make all changes in posture and all movements purposeful; avoid random movements.

4. *Facial expression.* Formerly, students of elocution spent torturous hours over charts of facial expressions. The instructions gave formulas for each emotion: to express anger, you were instructed to frown, draw your eyebrows down, pull your lips together, and look fierce; to show fear, you were instructed to draw back, open your mouth wide, and enlarge the openings of your eyes in an expression of stark terror; for expressing love, joy, and other emotions, equally absurd instructions followed. Obviously such rules caused the worst kind of artificiality. The bewildered elocutionist so concerned himself about his facial expressions that he could not concentrate on his ideas.

Today, speech instruction advises naturalness of expression. Almost all people show their feelings by their facial expressions; only poker players and the feeble-minded have vacuous expressions. To be sure, many normal people do not show their true feelings when self-conscious. The solution to unnatural facial expression is to bring apprehensions under control. As you conquer tenseness, become familiar with your subject, and believe fully in yourself, your facial expressions will reflect your true feelings.

The face of a speaker who has brought his anxieties under control indicates attitudes and opinions almost as well as what he says. The insincerity of the fixed smile of professional good will, the strive-to-please attitude, and the overanxious look are easily detected. To assist in correcting distracting facial expressions, give conscious attention to facial expressions during practice; seek the frank criticism of your instructor; and make movies of class speeches. When before an audience, concentrate on subject matter; as you bring your apprehensions under control, the corrective measures practiced in rehearsals will gradually predominate.

Characteristics of Good Gestures

Half-made and poorly timed gestures may be worse than no gestures since they call attention to themselves. Do not consider gesturing an absolute requirement; gestures should help you express yourself, but you should not gesture simply because you consider it customary. A study of the requirements for gestures should help you understand their function and purpose.

1. *Good gestures are spontaneous and natural.* As has been said of bodily action in general, gestures must also come in response to an inward urge. Do not force gestures; unless they come from a desire to express ideas, they will appear unnatural and affected. To gesture simply for effect invites ridicule. Develop a desire to share your ideas, and gestures will come naturally and spontaneously.

2. *Good gestures require a coordinated use of the whole body.* This requirement does not mean a perceptible change in the position of the body, but it does mean that the body must be attuned to the gesture. If you attempt to show disapproval of an idea by turning the palms downward at the same instant that you show an approving smile, the meaning of the gesture will be lost. Your audience will be perplexed because you indicate contradictory feelings simultaneously.

Suppose you ask for acceptance of a proposed plan. We discussed earlier the fact that acceptance gestures are made with the palms upward and the hands extended. Natural accompanying bodily action includes a step forward and a slight forward bending at the waist. The entire body becomes attuned to the idea expressed.

3. *Good gestures show proper timing.* The stroke of the gesture should come at the exact time that you say the word or syllable to be emphasized. If it precedes or follows the point emphasized, the gesture appears misplaced and calls attention to itself. Comedians of the silent-picture age used ill-timed gestures as a source of comedy. Poor timing of gestures to express serious thoughts makes the speaker appear ridiculous.

Poor timing usually results when a speaker fails to think about what he is saying. If you rehearse a gesture, poor timing results because you focus your attention on the gesture, not on the thought. Suppose you say, "What is the essence of democracy? It involves many factors, but *freedom* is the basis of all other factors." *Freedom* is the point of emphasis; the climax of the gesture should come as you utter this word.

4. *Good gestures are definite and fully made.* Many gestures appear like slight, fidgety movements of the hands. The speaker apparently desires to gesture but refrains from doing so because of his inhibitions. To be effective, movements must start somewhere and end somewhere. Consider gestures as having three stages—the beginning, the climax, and the return. A gesture that includes use of the hands and arms should begin with the movement from the shoulder joints, not the elbows or wrists. It should reach a climax well away from the body on the emphasized word. The arms and hands should then return to the sides in an unobtrusive manner. Never drop the hands to the side from midair purposelessly.

Make gestures definite and full-sweeping. Exaggerate the sweep of gestures in practice so as to accustom yourself to let go. When speaking before an audience, forget about how sweeping gestures should be made; concentrate on the ideas of your speech.

5. *Good gestures vary in vigor with ideas expressed.* This requirement does not mean that you should pound the table or beat the air aimlessly; it does call for enthusiasm and energy. The vigor of the gesture should conform to the idea expressed. To move your arms slowly through the air when you say, "The jet plane screamed through the air at a speed exceeding sound," would appear humorous and absurd. This statement should be accompanied by a swift movement of the arms to simulate the speed of the plane. You would not strike the palm of one hand with the fist of the other when saying "The gradual rise in prices resulted in decreased consumption." Use a slow, upward-moving arm gesture for this statement. Make the vigor of the gesture conform to the spirit of the idea.

6. *Good gestures are appropriate.* The number and kind of gestures depend not only upon the meaning to be conveyed, but also upon the size and type of audience and the occasion. Before large audiences gestures should be wider and more sweeping than before small groups. Conversely, descriptive gestures would be more appropriate when talking to small audiences than when talking to

large audiences. Gestures need to be adapted to type of audience, also. For instance, as a general rule, young people like more action than do older people.

The type of occasion also affects the use of gestures. The speaker at a funeral naturally would not use the vigorous type of gestures that one would use at a patriotic rally. The speaker at a workshop session would probably use descriptive gestures more than the other types, while the speaker at a political rally would normally use emphatic and conventional more than descriptive gestures.

7. *Good gestures have variety.* Some speakers use only one or two gestures throughout a speech. They use the same gesture to show disapproval, to ask acceptance, to emphasize an idea, or to show extreme feeling. One gesture frequently overworked is the hand-and-arm pumping movement. The speaker stands rooted in one spot or wanders about the platform, pumping his hand and arm up and down for emphasis.

The monotony of the use of one gesture detracts from what the speaker talks about; worse, it is confusing, for the gesture and the idea are incongruous. Most speeches contain many ideas that should be emphasized and clarified by a variety of movements, gestures, and facial expressions.

In summary, gestures serve the speaker well, but they should be used to make ideas meaningful, not as an end in themselves. The seven requirements discussed in this section should assist in making gestures feel natural and be meaningful.

II. Distracting Mannerisms of Delivery

A mannerism means any behavior in presentation employed with such frequency that it calls attention to itself. Actions of delivery tend to become objectionable because of overuse. One student reported that his teacher removed his glasses and replaced them twenty-three times during a class lecture. A college debater said "ladies and gentlemen" thirty-five times in a single speech. A business executive buttoned and unbuttoned his coat eighteen times in a twenty-minute speech, and a minister used the word "permissive" sixteen times in his sermon. That students took time to count and report these incidents indicates that they probably found the mannerisms more interesting than the speeches.

Often the speaker may be unaware of his mannerisms. The student who said "ladies and gentlemen" excessively reported that he did not realize that he used the phrase at all. Speakers acquire mannerisms as a release to nervous energy, as a substitute for a pause, as a rest period for thinking of what to say next, and as a release from the necessity for rapid thinking. Unless someone calls your attention to your mannerisms, they may become habitual.

The following mannerisms constitute the most common, except for those already discussed in the preceding three chapters. Have your instructor or a friend watch and listen especially for your mannerisms at your next class speech. If possible, make a recording of your speech for self-evaluation. A majority of the mannerisms that follow apply to errors in bodily action; some apply to language and other factors.

Misusing the Lectern

Perhaps you use the lectern more as a crutch than as an aid. You may lean on it habitually, rest a foot on its base, pull it toward you, push it away, or otherwise call the audience's attention to it. The lectern may serve a useful purpose but not in these ways. It is permissible to rest your hands on it occasionally, place your notes and other materials on it, or even lean on it at times. Refrain from using it, however, so excessively in any one way as to cause distractions.

Adjusting Clothing and Ornament

This mannerism may be termed the "fix-it" habit. Some speakers may remove their glasses, clean them, use them as pointers, put them back on, and repeat the process. Other speakers often look at their watches, crease and uncrease their notes, and wipe their faces periodically during their speeches. Men may button and unbutton their coats, adjust their ties, play with their watch chains, hoist their trousers, or jingle the coins in their pockets. Ladies may adjust their bracelets, play with their rings, twist their watches, smooth their hair, or readjust their scarves or hats. Any of these adjustments call attention to themselves when done excessively.

Lack of Direct Eye Contact

You may refuse to look at your audience. Some speakers continually look at their notes, out the windows, at the floor or ceiling, or otherwise away from their listeners. Eye contact serves a useful purpose in establishing audience communication. Direct eye contact indicates an enthusiasm for your subject and an interest in your audience. Learn your outline so well that you will not be forced to look at your notes excessively. Include all sections of the auditorium in your line of vision, not one section to the exclusion of others.

Excessive Bodily Action

Excessive bodily actions can become mannerisms. For instance, movements of the head may indicate approval or disapproval of an idea, but excessive movements back and forth or from side to side call the audience's attention to the movement. A speaker may lean forward to emphasize a point, but rocking back and forth becomes distracting. One may occasionally shift his weight from one leg to the other; but if he rests his weight on one leg while the other hangs limp, he presents an ungainly posture. Conversely, a speaker may stand too rigid and thus deprive himself of the values of bodily action. Controlled bodily actions aid the speaker; excessive movements become distracting.

Taking Pencil or Pen to the Platform

If you take a pencil or pen to the platform, you may use it as a pointer, wave it about, put it behind your ear, or perhaps play tricks with it. The audience becomes fascinated with your manipulations of the pencil and forgets to listen. Leave your pencil or pen at your desk or clamp it in your pocket before getting up to speak.

Making Extraneous Sounds

Do not clear your throat or smack your lips frequently during your speech, because these mannerisms prove irritating to audiences. Speakers frequently make such sounds when they begin a new point or during transitions. Many speakers do not realize that they have acquired these habits. An occasional recording of a class speech will reveal if you have these mannerisms. If you find that you do have them, pay particular attention to correcting them in practice sessions. If you can prevail on a classmate to listen to your speech, have him stop you each time you commit these mannerisms.

Vocalizing Pauses

Some speakers never seem to be able to pause. As explained in Chapter 12, a pause between ideas provides time for the audience to think about the previous point; a pause before an important point emphasizes its importance. During the normal time for pause, some speakers vocalize with "er," "ah," and "uh" or some connective word like "and," "but," and "so." If used excessively, such sounds and repetitious words detract from what the speaker says.

Talking on Way to Lectern

As explained in Chapter 10, some speakers do not show proper deliberation in beginning their speeches. The habit of starting to speak on the way to the lectern shows undue anxiety and does not permit the audience time to ready themselves to start listening. Take your place behind the speaker's stand and pause briefly before starting to speak.

The mannerisms of language and voice were discussed in Chapters 11 and 12. Some of the more common are talking too rapidly, using excessive and constant volume, indulging in an uneven rhythm or a singsong pattern, following a pattern of rising or falling inflection, overusing certain words, using of loaded words excessively, adhering too much to regional expressions, and using the wrong word. All these mannerisms have one thing in common—their frequent use interferes with oral communication by creating a distracting influence.

III. Summary

Bodily action constitutes an essential part of oral communication; an audience forms its impressions in part by the speaker's actions. Bodily action helps convey meaning, aids in holding attention, and increases energy and self-confidence.

Bodily action takes four forms: (1) movement of the whole body, (2) gestures, (3) posture, and (4) facial expressions. Gestures are of three types: (1) traditional gestures of the hands and arms; (2) emphatic gestures of the head, trunk, and shoulders; and (3) descriptive gestures. The requirements of good gestures include: (1) spontaneity and naturalness, (2) coordination of the whole body, (3) proper timing, (4) definiteness and completeness, (5) vigor, (6) appropriateness, and (7) variety.

Delivery mannerisms consist of any behavior employed with such frequency that it detracts from what the speaker says. Some of the more common include (1) misusing the speaker's stand, (2) adjusting ornament and clothing, (3) lack of direct eye contact, (4) using excessive bodily action, (5) taking pencil or pen to the speaker's stand, (6) clearing the throat excessively, (7) using vocalized pauses, and (8) talking on the way to the platform.

Questions and Exercises

A. Answer the following questions on Chapter 13.

1. How is bodily action important to oral communication?
2. Discuss three purposes of bodily action. Which do you consider the most important?
3. Discuss "movement of the whole body" as an aid to oral communication.
4. Define gestures. What are the principal types of gestures?
5. Of what value is posture to effective delivery? What constitutes acceptable posture?
6. Discuss facial expression as a part of bodily action. How do facial expressions help convey thought?
7. List and discuss briefly seven characteristics of good gestures discussed in this chapter. Can you add other requirements?
8. What is meant by delivery mannerisms? How do they affect delivery?
9. List and discuss several mannerisms resulting from ineffective use of bodily action. Voice. Language.
10. How should you set about to correct distracting delivery mannerisms?

B. For your oral speaking assignment you will have a choice between two types of speeches. Whichever assignment you choose, give particular attention to the use of bodily action; make abundant use of the types of action discussed in this chapter.

1. Prepare a "speaking for a cause" speech on a school or local problem about which you have strong feelings. Let yourself go; use bodily action frequently. Limit your speech to five minutes. The following topics are suggestions only; take the side of the question in which you believe.
   (a) The honor system, (b) the grading system, (c) dormitory rules, (d) library rules, (e) limit on extracurricular activities, (f) student loan funds, (g) athletic scholarships, (h) parking regulations, (i) censorship of the school paper, (j) required versus elective courses, (k) tuition costs, (l) social activities, (m) fraternities and sororities, (n) seating arrangements at football games, (o) semester versus quarter plans, and (p) entrance requirements.
2. Prepare a speech which explains a process or prepare a "how-to-do-it"

speech in which you use a physical object or some other type of visual aid. Review the section on visual aids in Chapter 7 and the instructions for the demonstration speech given in the exercises for Chapter 8 before preparing this speech. Limit your speech to five minutes. The following topics are suggested:
(a) How the law of supply and demand operates. (b) How to operate a brokerage house. (c) How to play golf. (d) How to play chess. (e) How the split-T formation works. (f) How tires are manufactured. (g) How an airplane operates in flight. (h) How to lay tile. (i) The operational plan for a bank. (j) How lumber is processed. (k) Merchandising in a department store. (l) The organization of a television station.

C. Attend a lecture or view a television speech: (1) discuss briefly the speaker's use of (a) movements of the whole body, (b) gestures, (c) posture, and (d) facial expressions. (2) List any mannerisms of the speaker that you noted.

D. What do you consider your principal weaknesses in the use of bodily actions while making a speech? List any distracting mannerisms that you think you have.

E. Check your list in Assignment D with the criticism that your instructor makes of your speech in Assignment B.

PART FOUR

Areas of Application

CHAPTER 14

Solve Problems Through Discussion

The basic principles of oral communication discussed in the three preceding divisions of this textbook apply to several specialized fields that are discussed in the three chapters of Part Four. Discussion, as a type of problem-solving, forms the subject of this chapter; conflict-resolving through debate is discussed in the following chapter; and speeches for special occasions are treated in the final chapter.

Author John W. Keltner of Kansas State College states,

> We can't live alone in our complex society. The day of the cave man making his way with a big stick is over. Our democratic way of living demands that we cooperate with each other through intelligent discussion to solve the problems of living together. It demands that we develop efficient methods of group decision-making.[1]

Much of the business of a democratic society is carried out through discussions; those problems that cannot be settled by discussion call for debate. Discussion and debate constitute the principal processes for solving problems and resolving conflicts. How are the two processes related?

[1] John W. Keltner, *Group Discussion Processes* (New York: Longmans, Green, and Co., 1957), pp. 2-3.

I. The Process of Problem-Solving

Consider the following situation, typical of the democratic process.[2] A faculty committee was appointed to study the problem of the semester, quarter, and term systems for arranging the school calendar. At the first meeting of the committee, the members discovered that they lacked sufficient factual information to proceed. The chairman appointed members of the committee to conduct investigations of the problem—to study the catalogues of other colleges, to write for the reports of committees from colleges that had recently conducted similar studies, and to study relevant articles in professional journals.

The committee members met later to report their findings. After all data were pooled, the question arose: "What specific recommendations shall we make?" Differences of opinion naturally arose. Criteria were set up to judge proposals, and each specific proposal was considered in relation to those criteria. With the possible recommendations before the group, the meeting adjourned to permit each member to study them.

At the next meeting, the members discussed the merits of the several proposals. After each had had his say, the chairman called for a vote. The motion carried favoring the recommendation to change to the semester system.

The proposal was then sent to the faculty senate—the faculty administrative body—where the chairman read and moved the adoption of the report. A debate ensued, and after all members had been heard, the motion passed. The recommendation then came up at the next meeting of the entire faculty, where the proposal was again debated and adopted.

Thus a democratic body faced and solved a problem. The solution was made possible by use of two essential tools of any democratic process—discussion and debate. Through discussion the original committee attempted to answer, "What should be done?" Debate was necessary to reach the final decision in the senate and faculty meetings, where the proposition was "Should the commit-

---

[2] See Glenn R. Capp, "Discussion and Debate in Life Activities," *The Bulletin of the National Association of School Principals,* XXXVIII: 199 (January, 1954), 67-70.

tee's recommendation be adopted?" Without discussion and debate, the solution would not have been possible. Without them, the deliberative bodies could not have functioned.

Courts of law constitute one of the principal areas for debate, but lawyers also utilize discussion techniques before they bring a case to trial. Recently, a citizen was summoned to serve on a jury panel. As the judge instructed the members of the jury about their rights and obligations, some lawyers came into the courtroom and called the judge aside. Upon returning to the jury panel, the judge announced that the case had been settled; the litigants had compromised their differences outside of court through discussion methods. The compromise had been effected by lawyers skilled in cooperative deliberation.

Conflict is inevitable in a democracy. So long as people govern themselves, disagreements will occur. Means may be devised to lessen conflict, but it cannot be eradicated. Our chief progress can be made in improving the methods of solving problems and settling conflicts, the methods employed in discussion and debate.

II. Limitations of the Discussion Method

Discussion permits group decision, a democratic means for solving problems. Usually the decisions reached through discussion are acceptable because each person contributes to the solutions. As a method, however, discussion has no magical powers for guaranteeing mature decisions.

A starting point for a study of the discussion method should be a consideration of its limitations. The principal limitations may be classified as three types: (1) limitations due to the process itself, (2) limitations due to participants, and (3) limitations caused by language difficulties.

Limitations of the Process Itself

Discussion recognizes thought-in-process; it requires the cooperative deliberation of problems and operates largely by trial and error. It is not the most efficient method of problem-solving. The greatest efficiency comes where one person has the right of decision. The absolute dictator has a high degree of efficiency in problem-solving, but he ignores the rights of the individual. Persons committed to the free-world concept consider individual participation in problem-solving, with all its inefficiency, superior to dictatorial decrees.

The discussion method is slow; it must allow persons time to pool their information and ideas and to consider their differences. If immediate decisions become necessary, discussion should not be used. We always move toward concentration of power in the executive branch of government during periods of stress such as wars and economic depressions. Increased executive authority becomes necessary because we must have quick decisions.

Limitations Due to Participants

By the same token that discussion permits a pooling of information and ideas, it allows a pooling of ignorance, misinformation, and immature ideas. The people that operate discussions constitute limitations.

The attitudes of the participants may make the difference between success and failure. The proper attitude reflects a desire to cooperate toward the end of a mutually satisfactory solution, a recognition that cooperation may mean compromise, and an earnest seeking for the best solution. If individuals assume the attitudes that their ideas must prevail at any cost, the discussion has little chance of success. If a person already has his mind made up as he begins a discussion, he will usually exert his efforts to coerce others. Thus cooperative deliberation cannot be attained. A cooperative initial attitude may well be termed a prerequisite for a successful discussion. It must be an investigative, discriminating, and an open-minded attitude.

The overly cautious person tends to impede the progress of discussions. Decisions should not be made without a consideration of the facts and varying points of view, but the deliberative attitude may be carried too far. Some persons pride themselves in never making decisions until "all the facts are in," but one can never know all the facts. It is the careful weighing of the *available* facts that makes for mature decisions.

Persons with fixed opinions also delay discussions. The person who weighs all proposed solutions in terms of how they affect his political, religious, or social viewpoints may refuse to consider worthwhile suggestions. Some persons pride themselves on the consistency of their standards for evaluation. Some always champion the cause of the little man, or favor capital over labor, or vote the Socialist ticket, or insist on the separation of church and state, while others hold just the opposite views. Regardless of how remote a particular proposal may be from these preconceived notions, such persons always evaluate it by their handy criteria. Such an attitude is usually accompanied by a suspicion of the motives of those who differ. Thus, if one expresses a mild opinion that perhaps the federal housing program has helped in slum clearance, he is immediately labeled as a New Dealer, a welfare-stater, or a liberal, and therefore a communist. For, "after all, they mean about the same thing"—so says the man with the ready-made standards for evaluation. Discussions operated by such persons have little chance for success.

Then there is the person who often resorts to oversimplification; he puts everything in a nutshell. "Give labor an inch and it will take a mile"; "Spare the rod and spoil the child"; "Bloods don't mix." Such persons usually judge most complex situations as all good or all bad; all black or all white, never grey. They allow no place for a middle course. Thus, either you believe in the welfare state or you do not; you are either a free enterpriser or a communist. No place exists for degrees or shades of belief. Such an "all-or-nothing" attitude deters conferences.

Thinking in a habitual pattern also retards discussions. With persons who think by set patterns, tradition bulks large. John Locke characterizes these persons as "men whose understandings are cast in a mold, and fashioned just to the size of a received hypothesis." [3] Such a person lacks flexibility of mind and the ability to adapt to change. He usually resists all change because he indulges his habitual reactions until they become solidified.

In short, discussions are limited by the participants. Discussion procedures cannot be made to work without competent people.

Limitations Caused by Language

Language often serves as a barrier to communication in discussion. What the speaker means may be understood by his hearers in different ways, depending upon the experiences they have had with what he talks about. Words are simply labels for things; they are not the things themselves. There is nothing in a word that keeps

---

[3] John Locke, *Essay Concerning Human Understanding*, ed. A. S. Pringle-Pattison (Oxford: The Clarendon Press, 1924-1927), p. 366.

people from having varied reactions to it. The word "table" may mean the desk at which one works, the mahogany table in his living room, or the battered table in his workshop. Confusion arises in discussions when one person uses a word in one way and another understands it in a different way. This may well be one of the chief detriments to harmony in industrial relations, and it constitutes a serious obstacle to communication in international organizations. Review the section on general semantics in Chapter 11 and apply it to the discussion process.

In summary, the principal limitations of discussion lie in the process itself, the participants, and the confusion occasioned by language. A recognition of the limitations of the discussion process should make those who use it more tolerant of it as a problem-solving device.

III. A Pattern for Discussion

In order to achieve a degree of success the discussion must be conducted according to an orderly procedure. The following pattern strives to give order and arrangement to the discussion process. It starts with a consideration of the problem and leads step by step through the solution. If all participants understand the pattern, wasted effort will be prevented. The steps in the process follow:

I. Define the terms and narrow the problem.
II. Analyze the problem.
    A. Consider the conditions that exist.
    B. Consider the causes that give rise to the problem.
    C. Consider standards for evaluating solutions.
III. Suggest and evaluate possible solutions.
    A. Explain each possible solution.
    B. Consider the advantages and disadvantages of each.
IV. Seek agreement on a solution.
V. Consider methods for applying the proposed solution.[4]

To explain these five steps, we shall use, throughout the rest of this section, a detailed outline for a hypothetical discussion that shows how the pattern may be applied.

[4] See James H. McBurney and Kenneth G. Hance, *Discussion in Human Affairs* (New York: Harper and Row, Publishers, Inc., 1950), Ch. VI, and John Dewey, *How We Think* (New York: D. C. Heath & Co., 1910), for more detailed discussions.

Define the Terms and Narrow the Problem

Define and explain terms so that all will have the same understanding of the terms. Time spent in striving for a meeting of minds on meaning, purpose, and scope of the discussion ultimately saves time.

Discussions sometimes fail because the group attempts too much for a single session. On problems involving major changes, several discussions may be necessary on different phases of the subject. Decide early how to limit the subject, how to dispose of irrelevant matter, and how to accomplish specific goals.

The following outline shows how this defining and narrowing process may be accomplished.

Question: How Can the Educational System of the United States Be Improved?

I. Define the Terms and Limit the Problem
   A. "Educational system" may refer to any one or more of its subdivisions: (1) elementary education, (2) secondary education, and (3) higher education.
      1. These divisions are defined as follows:
         a. *Elementary education* means the lower six to eight grades.
         b. *Secondary education* means the upper three to six grades, usually referred to as high school or junior and senior high school.
         c. *Higher education* means the training offered in colleges and universities.
      2. This discussion should include all three divisions because each is an integral part of our educational system.
   B. The educational system of the United States includes both public and private schools.
      1. *Public schools* mean those financed by taxation through governmental divisions.
      2. *Private schools* mean those financed by private organizations such as religious denominations.
   C. The *United States* includes the federal government, the fifty states, and their subdivisions.
      1. Today the states constitute the main governmental division for educational organization.
      2. Local school districts help finance and administer school programs.
      3. The federal government assists through offering long-term loans, lunch programs, and assistance to vocational education,

and by maintaining Army, Naval, and Air Force academies.

D. The term "improved" implies how education can be made more efficient in administration and instruction.

Analyze the Problem

After securing a meeting of minds on the meaning and scope of the problem, examine its nature and extent. What are the manifestations of the problem? How serious is it? What facts reveal its true condition? An objective analysis may reveal the problem to be less serious than first believed. An appraisal of the existing conditions should precede a consideration of solutions so that all will understand what conditions need correcting.

Next, determine what factors brought these conditions about. What caused the problem? Any solution decided upon should correct the causes; otherwise the solution will have no lasting effects. An aspirin may give temporary relief for a headache; to effect a lasting cure, one must get at the conditions that gave rise to it.

As a third step, decide on standards to evaluate proposed solutions. Each proposed solution can then be considered in light of the criteria agreed upon to measure the adequacy of possible solutions. Agreement on the criteria for evaluating solutions may pave the way for the ultimate decision.

The following section of the outline on education illustrates the analysis step.

II. Analysis of the Problem
- A. Many defects exist in the United States system of education.
  - 1. The curriculum is not sufficiently substantial.
    - a. Students avoid basic subjects.
    - b. Trivial courses have been added to the curriculum.
  - 2. The curriculum is geared to the average and slow student.
    - a. All students, regardless of ability, attend the same classes.
    - b. Superior students become disinterested; poor students become discouraged.
  - 3. The teaching profession attracts persons of low caliber.
    - a. Certification laws are regarded as a farce in many states.
      - (1) They require excessive pedagogy courses.
      - (2) They permit persons to teach with insufficient training in subject matter.
    - b. The pay for teachers is not commensurate with their training.
      - (1) Since 1940 only the teaching profession has failed to improve its status in real wages.
      - (2) Educational requirements have increased.

4. Differences in educational facilities and expenditures exist.
   a. Differences exist between rural and urban areas.
      (1) The farm population supports a greater percentage of school children in proportion to income than does urban population.
      (2) The expenditure per pupil in urban areas is almost double that in rural areas.
   b. Differences exist among states.
      (1) The wealthy states have the best-equipped schools.
      (2) The expenditures per pupil vary four-to-one among the wealthiest and the most impoverished states.
   c. Differences exist between Negro and white schools.
      (1) Some states still maintain separate schools.
      (2) In spite of recent advances, wide differences still exist.

B. The causes of educational problems still exist.
   1. Decentralization of the public school system prevents coordinated action.
      a. Local jurisdictions have too much authority.
      b. Some states will not permit coordination or financial support by a national agency.
   2. The states vary in their ability to support programs.
      a. Seven states receive 54 per cent of the national income.
      b. New York receives 17 per cent of the national income.
      c. The poor states do not have adequate taxable income.
   3. Local school programs are often controlled by school boards who do not understand educational problems.
   4. Emphasis on mass education lowers the quality of education.
      a. Poor students require too much of the teacher's time.
      b. The curriculum is watered down for poor students.

C. Criteria for judging solutions should be considered.
   1. Education should be available to all American youth.
      a. Superior students should not be neglected.
      b. Students should be given training commensurate with ability.
   2. Equality of educational training should be provided.
   3. The quality of education should be improved.
   4. Improvements in education should be made at the least expense consistent with sound policy.

Suggest and Evaluate Possible Solutions

This step considers possible solutions, not simply those solutions favored by various members. The question is "What are the possibilities?" Consider and explain each possible solution in detail. How would it operate? What are the principles on which it is based? What are its possible advantages and disadvantages? When these questions have been answered for each possible solution, the discussion group is prepared to seek agreement on the best solution. Although this procedure does not assure agreement, it does improve the chances for it.

The following section of the illustrative outline exemplifies this process.

III. Evaluation of Possible Solutions
  A. Revise and streamline state tax programs.
    1. Some states do not have income and sales taxes.
    2. Much personal property escapes taxation.
    3. Savings could be made by improving methods of tax collection.
      a. Small taxing districts could be abolished or consolidated.
      b. Overlapping tax jurisdictions could be prevented.
    4. The following issues should be considered:
      a. Can taxes be increased in the poor states?
      b. Can sufficient revenue be obtained by improving the collection and administration of taxes?
  B. A plan of school economy is a possible solution.
    1. Overlapping taxing districts cause excessive expense.
    2. School funds are inefficiently managed.
    3. The costs of administrative departments are exorbitant.
    4. The following issues apply:
      a. Is economy in administration possible?
      b. Would economy in administration and efficiency in operation provide sufficient funds?
      c. Is greater economy and efficiency practical?
  C. Raise educational standards and qualifications for teachers.
    1. Minimum standards for teacher training will tend to standardize education throughout the states.
    2. Increased teacher's pay will attract capable people.
    3. Basic courses will supplant soft courses.
    4. Segregation of students based on ability will permit proper attention to all students.
    5. The following issues are applicable:
      a. Can we raise educational standards and qualifications of teachers with the revenue available?
      b. Can we raise educational standards and maintain our concept of mass education?
  D. Increase federal aid to education.
    1. The federal government has left the management of schools to the states, vocational education excepted.
    2. In the United States fifty separate school systems exist without a unifying agency.
    3. The federal government controls taxation for national purposes.
    4. Education has overstepped state boundaries.

5. The following issues apply:
   a. Is additional federal aid needed?
   b. Would increased federal aid be practicable?
   c. Would further federal aid be accompanied by serious disadvantages?

Seek Agreement on a Solution

After considering possible solutions, the leader attempts to gain consensus on one of the solutions or on a compromise among two or more of them. Discussions sometimes break down at this point because the participants cannot compromise their differences.

The following section of the illustrative outline applies to the solution phase of the discussion.

IV. Development of Suggested Solution
- A. Plan D appears to be the best solution—increase federal aid to education.
- B. Reasons for this choice:
  1. Education has become a national problem which makes further federal support and regulation advisable.
     a. By federal regulation the states with poor systems can be brought up to a minimum standard.
     b. The federal support of vocational education has resulted in a well-planned national program.
     c. Mobility of population causes a person to be more a citizen of the United States than of any one state.
     d. Coordination of educational programs is possible only through federal aid and regulation.
  2. The federal government can raise taxes more efficiently than can the various states.
     a. It can avoid double taxation and overlapping taxing agencies.
     b. The federal tax program can equalize the burden on the several states.
  3. Federal support and regulation will raise standards.
     a. Backward communities will raise their standards to meet minimum requirements.
     b. The methods and policies of progressive communities will be extended to non-progressive communities.
- C. Disadvantages of federal aid to education.
  1. The federal government should not assume new burdens in view of its large national debt.
  2. Federal aid will result in federal control and thus remove the democratic spirit of American education.
  3. Federal aid would decrease local initiative.
  4. Federal aid would work to the disadvantage of private educational institutions.

5. Federal aid would cause the citizens of one state to pay for educating the children of other states.

Consider Methods for Applying the Proposed Solution

If the participants agree on a solution, as the final step they consider how to put the solution into operation. Even though the discussion group may not be involved with the execution of policy, its suggestions for application may be helpful. The practicality of the solution will no doubt have been considered in arriving at the solution; this phase of the discussion attempts to spell out a step-by-step procedure of execution.

The following section of the outline illustrates:

V. Suggestions for Putting Solution into Operation
   A. The federal government could establish minimum standards of education for each community; wealthy states could go beyond the minimum standard.
   B. The federal government could guarantee a minimum sum per student for each school district.
   C. The federal government could set up minimum standards and cooperate with the states and school districts in raising revenue.
      1. The "matching of funds" plan could be instituted.
      2. This plan would give the local districts more incentive for improving their schools.
   D. More substantial curricula should be enforced by the national agency.

This suggested pattern should not be considered as a panacea. It does help insure order and arrangement to the discussion process. As such, it enhances the opportunity for a successful discussion.

IV. Participating in Discussion

What constitutes successful participation in discussions? We learned earlier in this chapter that the participants often create a limitation. How can we participate in such a way as to help overcome this limitation? Successful participation may be judged by (1) the attitude of the participant, (2) the number of his contributions, and (3) the quality of his contributions.

Attitudes of the Participant

The attitude of the participant may mean the difference between the success and the failure of the discussion. The proper attitude may be characterized as follows:

1. *He adopts a cooperative attitude.* A cooperative attitude recognizes the common good of the group above selfish interests, a willingness to bypass personal desires for group interests. The discussion aims at compromising differences and arriving at solutions that represent the consensus of the group. A self-centered, individualistic, and competitive attitude defeats cooperation. Unless the participants strive to attain a cooperative spirit, the discussion has little chance of accomplishing its purpose.

2. *He assumes his share of the responsibility.* This responsibility involves (1) adequate preparation and (2) willing contribution. The discussion permits a pooling of information and ideas; but to have adequate facts and mature ideas, the participants must make proper preparation. The discussion will be no more productive than the ideas expressed by the participants. Each member should assume his proportionate share of the responsibility for getting ready for the discussion and participating in it.

3. *He avoids the passive attitude.* The participant does not withhold ideas simply because he has not had time to think them through thoroughly. Contributing ideas may sometimes come from spontaneous impulses, ideas that occur at the moment. Such ideas should not be thought of as reflecting the same maturity of judgment as those that are thought through in advance. Yet such spur-of-the-moment ideas may prove to be just what the group needs to settle a problem or move forward with it. Someone must express tentative opinions for the group's consideration. One should speak up if he thinks he has an idea that might be worth considering.

4. *He contributes objectively.* A participant should not hold tenaciously to a point of view because he advanced it originally. It may be that new facts or opinions make his original opinion seem unwise. His purpose is to help the group solve its problem, not to make his own ideas prevail. To be sure, he should defend any position that he considers valid and wise, but he should not hold to an original idea if further consideration causes him to doubt its validity. The objective participant keeps his remarks on the point at issue; he avoids personal statements designed to belittle persons associated with the issue or other members of the discussion group. The objective attitude helps to keep out dissension and strife.

5. *He is a good listener.* Good listening constitutes an essential part of the give-and-take processes in discussion. One cannot speak effectively on the point at issue unless he understands what others have said about it. The participant must be sure that he understands

another's point of view before indicating opposition to it. A good listener responds overtly to what others say, asks questions for clarification, and thinks before expressing agreement or opposition. If he spends his time thinking of what he plans to say next while others speak, his contribution may not be applicable. One must listen to understand.

Number of the Participant's Contributions

Is there a correlation between the number of times a person speaks and his general worth to the discussion group? To help answer this question, some experiments were conducted during practice sessions with college classes. One person tabulated the number of times that each participant talked. A panel of five speech teachers scored each participant on a qualitative rating scale.

The experiments showed in general that those who talked the most received the highest qualitative scores. There were, however, several individual exceptions. Some persons talked a great deal but did not say much. Others felt a compulsion to pass judgment on what everyone else said. Some were free in expressing opinions but had little factual information to back up their assertions. A few had competitive attitudes and attempted to argue each point. In spite of these exceptions, a majority of those who took the most active part made the most worthwhile contributions. A person can hardly speak too often in a discussion so long as he makes worthwhile contributions. He should be careful, however, not to monopolize the discussion to the extent that others cannot be heard.

Quality of the Participant's Contributions

The quality of contributions in a discussion may be measured by (1) the factual basis for opinions and (2) the maturity of judgments.

Sometimes discussions fail to produce results because no one has investigated the facts. In one class discussion, the participants argued about how much the price index had risen during the past year. This question should have been investigated, not argued. No amount of argument would change the facts or apprise the participants of them. Had someone known the facts, the stalemate could have been avoided. The tendency to "let George do it" seems to be a human tendency when students face the necessity of preparing for discussions. Yet a reasonable grasp of the facts constitutes an essential part of discussion participation. The pertinence and validity of facts should be carefully considered. Do they meet the qualifications of accuracy discussed in Chapter 7? Valid evidence is just as important for discussions as for public speaking.

Inferences from the facts also count heavily in discussion participation. What do the facts mean? What conclusion can be drawn from them? Maturity of judgment makes for the productive discussions characteristic of many conferences in industry. Reasoning, the process of drawing conclusions, is discussed in detail in Chapter 15.

V. Leading Discussion

The discussion leader must cultivate attributes of leadership conducive to a cooperative atmosphere that draws out the best from the participants. He succeeds in proportion to how well the discussion goes. He may be brilliant, stimulating, and eloquent—and thereby overshadow other members of the discussion. In so doing, he may defeat its primary purpose—cooperative group action. A good leader need not be the life of the party, but he must be a part of it. The leader performs the most important function in the discussion. To be successful, he must have the proper attitude toward the discussion process, realize the principles of leadership in a democracy, and understand the methods of procedure.

Attitudes on Discussion Leadership

An experienced professor of rhetoric observed many discussions in action during his twenty years of teaching the subject. Two leaders stand out as the poorest he encountered. They may be an object lesson to you in preparing for discussion leadership.

One was Major Proud, who had recently been promoted. A member of the reserves, he entered the armed services early in World War II and received rapid promotions. In civilian life he had held a position with few leadership opportunities; in the army he commanded many enlisted men and lower-ranking officers. Major Proud delighted in calling conferences on the slightest pretext. He used them primarily for the purpose of "putting his men in their places." He exemplified the class of dictatorial leaders. What methods did he use?

He furnished a detailed agenda and permitted no deviation from it. He dominated the discussions, insisting that his ideas be discussed and that army protocol be strictly enforced. He insisted on passing judgment on contributions by others and often assumed the role of an authority. He took sides on controversial matters and sometimes belittled those who differed with him. In short, he assumed the position of leader without the attributes of leadership.

What effect did his attitudes and actions have? At first, the participants prepared for the meetings and took active part in them. Later, they stopped preparing and deferred to the major for instructions. The conferences became occasions, not for mutual efforts in solving problems, but for the leader to give his orders.

The antithesis of this condition occurred in conferences led by Professor Mollycoddle. He assumed the chairmanship of his department because he was its most distinguished professor, not because he enjoyed administrative duties. He preferred to spend his time in reading and research and usually called conferences only when goaded into it. Unlike the major, he never prepared an agenda or seemed to know exactly why he had called the meeting. After starting a conference, he usually sat back without further comment and let it drift along. What happened in these conferences?

Other members of the staff vied for leadership and directed the discussions. Personal animosity often developed and shifted the discussions from the issues to personality clashes. Because the leader seldom made positive statements and did not intervene in personal clashes, the conferences drifted along without many productive results.

What can we learn from these two types of leaders? Neither exemplifies the proper type. A good discussion leader is a democratic leader. He works with the group in attempting to solve problems. He should not be dictatorial, nor should he let the discussion drift along without proper guidance. He works out an agenda but permits deviation from it if circumstances indicate the need. He plans the possible course that the discussion will take and attempts to keep down personal encounter by keeping the discussion on the issues. He asks discerning, thought-provoking questions. He attempts to create a cooperative atmosphere. He attempts to distinguish the essential from the non-essential and discourages uninformed opinions. If he has ideas and facts, he does not hesitate to contribute them, but he seldom takes sides on controversies that arise. He does not dominate the discussion, nor will he permit others to do so. He attempts to be objective rather than opinionated, patient rather than anxious, stimulating rather than dull, restrained rather than dogmatic. In short, he leads without its being obvious that he does so.

Principles of Leadership

The principles of leadership applicable to discussions closely parallel those in any activity in a democracy. A fundamental principle that distinguishes democracy from other concepts of government is its emphasis on the dignity of the individual. The individual has the freedom to speak up; his ideas count. Most business executives find that they can get more efficient production from their employees by leading them than by driving them. What principles of leadership in a democracy should guide the leader of conferences? They may be classified into three categories.

1. *People will support most readily those policies they help create.* If a leader wants whole-hearted support from his associates, he will give them a voice in determining policies. If he hands down an order, he will be likely to get compliance with the letter of the command but not with the spirit of it. Why do people in a democracy support best their own creations? They do so, in part, because those that help create policy understand the spirit and philosophy behind it. The human tendency to support that which one helps to create characterizes persons accustomed to the free-world concept.

In recent years big business has recognized this principle with beneficial results in productivity. Industries have instituted employee-participation plans that range all the way from suggestion boxes to a share of the profits. Years of service and importance of position receive reward by shares in the company. The unskilled and semi-skilled workers cooperate better because they help elect one of their kind to the managerial board. They produce better because they feel that they are a part of the organization.

How does all this apply to the discussion leader? He should keep in mind that if a person has a contribution to make, he should be encouraged to make it. He should include all those who will have a part in executing the policy. He should create a pleasant and friendly atmosphere conducive to a free exchange of ideas and opinions.

2. *Consider free discussion as the safety valve for democracy.* Persons with ideas desire to express them. If prevented from stating their views, they will seek more forceful means to express themselves. The failure of some civilizations dates from the time that freedom of speech became suppressed. Insurrection may result from continual suppression of free speech.

A tenet of the armed forces permits uninhibited griping among fellow soldiers. Uprooted from their customary mode of living and thrown into an entirely new environment, many soldiers naturally become frustrated and discouraged. Some soldiers testify to the relief they receive from "sounding off" to their buddies. Modern psychiatry utilizes free and uninhibited talk as a technique for treating nervous disorders. Perhaps you have sometimes felt better after having unburdened your troubles to a sympathetic listener. This principle has application to the discussion leader. By encouraging free expression of opinions, he paves the way for cooperation among the participants in the discussion.

3. *People in a democracy have the right to make their own mistakes.* The discussion leader must be patient; he must expect mistakes. He cannot rush the discussion process if he desires to realize its full advantages. He must not expect to arrive at decisions that satisfy everyone. He must realize that the people have the right to make their own mistakes. Fortunately, they often profit by their mistakes.

Techniques of Discussion Leadership

The procedural methods for discussion need not be formal or stilted. Parliamentary procedures may be necessary with large legislative groups, but informal procedures serve discussion groups best. Yet the leader cannot let the discussion drift along without any direction. What are his duties and obligations?

1. *He gets the discussion started.* The leader prepares the agenda. If possible, he sends the agenda to the participants prior to the meeting so they can make proper preparation. He gives any other necessary written materials to the participants before the discussion

begins. The reading of materials during the discussion diverts attention from the proceedings.

He sees that the proper physical arrangements are made beforehand: a rectangular-shaped table with writing pads, pencils, ash trays, and so forth are set at each place before the discussion starts. Avoiding possible disruptions makes for smooth-running discussions.

He arrives a few minutes early to introduce new participants and engage other arrivals in informal conversation. This act may aid in creating a friendly atmosphere and thus in setting the proper keynote. An unhurried atmosphere serves best; this spirit cannot be attained if the leader rushes in at the last minute.

After greeting other participants as they arrive and making the necessary introductions, the leader calls the meeting into session. In his opening remarks he stresses the purpose and importance of the problem. These opening remarks need not be long, but they should include any background about the origin and history of the problem that makes for a better understanding of it. If the discussion is one of a series on the same problem, he briefly summarizes accomplishments of previous sessions and states the purpose and scope of the present meeting. At the end of his introductory remarks, he raises the question of the definition of terms and limitations of the problem.

2. *He keeps the discussion moving constructively.* Once the discussion is underway, the leader keeps it moving constructively toward its goal by judicious use of the summary and skillful questioning.

The summary may be used for at least four important functions: (1) It is used to give the discussion order and direction. If the discussion has gone so far that no one seems to know where it is, the leader summarizes to bring it to a focal point. (2) It is used when the group has been discussing a single topic too long and it is necessary to move on. During the summary, the leader indicates what has been accomplished and suggests the direction the discussion should take. Here the summary serves as a transition from one phase of the discussion to another. (3) It is used when a delay procedure is indicated. Sometimes the discussion gets too heated and tends to get out of hand. At other times the group seems to lose perspective. Here the important thing is to delay. During the summary, the participants will have time to "cool off" and regain their composure. If the leader desires, he need not permit the discussion to return to the topic that gave rise to the dissension. (4) It is used when the leader becomes uncertain of what to do next. Occasionally the leader may become uncertain about the best procedure to follow. Usually during the process of summarizing, a new direction will be indicated. The summary gives him time to deliberate on the next move.

Skillful use of the question aids the leader in drawing out members of the group, in securing needed information, and in keeping the discussion moving. At times talk may lag and the meeting seem to bog down. When this condition arises, the leader asks searching inferential questions, not those that can be answered by *yes* or *no*. The following questions are some he may ask:

1. What experience have you had with this problem? How did you solve it?
2. How did this condition come about? How did that happen? What caused it to happen?
3. What do you think about the matter? Why?
4. Can you give an example of the situation you describe?
5. What other possibilities can you suggest?
6. Will you be a little more specific? Will you explain your suggestion in more detail?

The above types of questions may serve to keep the discussion moving constructively.

3. *He keeps down strife and dissension.* Undue personal conflict and bickering may kill the atmosphere of pleasantness that should prevail. The leader does not stifle honest differences of opinion, but he encourages differences of opinion agreeably. If he can keep the discussion on the issues of the problem, the occasion for personal conflicts will be lessened. If he knows that personal differences exist on certain matters, he delays their discussion until after the participants have discussed other matters upon which prejudices do not exist. Thus the group may learn to work together before the disputatious questions arise.

The leader does not permit argument or personal-opinion statements when the group is considering possible solutions. He restricts this phase of the discussion to an explanation of how the solutions will work and their advantages and disadvantages. With these facts before the group, the causes for personal differences may be lessened. Above all, the leader is fair and impartial if disagreements do arise. If matters tend to get out of hand, he can use the summary to help bring the conference under control.

4. *He provides the opportunity for all to participate.* It is desirable to have all members participate in the discussions and the leader tries to make it possible for all to contribute. However, a person talks best when he wants to talk, not when the leader calls on him. The leader avoids the *what-do-you-think-Mr. Jones* type of question; rather, he raises problems and asks inferential questions that will cause one to want to talk.

The leader may encounter two types of individuals with which he must deal: those who talk too much and have little worthwhile to say and those who do not talk enough.

The leader does not embarrass the talkative individual, because his embarrassment may dampen the fervor of the whole group and cause others to decline to participate. Unobtrusively he suggests that the aim of good discussion is to have all participate; the solution should be a joint endeavor. If Mr. Smith persists in talking the leader interrupts him politely, turns to the group, and states that he would like others to discuss Mr. Smith's idea. After one member concludes, he directs the discussion to another without letting it return to Mr. Smith. Again, the leader may listen to Mr. Smith without commenting on what he said, introduce a new idea and ask others to give their opinions of the new idea. In short, he lessens Mr. Smith's opportunities to speak without letting it be too obvious that he is doing so.

Quite a different problem arises when a person declines to participate. Capable people sometimes find difficulty in breaking into the discussion, as they do in any situation of social intercourse. Without being obvious, the leader attempts to bring such a person into the discussion; he bides his time for an opportune moment. For example, he might turn to Mr. Jones and say, "Mr. Jones, I recall that you had a similar problem arise when you served on the Chamber of Commerce Executive Board. How did you people cope with the problem?" This method points up Mr. Jones's importance and gives him an opportunity to speak from experience on the matter. If possible, the leader keeps him talking for some time by asking additional questions. Usually a reticent person will continue to participate once he has made his first contribution.

5. *He concludes the discussion.* The leader concludes the dis-

cussion so that it will not simply die out. He concludes it at the appointed time or when the group ceases to make progress, by giving a concise summary of what has been accomplished. He attempts to clarify what has been said in such a way as to give a sense of direction. If the discussion has reached a decision before the time is up, some time may be devoted to suggestions for putting the solution into operation. If another discussion is planned on the same problem, the leader should indicate the unfinished work and the phase of the problem for the next meeting.

VI. Summary

Discussion and debate form the principal methods for solving problems and resolving conflicts in a democracy. They find their expression in courts of law, legislative assemblies, and the everyday activities of citizens. Discussion offers the first approach to problem-solving. If discussion fails, debate applies for resolving the conflict.

Discussion has certain limitations: those of the process itself, those due to participants, and those caused by language.

A pattern for discussion gives the process order and arrangement. The pattern consists of five steps: (1) define the terms and narrow the problem, (2) analyze the problem, (3) suggest and evaluate possible solutions, (4) seek agreement on a solution, and (5) consider methods for applying the proposed solution.

Successful participation may be measured by the attitudes of the participants, the number of their contributions, and the quality of their contributions.

Discussion leadership depends upon the attitude of the leader, an understanding of the principles of leadership, and a knowledge of the techniques of discussion leadership. The leader must (1) get the discussion started, (2) keep it moving constructively, (3) keep down strife and dissension, (4) provide an opportunity for all to participate, and (5) conclude the discussion.

Questions and Exercises

A. Answer the following questions on Chapter 14.

1. What are the two principal methods for solving problems and settling conflicts in a democracy?
2. List and explain the three types of limitations of the conference method discussed in this chapter.

3. List and explain the steps in the pattern for discussion presented in this chapter. Why should discussion participants understand this pattern?
4. Why should discussion participants decide on criteria for judging solutions prior to considering possible solutions?
5. Upon what three bases may we judge effective participation in discussion?
6. Characterize the proper attitude for the participant as discussed in this chapter. Can you add to this list of characteristics?
7. How can you measure the quality of contributions of the participant?
8. Characterize the three types of discussion leaders discussed in this chapter. Do you agree that the democratic leader serves best? Why?
9. Explain three general principles of leadership in a democracy applicable to the discussion leader.
10. Discuss the five procedural techniques for the leader discussed in this chapter. Can you add to this list?

B. For your oral assignment, each member of the class will participate in a practice discussion. Five or six members of the class will constitute each discussion group and each group will elect its leader and select the topic for the conference.

Each conference will have a forty-five-minute time limit. Proceed as follows:

1. The instructor will divide the class into discussion groups. Each group will have a preliminary meeting to elect its chairman and select its topic. This meeting should be held several days prior to the conference.
2. In preparation for selecting the topics, each member of the class should bring to class three suggested topics. These lists will serve as the basis for decision in the preliminary meetings.
3. Each member of the class should make a preparation outline for his discussion. This outline should follow the steps in the pattern for discussion noted in this chapter. Use the outline for preparation purposes only; do not insist that the group follow your outline.
4. Follow each discussion with a critique with the instructor as leader.

CHAPTER 15

Resolve Conflicts Through Debate

An eminent lawyer who specializes in workman-compensation cases reported that only about 3 per cent of personal damage claims ever reach the courtroom. The other 97 per cent are settled outside the courts either by the litigants or by lawyers representing them. In deliberative bodies, solutions to a majority of problems are effected through discussion around the conference table. Only a small per cent require debate and a vote. In everyday business activities, decisions are reached largely through discussion, in conferences between the proponents of the proposal and the executives of the organization. Only a minority of proposals require action by the executive boards. In short, a majority of decisions in a democracy are made by means of investigation, discussion, and compromise. Yet the small per cent of decisions that cannot be made by compromise vitally affect the business of free people. Thus debate comes into play to complete the process by resolving conflicts that cannot be settled through discussion. Debate may be said to begin where discussion ends.

The debater performs an essential function in the democratic process. Without him, democracy could not operate. For example, in law the accused must have his case presented in its most favorable light or injustices may result. His lawyer uses debate to build the strongest case possible for him consistent with the facts. In deliberative assemblies, when legislative measures have been narrowed to a specific proposal, the advocate of each side presents the strongest case possible for his side. In human relations, any cause must have its ideals promulgated or progress becomes impossible.

The nature of a general textbook in oral communication does not permit a full treatment of the principles of advocacy, the process of pleading a case for another or for a cause. This chapter discusses only the salient principles of debate employed in college and high school forensic programs.[1] Although the procedural methods used in these training programs are somewhat simulated, the student thus trained can easily adapt his acquired skills to life situations of advocacy.

I. Procedural Principles of Debate

The procedures for college debate call for opposing teams, termed affirmative and negative. Each speaker on a team has a constructive and a rebuttal speech in which to build his case and tear down his opponent's case. The affirmative team proposes a change in an existing economic, social, or political policy. The affirmative side is analogous to the plaintiff in a law case or the proponent of a measure in a legislative assembly. The negative speakers oppose the proposed change and resemble the defendant in a law case or the opponent to a measure in a legislative body.

Each team proposes constructive cases consisting of the basic arguments on its side of the question. The basic arguments are known as the main issues; when stated in the form of arguments, the issues become the main contentions for the side advancing them. Not only must each side build a case, but each team must attack the case of the opposing team and defend its own arguments against attacks.

In brief, debate involves a threefold process: (1) a constructive process in which each team develops a case sufficient to prove its side, (2) a destructive process in which each team attempts to weaken or destroy the opposing case, and (3) a reconstructive process in which each team rebuilds its own case. These processes call for an understanding of procedural principles designed to give debate order and arrangement. What are these principles?

---

[1] For a detailed treatment see Glenn R. Capp and Thelma Robuck Capp, *Principles of Argumentation and Debate* (Englewood Cliffs, N.J.: Prentice-Hall, Inc., 1965).

The Affirmative Must Present a Prima-facie Case

A prima-facie case means one sufficient to prove the proposition. In a policy proposition the case must prove these issues: (1) A problem exists with sufficient force to demand a change. (2) The suggested proposal can solve the problem. (3) The solution will correct the evils in a satisfactory way. The case must be sufficient to overcome the natural advantage in favor of present conditions. Existing conditions are presumed to be best until proved deficient. Since the presumption of the argument favors the negative at the beginning of the debate, the affirmative must overcome this presumption by presenting a prima-facie case.

The Affirmative Assumes the Burden of Proof

This principle comes from legal procedures. In criminal law a man is presumed innocent until proved guilty. The burden rests on the state to prove its case by a preponderance of evidence. This same principle applies with any existing order—political, social, or economic; it cannot be condemned without cause. The affirmative side has the obligation to prove its case because it advocates a change. It must show that its proposal will be preferable to the existing order; otherwise, why change?

What obligations accrue because of the affirmative's burden of proof? The affirmative must prove a prima-facie case as explained in the preceding section. Furthermore, the affirmative side must gain the advantage on each basic issue. If the negative side can defeat any of the affirmative's main contentions, it will win. Each basic contention in the affirmative's case is essential to the case.

To illustrate, for the proposition, "Resolved, that the United States should adopt the essential features of the British system of education," the affirmative's main contentions may be stated as follows: (1) Defects in the United States' system of education demand a change. (2) Adopting the essential features of the British system of education will correct the defects. (3) The proposed plan is the best solution. All three contentions are essential to a prima-facie case and must be advanced and defended by the affirmative.

The negative side may choose to counter all the main issues, or it may concentrate on one or more. If the negative could prove that no defects exist, there would be no need to counter issues two and three. Conversely, the negative may admit the defects and concentrate its attack on the workability of the proposal.

The Affirmative Defines the Proposition

Since the affirmative side must prove its case, it has the right to say what the proposition means. This statement does not mean an unqualified right; it does mean that the affirmative has the right to define specific terms and give shades of meaning to the proposition. For example, the proposition that the United States should adopt the essential features of the British system of education gives the affirmative the right to name the essential features. Those features specified must in fact be essential, but their selection and order of presentation rest with the affirmative.

The affirmative should interpret the proposition so that the affirmative and negative positions are clearly distinguishable. For example, the affirmative on the proposition stated above must favor selective education, central control, compulsory study programs, and teacher certification based on subject-matter courses. Conversely, the negative must contend for mass education, decentralized control, individual choice in selecting programs of study, and emphasis on pedagogy courses for teacher certification. Why? Because these are, in fact, some of the basic differences between the British and American systems of education. The affirmative should interpret the proposition to bring out these basic differences.

The Affirmative Sets Forth the Basic Issues

The affirmative advances the main issues and the negative counters them. The right to set forth the issues does not mean an unqualified right, because the main issues inhere in the proposition. On policy questions the affirmative must show the problem, make a proposal to correct or improve the situation, and prove its proposal superior to others. The right to advance them in the order and manner desired resides with the affirmative.

Each Team Has the Burden of Rebuttal

This principle means that each team must respond to an argument advanced by the other or lose it by default. Once the affirmative presents its prima-facie case, the negative side must answer it. If the negative makes a successful rejoinder, the burden of rebuttal shifts to the affirmative. This burden shifts from one side to the other on each argument throughout the debate.

Constructive Cases Must Be Completed in the Constructive Speeches

The prima-facie case must be presented in its entirety in the constructive speeches; new issues may not be presented in the rebuttal speeches. This principle does not mean that new material cannot be presented in the rebuttals on issues already introduced into the debate. New supporting material and new alignment of arguments in rebuttals prevent these speeches from becoming a rehashing of the constructive speeches. Refutation may be included in constructive speeches, but no new issues can be introduced in the rebuttals.

The Negative Has a Choice of Stands

The negative may take one of four possible stands: (1) It may present an entirely destructive case of refutation of the affirmative contentions. The negative permits the affirmative to set the issues and argues its case with pure refutation. (2) The negative may uphold the status quo. It need not argue present conditions as entirely satisfactory, only that the system is sound in principle. (3) The negative may uphold the status quo with modifications. The proposed modifications should conform to the principles of the present system. Otherwise, the inadequacy of the status quo would be admitted. (4) The negative may present a counterplan—a program that differs from both the status quo and the affirmative proposal. This stand automatically admits the inadequacy of the present system and resolves the debate into a comparison of two proposed solutions. The negative assumes the burden of proof on its proposal and must show it superior to both the affirmative proposal and the status quo.

Not any of the above stands is superior to the others in principle, but one may be the best when applied to a specific proposition. The choice should be based upon reason, not upon simple preference.

II. Requirements of the Proposition

Only propositions, or resolutions, can be debated. They call for specific proposals that specify the affirmative and negative positions. For example, you cannot debate about law enforcement, but you can debate the proposition, "Resolved, that law enforcement agencies in the United States should be given greater freedom in the investigation and prosecution of crime."

Types of Propositions

There are three types of propositions—fact, value, and policy. (1) Propositions of fact pertain to the truth or falsity of an assertion; for example, "Resolved, that the open shop helps labor." Only questions of fact that cannot be determined by investigation are debatable. (2) Propositions of value question the worth of a proposal; for example, "Resolved, that extremism in defense of liberty is justifiable." Such questions involve the philosophy or worth of proposals, not whether they should be changed. (3) Propositions of policy propose a change in an existing order; for example, "Resolved, that the United Nations should establish a permanent military force." Such resolutions aim at a debate on the advantages of a proposed change in policy. Policy questions are superior for formal debate because they are the type most frequently argued in life, especially in conflict-resolving groups.

Phrasing of the Proposition

The wording of propositions often determines their worth as questions for debate. Poorly worded topics may be so ambiguous or one-sided as to render them useless. Observe the following suggestions for proper phraseology.

1. *State the topic in resolution form.* You do not argue *about* a proposition, but *for* or *against* it. For a discussion, the topic may be

"How can the United States improve its system of education?" Stated thus, the question has many sides and varying viewpoints. For debate, the topic must be stated in resolution form, as follows: "Resolved, that the United States should adopt a federal scholarship program." A resolution has only two sides—pro and con. The resolution does not ask, "What should be done about education?" It proposes, "A national scholarship program should be adopted." Thus, the affirmative and negative positions become apparent from the statement of the proposition.

2. *State the topic to provide a balance of arguments.* Excellent topics may be resolved into poor debate propositions by a statement that favors one side. "Resolved, that the United States should oppose communism" puts an imposing burden on the negative because almost all Americans dislike communism. "Resolved, that the Communist party should be outlawed in the United States" makes a better balanced proposition because Americans disagree on this method of opposing communism.

Properly balanced propositions set up a standard for comparison. "Resolved, that the ministry is a nobler profession than law" has no common standard for comparison because both professions are essential. They operate in different areas that are hardly comparable.

3. *State the topic as an affirmative resolution.* The affirmative must propose a change just as the plaintiff must bring the charge in a law case. Thus, the proposition must be worded affirmatively. "Resolved, that the United States should retain the income tax" does not call for positive action. The affirmative would have no burden to uphold. "Resolved, that the United States should establish a maximum income-tax rate of twenty-five per cent" properly calls for a change in policy.

4. *State the topic to embrace one central idea.* Propositions that include two or more proposals make poor resolutions. "Resolved, that the President of the United States should be elected by direct vote of the people for a six-year term" includes two proposals. The negative could win by defeating either proposal; it might deliberately ignore one proposal. Yet the affirmative must establish a case for each proposal to fulfill its obligation.

5. *State the topic to avoid ambiguous and prejudiced terms.* Terms subject to more than one legitimate interpretation lead to confusion. "Resolved, that the income tax is superior to the sales tax" involves the meaning of "superior." What standards measure

superiority? Does it mean which is more productive, easier to collect, more equitable, or meets better with public approval? The term instead of the basic principles of taxation might conceivably form the central point of controversy.

Avoid terms which assume points at issue. "Resolved, that unnecessary governmental restrictions on business should be abolished" assumes a point that the affirmative should be asked to prove. If governmental restrictions are assumed as unnecessary, who could prove that they should be retained? Avoid prejudiced terms that give either side an advantage.

6. *State the topic to restrict its scope.* "Resolved, that the American foreign policy should be revised for the space age" encompasses too broad a field. "Resolved, that the United States should recognize Communist China" restricts the proposition to one phase of our foreign policy. Some excellent topics are worded into poor propositions by failure to narrow and restrict them properly.

In summary, propositions for college debates resemble questions debated in life situations of advocacy. The prosecuting attorney charges the defendant as guilty; the proponent of legislation advocates a solution; the college debater proposes a change in an existing order. Properly worded propositions permit these comparisons to hold.

III. Analysis of the Proposition

Through analysis the debater breaks down the proposition into its component parts and discovers the main issues. The main issues are the inherent, vital points of controversy which form the basis of the case.

Types of Issues

To understand the importance of the main issues, consider the following types: potential, admitted, and real.

Potential issues inhere in the proposition. They must be established by the affirmative as prerequisite to a prima-facie case. On policy questions, they take the form of stock issues: (1) need, (2) solution, and (3) desirability of solution. The following issues illustrate for the proposition, "Resolved, that the United States should adopt the essential features of the British system of education."

I. Is a change in the United States system of education needed?
II. Would the adoption of the essential features of the British system of education meet the need?
III. Is the proposed solution the most satisfactory solution?

Potential issues are the issues of the proposition as distinguished from the issues of a particular debate.

Admitted issues consist of those affirmative issues conceded by the negative. Usually negative teams concede issues on which they feel they have a disadvantage and concentrate on those in which they anticipate an advantage in order to build a stronger case. For example, the negative may admit the problem and concentrate its attack on the proposed solution. All concessions should be made for cause, not simple preference.

The real issues of the proposition, as distinguished from the potential issues, become the ultimate points of controversy in a debate. They consist of the potential issues minus the admitted issues. It is upon the establishment of these that the case stands or falls. The real issues may vary from debate to debate, depending on whether the negative concedes one or more issues.

Steps in Analysis

You perform analysis as you do research in preparing the questions. Consider the following preliminary steps: (1) Determine the present significance of the question. (2) Study the origin and history of the question. (3) Dispose of irrelevant and admitted matter. (4) Interpret the proposition. (5) Discover the underlying philosophy of the proposition. (6) Contrast affirmative and negative main contentions.

1. *Determine the present significance of the question.* What changes in conditions give the proposition significance now? During the past twenty-five years, free trade has been chosen three times as the national intercollegiate debate topic. On each occasion changed world conditions gave the subject new significance. Debaters have discussed various phases of education for many years, but recent efforts in satellite development have given the subject new significance. Circumstances that give a question current interest aid in analysis.

2. *Study the origin and history of the question.* You cannot understand a question thoroughly without knowledge of its origin and history. Often history reveals the reasons for present problems which

may be interpreted best in the light of their historical development. A knowledge of the origin and history of a problem gives a basis for intelligent analysis.

3. *Dispose of irrelevant and admitted matter.* Not all matters about a proposition can be in dispute. Some may be irrelevant or trivial. You must separate the important from the unimportant. On the proposition that the United States should adopt the essential features of the British system of education, some differences do not apply as essential features; for example, length of school day, proportion of private to public schools, and the distinction between elementary and secondary schools are all irrelevant. The differences in basic principles, not differences in minor procedural methods, form the basis of argument. The disposal of irrelevant and minor differences permits concentration on the basic issues.

4. *Interpret the proposition.* An understanding of what the proposition involves forms an essential part of analysis. Unless both teams agree on what the proposition means, they may argue about its meaning and neglect to debate the issues. In arriving at a basic interpretation, you must consider specific terms first; then consider these terms together for an overall interpretation. A single term may point up the basic difference between the affirmative and negative sides. For example, the words *essential features* form such a term on the proposition stated above; it is the heart of the proposition.

5. *Discover the underlying philosophy of the proposition.* Almost all propositions that propose a change in an existing social, political, or economic order involve a fundamental change in philosophy. They introduce a change in basic concepts, in the implications that underlie the arguments. For example, for the proposition that the United States should adopt the essential features of the British system of education, the affirmative proposal calls for a change from the American concept of mass education to a restricted program of education for the superior student. This basic philosophy must permeate the entire case of the affirmative; it serves as a cohesive force which unifies all the arguments advanced to prove the case.

6. *Contrast affirmative and negative main contentions.* The preceding five steps provide the bases for contrasting the affirmative and negative positions on the main issues. On the first issue of *need* for a change in the education system, the affirmative must discover the main defects of the United States system of education that can

be corrected by adopting the British system. The negative side must decide upon the possible positions it may take. It may either contest the issue or admit it, depending upon which position will make the strongest case. If existing evidence favors the indictment, the negative should plan to admit the evils and concentrate on the practicality of the proposed solution. The mental process of weighing advantage against disadvantage should be applied to each basic issue during the analysis stage in deciding on the strongest case possible for presentation during the debate.

As a result of analysis you discover the meaning of the proposition and the basic arguments in support of each side. You learn to separate the essential from the non-essential, the fundamental arguments from the trivial, and the main issues from subordinate ideas.

IV. Proof of the Proposition —Evidence

Argumentation makes its basic appeal on logical proof. Evidence and reasoning form the basis of logical proof. Evidence consists of the facts and opinions used to support an argument; reasoning consists of the inferences made from the evidence. Proof is the result of both evidence and reasoning.

Types of Evidence

As explained in Chapter 7, evidence takes two forms: facts and opinions. Facts consist of the circumstances or conditions of a situation, the tangible or concrete findings. Opinions are statements of belief about the proposition. If you say, "The 586,000 square miles and 375 million acres in Alaska compose one-fifth the area of the United States," the statement is factual. If you say, "Alaska has the greatest potential for economic development of any of the states," the statement is opinion.

Note how one debater used factual material in debating the unicameral legislature.

> In 1777 Georgia adopted a one-house legislature which lasted for twelve years. . . . The Pennsylvania constitution of 1776 provided for a one-house legislature. In 1790 a convention was called which revised the constitution and provided for a two-house plan. . . . In 1777 Vermont adopted a constitution providing for a one-house legislature. . . . A Constitutional convention of 1836 scrapped the plan and substituted

a bicameral legislature. . . . We ask the affirmative to reconcile the failure of the plan they are proposing to these instances. . . .[2]

Later in his speech the debater quoted the opinions of experts to support his contentions.

Mr. William E. H. Lecky points out in his book, *Democracy and Liberty,* that ". . . of all the forms of government that are possible among mankind, I do not know any which are likely to be worse than the government of a single, omnipotent democratic chamber. . . ." Mr. Ellis P. Oberholtzer in *The Referendum in America* in discussing the reasons for the failure of the one-house plan in Pennsylvania stated, "A body of men upon whose action there was no vote, was a source of danger in the state. . . ." [3]

The first excerpt typifies factual evidence. The historical examples gave evidence of the failure of unicameral legislation. The circumstances of the examples constituted the evidence. This type of factual evidence compares to the facts elicited from witnesses in courts of law. Witnesses testify about the facts, not what they think about the facts.

The second excerpt illustrates opinion evidence. The two authorities gave their opinions about the effects of one-house legislatures. Opinions have probative force only if the persons quoted qualify through training and experience to make value judgments. This type of evidence is analogous to expert opinion in court trials. The courts may permit an expert to give his opinion about the facts. For example, the ballistics expert may testify if a particular gun fired the fatal bullet, or the doctor may testify about the sanity of the defendant.

Opinion statements are rarely sufficient within themselves to establish proof. On most policy questions the experts disagree. Although opinion statements lend prestige and dignity to conclusions, their effect may be more persuasive than logical. Review Chapter 7 for an explanation and tests of specific types of evidence.

Classification of Evidence

Knowledge of the legal classification of evidence will aid you in understanding the place of evidence in argumentation. The following are the kinds of legal evidence.

1. *Direct or circumstantial.* Direct evidence comes from persons

---

[2] Taken from classroom debate.

[3] Taken from classroom debate.

who witnessed the happening about which they testify. The witnesses testify about what they saw, not what they infer. Circumstantial evidence goes beyond the facts; it infers a conclusion from facts. If Jones saw Brown run the stop sign and crash with Johnson's automobile, he gives direct testimony about what he saw. Suppose that Brown passes Jones on the highway at an excessive rate of speed, in a no-passing zone, and with the highway patrol in pursuit. Upon arriving at the wreck Jones infers that Brown crashed into Johnson's automobile. In the first instance, what Jones witnessed constitutes direct evidence. In the second instance, he infers a conclusion based upon prior circumstances that he witnessed.

Direct evidence is factual evidence and applies the same in debate as in law. Circumstantial evidence in law is analogous to opinion evidence in debate; the conclusion requires a statement of belief.

2. *Oral or written.* Oral evidence consists of spoken statements. It constitutes the principal method for introducing evidence into legal trials. Written evidence comes from books, official documents, pamphlets, or other published materials. Written evidence serves the debater best because it may be more easily documented. Suppose your opponent challenges your source of evidence. If you can cite a published source, greater reliability accrues than if you give an oral source. The procedures for college debate do not allow for direct oral testimony.

3. *Expert or ordinary.* If facts come from a recognized authority, the evidence is expert; otherwise it is ordinary. The industrialist who testifies about the causes of labor unrest gives expert testimony; if the same industrialist expresses his opinion of the effect of cigarettes on lung cancer, he gives ordinary testimony. The courts rule out opinion evidence by non-experts. Before an opinion becomes admissible, the person testifying must be qualified as an authority. In debate, greater reliability is placed on opinions of qualified persons than on those of unqualified persons. Yet some debaters quote well-known persons without regard to their qualifications. Debaters often quote non-experts because they are known and respected by their immediate hearers, not because of their competence. To avoid this common mistake, quote persons in the field of their competence only.

4. *Original or hearsay.* Original evidence emanates from the person presenting it. Hearsay evidence consists of statements which one receives from another. If Smith sees the automobile accident, he

gives original evidence when he testifies. If Jones tells Smith what he saw, Smith gives hearsay evidence when he repeats what Jones told him. Courts of law rule out hearsay evidence except for clearly defined exceptions. Courts rule that the best evidence is more likely to come from an original than from a secondary source.

The hearsay rule has only partial application in debate. The debater gets much of his evidence from published sources. Material from source books, textbooks, or other recognized works carry more weight than evidence obtained from popular magazines, handbooks, or propaganda pamphlets.

5. *Positive or negative.* Positive evidence consists of existing facts or opinions. The presence of dust in the gun barrel indicates that it has not been fired recently. The worn steps in a building testify to its long use. The high price of food testifies to inflation. Conversely, the lack of evidence may serve as a basis for inference. That no marks were found on the victim's body indicates that he was not beaten. The absence of open criticism of the recreational program indicates either approval or apathy.

The absence of evidence where one might reasonably expect to find it may be significant. The lack of fingerprints on the open safe indicates that the robber took precautions not to leave evidence. The debater relies mostly on positive evidence.

6. *Real or personal.* Real evidence in law consists of objects such as the ransom note, photographs, or the lethal weapon. Personal evidence consists of statements of witnesses. A copy of a will illustrates real evidence; opinion of a witness about the testator's mental condition when he made the will exemplifies personal evidence. Real evidence applies more to law than to college debates. The procedural methods in contest debate prevent extended use of real evidence.

7. *Deliberative or casual.* Deliberative evidence consists of premeditated statements by witnesses with knowledge of their intended use. Casual evidence consists of spur-of-the-moment statements without knowledge of their future use. If the newspaper reporter asks your opinion of the poverty program, you will strive for a carefully reasoned opinion because you realize that you may be quoted. If a friend asks the same question, you would probably answer without much deliberation.

Industry makes use of casual suggestions through "brain-storming sessions." Subjects are broached without warning and participants make spontaneous suggestions. Some industries claim valuable benefits from such programs. Deliberative evidence is used more extensively in debate than casual evidence because most published material is deliberative.

In summary, a knowledge of the legal classification of evidence should cause you to weigh your evidence carefully. You will rarely need to make fine distinctions among the kinds of evidence, but a knowledge of the distinctions will aid you in the choice and effective use of facts and opinions.

Tests of Evidence

Review the tests for each type of evidence discussed in Chapter 7. In addition, consider the following general tests: (1) source, (2) quality, and (3) quantity.

1. *Sources of evidence.* In evaluating evidence, first inquire into the source from which the material came. The source may be deficient because of prejudice or lack of qualifications.

Prejudiced evidence comes from organizations or persons affected by the outcome of a problem; they disseminate only evidence favorable to their cause. Ordinarily they do not present false evidence, but they omit facts prejudicial to their position. The American Manufacturers Association presents facts favorable to capital while labor unions present facts favorable to labor. The White Citizens' Council publishes only facts unfavorable to social equality for Negroes, while the National Association for the Advancement of Colored People seeks evidence favorable to social equality. Democracy operates through pressure organizations; almost all professional and business organizations make use of propaganda agencies. The student of argumentation, however, must learn to distinguish the biased evidence they disseminate from objective evidence.

The research divisions of universities and educational foundations conduct objective studies. They seek true-to-fact information only. The evidence they publish is not prejudiced or biased.

The source of evidence may also be questioned on its qualifications. The person must be qualified by training and experience to know the facts and to interpret them properly. A history book written by a recognized historian has more prestige than one hurriedly written for popular consumption by an author not versed in history.

2. *Quality of evidence.* Evidence could meet the tests of source

and still be unreliable; it may be inconclusive or inconsistent. A limited survey may indicate a probable conclusion, not statistical certainty. The public-opinion poll may be worthless because the persons questioned were not objectively chosen. The questions in an interview may have been phrased to indicate the desired answer. The quotation may have been lifted from its context so that it distorts the author's views. These and other unscientific methods may make the evidence unreliable.

Reliable evidence is consistent within itself and with evidence derived from similar studies. One source of evidence may contradict another. Two sets of price indexes showed a discrepancy of ten per cent in the cost of living. The discrepancy occurred because one source used the base years 1947-49 and the other used the years 1957-59. Several tobacco companies advertise that their cigarettes contain less nicotine than other cigarettes. Obviously all these conflicting claims cannot be true. The inconsistency could probably be explained if we knew the basis of each test. Discrepancies in statistical material usually result from the use of conflicting units. Evidence published by pressure groups sometimes seems inconsistent because they choose only those facts favorable to their position.

3. *Quantity of evidence.* How much evidence is necessary to prove a contention? Much depends upon the nature of the argument and the beliefs of the audience. The sufficiency of evidence makes a perplexing question in legal procedure. Varying standards have been formulated, such as "beyond a reasonable doubt," "beyond a shadow of a doubt," and "sufficient to prove to the average reasonable and prudent person."

Debaters may state conclusions that go beyond the evidence. Such practices as quoting one or two unqualified authorities, citing limited statistics, and giving one or two isolated examples do not provide sufficient evidence to prove a contention. To prove that the evils of the United States system of education warrant the adoption of the British system takes considerable evidence. To prove that teachers are poorly paid requires less evidence. To prove that evils exist takes less evidence than to prove that the evils warrant a change.

The sufficiency of evidence also depends upon the beliefs of the audience. To prove that labor does not receive its just share of production would take less evidence for an audience of laborers than for an audience of industrialists. The adaptation of arguments to the beliefs of the audience should follow the analysis of the audience discussed in Chapter 4.

In summary, although the sufficiency of evidence presents a difficult problem, it is better to err with too much than with too little. Corroborate one type of evidence with other types. Variety in both types and sources helps avoid the error of insufficient evidence.

V. Proof of the Proposition —Reasoning

Suppose evidence shows that the United States system of education discriminates against superior students, encourages mediocre scholarship, makes ineffective use of facilities, and provides teachers of low caliber. What does this evidence mean? What caused this condition? How can the situation be remedied? The process of drawing inferences from evidence is termed reasoning. Evidence alone cannot establish a case; the proper relationship must be established between evidence and the conclusion drawn from it. Through inference we assess cause and effect relationships.

Argumentation appeals to understanding in order to influence belief. Conviction comes through reasoning. Logic distinguishes between good and fallacious reasoning. It tests the thinking processes to determine if they conform to established rules. Evidence and reasoning constitute the component elements of logic. This section shows how reasoning works with evidence to complete the process of logical proof.

Inductive and Deductive Reasoning Distinguished

Reasoning may be classified broadly as inductive and deductive. Inductive reasoning proceeds from the particular to the general; from an examination of specific cases we draw a general conclusion on the basis of the cases examined. Deductive reasoning reverses the process; it proceeds from a general statement to a particular conclusion. Given a general statement, we examine a particular case of the classification contained in the general statement and draw a conclusion relative to the specific case. The following illustrates:

Induction

School enrollments have increased in New York.
School enrollments have increased in California.
School enrollments have increased in Illinois.
School enrollments have increased in Florida.
Therefore, school enrollments have increased in the United States.

Deduction

School enrollments have increased in the United States.
The Far West is a part of the United States.
Therefore, school enrollments have increased in the Far West.

The Process of Induction

Inductive reasoning takes two forms, perfect and imperfect. Through perfect induction all members of a class are examined; if certain characteristics are found to be common among them, we conclude that the characteristics inhere in the class. For example, we investigate the state governments of the fifty states of the United States and find that all have welfare programs. We conclude that welfare programs are characteristic of the states of the United States. In reality no reasoning is involved; the conclusion is based on established fact. It involves no inference from the known to the unknown. The process resembles scientific investigation; a general rule is established by examining all cases.

Imperfect induction involves reasoning; it draws a general conclusion from an examination of part of the class. For instance, we conclude that welfare programs are characteristic of the states from an examination of five representative states—Oregon, Kansas, Pennsylvania, Maine, and Georgia.

The principal form of induction consists of reasoning by example, termed generalization. Reasoning by analogy and causal relation may also take the form of induction.

1. *Reasoning by example—generalization.* We generalize when we examine known instances of a class and draw conclusions regarding the entire class. If certain factors appear in the cases examined, we infer that they also exist in the cases not examined. The part represents the whole. For example, we infer that college debaters make superior academic records because we find this true at Northwestern, Harvard, Tulane, Stanford, and Kansas Universities.

If we assume that the five universities examined represent a true sampling of American universities, we establish a high degree of probability for our conclusion. We do not warrant that there are no exceptions, but we infer a probable general conclusion. To test the validity of generalization, apply the following tests:

a. HAVE A SUFFICIENT NUMBER OF EXAMPLES BEEN GIVEN? The number of examples required for a generalization depends upon the proposition. For example, we would be justified in concluding that full employment exists in the automobile industry by citing that this condition exists in Detroit, Dearborn, and Willow Run because they form the center of automobile manufacturing. If we wished to prove full employment in all of American industry, we should have to add cities that have full employment in a variety of industries. Usually the more cases cited, the stronger the generalization becomes. The fallacy of generalizing from too few instances is termed hasty generalization.

b. ARE THE EXAMPLES REPRESENTATIVE OF THEIR CLASS? The examples used for generalizing must be representative of those not used. You cannot generalize that all labor leaders are corrupt because a few have been exposed. That a few public officials have accepted bribes does not mean that the majority do. The fact that prices have risen little in the rubber industry, public utilities, and horse-drawn carriages cannot be used to generalize that prices in general have not increased. All may be exceptional cases. To show the true index of prices, use representative examples like steel, clothing, and housing.

c. CAN NEGATIVE CASES BE DISCREDITED? Negative cases are exceptions to those chosen for generalization. Negative instances do not necessarily invalidate a generalization if they can be shown as exceptions to the general rule. Suppose you conclude by generalization that minor league baseball is decreasing in popularity. Your opponent gives an example of Columbus, Ohio, where attendance reached an all-time high during the previous season. If you can show that Columbus led the league in a closely contested race, you will explain away the exceptional case.

Negative instances must be accounted for if they exist in appreciable numbers. Otherwise your generalization will be weakened or possibly destroyed. In choosing examples for generalization, make sure that either few negative instances exist or that you can satisfactorily explain them.

2. *Reasoning by analogy*. For purposes of reasoning, analogy as-

sumes that if two things are alike in germane known respects they will also be alike in unknown respects. We infer that the profit-sharing plan in Industry X will be successful in Industry Y because the two industries are similar in size and purpose. We reason that the honor system will be as successful in University X as it has been in University Y because the two universities are similar in size, curricula, student interests, and purposes. We infer that the resemblances in known particulars extend to unknown particulars. Apply the following tests:

a. Do THE SIMILARITIES OUTWEIGH THE DIFFERENCES? A multiplicity of differences between the things compared may weaken the analogy. Conversely, that many similarities exist between two objects does not always warrant an inference that they are fundamentally alike. The strength of the similarities counts more than the number. The comparisons are more qualitative than quantitative.

For example, in the analogy that a profit-sharing plan would be successful in Industry Y because it has been successful in Industry X, suppose that Industry Y is a marginal industry with little profits but that Industry X makes large profits. This major difference may outweigh many similarities. Irrelevant details cannot serve as the basis for a valid comparison regardless of their number. In using the analogy, check both the number and the importance of the points of similarity.

b. CAN THE DIFFERENCES IN THE CASES COMPARED BE EXPLAINED? Non-essential differences will not necessarily invalidate a comparison. For example, in the comparison that the honor system would be successful at University X because it has been successful at University Y, suppose that the two universities differ greatly in size of campus. This difference could hardly affect the success of an honor system because it has little to do with the point at issue.

On the other hand, suppose that University X has strict entrance examinations but University Y requires minimum academic standards. The opposing team could show the analogy to be false, for this difference applies specifically to the success of an honor system because it affects the quality of the student body. Superior students are less likely to cheat because they have little reason for cheating. In reasoning by analogy, show either that no differences exist between the things compared or that the differences are irrelevant.

3. *Reasoning by causal relation.* Reasoning from causal relation is based upon the universal belief in causation—nothing happens

without cause. Normally, every effect must be produced by some cause and every cause will produce its effect. For example, we note that labor unions obtained wage increases; we infer an increase in the cost of living. We observe a bumper cotton crop and infer that the farmers received adequate rainfall. We read about increases in unemployment and infer decreases in production. These inferences are based upon observation of numerous past instances. We assume high prices during periods of prosperity because high prices have always paralleled prosperous times. Thus, causal reasoning is largely inductive in form because it depends upon generalization. Our acceptance of the conclusion depends upon observation of past instances. The principal methods of causal reasoning are from effect to cause and from cause to effect.

a. EFFECT-TO-CAUSE REASONING. In effect-to-cause reasoning, we observe an effect and attempt to determine the cause. We contend that observed effects resulted from the cause or causes that we ascribe. The argument is from "what comes after" to "what has gone before." To illustrate, we observe many new automobiles on the highway; we infer prosperous times. We observe an increase in juvenile delinquency; we infer a break-up in home life. We observe riots in the South and East; we infer dissatisfaction with the enforcement of civil rights laws. We start with a known effect and attribute it to a specified cause or causes.

Effect-to-cause reasoning must establish a strong connection between the known effect and the alleged cause. For example, the teacher shortage may be attributed to poor pay as the cause. Equally important causes may be unwise certification requirements, low prestige for the profession, and the lack of summer employment. The probative force of argument from effect to cause depends largely upon the strength of the probability that no other cause or causes than those alleged could produce the known effect. Most effects result from several causes; beware of omitting contributory causes.

b. CAUSE-TO EFFECT REASONING. Reasoning from cause to effect infers an effect as probable because of operating causes sufficient to bring it about. We start with circumstances sufficient for a cause and infer what the effect will be. We note increased criticism of the party in power and infer a change in administration at the next election. We read about increasing tensions in Vietnam and infer that additional American troops will be called out. We observe the plentiful rainfall and anticipate a bumper crop. Argument from cause to effect attempts to establish the most probable effect of operating causes. For example, decreases in taxes tend toward stimulation of business, but that factor alone may not be sufficient to combat recession. Programs for combatting recessions include lessening of loan restrictions, increased governmental spending, and higher wages. In reasoning from cause to effect, make sure that the suggested cause is sufficient to produce the alleged effect.

A cause may be sufficient to produce an alleged effect but intervening conditions may prevent the cause from operating in its usual manner. For example, the wheat farmers anticipated low prices because of an oversupply of wheat, but the government adopted a price-support program. Normally, an oversupply of a product results in lower prices. In this case, the government's price-support program kept the cause from operating in its usual manner. If the opponent can show other forces sufficient to prevent the given cause from operating in its usual way, he can weaken the argument from cause to effect.

The Process of Deduction

We learned in the preceding section that through induction we arrive at general conclusions by examining specific cases. Conversely, deductive reasoning arrives at a particular conclusion about a specific case brought under the classification of a general rule. Deduction is a form of reasoning, not a method of argument. Thus we may reason logically from false premises and arrive at factually false conclusions. The deductive form does not test the validity of the premises. Unacceptable premises must be established by induction. Given two related statements, the deductive form arrives at a conclusion regarding their relationship.

1. *The syllogism.* The syllogism constitutes the principal form of deduction. It contains three propositions so arranged that the last can be inferred from the first two. These propositions are known as the major premise, minor premise, and conclusion.

The major premise takes the form of a general proposition. The minor premise brings a particular statement within the classification of the major premise. The conclusion relates to the particular case contained in the minor premise. The following illustrates.

Major premise: All basic industries have experienced price increases.
Minor premise: Steel is a basic industry.
Conclusion: Steel has experienced price increases.

There are three types of syllogisms: (1) categorical, (2) conditional or hypothetical, and (3) alternative or disjunctive.

a. THE CATEGORICAL SYLLOGISM. The categorical syllogism is exemplified by the example above. The term "all basic industries" is an unqualified statement. "Steel" comes under the classification of basic industries. The conclusion relates to "steel," a specific case. The following rules apply.

There are three and only three terms. The three terms are major, middle, and minor; each appears twice in the syllogism. The major term is always the predicate of the major premise and the conclusion; the middle term appears as the subject of the major premise and the object of the minor premise; the minor term is the subject of the minor premise and the conclusion. The following form illustrates:

Major premise: All successful industries (middle term) make a profit (major term).
Minor premise: Steel (minor term) is a successful industry (middle term).
Conclusion: The steel industry (minor term) makes a profit (major term).

The middle term must be distributed in the major premise. A distributed term is all-inclusive; it relates to all parts of a classification. "All successful industries" meets this qualification. Note the following example.

Major premise: Some successful industries make a profit.
Minor premise: The postal service is a successful industry.
Conclusion: The postal service makes a profit.

The minor term, "some successful industries," is undistributed; it does not include all parts of a classification. No conclusion can be made about the postal service.

No conclusion can be drawn from two negative premises. Two negative premises destroy the relationship among major, middle, and minor terms; the middle term is destroyed. To illustrate:

Major premise: No successful industries make a profit.
Minor premise: The carriage trade is not a successful industry.
Conclusion: The carriage trade does not make a profit.

The conclusion is not valid nor would any other conclusion follow from two negative premises.

The conclusion must be negative if one premise is negative. The conclusion is negative with either a negative major or minor premise. For example:

Major premise: All successful industries make a profit.
Minor premise: The carriage trade is not a successful industry.
Conclusion: The carriage trade does not make a profit.

or

Major premise: No inefficient industries make a profit.
Minor premise: Marginal farming is an inefficient industry.
Conclusion: Marginal farming does not make a profit.

No conclusion can be drawn from two particular premises. Since a particular premise includes only a part of a class, the following conclusion does not follow:

Major premise: Some inefficient industries make a profit.
Minor premise: Some textile industries are inefficient.
Conclusion: Some textile industries make a profit.

The conclusion must be particular if one of the premises is particular. In the following illustration, the minor premise and the conclusion are particular; therefore, the conclusion follows:

Major premise: All successful industries make a profit.
Minor premise: Some automobile manufacturers are successful industries.
Conclusion: Some automobile manufacturers make a profit.

b. THE CONDITIONAL OR HYPOTHETICAL SYLLOGISM. The hypothetical syllogism has in its major premise a condition; it states that if one proposition is true, another follows. For example:

Major premise: If Congress increases taxes, industry will decrease capital investment.
Minor premise: Congress will increase taxes.
Conclusion: Industry will decrease capital investment.

The major premise contains a condition; the minor premise comes within the class of the hypothesis expressed in the major premise. The conclusion states that the generalization expressed in the major premise also applies to the particular instance contained in the minor premise.

The conditional clause, "if Congress increases taxes," is the antecedent; the clause to which the condition applies, "industry will decrease capital investment," is the consequent. The following rules apply:

If the minor premise affirms the antecedent, the conclusion must affirm the consequent. This rule applies in the preceding example and constitutes the most common form of the hypothetical syllogism. The minor premise affirms the antecedent; the conclusion affirms the consequent.

If the minor premise denies the consequent, the conclusion must deny the antecedent. The minor premise of the above example may be changed to illustrate this rule.

Major premise: If Congress increases taxes, industry will decrease capital investment.
Minor premise: Industry will not decrease capital investment.
Conclusion: Congress will not decrease taxes.

If the minor premise affirms the consequent or denies the antecedent, no valid conclusion may be made. Arrange the above syllogism into these forms and note the effect; no conclusions can logically follow from the premises.

C. THE ALTERNATIVE OR DISJUNCTIVE SYLLOGISM. In the disjunctive syllogism, the major premise contains alternate possibilities; the minor premise either affirms or negates one of the alternatives; the conclusion negates the alternative not affirmed or affirms the alternate not negated in the minor premise. The following example illustrates:

Major premise: Either Congress must increase taxes, or inflation will continue.
Minor premise: Congress will not increase taxes.
Conclusion: Inflation will continue.

or

Major premise: Either Congress must increase taxes, or inflation will continue.
Minor premise: Congress will increase taxes.
Conclusion: Inflation will not continue.

The following rules apply:

The possibilities enumerated in the major premise must be all-inclusive. Many problems cannot be resolved into "either-or" statements; there may be more than two possibilities. The conclusion may be invalid if all alternatives are not included in the major premise. For example:

Major premise: To prevent inflation, either taxes must be increased or savings must be expanded.
Minor premise: Savings cannot be expanded.
Conclusion: Taxes must be increased.

The major premise overlooks other preventives of inflation, such as decreased wages, increased production, or increased sale of government bonds. Inflation could be prevented without either increasing taxes or expanding savings.

The possibilities enumerated in the major premise must be mutually exclusive. If the possibilities enumerated in the major premise overlap, the destruction of one alternative weakens or destroys the other. Note the following illustration:

Major premise: To prevent inflation, either savings or sale of government bonds must be increased.
Minor premise: The sale of government bonds cannot be increased.
Conclusion: Savings must be increased.

The sale of government bonds is one of the methods for increasing savings. If the sale of government bonds cannot be increased, savings cannot be expanded. The alternatives are not mutually exclusive.

If the minor premise affirms one of the alternatives of the major premise, the conclusion must deny the other. For example:

Major premise: To increase purchasing power, either wages must be increased or prices must be decreased.
Minor premise: Wages can be increased.
Conclusion: Prices need not be decreased.

If the minor premise denies one of the alternatives of the major premise, the conclusion must affirm the other. To illustrate:

Major premise: To increase purchasing power, either wages must be increased or prices must be decreased.
Minor premise: Prices cannot be decreased.
Conclusion: Wages must be increased.

2. *The enthymeme.*[4] Arguments in debate are rarely presented in formal syllogistic style. Either one of the premises or the conclusion

[4] For a discussion of the enthymeme and probability, see James H. McBurney and Glen E. Mills, *Argumentation and Debate: Techniques of a Free Society* (New York: The Macmillan Company, 1964), pp. 145-51.

is assumed. This incomplete type of syllogism is termed *enthymeme.* For example, the foregoing syllogism would be stated as follows:

Major premise: To increase purchasing power, either wages must be increased or prices must be decreased.
Conclusion: Wages must be increased.

The minor premise, "prices cannot be decreased," is assumed. In the same manner, the major premise or the conclusion may be assumed with the presence of the other two parts of the syllogism.

3. *Sorites.* Deductive reasoning may be expressed as a chain of reasoning termed *sorites.* This form consists of a chain of syllogisms or enthymemes with all but the last conclusion suppressed. For example:

High wages increase purchasing power.
Increased purchasing power causes expansion of production.
Expansion of production decreases unemployment.
Full employment leads to inflation.
High wages lead to inflation.

VI. Rebuttal and Refutation

An important part of debate consists of tearing down the arguments of the opposing side and rebuilding one's own arguments. The processes are termed rebuttal and refutation.

The terms *rebuttal* and *refutation* are sometimes used synonymously. One distinction should be understood: refutation consists of attacks on opposing arguments; rebuttal consists of attacks on one's opponent's arguments and the reconstruction of one's own arguments. In formal debates, separate speeches are assigned for rebuttal as distinguished from the constructive speeches. Refutation may be an important part of both the constructive and rebuttal processes.

Methods and Forms of Refutation

You may weaken your opponent's arguments by attacking either the reasoning or the evidence, or both. Errors in reasoning are termed fallacies. Fallacies are committed by violating any of the tests for inductive and deductive reasoning discussed in the preceding two sections of this chapter.

Errors in evidence may be committed by violating the rules of evidence explained in Chapter 7 and in Section IV of the present chapter. You may show the insufficiency of your opponent's evidence, its misapplication, its inaccuracy, or its unreliable source.

Rebuttal arguments may be classified as follows:

1. *Reduce an argument to an absurdity.* This form, termed *reductio ad absurdum,* assumes the truth of an opponent's statement, extends the argument to its ultimate conclusion, and shows the absurdity of it. For example, your opponent argues that the United States should not adopt the principle of selective education because it is an untried plan. By the same process of reasoning, we should never have attempted public education, coeducation, or mass education because they were untried plans when adopted. Extending the argument further, nothing new should be adopted, for all original proposals are untried. The absurdity of the argument appears by extending the reasoning to its logical conclusion.

2. *Reduce an argument to a dilemma.* The dilemma claims an argument leads logically to only two conclusions, each untenable. The two untenable alternatives become the horns of the dilemma. The classic example, "Have you quit beating your wife?" illustrates the dilemma. If you answer "yes," you admit you once did beat her; if you answer "no," you imply you are continuing the practice.

To illustrate: suppose your opponent argues that to improve education, the United States must either increase revenue or divert to education funds now used for space development. You argue that either procedure would be unsatisfactory; thus, no satisfactory method remains for increasing revenue.

3. *Expose inconsistencies.* An inconsistency contains a contradiction within an argument or between arguments. Inconsistencies apply either to reasoning or to the presentation of evidence. If your opponent claims mass education superior to selective education in one argument and then later claims that many cities are correcting the evil of mass education through adopting selective-education plans, you can weaken his argument by pointing out that the one contention contradicts the other.

4. *Appropriate opposing arguments.* The process of appropriating opposing arguments may be called "turning the tables." By this method, you interpret the evidence or the reasoning of your opponent so as to prove your contentions. To illustrate, your opponent claims that the United States extends education to the masses and thus discriminates against superior students. You counter that best

results accrue in a democracy from educating the masses and that a system of mass education need not discriminate against superior students. Education can be extended to the masses with special consideration for superior students through honors programs. Thus, you appropriate an opponent's argument to prove your case.

5. *Expose opposing arguments as irrelevant.* You expose an opponent's argument as irrelevant by showing that it does not advance his case. This method is sometimes called the "so what?" method; granted the argument, what does it prove? For example, your opponent claims that rural sections do not have schools comparable to urban areas; thus, the American system discriminates against rural communities. You counter by claiming this charge irrelevant. Students from rural districts are transported to the better schools in urban areas. They receive superior training without the added cost of maintaining expensive facilities in sparsely settled districts.

Preparing for Rebuttal and Refutation

Although final organization of rebuttal points must be made during the debate, some preparation can be made in advance. You can anticipate many of your opponent's arguments and plan your answers. This prior preparation may take the following forms:

1. Through analysis, decide on the possible arguments of your opponent.
2. Plan possible methods of attack on each anticipated argument.
3. List reasons and assemble evidence on each anticipated point.
4. Decide on methods of attacking specific items of evidence.

Let your plans remain adaptable to your opponent's specific arguments. Your prior plans and preparation should enable you to adapt to your opponent's arguments during the debate.

Organize your rebuttal points into a logical sequence of ideas during the debate. Do not take notes in a haphazard manner, but group your points under headings of main issues. Answer all arguments pertaining to an issue before proceeding to the next issue.

Each rebuttal point includes three steps: introduction, body, and summary. In introducing a rebuttal point, make clear what point you plan to refute and the issue to which it pertains. In the body of the point, present reasons and evidence to refute your opponent's argument and to rebuild your own. In summary, show clearly wherein your refutation has weakened your opponent's argument and the status of the debate as the result of your refutation.

VII. Summary

Many problems are solved through discussion in a democracy. If they cannot be solved in this manner, debate must be employed to settle the conflict.

To participate effectively in debate, you must understand certain procedural principles: (1) prima-facie case, (2) burden of proof, (3) right of definition, (4) right of setting forth issues, (5) burden of rebuttal, and (6) no new issues in rebuttal speeches.

Debate requires a proposition. There are three types: fact, value, and policy. Policy questions are best for debate. The question must be phrased properly, as follows: (1) in resolution form, (2) for equal balance of arguments, (3) as an affirmative resolution, (4) to include one central idea, (5) to avoid ambiguous and prejudiced terms, and (6) to restrict its scope.

Through analysis the main issues emerge; they include three types: potential, admitted, and real. The steps in analysis include: (1) determining present significance of topic, (2) studying its origin and history, (3) disposal of irrelevant and admitted matter, (4) interpretation of the proposition, (5) discovery of the underlying philosophy, and (6) contrast of affirmative and negative main contentions.

Evidence constitutes an essential part of logical proof. Evidence consists of facts and opinions. Evidence may be classified as (1) direct or circumstantial, (2) oral or written, (3) expert or ordinary, (4) original or hearsay, (5) positive or negative, (6) real or personal, or (7) deliberative or casual. To test evidence, consider its (1) source, (2) quality, and (3) quantity.

Reasoning forms a component part of logical proof. Reasoning may be broadly classified as inductive and deductive. Inductive reasoning proceeds from the specific to the general and includes reasoning by example, analogy, and causal relations. Deductive reasoning proceeds from the general to a specific conclusion. The syllogism constitutes the main form of deduction. The types of syllogisms include: categorical, conditional or hypothetical, and alternative or disjunctive. The enthymeme and sorites are other methods of deductive reasoning.

Rebuttal and refutation form an essential part of advocacy. Refutation may question evidence or reasoning, or both. Rebuttal points may take the form of (1) *reductio ad absurdum,* (2) exposing a dilemma, (3) exposing inconsistencies, (4) appropriating opposing arguments, and (5) exposing irrelevant arguments. Rebuttal points should be organized during the debate. General preparation for rebuttal should be made prior to the debate.

Questions and Exercises

A. Answer the following questions on Chapter 15:

1. Explain how debate applies in a democracy.
2. Explain briefly the following procedural principles of debate: (1) burden of proof, (2) prima-facie case, (3) burden of rebuttal, and (4) right to interpret the proposition.
3. Distinguish among fact, value, and policy questions. Which type serves college debate best? Why?
4. State and explain six requirements for phrasing a debate proposition. State the principles of each requirement.
5. What is the ultimate purpose of analysis of the proposition?
6. Distinguish among potential, admitted, and real issues. Illustrate your answers.
7. State and explain six steps in analysis. Why are these steps important to analysis?
8. Distinguish between fact and opinion evidence. List and explain several ways that evidence may be classified.
9. State and explain the principal tests for evidence.
10. Define reasoning. Distinguish between the inductive and deductive processes.
11. List the three principal forms of inductive reasoning. Explain several tests for each.
12. List and explain three types of syllogisms. State several rules for each.
13. How does the syllogism differ from the enthymeme or sorites?
14. Distinguish between rebuttal and refutation. How are they related to the total process of advocacy?
15. State and explain several forms that refutation and rebuttal points may take.
16. List several steps in preparing for a rebuttal. Why must the final organization of your rebuttal points be made during the process of the debate?

B. For your oral assignment you may have a choice of two plans. The choice should be made by vote of the class upon recommendation by the professor. If class time permits, both exercises should prove profitable. Plan

A requires less class time and is probably more interesting. Plan B permits more individual participation.

1. Plan A includes the following steps:
   a. Organize the class into a legislative assembly. Let each member of the class suggest topics for a debate. Discuss the suggested topics in class and select one, by vote if necessary.
   b. Conduct a public-opinion poll among class members to determine their attitudes toward the selected topic. On the basis of this poll, divide the class into three sections: (1) those favorable to the proposal, (2) those opposed, and (3) those who are neutral. The favorable and opposed group should be near the same size. The neutral group may be smaller.
   c. Seat the favorable group on the left side of the classroom; they constitute the liberal party. Seat the opposed group on the right side of the classroom; they are the conservatives. Seat the neutral group in the rear of the classroom; they hold the balance of power.
   d. Elect a chairman from the neutral group, preferably one who understands parliamentary procedure. Through an understanding with the neutral group he shall see that no motion to adjourn, to table the motion, or to cut off debate will receive a favorable vote until near the end of the class period.
   e. The liberals introduce the proposition, move its adoption, and speak for it in an opening speech of not more than eight minutes. Next, the chairman recognizes the leader for the opposition for a speech of not more than six minutes. Thereafter, he recognizes alternating speakers for each side who will be limited to four-minute speeches. A timekeeper should be appointed from the neutral group.
   f. Near the end of the class period the chairman will see that the measure is brought to vote. The neutral group will vote individually on the basis of which side did the most effective debating. In case of a tie the chairman may vote.
   g. Members of the neutral group may ask questions of either side but shall not speak to the issue unless they join one side during the debate. In that event they give up their neutral position.
2. Plan B calls for individual debates on different topics selected by the class.
   a. Form two-member teams, the number depending on the size of the class. Assign an affirmative and a negative team to each proposition.
   b. Each speaker shall have a seven-minute constructive speech and a three-minute rebuttal speech. The affirmative shall speak first in the constructive speeches and the negative first in rebuttal.
   c. The class shall vote at the conclusion of the debates on the basis of which side did the most effective debating, not on their beliefs on the proposition.

C. Perform the following exercises:

1. List properly phrased policy propositions as follows:
   (1) two school problems, (2) two state problems, (3) two national problems, and (4) two international problems.
2. Point out the errors, if any, in the statement of the following propositions:
   a. Resolved, that the United States foreign policy should be changed.
   b. Resolved, that the federal government should adopt a public-works program to alleviate poverty.
   c. Resolved, that the unjust laws restricting civil liberties should be repealed.
   d. Resolved, that the dog is more intelligent than the horse.
   e. Resolved, that the President should be elected for a single six-year term and by direct vote of the people.
3. State the importance of the immediate cause for discussion in the following propositions:
   a. Resolved, that further development of nuclear weapons should be prohibited by international agreement.
   b. Resolved, that the United States should join the European Common Market.
   c. Resolved, that the United States should encourage trade with the communist countries of Europe.
   d. Resolved, that the federal government should establish a national program of public works for the unemployed.
4. Underscore the terms in the above propositions that should be defined. What methods would you use to define them?
5. Point out the weaknesses, if any, in the following sources of evidence:
   a. An opinion statement issued by the secretary for the National Association for the Advancement of Colored People on the subject of integration. An opinion statement on the same problem by the secretary of the White Citizens' Council. An opinion statement on the same problem by the President of the United States.
   b. Mickey Mantle's opinion of the effect of baseball on leisure activities.
   c. George Romney's opinion on the foreign-car market in the United States. His opinion on civil rights.
   d. Barry Goldwater's opinion of the 89th Congress. His opinion of economic conditions in Oregon.
   e. William Scranton's opinion of labor leaders.
      George Meany's opinion of labor leaders.
      Arthur Goldberg's opinion of labor leaders.
6. Rearrange the following syllogisms into proper form:
   a. All dogs are mammals.
   b. Mickey is a mammal.
   c. Mickey is a dog.

a. Labor unions cause inflation.
b. Labor unions cause high wages.
c. High wages cause inflation.

a. Wages cannot be decreased.
b. Either savings must be increased or wages must be decreased.
c. Savings must be increased.

a. Tubby is a dog.
b. Tubby is not a cat.
c. Tubby is either a dog or a cat.

7. Label each of the above syllogisms as (1) categorical (2) hyothetical, or (3) disjunctive.
8. Label the major, middle, and minor terms in the above syllogisms after they have been arranged in proper form.
9. Bring to class three examples of generalizations that you have heard or read.
10. Give examples that justify the following generalizations:
    a. Americans enjoy a high standard of living.
    b. A college education is a good investment.
    c. Americans believe in freedom of speech.
    d. War scares cause inflation.
11. Bring to class three examples of reasoning by analogy that you have heard or read.
12. Bring to class three examples of causal reasoning that you have heard or read.
13. Give one original example of the following types of fallacies: (1) hasty generalization, (2) false analogy, (3) mistaking the cause, and (4) mistaking the effect.
14. Find two examples in the newspapers of errors in the use of evidence.

CHAPTER 16

Adapt Skills to Special Occasions

The basic principles of oral communication discussed throughout this textbook apply to speeches for all occasions. Application has been made to the principal types—informative, persuasive, and argumentative. This chapter will apply the principles to special types of speeches and make suggestions for their composition and delivery. The discussion includes the following types of speeches: (1) introduction, (2) welcome and response, (3) presentation and acceptance, (4) eulogy and dedication, (5) after-dinner speeches, and (6) radio and television speeches.

I. The Speech of Introduction

Speeches of introduction apply on almost all speaking occasions except those like religious services, classroom lectures, and workshop programs that have permanent lecturers. In spite of their frequent use, speeches of introduction are often execrably done. Two examples illustrate. A professional organization employed a principal speaker for its convention. The speaker was allotted forty-five minutes at a breakfast session, but the toastmaster took twenty minutes to introduce him. The toastmaster made such extravagant statements about the speaker's qualifications that he embarrassed him. He anticipated the speaker's address and stated his own views on the subject. He talked about himself, his experiences, his accomplishments; finally, he made several unsuccessful attempts at humor. Most objectionably, he talked much too long.

On another occasion, the superintendent of schools in a small town introduced the commencement speaker as follows:

> We are happy to have Professor Jones as our speaker tonight. I know nothing about him since I met him only a few minutes ago. He was secured by the commencement committee. However, he should be good because he has been a speech teacher at Poe University for more than twenty years. I had better turn the meeting over to Professor Jones now before I reveal my own poor speech; speech teachers make me nervous. Anyway, the college that I attended—how many years ago is top secret—didn't teach expression. Professor Jones is such a permanent fixture around these parts, however, that he needs no introduction. Professor Jones, it's all yours.

These two speeches exemplify most of what is bad in speeches of introduction, and little that is good. Unfortunately, they are real instances, not hypothetical. How can we avoid the mistakes of these negative examples? Consider the following discussion.

The Purpose

The purpose of the speech of introduction is threefold: (1) to create a pleasant atmosphere, (2) to give the qualifications of the speaker, and (3) to stress the importance of the subject. The introducer should not be the "life of the party," call attention to himself, or give the speaker's speech. Consider the introducer as the advance agent of the speaker; he should unobtrusively increase the audience's respect for the speaker. The audience should hardly be aware of the introducer, because he should center attention on the speaker.

On some occasions, it may not be necessary to stress all three purposes listed above. For example, prior events on the program may have created the proper atmosphere; the speaker may be well known to the audience; the importance of the subject may be obvious. The introducer must analyze the speaking situation and adapt his speech to prevailing conditions.

Suggestions for Preparation

What principles can we isolate from the foregoing examples of poor speeches of introduction? Four positive and four negative suggestions follow:

1. *Consult the speaker.* Consult the speaker for ideas he might like included and for advice on what you plan to say. Be a good host to the speaker. Be prepared to answer his questions about the audience and the occasion and to provide materials that he might request.

2. *Make the speech of introduction a separate speech.* Do not

make the speech a part of announcements or expressions of courtesy. If the presiding officer does not know the speaker well, he may ask an acquaintance or a close associate of the speaker to introduce him. If the chairman presents the speaker, he should make a transition from his previous remarks to the speech of introduction; for example, "Now we come to the main feature of our program—the principal speaker. I shall present him at this time."

3. *Be brief but thorough.* The length of the speech depends on how well the speaker is known to the audience; the better-known the speaker, the shorter the introduction. Because of the prestige of the President of the United States, he is usually presented simply as "Ladies and gentlemen, the President of the United States." Yet to present a less-known person so briefly shows poor taste and leaves the audience dissatisfied. Unless the listeners already know about the qualifications of the speaker, the introducer should state them. The length of the speech of introduction will, therefore, vary with the circumstances. If you should introduce the president of your university to a campus organization, you would need few qualifying statements. If you presented him to a club in your home town, you would need to say more. Rarely should the speech of introduction run less than thirty seconds or more than three minutes.

4. *Use humor in good taste.* The introducer may create a pleasant atmosphere by the judicious use of humor. Humor should never be used, however, to depreciate the qualifications of the speaker or to minimize the importance of the subject or occasion. Humor can help set the keynote of a meeting. Ask yourself, "What atmosphere would serve the speaker best?" If he plans an entertaining speech, use humor in the introduction. If he plans a serious speech, use humor sparingly.

5. *Do not overpraise the speaker.* To attempt to make an ordinary mortal appear superhuman embarrasses both the speaker and the audience. Stress the speaker's qualifications and prestige with restraint and in good taste. Avoid flowery language, extravagant claims, and an effusive manner.

6. *Do not talk about yourself.* As the introducer, you are the agent of the main speaker, not the main speaker. You succeed in proportion to how well you cause the audience to respect the speaker, not to how well the audience thinks you speak. Statements about your previous association with the speaker may help estab-

lish a bond between you, the speaker, and the audience; but such statements should enhance the speaker's prestige, not yours. One introducer told about an incident when he was president and the speaker was vice-president of their class in college. This incident obviously violates the principles discussed here.

7. *Do not stress the speaker's speaking ability.* Such statements as "The speaker should be good because he teaches speech" or "The speaker has established an outstanding reputation as an orator" put the speaker at a disadvantage. The listeners will likely center their attention on the speaker's skills instead of his ideas. Stress the speaker's training, experience, and honors; avoid mention of his speaking ability.

8. *Avoid trite and hackneyed language.* Speeches of introduction often include worn-out phrases, such as "The speaker needs no introduction," "It gives me great pleasure," "I am pleased and honored," "I consider it a unique privilege," "It is appropriate to this auspicious occasion," and "I am too pleased for words." Use fresh and original expressions appropriate to the occasion.

The Arrangement of Ideas

Organize the speech of introduction through four steps: (1) direct attention to the occasion, (2) focus attention on the speaker, (3) stress the importance of the subject, and (4) present the speaker. These steps can best be accomplished by the traditional organizational pattern—introduction, body, and conclusion.

1. *The introduction.* In the introduction, catch the immediate interest of the audience and set the keynote for the speech to follow. Use any of the methods explained in Chapter 8 for these purposes. For example, the late Irving T. Bush, President of Bush Terminal Company of New York City, opened his speech introducing former Chief Justice Charles Evans Hughes with humor: "I have always thought that the ideal introductory speech was that of a certain gentleman of German extractions from the Middle West who was asked to introduce the Senator of his state. He said, 'I am asked to introduce Senator Jones who will speak to you. I have done it. He will do it.' "[1] Former Professor at Ohio State University Henry R. Spencer's opening sentence when introducing columnist and Pulitzer prize-winner Anne O'Hare McCormick was: "If this

---

[1] W. P. Sandford and W. H. Yeager, *Business Speeches by Business Men* (New York: McGraw-Hill Book Co., 1930), p. 697.

is a man's world, we have surely made a mess of it. But as we are young we are resolved to learn, and we turn therefore to the other sex." [2]

2. *The body.* In the body of the speech, present information to increase the prestige of the speaker and to enhance interest in the subject. Tell about the speaker—his position, his training, his experiences, and any honors or distinctions that increase his prestige. If the speaker has traveled widely, written books, or headed important enterprises that bear on his subject, stress these points. Show the importance of his subject to the audience, but do not try to anticipate how the speaker will develop his subject or to express your opinion about it. If your opinion about the speaker's subject differs from his, expressing it might make his task more difficult. Arrange your points in climactic order, ending with the presentation of the speaker.

3. *The conclusion.* As the final step, present the speaker and give the title of his speech; for example, "I present Mr. John Doe, who will speak on the subject, 'Hook Your Wagon to a Star'—Mr. Doe"; or "For a discussion of the important subject, 'Government in Business,' I present Senator Peter Poe."

The Manner of Presentation

Effective presentation follows the suggestions made in Part Three—reasonable poise, pleasing and intelligible voice, uninhibited bodily action, and communicative language. Enthusiasm, tact, and sincerity should characterize your manner. Do not read a speech of introduction. Speak extemporaneously from a mental outline with as original an approach as you can devise.

Sample Speech

The following speech of introduction was given at the annual banquet of the Baylor University Chapter of the American Association of University Professors. The principal speaker was known by some members of the audience, but not intimately.

> "If a man be endowed with a generous mind, this is the best kind of nobility." This statement by Plato characterizes our speaker for tonight. During the more than twenty years that I have known Dr. Sartain, I

[2] William Hayes Yeager, *Effective Speaking for Every Occasion* (Englewood Cliffs, N.J.: Prentice-Hall, Inc., 1951), p. 127.

have become increasingly impressed, not only with his generous and penetrating mind, but with his kindly spirit.

A risk that one runs in introducing a cherished friend is that he may deal in extravagant statements. I find myself in somewhat of a paradoxical situation this evening because a simple factual recital of the training, accomplishments, and contributions of Dr. Sartain appears to be overstatement. I am tempted to dwell at length on such matters as these:

1. His writings, which include co-authorship of a recent textbook, "Human Behavior in Industry," his forthcoming textbook to be published by Prentice-Hall, and numerous articles in professional journals.
2. His important positions which he has held at Southern Methodist University, where he was first the Director of Forensics, later Professor of Psychology, and now is chairman of the Department of Personnel Administration. He also has more than a passing interest in Baylor University, having taught recently as visiting professor in our summer session.
3. His membership in important organizations. For example, he served recently as president of the Southern Methodist University chapter of the American Association of University Professors. He is president of the Southwestern Psychological Association, a fellow of the American Psychological Association, and a member of the Association for the Advancement of Science.

Rather than dwelling on these matters, may I say simply that I congratulate you for securing Dr. Sartain for this occasion. In my association with Dr. Sartain, I have been impressed with the excellence of his forensic teams but even more with him as a man—his pleasant disposition, his sense of fair play, his high ethical standards, and his ability as a scholar. I present to you my friend and the friend of all teachers—Dr. A. Q. Sartain.[3]

II. The Speech of Welcome

Numerous occasions call for speeches of welcome in our modern society. Most Americans belong to several organizations which sponsor meetings that call for speeches of welcome. The principal occasions for speeches of welcome are these: (1) conventions of professional organizations; (2) meetings such as home-coming gatherings, speech tournaments, workshops, institutes, orientation programs, and career-day programs; (3) ceremonies for welcoming a distinguished guest to a city; and (4) programs for welcoming new members to an organization. Speeches of welcome to convention delegates and distinguished guests are usually made by public offi-

[3] Unpublished speech, Glenn R. Capp.

cials; for special gatherings and for welcoming new members to organizations, the president of the sponsoring group makes the speech.

The Purpose

The purpose of the speech of welcome is twofold: (1) to express appreciation for the organization or person welcomed and (2) to create good will. Look upon the speech as a public act of courtesy; the host desires to establish friendly relations with the visiting organization. The speaker should indicate by his manner and words that he considers the meeting important and that he hopes it will be profitable for the visitors. The sentiment expressed should be genuine, the manner pleasant, and the spirit friendly.

Suggestions for Preparation

Speeches of welcome are often stereotyped and perfunctory, especially when given by busy public officials. To keep them individual and original, consider the following suggestions.

1. *Use tact and good taste.* Try not to leave the impression that you are performing a routine assignment or that the meeting imposes on your time. If you must leave immediately after your speech, have the chairman comment on the reasons; for example, "Thank you, Mayor Jones. The Mayor has a council meeting at ten o'clock. We hope that he may have the opportunity to drop in on some of our future sessions." If possible, remain for a few minutes until there is a break in the meeting; then leave as unobtrusively as possible.

2. *Be optimistic and enthusiastic.* Speeches of welcome are usually arranged for the opening sessions of conventions or at the beginning of programs when new members are received into organizations. These speeches usually precede other expressions of courtesy, explanations, and announcements. Opening sessions aim at creating a friendly and optimistic atmosphere; they set the keynote for future sessions. The speech of welcome should conform with this purpose.

3. *Make the speech brief.* Rarely should the speech of welcome exceed five minutes except when included as part of a principal address. When so arranged, the speaker gives the welcome as a part of the introduction to his principal address. The length of the speech of welcome depends in part on how closely the speaker is associated with the sponsoring organization. For example, if the

mayor of a city gives the welcoming speech to a convention of educators, the speech normally will be brief; if the president of the local university gives the speech, it will perhaps be longer because of the community of interests between the president and the delegates. On some occasions, two or more speeches of welcome may be arranged representing different interest groups. For example, both the mayor of the city and the president of the local university may welcome the convention of educators. For occasions that have multiple speeches of welcome, brevity becomes increasingly important.

4. *Avoid emotionalism.* Although optimism and friendliness should characterize the speech of welcome, emotionalism has little place in it. For occasions that welcome convention delegates and workshop participants, the mood may be somewhat dignified and formal. For ceremonies that welcome a guest to a city, the program may take the form of a ritual. Little cause for emotionalism exists. Conversely, meetings such as home-coming gatherings, reunions, and programs for welcoming new members lend themselves to emotionalism. To guard against excessive emotionalism on such occasions, keep your remarks in a light vein; inject well-chosen humor and emphasize the festive nature of the occasion.

5. *Avoid flowery platitudes and stereotyped forms.* The following objectionable expressions have been noted in speeches of welcome: "You people are the salt of the earth." "Our hearts glow with pride because of what you have accomplished." "Welcome back to your dear old alma mater." "You represent the Alpha and Omega of all that is good." "I know you will work like a Trojan, but. . . ." "A Herculean task confronts you." "There are no losers in a speech contest." "Like the sword of Damocles. . . ." "Let's make them eat crow." "Let us not rob Peter to pay Paul." "We find ourselves on the horns of a dilemma." "Yours is no fool's paradise." Although such forms are expressive, they have lost their force through overuse. Attempt to make the speech of welcome novel, fresh, and alive; avoid overpraise and exaggeration.

The Arrangement of Ideas

The speech of welcome calls for novel and original treatment; as in the speech of introduction, this can be achieved best within the framework of the traditional pattern—introduction, body, and conclusion.

1. *The introduction.* Attempt to capture the attention and inter-

est of the audience with your opening statement; for example, one public official began his speech to a convention of funeral directors with, "I presume you have come to praise Caesar, and not to bury him." A mayor began his speech at a convention of theater teachers with "All the world's a stage; the mayors simply give speeches of welcome." Another public official opened his speech to a workshop of law-enforcement officers with "I understand there are two types of pedestrians—the quick and the dead."

Indicate for whom you speak. Speeches of welcome are made in behalf of an organized group—a city, a university, another organization—or by the representative of the sponsoring organization to its various branches. Identify your relation to that group unless the chairman does so in introducing you.

2. *The body.* The body of the speech should perform two functions: (1) express appreciation for the group welcomed and (2) give information about the place where welcomed. Seek out the philosophy behind the organization welcomed; learn about its background and history, and facts about its aims and purposes; demonstrate your knowledge of these facts by complimenting the visiting organization. Tell about the city or organization which you represent—places of interest which the delegates may visit, recreational facilities, and unusual places to eat. In short, pay tribute to both the visiting delegation and to the organization that welcomes them.

If an out-of-town representative of the sponsoring organization welcomes the convention delegates, he would omit information about the local city and would stress the purpose of the meeting and the common aims of the delegates. If a local person preceded him with a speech of welcome, the organization's representative would reply briefly by expressing appreciation to the local speaker before giving his speech welcoming the delegates.

3. *The conclusion.* Conclude the speech of welcome by expressing hope that the meeting will be successful, by pledging the cooperation of the welcoming organization, and by inviting the delegates to return for a future meeting. James G. Stewart, the mayor of Cincinnati, ended his speech with, "And we hope you will like it [Cincinnati] so much that, in the words of the late President, 'you will come here again, again, and again.' "[4]

---

[4] Yeager, *op. cit.*, p. 134.

The Manner of Presentation

In presenting the speech of welcome, utilize all the principles of effective voice, bodily action, language, and poise previously discussed. The manner should be sincere, cordial, and gracious. Make the spirit fit the occasion. Use direct, conversational, communicative speech without oratorical flourish.

Sample Speech

The following speech of welcome was given at the twenty-fifth annual high school speech tournament sponsored by Baylor University.

We welcome you this morning to our twenty-fifth birthday celebration —to the original and oldest college-sponsored tournament in Texas for high schools. Since the first meeting in the Spring of 1935, the tournament has grown to perhaps the largest debate tournament held annually in the United States. This year we have 958 registered speakers and an additional 250 forensic directors, chaperons, and alternate speakers—a total attendance of over 1,200.

The 324 debate teams and 652 speakers in the other speaking contests will require 866 judging assignments and 162 contest rooms. You may wonder how all these facilities are possible. They would not be possible without the cooperation of a large number of people. The tournament is now sponsored jointly by Baylor University, Waco High School, and the Heart O' Texas Lions Club; also cooperating are the Waco Chamber of Commerce. *The News Tribune and Times Herald,* Waco civic clubs, the Waco Hotel Association, and the Seventh and James Street Baptist Church.

You may wonder why we would go to all the trouble. The answer is partly selfish—we would like to have many of you as future students. Further, we think you are engaged in an extremely worthwhile activity. I agree with the famous American philosopher Alexander Meiklejohn when he said, "It seems to me that stronger than any other group, tougher in intellectual fiber, keener in intellectual interest, better equipped than any others to battle with coming problems are the debaters—the students who, apart from their regular studies, band themselves together for intellectual controversy with each other and with their friends from other schools."

The large folders of letters of appreciation which I have in my files from former participants and from my own favorite exdebaters proclaim that the activity is more than worthwhile. Numbered among these letters are those from United States Senators, ambassadors to foreign countries, college presidents and teachers, the owner of a fifty-million-dollar corporation, and ministers, lawyers, and doctors of prominence. Almost without exception, these former students testify to the interest created by the competition for the loving cups which you see on display here on the stage. More important, they testify to the permanent assets received from their training in forensics. These benefits will be remembered long after you have forgotten whether you won or lost. We welcome you this morning to membership in the distinguished club of more than twenty thousand former participants in this meeting. We wish for you both a pleasant and profitable visit in our city and on our campus.[5]

Reply to Speech of Welcome

Some occasions call for a response to a speech of welcome; others do not. At conventions the presiding officer usually thanks the speaker and the sponsoring organization in behalf of the convention. Responses are rarely made to speeches of welcome on occasions such as workshops, institutes, tournaments, and festivals or to a speech welcoming several new members into an organization. If the speaker singles out one person for extended praise or if a city welcomes a distinguished guest, a response is expected.

The speech of response follows the same general principles as the speech of welcome. The speaker should respond to the mood created by the speech of welcome. Normally, he should arrange his ideas in the following order: (1) Indicate for whom he speaks if he represents a welcomed group. (2) Express appreciation for being honored. (3) Compliment the group that gives the welcome. (4) Express pleasant anticipations for the meeting or for the personal honor.

Although the speech of reply must remain adaptable to the speech of welcome, it should not be impromptu. Plan the speech in advance and make whatever changes seem advisable at the moment. The speech should be brief, cordial, and sincere.

III. The Speech of Presentation

Our society is replete with occasions that call for speeches of presentation. Civic organizations honor citizens for outstanding service to the community; industrial and educational institutions honor employees for years of service when they leave their places of employment or when they retire; universities and colleges confer honorary degrees on outstanding citizens; fraternal and service organi-

[5] Unpublished speech, Glenn R. Capp.

zations present earned degrees and awards for superior accomplishments; schools, clubs, and industries award scholarships, medals, trophies, and plaques for competitive winners; and political organizations honor public officials upon retirement from office. Almost all of these occasions call for speeches of presentation and the awarding of symbolic tokens of appreciation.

The Purpose

The purpose of the speech of presentation is threefold: (1) to honor the recipient, (2) to honor the donor, (3) to increase morale in an organization. Tribute to the recipient constitutes the primary purpose, because the person or organization making the presentation desires to reward faithful service and outstanding accomplishment. Tribute to the donor serves to recognize those who have supported the organization by making the awards possible. By suggesting attributes of the recipient and the donor that others may emulate, the spirit and morale of others may be enhanced.

Suggestions for Preparation

Speeches of presentation allow for more individual differences than do most speeches for special occasions because of the variety of occasions that utilize them. The suggestions that follow apply generally and can be adapted to these occasions.

1. *Know the recipient.* The speech of presentation may be cold and impersonal unless the speaker knows the recipient well. To create a friendly spirit and improve morale, the speech must show warmth and sincere feelings of appreciation. If the presiding officer does not know the recipient well, he should appoint someone familiar with his virtues to make the presentation speech. For competitive awards, the director of the program or the donor should make the presentation speech. Above all, the speech should be personal; stereotyped speeches of presentation are easily detected.

2. *Know the occasion.* The speaker should be familiar with the occasion, the origin and history of the award, and the standards by which one qualifies. On one occasion the president of a university agreed to present the awards in a competitive speech tournament. He arrived late and apparently without proper instructions. His speech revealed that he knew little about the meeting; he was not aware of the distinction among the various awards or the basis

upon which they were awarded. The winners felt disappointed because they did not receive appropriate recognition. An understanding of the occasion makes for a successful presentation speech.

3. *Show proper restraint.* Speeches of presentation sometimes tend to overpraise and exaggerate. Service awards, competitive trophies, and scholarship honors are usually given annually; although the winners should be congratulated, they should not be praised too highly. Beware of emotionalism when presenting awards to persons upon their retirement. Emphasize the happy side, inject well-chosen humor, and keep the spirit of the occasion light. Restraint is important on most occasions, but especially when making speeches of presentation.

4. *Recognize the losers.* Often competitive events are won by the narrowest of margins. The bounce of the ball may decide the football game; the system for breaking ties may determine the oratory winner; the peculiarities of the judge may decide the band competition; and a figurative toss of the coin may award Miss America her title. Although we seem committed to deciding the "champion," most people recognize that chance often plays a deciding factor. Without detracting from the honor of the winners, bring the losers into your speech for recognition.

5. *Speak briefly and extemporaneously.* There is little need for long speeches of presentation. The length will vary with the occasion, but brevity has its merits regardless of the occasion. When presenting awards of the same type to several persons, make one presentation speech; then have the recipients come forward for their awards without additional speeches. When honoring one person on his retirement or because of unusual accomplishments, the presentation may be a part of a major address; the presentation usually comes at the end of the address.

Rarely should a speech of presentation be read. Parts of the speech may be read without prejudice, such as special citations or the standards for the award; but the overall approach calls for extemporaneous speech. A spirit of spontaneity and informality can best be achieved by speaking extemporaneously.

The Arrangement of Ideas

The organization of speeches of presentation may vary with the type of occasion and the intent of the speaker. The following general instructions follow the pattern of introduction, body, and conclusion.

1. *The introduction.* Capturing attention and holding interest usually present little problem with speeches of presentation. The spirit of enthusiasm of the occasion performs these functions. The introduction should serve to give pertinent information about the award—its origin and its history, including the standards upon which the award is made, the name of the donor, and the names of previous winners.

2. *The body.* The body should be organized to bring out three factors: (1) the virtues and accomplishments of the recipient, (2) appreciation for the donor, and (3) a brief description of the gift or award. Support these points with specific information. In praising the recipient, give instances of his deeds and virtues; show how the donor has advanced a worthy cause by his award; display the award and explain its significance.

3. *The conclusion.* In concluding the speech of presentation, call the recipient forward, congratulate him, and shake his hand as you present the award. Then express your appreciation of the recipient in your closing statement. For example:

> In behalf of all civic clubs in the city, Dr. Wiles, we express our sincere appreciation for your pioneering work in establishing the Civic Welfare Center. To show our love and appreciation, and to make your future work a little easier, we present you with these keys to a new automobile which is now parked in front of this banquet hall. With this token of appreciation go our best wishes for your continued success.

The Manner of Presentation

Let your manner of speaking reflect sincere sentiment. Speak in a conversational, communicative style without flowery language or an effusive manner. Call the recipient forward at the conclusion of your speech; to keep him standing while you speak may be awkward and embarrassing to him. Identify the award, and do not obstruct its view as you present it. Put into practice the principles of voice, bodily action, poise, and language discussed in Part Three.

Sample Speech

The following speech awarded the honorary degree of Doctor of Laws to Mr. Joe L. Allbritton, a distinguished alumnus of Baylor University, at its annual commencement exercises on May 22, 1964.

Mr. President, Members of the Board of Trustees, Members of the Graduating Class, Ladies and Gentlemen:

I take more than the usual pleasure in presenting Mr. Joe Allbritton for the degree of Doctor of Laws because he is one of my favorite former students who has remained a cherished personal friend since his college days. I first recognized Mr. Allbritton's unusual ability while he was still a high school student, a debater for Sam Houston High School in Houston. A special invitation to him to come to Baylor resulted in four years of pleasurable association in a student-teacher relationship. In the fifteen years since his graduation I have watched his unusual successes with increasing pleasure and pride—for no greater satisfaction can come to a teacher than to observe the successes of his former students.

Mr. Joe L. Allbritton was born on December 29, 1924, at D'Lo Simpson County, Mississippi, the son of Lewis A. Allbritton and Ada Carpenter Allbritton. He attended public schools in Houston, Texas, and was graduated from Sam Houston High School in 1942. After attending Baylor University for one year, he joined the Navy in which he served for three years. After World War II, he returned to Baylor where he received the LL.B. degree in 1949, and was admitted to the Texas Bar the same year.

Mr. Allbritton is honored first for his accomplishments—both in the field of business and the professions. Time prevents naming all of them but among his accomplishments are: (1) Chairman of the Board, Pierce National Life Insurance Company, Los Angeles; (2) President and Director, San Jacinto Savings Association, Houston; (3) Chairman of the Board, Mineral Oil Refining Company, Dickinson, Texas; (4) Chairman of the Board, Pierce Brothers Mortuaries, Los Angeles; (5) Partner in the law firm of Allbritton, McGee, and Hand, Houston; (6) Director, Bank of the Southwest National Association, Houston. For his accomplishments, Mr. Allbritton ranks high.

Second, Mr. Allbritton is honored because of his contributions to civic, educational, and religious enterprises. In many ways what a man contributes to his society in time and effort counts more heavily than what he accomplishes. Mr. Allbritton has contributed in many ways: (1) Vice Chairman of the Board of Trustees, Baylor University College of Medicine; (2) Trustee and Member of Executive Committee, Baylor University; (3) Member, Texas Medical Center Joint Administrative Committee, Houston; (4) Chairman of Trustees, Garden Oaks Baptist Church, Houston. For his contributions to society, Mr. Allbritton ranks high.

More important, Mr. Allbritton is honored because of the type of person that he has become. Emerson once said that what a man is speaks so loudly that I cannot hear what he says. Mr. Allbritton has spoken eloquently today, but his life speaks even more eloquently than what he has said. In our long acquaintance, I have been impressed by the many things which Mr. Allbritton has accomplished, but I have been even more impressed with him as a man—what he is: his pleasant disposition, his kindly spirit, his modesty, his sense of fair play, and his desire to be of service to mankind. For the type of life that he lives, Mr. Allbritton ranks highest.

For these reasons, President McCall, I take pleasure in presenting Mr. Joe L. Allbritton for the conferring of the degree Doctor of Laws.[6]

Reply to Speech of Presentation

Some speeches of presentation call for speeches of acceptance. When several people receive similar service awards or competitive trophies, one person may be chosen to represent all the recipients, or the presiding officer may express their appreciation. On occasions honoring one or a few individuals, separate speeches of acceptance are in order. In accepting a gift, conform to the mood created by the speaker who presented it. Avoid sentimentality or emotionalism. Injecting well-chosen humor helps keep the spirit in a light vein.

Organization of the speech of acceptance may follow the following sequence: (1) In the introduction, express sincere appreciation for the honor. (2) In the body, recognize the help of others or refer to the other competitors in the contest and pay tribute to the donors. (3) In the conclusion, accept and display the gift as you again express appreciation for the award.

Beware of both self-depreciation and self-glorification. Let your manner reflect sincere appreciation. Avoid phrases such as "I am speechless," "I don't know what to say," "I don't deserve all this," and "I can't thank you enough." A simple "I thank you" is preferable to a stammered expression of irrelevant remarks; conversely, expressions of surprise hardly apply if you have a well-prepared speech of acceptance. Show appreciation both by what you say and by your manner of saying it.

IV. The Formal Eulogy

The formal eulogy resembles the speech of presentation except that it is more formal and does not include a gift. Formal eulogies apply in at least four situations: (1) a tribute to a living person for unusual accomplishments; (2) a tribute upon the death of a person, or shortly thereafter; (3) a tribute on the anniversary of the birth or death of a person; and (4) a speech nominating a person for office. Eulogies are usually given on formal occasions such as the

[6] Unpublished speech, Glenn R. Capp.

founders-day programs of organizations and institutions, patriotic meetings before school assemblies or civic organizations, or special occasions like United Nations Day or Fourth-of-July celebrations.

The Purpose

The eulogy serves one or a combination of the following purposes: (1) to pay tribute to a person for an outstanding accomplishment or because of his influence on some movement or institution; (2) to increase respect for a person because of his influence on principles and institutions; (3) to set forth principles in a distinguished person's life for emulation by the listeners. The following occasions serve as illustrations: a school assembly honors Abraham Lincoln on the anniversary of his birth; a convention of labor union leaders honors Samuel Gompers for his influence on the union movement; a convention of scientists honors Albert Einstein for his influence on scientific development.

Suggestions for Preparation

The speech commemorating a person requires more knowledge and preparation than most types of speeches for special occasions. The following suggestions apply:

1. *Know the subject well.* A speaker usually uses incidents in the life of the person eulogized to illustrate his points. A thorough understanding and feeling for the person affect the speaker's manner; his knowledge of his subject must come from more than a surface study of facts to be found in encyclopedias or biographical references. He must know the problems and issues of the era in which the person lived and his significant contribution to the solution of those problems. He must understand the influence that the person had on important movements or institutions. Knowledge of one's subject helps on all occasions; it is essential to a successful eulogy.

2. *Evaluate subject accurately.* In the speech of eulogy, do more than enumerate the accomplishments, virtues, or incidents in a person's life. Omit unimportant events and insignificant details; stress major beliefs and philosophies. Emphasize his ideas, ideals, and basic contributions. Recognize his weaknesses as well as his strengths. Often a person's major accomplishments result from his struggle to overcome handicaps or from his strong convictions. Franklin D. Roosevelt made a significant contribution to the treat-

ment of infantile paralysis largely because of his efforts to overcome his own physical handicap; Clarence Darrow's aversion to capital punishment was partly responsible for his phenomenal success as a criminal lawyer; Booker T. Washington's efforts to overcome his early environment account in part for his efforts to improve the plight of his race. Assess cause-and-effect relationships in evaluating your subject, and humanize him by making an accurate and objective appraisal.

3. *Avoid flowery style and oratorical flourish.* The eulogy tends toward exaggeration, one-sided evaluation, and the use of a flamboyant manner. Regardless of how much you may admire your subject, show restraint in your feelings and in your choice of language. Avoid such statements as "The greatest man of his day," "The most significant contribution in history," and "The most beloved man of his era." Show your admiration for his qualities and contributions, but do so in a direct, conversational manner.

4. *Choose interesting support.* Since the means of developing the eulogy consists largely of biographical data, select incidents that have human interest and appeal. The speech may appear dull if one simply lists such facts as date of birth, places of residence, positions held, and honors received. Select those facts that contribute to the person's greatness or that show qualities important in his life. Examples that show action and that appeal to basic drives hold interest well. We remember incidents like Washington's chopping down the cherry tree, Lincoln's walking many miles to return a borrowed book, and Theodore Roosevelt's hunting big game. Such incidents show action, exemplify human traits, and appeal to the factors of interest. They help in getting attention and holding interest.

The Arrangement of Ideas

The organization of the speech of eulogy may be either biographical or selective. The biographical method selects events in a person's life and develops them chronologically from birth to death. The selective method chooses such factors as the person's virtues, accomplishments, or characteristics as the main points of the speech.

1. *The introduction.* The occasion which gives rise to the speech of eulogy is usually well understood; therefore, little time need be given to centering the listener's attention on the occasion. Start with an interesting incident from the life of the person eulogized,

a pertinent virtue that characterizes him, or a reference to how you became interested in him. Then indicate how you intend to develop your speech, by either the biographical or the selective method.

2. *The body.* The biographical method divides the person's life into divisions that form the main points of the speech. Chronological order determines the arrangement of material. For example, for a speech eulogizing George Washington, the main points may be (1) Washington's boyhood and training, (2) Washington's military experiences, (3) Washington's administration as President, (4) Washington's declining years. His life is developed chronologically, with facts and incidents of his life as supporting material.

In the selective method, a person's virtues, characteristics, or accomplishments become the main points of the speech. The speaker uses only the biographical incidents that support the main points in this organization. For example, a speech stressing Washington's accomplishments might include (1) Washington's contributions to agriculture, (2) Washington's contributions to the military, and (3) Washington's contributions to the government. Again, a speech on Washington's characteristics may use these main points: (1) Washington's personality, (2) Washington's commanding physical presence, and (3) Washington's leadership qualities. The selective method uses biographical data as supporting material but not as the basis for the organizational pattern.

3. *The conclusion.* Conclude the eulogy on a note of praise—a personal tribute, a striking statement, or a provocative quotation. Rarely is a detailed summary needed, although a brief reiteration of the main points may be included in the statement of praise. For example, consider the following conclusion to a speech eulogizing George Washington:

> Let us pledge anew our faith in the founders of our nation. The freedom that we now enjoy was gained by the sacrifices of men like Washington. We can best honor his memory by assuming our obligations and responsibilities to the nation which he helped establish.

The Manner of Presentation

Occasions for the speech of eulogy are usually formal and dignified; the manner of speaking should conform to the occasion. Direct, communicative speaking is preferred to bombastic oratory; simple and colorful language fits the occasion better than a flowery or ornate style; restrained bodily action proves more appropriate than gross action. Although the occasions for eulogies may be charged with emotion, show restraint in expressing genuine feelings of appreciation for the person eulogized.

Sample Speech

The following eulogy was presented by Senate Majority Leader Mike Mansfield of Montana as a tribute to former President John F. Kennedy on Sunday, November 24, 1963. It was given in the Capitol Rotunda where the President's body lay in state. The speech is based on an occurrence immediately after the President's assassination while his body was at the Dallas Parkland Hospital. Mrs. Kennedy took the wedding band from her finger, placed it in her late husband's hand, gently kissed his cheek, and walked beside the casket to a waiting hearse.

Although the speech departs in many ways from an ordinary eulogy, it was presented at no ordinary occasion. The intense interest of the people and knowledge of the setting for the speech called for an unusual speech. The moving, poetic words of Senator Mansfield follow:

> There was the sound of laughter and, in a moment, it was no more. And, so, she took a ring from her finger and placed it in his hands. There was a wit in a man neither young nor old; but a wit full of an old man's wisdom and of a child's wisdom and, then, in a moment it was no more. And, so, she took a ring from her finger and placed it in his hands. There was a man marked with the scars of his love of country, a body active with the surge of a life far, far from spent and, in a moment, it was no more. And, so, she took a ring from her finger and placed it in his hands. There was a father with a little boy and a little girl and the joy of each in the other and, in a moment, it was no more. And, so, she took a ring from her finger and placed it in his hands. There was a husband who asked much and gave much and, out of the giving and the asking, wove with a woman what could not be broken in life, and, in a moment, it was no more. And, so, she took a ring from her finger and placed it in his hands, and kissed him, and closed the lid of a coffin. A piece of each of us died at that moment. Yet, in death he gave of himself to us. He gave us of a good heart from which the laughter came. He gave us of a profound wit, from which a great leadership emerged. He gave us of a kindness and a strength fused into the human courage to seek peace without fear. He gave us of his love that we, too, in turn, might give. He gave that we might give of ourselves, that we might give to one another until there would be no room, no room at all, for the bigotry, the hatred, the prejudice, and the arrogance which converged in that moment of horror to strike him

down. In leaving us—these gifts, John Fitzgerald Kennedy, President of the United States, leaves with us. Will we take them, Mr. President? Will we have, now, the sense and the responsibility and the courage to take them? I pray to God that we will.[7]

The Speech of Nomination

The speech nominating a person for office often takes the form of a eulogy. The instructions for the eulogy apply with this additional suggestion. An appropriate speech of nomination discusses (1) conditions and problems of the office which must be met, (2) qualifications for the office which the candidate must meet, and (3) qualifications of the proposed candidate to meet the needs of the office.

In informal situations like club meetings, a brief statement such as "I nominate Mr. Jones" will suffice. In situations like nominations for political office or for officers in professional organizations, the nomination speech should employ the principles of persuasion discussed in Part Two. Develop each point with reasoning and evidence. Support your opinions about the candidate with proof. Use positive suggestion; do not talk about the weaknesses of other candidates; stress the virtues and qualifications of your proposed candidate.

The Speech of Dedication

On some occasions, institutions or movements are eulogized rather than persons. Typical situations are (1) programs commending some great movement or organization such as universities, political parties, and labor unions; (2) programs commending great occasions such as American Independence Day, Lincoln's Emancipation Proclamation, or Veterans' Day; (3) programs laying the cornerstone or dedicating buildings and monuments.

The purpose of the dedication speech may be (1) to eulogize the occasion and increase the listeners' respect for it, (2) to cause increased devotion for the cause represented by the dedication, (3) to bring about a renewed striving for the objectives of the thing eulogized, and (4) to lay down principles and ideals which the listeners may emulate. These formal and dignified occasions pay tribute to organizations, institutions, and movements and have much in common with occasions that eulogize persons.

In preparing for the speech of dedication, familiarize yourself

[7] Published by permission of Senator Mike Mansfield.

with the events and circumstances of the thing dedicated. Develop the philosophy behind the movement or institution, not trivial problems relative to its function. The chronological order, past-present-future, suggests an appropriate organizational pattern. In developing the past, explain the principles and aims upon which the organization was founded; in developing the present, show how the movement has attained its aims and lived up to its principles; in developing the future, enumerate the tasks ahead, the new ideals for which the listeners should strive.

Since the occasion is formal and dignified, the manner of speaking should conform to the occasion. Sincerity and restraint should mark the delivery. Avoid overstatement, flowery language, and oratorical style. Speak in a conversational and communicative manner, with the aim of communicating ideas and genuine feelings.

V. The After-Dinner Speech

In Chapter 5 the entertaining speech was discussed as one of the three basic types, the others being the informative and the persuasive. Entertainment may be a part of any speech, but the entertaining speech uses humor and interesting diversion as its primary purpose. Numerous occasions, such as club meetings, assemblies, parties, dinners, and any gathering where weighty discussions appear inappropriate, call for entertaining speeches. Dinner or banquet occasions provide the most common setting, thus the term "after-dinner speech."

Not all after-dinner speeches have entertainment as their primary purpose. Some dinner occasions call for speeches with a serious purpose; the banquet or dinner simply provides the setting for speeches of explanation or persuasion. The instructions given in other parts of this textbook apply to the serious after-dinner speech; this section discusses the entertaining after-dinner speech.

The Purpose

The after-dinner speech aims to provide interesting diversion and pleasantry. It develops a trend of thought in a pleasant and entertaining manner. It may be informative or persuasive so long as these ends do not constitute the principal purposes. The chief purpose, to entertain, forms the main highway which the speech travels. As expressed by Professor Clark S. Carlile of Idaho State College,

"The humor is achieved by hitting a few bumps, skidding around a bit, getting stuck in a mud hole, having a flat tire, and flirting with the farmer's daughter, all the time keeping to the main highway. Thus when you arrive at your destination, you have traveled a straight road but you've had a pleasant time doing it." [8] The after-dinner speech has a specific purpose, a central idea, and main points, the same as do other types; but, unlike other speeches, the forms of support are chosen for their entertainment value, not for their logical adequacy.

Suggestions for Preparation

For many speakers, the after-dinner speech is the most difficult type. Some speakers lack a flair for the unusual, a light touch; others lack knowledge about how to plan an entertaining speech. The following suggestions should help one gain knowledge about the speech.

1. *Seek novel subjects and original ideas.* The choice of subjects for after-dinner speaking has few limits so long as fresh points of view appropriate to the audience and occasion are presented. Choose subjects from your field of specialization, interests, and experiences that you can treat in an original manner. For example, one student talked about the presidential election at a banquet of his fellow political-science majors during a presidential campaign. He used the topic as a springboard for relating much of the fresh humor then prevalent about the youth, inexperience, beliefs, and campaign promises of the candidates. He succeeded because he chose a timely and appropriate subject, had a basic understanding of his subject, knew the interests of his listeners, and used fresh and appropriate humor.

A forensic director talked on "The Lighter Side of Debate Coaching" at an annual banquet of forensic students. He related humorous incidents in his own experiences as a forensic director under three headings: (1) slips of the tongue by debaters, (2) peculiarities of debate judges, and (3) unusual happenings at tournaments. He succeeded because he chose an appropriate subject in which his audience was interested and because he had a long experience upon which to draw for subject matter.

2. *Adapt plans to the audience and occasion.* Stereotyped plans

[8] Clark S. Carlile, *Project Text for Public Speaking* (New York: Harper and Row, Publishers, Inc., 1953), p. 125.

and stock humor will not do. The after-dinner speech must be planned for a particular audience and adapted to the occasion. A speech on devices used to induce speech teachers to give free talks would probably be hilarious to an audience of speech teachers, only mildly entertaining to other faculty members, not at all entertaining to businessmen, and insulting to women in a study club. Humor must be personal; to use the same type of humor for all audiences invites failure. Badinage may be an excellent source of humor; but one cannot rail against the weaknesses or beliefs of people without intimate knowledge of how they think and feel; otherwise, what may be intended as good-natured fun may prove offensive.

A good after-dinner speaker remains adaptable to the occasion; he capitalizes on remarks of the toastmaster or previous speakers, pokes fun at well-known persons in the audience, and treats the commonplace in a novel way. He uses such devices as exaggeration, clever wording, and twisting ideas in an original and amusing manner.

3. *Avoid heavy subject matter and complicated arrangement.* Weighty problems and controversial issues have little place in the after-dinner speech. An audience expects to be amused, not burdened, by speeches on social occasions. Avoid a complicated arrangement of ideas; use main points as a cohesive force for light illustrative material and well-chosen humor. Use anecdotes and illustrative material in preference to statistics and detailed examples. Avoid contentiousness; amuse your listeners, do not antagonize them. Tell amusing stories, jokes on yourself, and stories with surprise endings; use a variety of support for an uncomplicated arrangement of ideas.

4. *Avoid a string of unrelated jokes.* After-dinner speeches that do not have a central theme usually result in a series of unrelated and disconnected jokes. If a speaker selects his ideas to permit him to use his stock stories, his illustrations will be likely to appear irrelevant. Neither should the after-dinner speech consist of a single story or narrative. Jokes, episodes, and stories should be used to illustrate the theme of the speech and to develop the main points. The central theme, not the illustrative material, should govern the organization of the speech.

5. *Use a variety of humor.* The excessive use of one or two types of humor may tire an audience; use a variety. In addition to the

methods for achieving humor already discussed, consider the following:

a. INCONGRUITY—present the familiar in an unusual way, make unfamiliar combinations of familiar things, or put unfamiliar things into familiar surroundings.

b. PUNS—use words that are pronounced alike to produce an incongruous idea or double meaning; for example, "She looks to be in her middle flirties." "Keep drinking and you will become a grave man."

c. EXAGGERATION—overstate an idea to the extent that the exaggeration becomes obvious. The overstatement may be either in the idea or in the language used to express the idea.

d. IRONY—say a thing in such a way that the opposite is obviously intended. The statement contains a contradiction between the literal and intended meaning.

e. BURLESQUE—present a humorous caricature that treats lofty material ludicrously or ordinary material with mock dignity. Burlesque may take the form of a parody in which something insignificant is treated as important.

6. *Use appropriate humor.* Humor should be in good taste, never low and degrading. It should be adapted to the occasion and to the cultural level of the audience. On some occasions broad, obvious humor may be in order. On other occasions delicate, subtle humor applies best. On all occasions humor should be spontaneous and relevant to the discussion. Genial and light humor should never give way to biting sarcasm and scathing barbs. Humor should provide relaxation, enjoyment, and entertainment for the listeners.

The Arrangement of Ideas

Like other types of speeches, organization of the after-dinner speech may be considered under the divisions—introduction, body, and conclusion.

1. *The introduction.* Strive for an immediate, overt response from the audience. Set the keynote for the speech and prepare the audience to be entertained. Begin with an incongruous statement, capitalize on a remark made by the chairman or a previous speaker, tell an amusing story, refer to a recent humorous happening, or poke fun at yourself or someone in the audience. Let your opening remarks lead directly to the body of the speech. One speaker, who

had obviously been lauded excessively by the chairman, began, "I have never heard so many deserved compliments about a speaker." Another speaker said, "What a splendid speech of introduction; I thought it was pretty good when I wrote it for the chairman."

2. *The body.* The points in the speech should be stated simply. Avoid a complicated arrangement of ideas. Introduce the points with an amusing anecdote or illustration; then expand the basic idea of each point by additional illustrations, stories, and jokes. Do not attempt to maintain sustained amusement; give the listeners time to rest during explanations and transitions. Build each point to a climax of interest; reserve some of the most amusing illustrative material for the last part of the speech.

Present ideas through illustrations, analogies, anecdotes, allusions, and figures of speech; use a minimum of explanation, reasoning, statistics, and restatement. Any method for arranging ideas discussed in Chapter 8 may be adapted to the after-dinner speech. For example, the problem-solution method may be used by presenting an obviously fictitious problem and suggesting an absurd solution. The method of arrangement is not so important as the novelty and originality employed in using it.

3. *The conclusion.* The conclusion for the after-dinner speech differs from that of other types. In many instances, the formal conclusion may be omitted; simply end on a point of amusement. When a conclusion seems advisable, omit a detailed summary as used in informative or persuasive speeches; restate the barest suggestion of the points, preferably in a statement which epitomizes them. Do not let the conclusion become an anticlimax. Close swiftly by an amusing illustration, a story of action, or a brief restatement of your theme.

The Manner of Presentation

Make the delivery of the after-dinner speech swift-moving and vivid. Let your manner suggest enjoyment. Be optimistic, genial, and good-natured. A pseudo-serious speech given in a "dead-pan" manner often serves well. Your manner of speaking should reflect the mood of the occasion; avoid contentiousness, dogmatism, and argumentation. Converse with your audience with intimacy and good humor.

VI. Adapting Speeches to Radio and Television

It appears that radio and television, like the automobile and airplane, are here to stay. We need to recognize their enormous potential. Almost every family in the United States owns from one to a half-dozen radios, and the number of television sets in use is increasing by the thousands yearly. Famous speeches of a century ago were heard by only a few thousand people; epic-making speeches of recent years have been heard by radio and television audiences estimated at between eighty and ninety million. Radio and television have revolutionized the leisure-time activities and cultural opportunities of Americans. Furthermore, television has the potential for revolutionizing the American educational system and has already made steps in that direction. Fifty years ago the average citizen rarely came in contact with the great minds, artists, and speakers of that age; now all these opportunities are available at the turn of a dial. Although the scope of this text prevents a full discussion of radio and television, the adaptation of public speaking to these media is considered briefly.

We can begin with the premise that good speech is good speech regardless of the medium for disseminating it. The instructions given in Parts Two and Three about the composition and delivery of a speech apply to radio and television speaking the same as to other types. Differences in application do apply, however. What are these differences?

Differences in Audiences

Chapter 4 treats audience analysis in detail from the viewpoint of listeners' interests, attitudes toward the speaker, attitudes toward the speaker's subject, and varying facts about different audiences. These factors can be pinpointed with considerable accuracy for live audiences; they are less easily gauged for the radio and television audience for the following three reasons.

1. *Greater variety of interests.* Assembled audiences frequently have common primary and secondary interests, similar attitudes toward the speaker and his subject, and like educational and cultural backgrounds. Conversely, radio and television audiences have a diversity of interests, attitudes, and backgrounds. Furthermore,

radio and television audiences are sometimes less motivated to listen than assembled audiences because they have many factors competing for their attention. The man who listens in the privacy of his home may be torn between his desire to read the evening paper and his desire to listen to the television program; he may even decide to do both at the same time. If he decides in favor of the television program, he may have several interruptions—the telephone may ring, his son may ask for help with his homework, or his wife may decide to rearrange the furniture. As a result he may only half-listen.

On the other hand, on some occasions a broadcast audience may be highly motivated. The speaker, the topic, or the occasion may be of such interest as to command undivided attention. These conditions prevailed on such occasions as when Franklin D. Roosevelt spoke for declaring war on Japan, when General Douglas MacArthur addressed Congress upon being relieved of his command, when President John Kennedy addressed the nation on television about the Cuban crisis, and when President Johnson discussed the civil rights crisis in Selma, Alabama. Motivated listening conditions prevail when students take classes by television, when speeches in political campaigns become intense, when issues of momentary interests are discussed. Furthermore, under ideal listening conditions, fewer distractions may be evident for broadcast listeners than for assembled audiences. Those who listen alone or in small groups may be less subject to the distractions of a crowd or outside noises than those who listen in assembled audiences. These ideal listening conditions are, however, the exception. In speaking over radio or television, the speaker normally loses the advantages of the psychological factors which motivate an assembled audience to listen. Why are these factors important to the radio and television speaker?

The television speaker must make his appeals to interests as universal as possible. Since his audience consists of people of all ages, economic and cultural backgrounds, professions and businesses, he cannot find a community of primary interests to which he may appeal. He must, therefore, appeal to factors of unusual momentary interests, factors that concern all people. Furthermore, his appeals to the factors of motivation must be universal. Chapter 3 discusses seven basic motives of man to which speakers must appeal to insure efficient listening. These factors of self-preservation, property, power, reputation, affection, sentiment, and taste affect the basic desires and needs of people. Different motives apply to different groups of people, so a speaker must use a variety of appeals; what may motivate a young, well-educated, professional man may not motivate an elderly, uneducated, unskilled laborer.

2. *Widely dispersed groups.* An assembled audience constitutes a social group that imposes restraints on each listener. Listeners rarely walk out on a speaker, eat their lunch, read newspapers, or talk back audibly, because they feel the inhibiting pressures of a social group. Radio and television listeners do all these things; they make up many small, widely dispersed, intimate groups that feel few pressures of a social gathering. They feel comfortable, relaxed, and uninhibited. The speaker who talks in the grand style appears ridiculous. Family groups do not invite speakers into their living rooms to be harangued; they expect the speaker to be warm, intimate, informal. The television speaker should, therefore, speak in a direct, communicative manner, much as he would in conversing with a half-dozen people.

3. *Inability to gauge response.* A speaker can learn much from an assembled audience by observing his listeners' physical and audible reactions. He can gauge whether the listeners understand, accept, or enjoy his speech. His impressions of audience response may cause him to modify his speech as he talks—to restate an idea, to omit an illustration, to show more animation, or to inject humor. The radio and television speaker has no way of determining audience reaction and cannot adjust to listeners' response. Furthermore, he loses the effect of audience stimulation, "the feel" of an audience. He feels no encouragement to reach emotional heights, to put forth his best efforts, to please his audience.

All these differences between an assembled audience and a broadcast audience point up the difficulties in interesting radio and television audiences; they add to the complexity of the speaking situation. These added complexities may be met, in part, by adjustments in the methods of preparation and delivery.

Preparing the Broadcast Speech

The principles of analyzing and evaluating material, selecting forms of support, deciding on main points and subpoints, and arranging ideas as discussed in Part Two apply to radio and television speaking. The following factors pertain to the adaptation of these principles to the broadcast audience.

1. *Decide on the desired audience.* On many occasions speeches given before live audiences are also broadcast. For example, President Roosevelt spoke to a joint session of Congress on December 8, 1941, for declaration of war against Japan; the speech was also heard by a radio audience estimated at sixty million people. President Johnson gave the commencement address at Baylor University on May 28, 1965; his immediate audience consisted of some ten thousand people, but his radio and television audiences numbered in the millions. On history-making occasions such as these, interest in the occasion is sufficient to hold the broadcast audience; the speaker may direct his speech to his assembled audience. On television the presence of the microphone adds importance to the occasion. But what about the politician who campaigns for election or the organization's representative who desires to influence public opinion? Their assembled audiences may consist of only a few hundred people, but the broadcast audiences may number into the hundreds of thousands. Such speakers may accomplish their objectives better by directing their speeches to the broadcast audiences. Use the informal, direct methods discussed in the preceding section because they apply best to intimate, dispersed groups with a disparity of interests.

2. *Use simple patterns of organization.* Since the attention of the broadcast audience may be easily diverted, avoid a complicated arrangement of ideas. With the broadcast audience in mind, review Chapter 8 on "Organize Your Speech." Begin with an unusual statement or a striking illustration to get immediate interest in your subject. State the central theme in a brief, slogan-like phrase and repeat it often. Either make your main points few in number or develop only one main point. State the main points in short sentences that bear easy repetition. Use a simple organizational pattern like the "problem-solution" form, or the chronological, simple enumeration, or logical order. Proceed from the simple and familiar to the more complex and unfamiliar ideas. In concluding, give a brief summary, restate the central idea, and indicate the desired action. Beware of overamplification of ideas; make each statement count. Arrange your speech so that your audience can capture your central theme and follow your sequence of ideas.

3. *Select interesting and concrete forms of support.* Use illustrative material liberally, especially examples and analogies. Specific instances serve better than detailed examples because they are easier for the audience to grasp and take less time to develop. Keep in mind the diversity of interests in the broadcast audience; select supporting material that has broad appeal. Avoid technical and philosophical discussions that require detailed explanation and abstract theorizing. Leonard Bernstein interested many people in classical music by his non-technical discussions and demonstrations. Carl Sandburg and Robert Frost introduced poetry to many people by their interesting television speeches.

Visual aids may be particularly valuable on television because they enable the speaker to use both visual and auditory methods. Through the use of close-up shots, such visual aids as maps and drawings may be shown in detail. Visual aids also provide the action and variety necessary for holding audience interests. The instructions given in Chapter 7 on the preparation and use of visual aids apply to television speeches with these added suggestions: (1) Avoid visual aids that reflect light unduly, such as glossy prints, slick paper, or drawings with a white background. Television studios have the proper type of display boards for visual aids. If you prefer to hold the visual aid in your hands, mount it on dull-finish cardboard and use black lettering. (2) Use visual aids which correspond with the shape of television screens. For example, use a cardboard mounting nine inches high by twelve inches wide or twelve inches high by sixteen inches wide. (3) Do not use visual aids simply because television lends itself well to their use. Use only those aids that will help make your ideas and explanations meaningful.

4. *Prepare the manuscript and outline carefully.* Proper timing of the broadcast speech is essential since broadcast stations operate on a strict schedule. Time the manuscript carefully during rehearsal; but to allow for variations, include a paragraph near the end which may be either included or omitted to adjust to the time limit. Allow time for the station break, the commercials, and the introduction of the program.

Broadcast speeches may be read from the manuscript, read by use of a teleprompter for television, or spoken extemporaneously. Formerly radio stations required a written manuscript, but today most stations permit individual preferences. Reading from a manuscript finds favor with many radio speakers because preparation of the manuscript permits careful choice of language and prevents digressions. Conversely, reading may prove least effective for television because the manuscript decreases eye contact and directness. The teleprompter, a mechanical device placed outside the range of the camera, permits the television speaker to read while facing the camera. This method rarely succeeds in camouflaging a read speech; the constant stare of the speaker appears artificial. Those who speak fluently from an outline prefer to speak extemporaneously. This method permits easy adaptation to the time limit and encourages direct, conversational communication. The use of the extemporaneous method, however, does not relieve one of the necessity for careful preparation. When using this method for television, arrange a system of signals or provide advanced instructions to the cameramen for the use of visual aids.

Leave nothing to chance when preparing the broadcast speech. A well-prepared manuscript or outline and several rehearsals will improve the chances of successful communication.

Presenting the Broadcast Speech

The principles for effective presentation—poise, language, voice, and bodily action—discussed in Part Three apply to the broadcast speech. In addition, consider the following factors.

1. *Adjust to the microphone.* For radio, talk into the microphone in much the same manner as explained in Chapter 10 for using a public-address system. In using the microphone, observe these precautions: (1) Avoid sudden changes in volume that may cause a blasting effect on the amplifier. Speak in an animated, conversational style much as if you were talking to a few people in the privacy of your living room. (2) Do not move outside the range of the microphone. Avoid swaying movements or changes in stance that cause variations of volume. Maintain a constant position as you talk directly into or slightly across the microphone. (3) Beware of extraneous noises caused by the rustling of papers, the rattling of coins, the shuffling of feet, or the drumming on the table. The sensitive microphone picks up these noises, which often prove irritating to listeners. Use an inexpensive pulp paper for your manuscript; it causes less noise when the pages are turned or shuffled than does bond or onion skin paper. (4) Be particularly careful when pronouncing the sibilants: *s, sh, z, zh, j,* and *ch.* A

noticeable hissing sound irritates listeners. Speaking across the microphone may help eliminate these hissing sounds.

For speaking on television, the microphone presents less difficulty than for speaking on radio. Television stations use several types of microphones that may be moved as the speaker moves. The instructions, however, on sharp changes of volume and the avoidance of extraneous noises and hissing sounds apply to television as well as to radio speaking.

2. *Adjust to the invisible audience.* The lack of a visible audience constitutes an important adjustment that speakers must make for radio and television. The adjustment may be made in part by simply visualizing the listening audience; visualize people sitting before their radio and television sets; imagine their reactions as being much like those of assembled audiences that you have previously addressed. By projecting your imagination, you can acquire the "feel" of your listeners, although you cannot see them.

You may prefer to invite a few people into the studio to serve as a live audience. By speaking to them in a conversational manner, you can approximate the condition of your invisible listeners as they sit in small groups before their radio and television sets. This practice will make you less inclined to use the grand manner; instead, you will speak directly and communicatively.

3. *Avoid delivery mannerisms.* For radio, voice and language must carry the load of the presentation skills; television adds bodily action. Many speakers prefer to use bodily action in radio speaking because it helps them to become animated and to visualize the invisible audience. In speaking on television, avoid sweeping and sharply made gestures. Facial expressions and the lesser bodily movements of the head and shoulders serve best.

The delivery mannerisms discussed in Chapter 13 apply with force to radio and television speaking. As explained previously, a mannerism of delivery consists of any action used with such frequency that it calls attention to itself. In speaking on radio, be careful of long pauses; since the listeners cannot see the speaker, they become impatient with excessive deliberation. Unusual dialects, mispronounced words, and halting speech prove especially distracting. Check the manuscript carefully for the pronunciation of words; rehearse the speech until it can be read or spoken fluently. Avoid such mannerisms as clearing the throat, repeating words and phrases, and vocalizing pauses with "ah" and "uh" or with connective words like "and," "thus," "but," and "so."

When speaking on television, add the mannerisms of bodily action to the above list. The following mannerisms became especially noticeable on close-up shots: (1) adjusting glasses or clothing; (2) looking away from the camera; (3) showing a "dead-pan" facial expression; (4) using notes or other materials excessively; (5) moving the head and arms frequently; (6) carrying pencil, pen, or other articles in the hands; and (7) sitting or standing in a slouched position. Attempt to give an informal but poised appearance; avoid mannerisms that may detract from the thought of the speech.

4. *Adjust to the technical aspects of broadcasting.* Many people complain about the distracting influences of broadcasting. For those inexperienced in broadcasting, a brief discussion of what to expect should prove helpful.

Almost all radio and television stations will ask you to report from thirty to forty-five minutes early. The director will show you the broadcast set-up and instruct you on how to proceed. He will ask you to speak into the microphone so that he may adjust for your volume and position. He may ask you to rehearse the entire speech. During your speech you will face the control room so that you may see visual instructions from the engineer. The director will instruct you on the timing signals, but you may want to check the position of the studio clock so that you can glance at it from time to time. Ask the director for the exact time that you must conclude.

For television, the bright floodlights, the activities of the cameramen, and the visual instructions of the director may prove distracting at first. Others in the studio may go about their business of adjusting equipment or setting up for the next program without apparent concern for your speech. If the station uses two or more cameras, the cameramen may communicate with each other through hand signs, or the director may motion for you to face the live camera or make other adjustments in your position. The live camera always has a small red light termed the tally light just below the lenses; remember to face the camera with the red light.

How can you cope with these distracting influences? Although you must heed the visual instructions, the time signals, and the tally light, attempt to ignore the other activities in the studio and control room. Concentrate on the thought of your speech and the invisible listeners. "Think the thought" of your speech and visualize your listeners' reactions.

The floodlights generate considerable heat. Avoid wearing woolen suits or other heavy clothing. Also avoid wearing accessories such as tie pins, bracelets, or other articles that reflect the bright lights. White shirts or blouses also reflect light excessively. Light grey or blue appear white to the viewer and do not cause glare. Clothing with prominent stripes and figures should not be worn. Although proper dress and grooming matter little for radio speaking except for the psychological effect they may have on the speaker, they matter a great deal for television. Rumpled clothing, crooked ties, peculiar hats, and unusual adornment may prove more interesting than what you have to say.

VII. Summary

The basic principles of composition and delivery apply to speeches for special occasions, namely: (1) speeches of introduction; (2) speeches of welcome and response; (3) speeches of presentation and acceptance; (4) speeches of eulogy, nomination, and dedication; and (5) after-dinner speeches. The same principles apply in preparing speeches for radio and television.

The speech of introduction attempts to create a pleasant atmosphere, to give the qualifications of the speaker, and to show the importance of the subject. Suggestions for preparing the speech of introduction include: (1) consult the speaker for advice and information, (2) make the introduction a separate speech, (3) make the speech brief but thorough, (4) use humor, (5) avoid overpraise, (6) avoid talking about yourself, (7) avoid stressing the speaker's speaking ability, and (8) avoid trite and hackneyed language. The introduction attempts to get immediate interest and to set the keynote for the speech. The body presents information to increase the prestige of the speaker and to enhance interest in the subject. The conclusion presents the speaker and the title of his speech. Enthusiasm, tact, and sincerity should characterize the speaking manner.

The speech of welcome applies on occasions like meetings of convention delegates, meetings for special occasions, meetings to honor distinguished guests, and meetings to welcome new members to an organization. Its purpose is to express genuine appreciation to the organization or person welcomed and to set the keynote for the ensuing meeting. Attempt to bring freshness and originality to the occasion by (1) using tact and good taste, (2) being optimistic and enthusiastic, (3) speaking briefly, (4) avoiding emotionalism, and (5) avoiding flowery platitudes and stereotype forms. In organizing the speech, attempt to capture the immediate interest of the audience and establish a pleasant keynote in the introduction. In the body, a local person would express appreciation for the group welcomed and give information about the place or organization to which the group is welcomed. An out-of-town representative of the sponsoring organization would stress the purpose of the meeting and the common aims of the delegates. In the conclusion, express your best wishes for a profitable meeting and pledge the support of your organization. Be sincere, cordial, and gracious by your manner. Response to the speech of welcome should follow the principles suggested for the speech of welcome.

Speeches of presentation apply when presenting gifts or awards to those (1) who are leaving a place of employment or who are retiring, (2) who have earned service awards, (3) who have won prizes, and (4) who are honored by their co-workers or employers. The purpose of the speech is to honor the recipient, honor the donor, and increase morale in an organization. Suggestions for preparing the speech of presentation are: (1) know the recipient, (2) know the occasion, (3) show proper restraint, (4) recognize the losers, and (5) speak briefly and extemporaneously. In organizing the speech of presentation, use the introduction to give pertinent information about the gift or award. Organize the body of the speech to bring out the virtues and accomplishments of the recipient, show appreciation for the donor, and briefly describe the gift or award. Avoid flattery, flowery language, and an effusive manner. Replies to speeches of presentation should be brief and sincere.

The formal eulogy pays tribute to persons for significant accomplishments or for influence on movements or organizations. For proper preparation, (1) know the subject well, (2) evaluate the subject accurately, (3) avoid a flowery style, and (4) choose interesting illustrative material. In the introduction, focus attention on the person eulogized. The body of the speech may arrange the divisions of the speech chronologically or on a selective basis. Conclude the speech on a note of praise with a personal tribute. Speeches of nomination and dedication are special forms of tribute.

The after-dinner speech provides entertainment. It develops an idea in a pleasant and humorous manner. To help make the speech a success, (1) seek novel subjects and original ideas, (2) adapt plans to the audience and occasion, (3) avoid heavy subject matter and complicated arrangement, (4) avoid a string of unrelated jokes, (5) use a variety of humor, and (6) use appropriate humor. The introduction should capture the immediate interest of the audience and set a keynote of pleasantry. The body should state the points simply and support them with abundant illustrative material. Conclude the speech on a note of pleasantry.

Speaking on radio and television requires certain adaptations of the basic principles of speech. Differences of broadcast audiences from assembled audiences should be noted: (1) the broadcast audience has a greater variety of interests than the assembled audience; (2) the broadcast audience consists of widely dispersed groups; (3) the broadcast audience cannot enable the speaker to gauge audience response. In preparing the broadcast speech: (1) decide whether to speak primarily to the broadcast audience or to the assembled audience in cases where the broadcast is being made of an attended event; (2) use a simple pattern of organization; (3) select interesting and concrete forms of support; and (4) prepare the manuscript and outline carefully. Factors of importance to presentation include (1) adjustment to the microphone, (2) adjustment to the invisible audience, (3) avoidance of delivery mannerisms, and (4) adjustment to the technical aspects of broadcasting.

Questions and Exercises

A. Answer the following questions on Chapter 16:

1. What is the principal purpose of the speech of introduction? Discuss several suggestions for preparing the speech.
2. What are the principal steps for organizing the speech of introduction? Characterize the manner of presentation.
3. What occasions call for the speech of welcome? Discuss briefly the five suggestions for preparing the speech of welcome. Can you add to this list?
4. Characterize the organization and the manner of presenting the speech of welcome.
5. What purposes does the speech of presentation serve? List suggestions for preparing this type of speech.
6. Contrast the methods of organizing the speech of presentation with those of organizing the reply to the speech of presentation. What principles should govern the delivery of these speeches?

7. How does the formal eulogy differ from the speech of presentation? List several occasions that call for the eulogy.
8. Discuss briefly the characteristics of organization and presentation of the formal eulogy.
9. What is the principal purpose of the after-dinner speech? Characterize the types of humor applicable to this type speech.
10. Discuss briefly the introduction, body, and conclusion of the after-dinner speech. How should the manner of presentation of an after-dinner speech differ from that of a persuasive speech?
11. What are the principal differences between a broadcast audience and an assembled audience? Of what importance are these differences in adapting public speaking to radio and television?
12. List several factors which should be considered in preparing the broadcast speech. Can you add to the list given in this chapter?
13. What can the speaker do to help compensate for the lack of a visible audience in a broadcast speech?
14. Discuss several technical considerations in speaking on radio and television. How may you compensate for the distracting influences encountered in staging the broadcast speech?

B. Your final performance assignment will consist of three parts.

1. Write out brief speeches of introduction, welcome, and presentation. State an imaginary setting for each speech. Your instructor will ask you to read one of these speeches before the microphone as he records the speech. Hand in all three speeches to your instructor.
2. Find an example of a formal eulogy in one of the collection of speeches listed in Chapter 6. Write a brief oral report of this speech to be handed in to your instructor. Include the following factors in your analysis of the speech.
   a. What was the setting for the speech?
   b. What was the central theme of the speech?
   c. How well did the speaker conform to the principles of organization discussed in this chapter?
   d. Criticize the speaker's use of language.
   e. Rate the speech as excellent, good, average, fair, or poor. Justify your rating.
3. Prepare a five-minute entertaining speech suitable for an after-dinner setting. Present this speech in class. Choose a topic from your background of information and experiences. Seek an original idea and use humor in developing your theme. Observe the precautions discussed in this chapter. Remember that your main purpose is to provide an interesting and pleasant diversion for the class.

INDEX

Index

E

P

Q

R

W

Y